THE STATE OF THE NATION

FALI S. NARIMAN

HAY HOUSE

HAY HOUSE INDIA

New Delhi • London • Sydney

Carlsbad, California • New York City

Hay House Publishers (India) Pvt Ltd
Muskaan Complex, Plot No. 3, B-2, Vasant Kunj, New Delhi – 110070, India

Hay House LLC, P.O. Box 5100, Carlsbad, CA 92018-5100, USA
Hay House UK Ltd, 1st Floor, Crawford Corner, 91-93 Baker Street, London W1U 6QQ, UK
Hay House Australia Publishing Pty Ltd, 18/36 Ralph St., Alexandria NSW 2015, Australia

Email: contact@hayhouse.co.in
Website: www.hayhouse.co.in

The cartoons on pp. 242 and 284 have been reproduced with the permission of Bennett, Coleman & Co. Ltd. The other cartoons have been reproduced from Dr Dharmendra Bhandari's book *R. K. Laxman – The Uncommon Man* with the author's permission.

Cover photograph © Ananth Padmanabhan

First published by Hay House India, 2013
First paperback edition, 2015
Reprint, 2025
24 23 22 21 20 19 18 17 16 15

ISBN 978-93-84544-06-5
Printed at Repro India Ltd

FSC www.fsc.org
MIX
Paper from responsible sources
FSC® C047271

Hay House is committed to a sustainable future for our business, our readers and our planet. This book is made from Forest Stewardship Council® certified paper.

Fali S. Nariman was a distinguished senior advocate at the Supreme Court of India. He served as chairman of the executive committee of the International Commission of Jurists (ICJ) in Geneva from 1995 to 1997. Nariman was a member of the London Court of International Arbitration (LCIA) from 1988 to 2003 and served as vice-president of the ICC International Court of Arbitration in Paris for over fifteen years, from 1989 to 2005. He was elected president of the International Council for Commercial Arbitration (ICCA) from 1994 to 2002 and later became its honorary president. In recognition of his distinguished services in jurisprudence, he was awarded the Padma Bhushan in January 1991 and the Padma Vibhushan, India's second-highest civilian award, in January 2007 for exceptional contributions to public affairs. Additionally, he served as a nominated member of the Upper House of India's Parliament from 1999 to 2005.

BY THE SAME AUTHOR

A revelatory, comprehensive and perceptive autobiography – candid, compelling and authoritative

Over the decades, Fali S. Nariman has attained the status of a pre-eminent advocate whose views are not only heard by those in the corridors of power – both judicial and political – but also respected. This volume presents his life journey right from his childhood in Rangoon to the present. Starting with his formative years, when he had the good fortune to interact with many eminent judges and advocates, the author moves on to deal with a wide variety of important subjects, such as:

- The sanctity of the Indian Constitution and attempts to tamper with it.
- Crucial cases that have made a decisive impact on the nation, especially on the interpretation of the law.
- The relationship between the political class and the judiciary, and how political power can be asserted in the guise of judicial interpretation.
- The cancer of corruption and how to combat this menace.

The author also outlines measures to restore the now-low credibility of the legal profession. He delineates his role in several high-profile cases and describes the highlights of his tenure in the Rajya Sabha. This book is a must for both members of the legal profession and the lay reader who will find the contents informative, educative and thought-provoking.

To
The little Indian
in whom rests
the future of the nation

Bapsi F. Nariman
The inspiration for this book

CONTENTS

PREFACE

In the thirtieth anniversary edition of the Collins English Dictionary *(2009), NATION is defined as: '(i) an aggregation of people or peoples of one or more cultures races, etc., organized into a single state: e.g., the Australian nation; (ii) a community of persons not constituting a state but bound by common descent, language, history, etc.: e.g., the French-Canadian nation.' The word itself is derived from the Latin,* nātiō, *which literally means 'to be born'.*

It was with the promulgation of India's Constitution on 26 January 1950 that the Indian NATION was born, bringing, for the first time in over 2000 years, geographical and political unity in a vast subcontinent. Not since the time of Chandragupta Maurya and his immediate successors,[1] had Hindustan been under one ruler or government.

A contemporary assessment of the record of the first 65 years in the life of a nation is bound to be faulty. It lacks perspective. It does not have the historical advantage of time and distance. Yet, during the past six-and-a-half decades, the Indian experiment with unity-amidst-diversity has been continuing: a major plus point during a period when the country has witnessed much upheaval, both political and social, but during which it has also experienced material progress with remarkable achievements in the fields of medicine, science and technology.

***

In the months after independence (August 1947), the choice of a national language got mired in acute controversy; emotionally, it has still not been resolved. What prevails is only a temporary truce, with two national languages (Hindi and English) in one nation! But more than 60 years of the Constitution has ensured for religious and linguistic minorities, and for religious denominations of every kind, a freedom from state interference that is quite unique; the autonomy these groups enjoy in Indian polity is unsurpassed amongst the world's developing societies.

We have not yet resolved the complexities that lie buried in the great, but elusive, doctrine spelt out in Article 14.[2] The tension between a commitment to non-discrimination as well as to equality was poignantly expressed by India's prime minister, Jawaharlal Nehru, during the debate in Parliament at the time of the Constitution's First Amendment Bill (in May 1951):

> *We cannot have equality because in trying to attain equality we come up against some principles of equality* .... We cannot have equality because we cannot have non-discrimination because if you think in terms of giving a lift up to those who are down, you are somehow affecting the present status quo undoubtedly. Therefore you are said to be discriminating because you are affecting the present status quo. Therefore if this argument is correct, then we cannot make any major change in that respect because every change means a change in the status quo, whether economic or in any sphere of public or private activity. Whatever law you may make, you have to make some change somewhere. Therefore we have to come to grips with this subject in some other way.[3]

Over the past 60 plus years, we have not yet 'come to grips with this subject'. To what extent should the claim based on merit and on the Fundamental Right to Equality be ignored? How far does our document of governance, truly interpreted, direct us to go? How soon are we to atone for the oppression of centuries? Should we go on equalizing under a regime of enforced downward uniformity? And for how long? These questions keep surfacing periodically, but the answers given are never quite satisfactory or convincing: even when articulated by the distinguished and the knowledgeable. In 1964, Justice K. S. Hegde, when sitting as a judge in the High Court of Mysore wrote: 'It is cynical to suggest that the interest of the Nation is best served if the barber's son continues to be a barber and a shepherd's son continues to be a shepherd .... The goal of a welfare State cannot be reached if we overemphasize the *merit theory*.'[4] And a few years later (in 1971), when sitting in the highest court of the land he wrote:

> Undoubtedly we should not forget that it is against the immediate interest of the Nation to exclude from the portals of our medical colleges qualified and competent students but then the immediate advantages of the Nation have to be harmonised with its long-range interests. It cannot be denied that, unaided, many sections of the people in this country cannot compete with the advanced sections of the Nation. Advantages secured due to historical reasons should

> not be considered as fundamental rights. Nation's interest will be best served – taking a long-range view – if the backward classes are helped to march forward and take their place in line with the advanced sections of the people.[5]

Even in 2011-12, the representation of the underprivileged in public employment has continued to remain grossly disproportionate when compared to those belonging to the more privileged classes; as Ralph Bunche* once said: 'Inalienable rights can never be enjoyed posthumously!'

But on the other side of the argument, there is the spectre of agitated public opinion, which cannot be ignored: an increasing resistance to the view that the sins of generations of forefathers in the higher castes should be expiated here and now – in just a couple of generations. Even the Hindu law of 'pious obligation' requires the son to meet the financial obligations only of his father, not of all the forebears of his father! The judges, who have the final say in all constitutional matters, have interpreted compensatory discrimination clauses in our Constitution differently at different times. A perceptive commentator, has said that (in this area) 'the law does not evolve – *it meanders*!'[6] On occasions, the courts have prodded and energized governments to live up to their constitutional commitment to alleviate the lot of the downtrodden, but the ground rules have kept changing. A sympathetic critic explains why:

> In an area of law founded on the constitutional embrace of conflicting principles, it should not be expected that courts would provide an enduring synthesis that transcends and encompasses them and settles disputed issues with finality. Rather, we would expect – if the courts are at all representative of the larger society – some ambiguity and vacillation. And the courts have vacillated, sometimes emphasising compensatory discrimination; other times, formal equity; sometimes, rectification of communal disparities, at other times, non-recognition of communal units ... a number of factors operate to relax the pressure for consistency and economy

*Ralph Bunche (African-American) was an academic and diplomat who bagged the 1950 Nobel Peace Prize.

> and to facilitate the admission into the corpus of authority a variety of doctrines, not all of them reconcilable, which reflect the tensions between antagonistic principles.[7]

But amidst 'the tensions between antagonistic principles', one thing is certain: so long as poverty – dire poverty – continues to stalk the land and so long as gross disparities between the very rich and the very poor get accentuated (as they have in recent years), the ideal of an egalitarian society envisaged in our basic document of governance remains an evanescent dream. Whatever the nation's karma, our founding fathers cannot be faulted for a lack of idealism; nor can Providence. It is not in our stars but in ourselves that we are thus. It is not *because* of our Constitution, but, *despite* its provisions that, as a nation, we have failed to fulfil what were naïvely assumed to be achievable goals. We the people of India boldly abolished *untouchability* in our Constitution – but after more than 60 years of its working we have not been able to eliminate it from our hearts!

***

When members of India's Constituent Assembly first resolved to dedicate themselves, in all humility, to the service of the country and its people, Dr S. Radhakrishnan (later president of India) – who had seconded the resolution – warned that '*when power outstrips ability, we will fall on evil days*'. Power has overtaken ability. We *have* fallen on evil days. There is a crisis of competence, along with a conspicuous lack of integrity, in almost all fields of activity – more markedly in the political. And the entire country is submerged in a tidal wave of corruption. The public is fed up with politicians as a class, not only in India but in other parts of the world as well. In that delightful television series *Yes Minister*, there is an opinion expressed, which, if it had been recorded in a serious programme, would have rung alarm bells:

> When civil servants will remove politicians on grounds of incompetence it would empty the House of Commons, and remove the Cabinet – and that would be the end of democracy – *but it would be the beginning of responsible Government*!![8]

I believe that what has sustained the freedom enjoyed by our people has been *basic horse sense*, which has been defined as the good sense that horses have in not betting on people! But, in a democracy, we *have* to bet on people, set store by them and take to heart the decisions they make.[9]

Mercifully, despite tremendous odds, we have so far managed to pull through with our written Constitution. *And we are still one nation.* What we appear to have lost over the last 60-plus years is the fine art of conserving the political freedom we had won and the spirit in which the Constitution itself was drafted – a spirit of accommodation and consensus, so wanting now in all fields of activity.

* * *

To the question – how long will our Republic last? –the answer is: hopefully, forever, but, no one can tell. There is a story – a true story – of the time when the United States of America (like India today) was rid with dissension bordering on chaos – which ultimately led that nation into a civil war from 1861 to 1865. It was at this time that the French ambassador to Great Britain – himself a historian – pontifically enquired of his colleague the US ambassador (a poet and littérateur):

> Tell me, Excellency, tell me: how long will *this* republic of yours last?

The response of Ambassador James Lowell was as restrained as it was prophetic:

> Excellency, as long as its leaders live up to and cherish the ideals of its founding fathers.[10]

In India, our present leaders have failed to live up to the ideals of the founding fathers. Let us ignore them with the biblical condemnation: '… thou art weighed in the balances and found wanting.'[11] Let us pin our hopes on the leaders of *tomorrow*. This book is written in the expectation that they will get inspired with the ideals of those who framed the nation's Constitution.

– Fali S. Nariman

March 2013

Notes and References

1. 322 to 185 BCE (before the Christian era).
2. Article 14: *Equality before law:*

   The State shall not deny to any person equality before the law or the equal protection of the laws within the territory of India.
3. Parliamentary Debates, Vol. XII-XIII, Part II, Col. 9617, 29 May 1951.
4. See AIR 1964, Mysore, 132 at 136.
5. See *A. Periakaruppan* vs *State of Tamil Nadu*, AIR 1971, SC 2303, p. 2309.
6. Rajeev Dhavan: *The Supreme Court of India: A Socio-Legal Critique of Its Juristic Techniques*, Bombay, N. M. Tripathi, 1977. Dhavan (a Supreme Court advocate and a human rights activist) suggests that this is India's version of the '*happy mean*', a broad margin of tolerance, which is in keeping with the pattern of the common law.
7. Marc Galanter: *Competing Equalities: Law and the Backward Classes in India*, University of California Press, Los Angeles, 1984. p. 539. (An Indian paperback version of the same book was published in 1991.)
8. 'A Real Partnership', *Yes Minister*, Series I, Episode 5, 1986.
9. A most recent example has been the response of the government of the day to the growing pressure of public opinion stirred up by social activist Anna Hazare over the inordinate delay in the introduction of an effective Lokpal Bill in Parliament. In a government notification gazette issued on 9 April 2011, members of Hazare's team (or Team Anna) were officially associated in the drafting of the Bill! That all this ultimately came to naught is of little consequence; what is noteworthy and significant is the realization that Members of Parliament (once elected) can no longer be unresponsive to the views and protests of large sections of *We the People*.
10. Recounted in Lowell's Independence Day speech delivered in the United States on 4 July 1883.
11. The Old Testament, Ezekiel: V, 25.

Chapter I

One Nation

In 1888, after retirement as member of the Governor-General's Council, John Strachey (1823–1907) wrote about his experiences in the subcontinent in a book titled India *.... To Strachey, the thought that the men and women of the Punjab, Bengal, the North-west Provinces and Madras should ever feel that they belonged to one nation was 'impossible'. He wrote: 'You might with as much reason and probability look forward to a time when a single nation will have taken the place of the various nations of Europe.' But John Strachey was English; he did not belong to India and was not enthused with the idea of India. Fifty years later, free India's first prime minister, Jawaharlal Nehru, was obsessed with it!*

MY, MY! WHAT'S HAPPENING TO MY COUNTRY!
INDIA
R.K. Laxman

India's diversity begins with its geography. The subcontinent of Hindustan – which now includes the independent nations of Pakistan (since 1947) and Bangladesh (since 1971) – was once a separate geographical entity bounded by high mountains in the north and great oceans to the west, south and east. In this great land mass of nearly 4.4 million square kilometres, there lived more than one-fifth of humanity. Until about 85 years ago, it could be approached only by sea or through the narrow passes in the north-west. Protected by natural barriers, it formed a cul-de-sac to successive migratory waves of invaders, who were halted, and who intermingled with the indigenous inhabitants to such an extent that radically distinct categories of people became hard to identify. Language and religion, rather than ethnic origin, became the primary distinguishing features of the myriad peoples of India.

Within the subcontinent, in that vast triangle narrowing down from the everlasting snows in the north to the perennial sultry heat at Cape Comorin (Kanya Kumari) in the south, there are separate geographical regions:

- In the far north, north-east and north-west are the great mountain ranges of the Himalayas[1] – where stand the world's highest peaks – revered as holy by most of the inhabitants of Hindustan.[2]
- Immediately below the Himalayas, a vast alluvial plain stretches in an unbroken surface for some 2720 kilometres across northern India, formed by the three great rivers of the north: the Indus, the Ganges/Ganga and the Brahmaputra. Scorching hot in summer and bitterly cold in winter, the Indo-Gangetic plain is one of the more densely populated regions in the world.
- In the far west, lie the desolate salty marshlands of the Great Rann of Kutch[3] – home to the world's dwindling population of

the onager (the Asian wild ass) and the only breeding ground in the entire subcontinent for that gregarious bird, the flamingo.

- Nearer, but still in the west, are a hundred thousand square kilometres of dune-covered deserts of (what is now) Rajasthan.
- Then, in the far east, at the mouth of the Ganges, are the Sunderbans – the world's largest single block of tidal mangrove forest – home of the Bengal tiger.
- A range of hills in central India (the Central Highlands) separates (as it always did) the southern two-thirds of the subcontinent, whose main geographical feature is a massive tableland that protrudes way down into the Indian Ocean. Hugging its western side (along the Arabian Sea) are located some of the world's most ancient mountain ranges called the Western Ghats, whilst running parallel to the Bay of Bengal, along the eastern coast are the Eastern Ghats.
- The Deccan Plateau occupies a major portion of the southern part of the country: it consists of a gigantic triangular block, a hundred metres high in the north and almost a kilometre tall in the south. It contains much of India's mineral wealth.

* * *

The people of Hindustan were (and still are) as diverse and disparate as its geography. After retirement as member of the Governor-General's Council, John Strachey (1823–1907) wrote about his experiences in the subcontinent in a book titled *India* (first published in 1888). To Strachey, the thought that the men and women of the Punjab, Bengal, the North-west Provinces and Madras should ever feel that they belonged to one nation was 'impossible'. He wrote: 'You might with as much reason and probability look forward to a time when a single nation will have taken the place of the various nations of Europe.'[4] But John Strachey was English; he did not *belong* to India and was not enthused with the *idea of India*. Fifty years later, free India's first prime minister, Jawaharlal Nehru, was obsessed with it!

Writing in the quiet seclusion of a British prison in 1944 (during his ninth term of imprisonment for revolting against the British), Nehru contemplated the *cultural unity* of India:

> The diversity of India is tremendous .... It is fascinating to find how the Bengalis, the Marathas, the Gujaratis, the Tamils, the Andhras, the Oriyas, the Assamese, the Canarese, the Malayalis, the Sindhis, the Punjabis, the Pathans, the Kashmiris, the Rajputs, and the great central block comprising the Hindustani-speaking people, have retained their peculiar characteristics for hundreds of years, have still more or less the same virtues and failings of which old tradition or record tells us, and yet have been throughout these ages *distinctively Indian*, with the same national heritage and the same set of moral and mental qualities .... Christians, Jews, Parsees, or Moslems, who professed a religion of non-Indian origin, on coming to India, settled down there, became *distinctively Indian* in the course of a few generations. Indian converts to some of these religions never ceased to be Indians on account of a change of their faith. They were looked upon in other countries as Indians and foreigners, even though there might have been a community of faith between them.[5]

Nehru was speaking of undivided British India, home to more than 14 major languages (and 33 main dialects) belonging to separate language families, wholly unrelated to one another. The Indian National Congress, of which he was the most frequently elected president,[6] looked upon the entire subcontinent as a single country, its diverse inhabitants as one people.[7] Its rival political organization, the Muslim League, pressed for territorial adjustments – on the basis of areas predominantly inhabited by Muslims – which led, ultimately, to the establishment of the separate state of Pakistan.[8]

* * *

In New Delhi, in the first week of June 1947, a plan to partition India was announced by Viceroy Lord Louis Mountbatten[9] – not entirely out of altruistic motives! In the second week of June, Britain's foreign secretary, Ernest Bevin, had told the British Labour Party Conference in Margate (UK) that the division of India 'would help to consolidate Britain in the Middle East'![10] But conservative public opinion in the UK now looks upon the partition of India as the starting point of the dissolution of the British Empire; a few recall the warning of a previous viceroy, in a prior century, that 'the loss of India would mean that Britain drops straightaway to a third rate power'.[11]

Since a separate homeland for Muslims was ultimately acceptable to leaders of the Indian National Congress, the Indian Independence Act 1947 was drafted and rushed through Britain's Parliament. A fascinating, though otherwise disturbing, account of those times has been recorded by one of India's most respectable statesmen, Maulana Abul Kalam Azad.[12] He has described how the leading figures in the Congress – one by one – acquiesced in the idea of a separate state on the subcontinent; one of the few who did not was the Maulana himself!

The Indian Independence Act 1947 (a Westminster statute) declared that there would be two 'dominions' in the subcontinent: the Dominion of India and the Dominion of Pakistan. The predominantly Muslim-inhabited areas (East Bengal,[13] West Punjab, Sind, Baluchistan and the north-western provinces) were to go to Pakistan. The rest, which included Madras, Bombay, West Bengal, the United Provinces (Uttar Pradesh), East Punjab, Bihar, the Central Provinces and Berar, Orissa and Assam, was to remain a part of India.[14]

***

Pre-partition India comprised not only British India but more than 550 separate political units (Indian States) that owed their existence to the 'paramountcy' of the British Crown.

'Paramountcy' meant that internally as well as externally the Indian States were under the protection of the supreme political power in India. The unavoidable consequence of such complete dependence was the acknowledged suzerainty of the 'protecting power'.[15]

A few of the Indian States, such as Hyderabad and Jammu and Kashmir, were as large in size as the United Kingdom, while many others consisted of areas admeasuring a few thousand square kilometres. During the British Raj, a wide variety of titles were invented for (and conferred on) the rulers of different Indian States, and a formal hierarchical system of 'gun salutes' was institutionalized, which greatly pleased the princes – great and small! The 101-gun imperial salute was reserved only for the British monarch, and the hundreds of what were recognized in international law as 'vassal states'* were classified (in diminishing order of importance) by the number of cannonballs that were required to be fired when paying honour to them! It helped to signify their prestige in the eyes of the British! The seniormost of these 'salute states' were Hyderabad and Berar, Mysore, Jammu and Kashmir, Baroda, and Gwalior, the rulers of which were entitled to a 21-gun salute.

The main feature that distinguished the Indian States from the provinces, in pre-partition India, was that they had not been annexed as part of British India. These states had no international status: their foreign relations remained the exclusive right and responsibility of the British Government. Pledging loyalty to the British Crown, the ruler within each state was an absolute monarch. All local laws flowed from his edicts. In turn, the British Government granted the ruler safety from external attack and internal revolt. Forty-five per cent of the area of pre-partition India (roughly 600,000 square miles or about 1.5 million square kilometres) was located in the Indian States, in which lived one-fourth of the total population of British India! These states were scattered – in bits and pieces – throughout the subcontinent. Their geographical distribution, however, did not coincide with any ethnic, religious, or linguistic division. The peoples of the provinces of British India and of the Indian States had suffered alike from successive waves of invasion and foreign domination. Close ties of cultural affinity, as also of blood and sentiment, bound together the people in the Indian States and in the provinces.

* * *

Under Section 7 of the Indian Independence Act of 1947, the 'paramountcy' of the British Crown in relation to Indian States 'lapsed' on 15 August 1947, leaving their rulers 'finally bereft of all authority, little lost pools of sovereignty, left behind on a barren shore, by the receding tide of history', as picturesquely expressed by Malcolm Muggeridge.[16]

Most of the rulers of the Indian States were persuaded (or *compelled*, by circumstances) to sign instruments of accession to the Union of

*A vassal state is one that is completely under the suzerainty of another state (vassalage is an institution that has now fallen into desuetude). Internationally, its independence is so restricted as scarcely to exist at all. (Source: Wikipedia.)

India.[17] In British India, the largest Indian State of Hyderabad (which included Berar) refused to do so, raising the banner of revolt. On orders from the Central Government, when Indian troops marched into Hyderabad and Berar, the Nizam characterized this as an 'invasion'; the Government of India treated it as an act of 'liberation' of the people living there.[18]

The smaller Indian States were merged into former Indian provinces, which became Part A states under the 1950 Constitution of India. Some of them were grouped together into more viable units and designated as Part B states. The remaining became chief commissioner's provinces (later union territories) administered directly by the Central (or Union) Government.[19] The Indian States were thus wholly absorbed into the Union of India. By an accident of history, however, the British Indian State of Sikkim, in the strategic north-east, stayed out; it was admitted into the Union only in 1975 as India's 22nd state.[20]

Another small but notable Princely State in the north-east was Manipur; notable, because, when still under a constitutional monarchy, it had the unique distinction of having held elections in June 1948, based on adult franchise! Manipur merged with the Indian Union in October 1949, an event that till this day troubles members of the majority Meity community living there; it is also a contributing factor to the insurgency in the Imphal Valley.[21]

***

With the passing of the Indian Independence Act 1947 (creating two dominions – India and Pakistan) political control of the Crown over British India came to an end.

In India, a Constituent Assembly was convened, which claimed to have '*derived from the people* all power and authority to frame a Constitution'[22] – a hugely exaggerated assertion! Members of the Constituent Assembly had been elected, not *by the people,* but by sitting members of already existing provincial legislative assemblies (set up under the Government of India Act 1935)! India's Constituent Assembly had, in all, 217 members, predominantly male, with only 15 women. The representation of the provinces and of the Princely States in the Constituent Assembly was fixed on the basis of one member for every one million of the population.[23] Special representation was given to the Sikhs (in the East Punjab) and to the Muslims, although the Muslim League had boycotted the Constituent Assembly on a call given by Mohammad Ali Jinnah way back in July 1947.

Of the Muslims remaining in India after partition (and there were hundreds of thousands of them), some were members or supporters of the Congress Party; others looked to Muslim stalwarts in the Constituent Assembly, as well as to Congress leadership, to protect their interests.

Have they been well served? Have the interests of the Muslims who remained behind in India at the time of partition (and of their progeny) been adequately secured and safeguarded? Not according to Jaswant Singh – cabinet minister in the National Democratic Alliance (NDA), which was in power at the Centre from 1999 to 2004 – in his book titled *Jinnah: India-Partition-Independence* (Rupa, New Delhi, 2009). He gave the reasons in a television interview (in August 2009) over CNN-IBN with Karan Thapar, a noted broadcaster. Here are excerpts from a transcript of this interview:

> Karan Thapar: Your book also raises disturbing questions about the partition of India. You say it was done in a way 'that multiplied our problems without solving any communal issue'.
>
> Then you ask 'if the communal, the principle issue, remains in an even more exacerbated form than before, then why did we divide at all?'
>
> Jaswant Singh: Yes, indeed why? I cannot yet find the answer. Look into the eyes of the Muslims who live in India and you truly see through the pain they live – to which land do they belong?
>
> We treat them as aliens, somewhere inside, because we continue to ask even after partition: *you still want something*?
>
> These are citizens of India – it was Jinnah's failure because he never advised Muslims who stayed back.
>
> Karan Thapar: One of the most moving passages of your biography is when you write of Indian Muslims who stayed on in India and didn't go to Pakistan. You say they are 'abandoned', you say they are

'bereft of a sense of kinship', not 'one with the entirety' and then you add that 'this robs them of the essence of psychological security'.

JASWANT SINGH: That is right, it does. That lies at the root of the Sachar Committee report.[24]

KARAN THAPAR: So, in fact, Indian Muslims have paid the price in their personal lives.

JASWANT SINGH: Without doubt, as have Pakistani Muslims.

KARAN THAPAR: Muslims have paid a price on both sides.

JASWANT SINGH: I think Muslims have paid a price in partition. They would have been significantly stronger in a united India, effectively so much larger land, every potential is here. Of course Pakistan or Bangladesh won't like what I am saying.

* * *

India's constitutional historian (Professor Granville Austin) has accurately described the Constituent Assembly as 'a one-party body in an essentially one-party country. The Assembly was the Congress and the Congress was India'.[25]

Although elected on the basis of a very limited franchise, the Constituent Assembly performed its function of constitution making as if it was truly representative of all sections of Indian society: this was simply because it consisted of persons with vision, persons who were acutely conscious of the historic (though difficult) task of creating an egalitarian society from out of a bewildering mass of religions, communities, castes and races, out of peoples speaking different languages, and having separate beliefs and practices. The members of the Constituent Assembly knew well their country and its people. They understood the problems of the society in which they lived. They were aware of the historic injustices and inequities afflicting the large mass of people and they realized the imperative of redressing them by constitutional means as early as possible – since the alternative was too frightening to behold. Ignorance, illiteracy and, above all, mass poverty, were taken note of by members of the Constituent Assembly; they were also conscious of the fact that the Hindu religion – '*the religion of the overwhelming majority of people as it was being practised – was not known for its egalitarian ethos*'![26] The debates in the Constituent

Assembly fill 11 large volumes. Large parts of its deliberations reflect the anxiety of members of that body for the need to forge political unity out of a multilingual, multireligious assortment of people at varied stages of development.

* * *

The most remarkable feature of the debates in the Constituent Assembly was that, because of India's immediate political past, they were conducted almost entirely in English!

When the British came, saw and conquered India in 1774, Warren Hastings, the first governor-general of Bengal, decreed that the English residing in India should acquaint themselves to the fullest extent with Indian languages and culture in order to better associate themselves with (what were then called) 'the Orientals'. This led to the establishment of a famous college at Fort William in Calcutta, where Arabic, Persian and Sanskrit were taught, and students could avail themselves of courses in Hindu and Muslim laws as well as in English law. This new policy continued for the next 50 years and more, till the mid-1830s, when it was reversed. Lord Thomas Babington Macaulay's now-infamous Minute on Education – compiled in the spring of 1835 – was responsible for changing the entire course of British educational policy. Macaulay favoured English, and the curriculum was adapted accordingly. It had fateful consequences, both for the Indians and the British. For Indians, the changed educational policy did not produce a learned class imbued with the best that the English language and literature could offer, but, rather, an English-speaking secretarial and professional class, 'without a tradition of responsibility and power'.[27] 'Education for clerks' was how Nehru[28] summed up the British educational policy in India during the nineteenth century. As for the British, looking back in 1964, Malcolm Muggeridge said, in a broadcast over the BBC, that 'education was about the worst thing the British did to India and appropriately enough this contributed to our departure.'[29] He then embellished his assertion with a rhetorical query: 'Was it not the enraged and unemployed graduates who chased us out, hurling after us curses, and copies of the *Oxford Book of English Verse*?'

Many years before, C. F. Andrews, a vigorous supporter of Indian independence, had expressed different sentiments, with less rhetorical flourish! In a letter addressed to the private secretary of the then viceroy of India (the Earl of Minto - 1905 to 1910), Andrews wrote:

> English as the language of education has justified itself, in spite of great drawbacks. It has had a supreme political justification. It has made India no longer only a geographical expression but a political unity. *It has created the hope and the possibility of an Indian Nation.* English history and literature have fashioned the political thought of modern India and fashioned it inevitably on national lines.[30]

'The hope and the possibility of an Indian Nation' were achieved, almost fortuitously, when the British quit India in 1947 – in haste and confusion – leaving its inhabitants to fend for themselves as best as they could![31]

It is in the above background that our document of governance was drafted – by persons elected by members of already existing legislative assemblies. Most of the men and women so elected were not only fluent in the English language but also they worked and even thought in English!

* * *

On the eve of independence, grave misgivings had been expressed about the legal system inherited from the British.

Staunch followers of Mahatma Gandhi accused the British of wreaking havoc in India by replacing quick, cheap and efficient *panchayat* justice with *courts*, '*which were expensive and dreadfully slow*, and, which promoted endless dishonesty, and degraded public morality'. They would rather have panchayats dispense justice at the village level, thereby eliminating the need for lawyers and complex laws! One of Mahatma Gandhi's followers, Shriman Narayan Agarwal, drafted what he called a 'Gandhian Constitution for Free India', which had the Mahatma's tacit approval.[32] In Agarwal's draft constitution, the primary political unit was to be the village panchayat, whose members would be elected by all adults in the village. Above the village panchayats would come a hierarchy of indirectly elected bodies. First, the *taluka* and district panchayats, each comprising the sarpanchs (panchayat leaders) of the next lower panchayats and having only advisory powers over them. Members from district and municipal panchayats would make up the provincial panchayat, which would elect a president to serve as head of provincial governments. Presidents of provincial panchayats would comprise the All-India Panchayat, whose president, in turn, would be the head of state and of government, which would be ministerial in character. But Agarwal's draft was not adopted. When the Constituent Assembly first debated the Objectives Resolution (which Nehru had drafted), it became certain that India would have a centralized parliamentary system of government. The Objectives Resolution of 9 December 1946 declared that the new Constitution would be dedicated to the goal of a social revolution, but did not specify how this would be achieved. Neither panchayats nor indirect forms of government were mentioned. It became clear that the Constituent Assembly was not contemplating a Gandhian-type constitution; in the debate on the Objectives Resolution, there was neither approval nor criticism of the omission of Panchayati Raj. The subject was just not mentioned! Members of the Constituent Assembly spoke of democracy, socialism and the responsibilities of legislatures, but not of the need for an '*Indian*' type of government. Attempts by Gandhians and 'traditionalists' to form a polity based on village autonomy and self-sufficiency were not accepted since the draft Constitution had deliberately opted for a federal and parliamentary republic, with a centralized bureaucratic administration. The only concession made to the Gandhians was in one of the Directive Principles of State Policy (set out in Article 40 of the Constitution), which provided that the state shall take steps to organize village panchayats and endow them with such powers and authority as may be necessary to enable them to function as units of self-government.

* * *

The Constitution of India of 1950 – one of the longest ever framed for an independent country – was proclaimed on 26 January 1950.

The Constitution contained 395 articles and eight schedules occupying, in the official edition, 251 pages. 'Too long, too detailed and too rigid' was the laconic comment of Sir Ivor Jennings, chronicler of Westminster-type constitutions around the common-law world.[33] It was 'a lawyer's constitution', Jennings had said (with a sneer!), 'framed only for lawyers'! That may have been true. But looking back, what is of importance is that this 'lawyer's constitution' has endured; it has so far lasted 60 odd years – and still going strong!

But the record of two (now independent) countries in the subcontinent has not been the same: Pakistan (since 1947) and Bangladesh (since 1971). The reason is that the life of a written constitution – like the life the law – depends not on logic or draftsmanship but on experience. In Pakistan, since August 1947, there have been drafted three separate documents of governance at different times – but interspersed with periods of martial law and civil and military dictatorships. So too with Bangladesh: the Constitution of the People's Republic of Bangladesh 1972 has undergone periods of suspension (when martial law was imposed) and of radical changes over the years. A brief history of constitution making (and unmaking) in Pakistan and in Bangladesh is recorded in the Appendix.

In the subcontinent, one useful lesson about written constitutions is *that they do not work on their own*. A special effort has to be made by those entrusted to work them to see that they do not flounder. When India's Constituent Assembly was about to complete its task (in November 1949 – just a day before the adoption of the Constitution of India), the chairman of the Drafting Committee, Dr B. R. Ambedkar, in his reply to the entire debate, said:

> However good a Constitution may be it is sure to turn out bad because those who are called upon to work it happen to be a bad lot. However bad a Constitution may be, it may turn out to be good if those who are called to work it happen to be a good lot. The working of a Constitution does not depend wholly upon the nature of the Constitution.[34]

* * *

The length of India's Constitution was due not only to the size of the country but also to the problems of accommodating, in a federal-type constitution, the points of view of representatives of people speaking different languages and observing different faiths, all striving at the same time to transform a rigid, hierarchical social order into an egalitarian society.

The chapter on Fundamental Rights (Part III of the Constitution) owed much to the standard-setting Charter of the United Nations (1945) and to the almost contemporaneous Universal Declaration of Human Rights (1948).

The Constitution is divided into 22 parts dealing with various aspects of the country's governance. In some places, it suffers from an excessive emphasis on detail, which could have been left to ordinary legislation. It often shows (not surprisingly) a hybrid mixture of different, almost conflicting, concepts. India is a land of contrasts: the Ganga (the Ganges) is revered and worshiped by millions as India's most sacred river, but it is also the most polluted. In a land of conflicting ideas and ideals, even the basic document of governance is replete with incongruities:

- With more than 30 main indigenous languages and dialects from which to choose, the Constitution recognized English as one of the two official languages.
- Among the regional languages listed in the Eighth Schedule in 1950 was Sanskrit, which was (and is) hardly ever spoken – except in prayer[35] – like Latin in the West.
- Though conceived as a *secular* Republic, the chapter on Fundamental Rights (Part III) has recognized and protected India's six main religions and nearly 200 'religious persuasions'.[36]
- The right to equality was guaranteed, and the state was prohibited from discriminating against any citizen on grounds only of race, religion, caste or place of birth, but, at the same time, the Constitution also recognized and encouraged 'compensatory discrimination' in favour of socially and *educationally backward classes of citizens.* But mere economic backwardness arising out of dire poverty was not recognized as a basis for preferential treatment in educational institutions in the state or in employment under the state.
- While adopting adult suffrage as the basis for periodic elections to Parliament and state assemblies and abolishing special electoral rolls based on race, religion, caste or sex, the Constitution made provision for the reservation of seats in the House of the People

(the lower house of Parliament or Lok Sabha), and in the Legislative Assembly of every state, for Scheduled Castes and Scheduled Tribes: for centuries, the outcastes of Hindu society.[37]

Despite these seemingly disparate and contradictory provisions necessitated by social, historical and political considerations, if there is one overriding concept discernible in the Indian Constitution, it is the *unity of the nation*.

* * *

It was the ideal of a unified India mentioned in the Preamble to the Constitution ('integrity of India') that inspired provisions for a common citizenship.[38]

Geographically, British India was never one cohesive unit. Even during British rule, India was interspersed with a proliferation of states. Politically, with the lapse of paramountcy and the loss of protection of the British Crown, the inhabitants in the Princely States became virtually 'stateless'. This condition contributed directly to the relatively smooth absorption of almost all the Princely States into the Union of India. The Constitution provided a common citizenship not only for the former inhabitants of British India but also for those of the former Indian states. With their accession to India, the territory of these states became a part of the territory of India. Every person domiciled in India who was born (or either of whose parents was born) in India, or who had ordinarily been a resident in India since 1945, was deemed to be a citizen of India (Article 5). The Constitution also guaranteed to every citizen the Fundamental Right to move freely throughout India and to reside and settle in any part of India (Article 19[l][d] and [e]).[39]

Common citizenship meant non-discriminatory participation in the political life and affairs of the country. Communal representation in legislative bodies and separate electorates for separate communities (introduced by the British in 1909) was abolished. There was to be one general electoral roll for every territorial constituency (Article 325) and every adult citizen of India was entitled to be registered as a voter at every election to the Lok Sabha and to the Assembly of the state in which he or she resided (Article 326). Anyone – man or woman – Hindu, Muslim,

Sikh, Christian, Buddhist, Jain or Parsi, who is a citizen, is eligible to be elected to any office in the land, even the highest. Each decennial census (after 1951) has recorded that more than 80 per cent of the Indian people profess some form of the Hindu religion; in the census of 2001, the Muslims constituted about 12.4 per cent of the population and the Sikhs less than 2 per cent.

From 1950, there have been 12 presidents of India (an elected office): three of them have been Muslims, one has been a Sikh, and from 2007 till 24 July 2012, we had a woman as president.

* * *

If the provision of a common citizenship raised few or no problems, the next step – that of a common language – presented manifold difficulties leading to long and acrimonious debate in the Constituent Assembly.

The languages spoken by the majority of the people of India fell into two major unrelated language families: in the North were the Sanskrit-based Indo-Aryan languages (Assamese, Bengali, Gujarati, Hindi, Marathi, Oriya, Pahari and Punjabi) and, in the South, the Dravidian languages (Kannada, Malayalam, Tamil and Telugu).[40]

Then there was the language of the conquerors. Under Mughal rule (which preceded the British), Persian was the court language, but with the fall of the Mughal Empire, Persian was replaced by Urdu.[41] The name 'Urdu' is derived from 'Zaban-e-Urdu-Muala', which means 'the language of the exalted camp', that is, the camp (or court) of the ruling sultan of Delhi. With the establishment and consolidation of British rule, English came to be adopted as the language in which official correspondence was carried on at higher levels throughout the country. Higher education was also imparted in English, which became increasingly the language linking the intelligentsia of the country. It was also the language of the superior courts (the high courts and the federal court of India[42]). It served as a force for national unity and for the development of a national consciousness.

Competing claims were made in the Constituent Assembly for recognition of one or another language as the official language. Tempers ran high. To assuage them, Mahatma Gandhi suggested the adoption of Hindustani – a mixture of Hindi and Urdu – as the common language, its use being recognized in both the Devnagari and the Urdu scripts. But this was rejected: Hindustani was not acceptable to the people of the South. The Constituent Assembly commenced its debate on the official language, and on recognition of regional languages, in a tense atmosphere. More than 400 amendments to the Language Resolution were tabled. Language, which contributed to the diversity and cultural richness of India, was now threatening to divide it. Statesmanship compelled a compromise, and this compromise is reflected in the 'Language Clauses' that were finally adopted in the Constitution (Part XVII).[43] The official language of India was declared to be Hindi in the Devnagari script, but English was to continue in use for all official purposes for an initial period of 15 years, extendable by Parliament (Article 343).[44] The period for the concurrent use of English has been extended indefinitely with the enactment (by India's Parliament) of the Official Languages Act 1963. Accordingly, both Hindi and English have become official languages of the Union of India. Both are used to transact business in the Houses of Parliament (the House of the People or Lok Sabha and the Council of States or Rajya Sabha) and for all official communications between the Union Government and the government of a state that has not adopted Hindi alone as its language (see Article 346). The official language in each state was left to be decided by the state legislatures – each could adopt the regional language or Hindi (Article 345). In 1950, the states were multilingual as several languages were spoken in different regions of each state. The Constitution therefore provided that the president be empowered to direct that a language be recognized officially throughout a state when a substantial portion of that state's population spoke that language (Article 347).

* * *

The territorial division of states was a legacy from the past.

The demarcation had been determined partly by the sporadic growth of British power in India and partly by the process of integration of 550 Princely States. Shortly after the Constitution came into force, there was a demand for a 'rational' reorganization of states, on a linguistic and cultural basis. This was first conceded (in 1953) in the case of the Telugu-speaking areas of Madras and Mysore states, which, in 1956 were merged with the Telugu-speaking areas of the former state of Hyderabad to form India's first and largest linguistic state, Andhra Pradesh. This new state had to contend with many growing pains. Shortly after its formation, people of the same stock, united by a common language, again threatened to divide. There were demands for the formation of a separate state for the Telangana region, which was economically and culturally more backward than the rest of Andhra. For a while the problems were contained. The bifurcation of the state was averted, but not before a constitutional guarantee was secured that, in matters of public employment and education, equitable opportunities would be provided for the people of the Telangana region (Article 371-D, introduced in the Constitution in 1973). The formation of Andhra is a reminder that a feeling, amongst a section of the people of being oppressed and outflanked by the more fortunate, can transcend, and even disrupt, bonds of racial and linguistic affinity.[45]

On the recommendation of a commission presided over by a sitting judge of the Supreme Court of India,[46] the territories of other existing states were redrawn and territorial boundaries were readjusted to fit the linguistic and cultural similarities of inhabitants in various areas. 'Nothing gives rise to so much anger, hostility and even hatred,' wrote the distinguished civil servant Nari Rustumjee, with first-hand experience in the north-eastern region, 'as the apprehension of *cultural aggression* and it is this apprehension that has been at the root of unrest in India's north-eastern frontiers since British withdrawal.'[47] In north-eastern India an attempt had been made to enforce a regional language. The composite state of Assam, as defined by the Constitution, included the hill and tribal areas. In their zeal to promote unity among diverse elements in the state, the Assamese insisted that theirs should be the only recognized regional language. This alienated the people of the hill areas.[48] The result was the formation of smaller, non-viable states and union territories in the north-east. Today, India (which is described in the opening article of the Constitution as 'a Union of States') includes 28 *linguistic* states[49] and seven union territories that are directly administered by the Central Government.

Each linguistic unit has adopted its own regional language – at times more than one. Hindi is the regional language in what used to be the five northern states[50] (Bihar, Madhya Pradesh, Rajasthan, and Uttar Pradesh[51]); Urdu in Jammu and Kashmir;[52] Punjabi in Punjab; Hindi and Gujarati in Gujarat; Pahari in Himachal Pradesh (a hill state carved out of the former state of East Punjab); Marathi in Maharashtra (whose principal city is Mumbai; earlier called Bombay); Oriya in Orissa (now Odisha); Assamese in Assam; Bengali in Tripura and West Bengal; Manipuri in Manipur; English (along with Lepcha, Bhutia, and Nepali) in the eastern hill state of Sikkim; English and Khasi in Meghalaya and in the tribal and mountainous state of Nagaland; and English and Mizo in Mizoram[53] and Arunachal Pradesh.

In the South, the regional languages are: Telugu in Andhra Pradesh;[54] Kannada in Karnataka (the former state of Mysore); Malayalam in Kerala and in the offshore union territory of Lakshadweep (the Laccadive Islands); and Tamil – the oldest Dravidian language – in Tamil Nadu (originally, the state of Madras). In the former Portuguese possession of Goa on the west coast, the languages of administration are Konkani and Marathi and in the former French enclaves of Pondicherry (also known as Puducherry) and Mahe on the east coast, French, English, Tamil, Telugu and Malayalam are used for official purposes.

The framers laid the constitutional groundwork for strengthening Hindi – one of the two official languages of the Union. Article 351 has imposed a duty on both Parliament and the Central Government to promote and strengthen the language, drawing sustenance from, but not interfering with, the 14 other main languages specified in the Eighth Schedule (now extended to 22). The Constitution has also directed that a commission be constituted every 10 years to make recommendations for the progressive use of the Hindi language for the official purposes of the Union (Article 344).

* * *

Because of a desire not to disturb the broad pattern of the legal system introduced by the British,[55] all proceedings in the Supreme Court of India as well as in the high courts, located in the states, were to be conducted in English.

Bills introduced in, and all Acts passed by, the Parliament and state legislatures were also to continue to be in English (Article 348).

A provision authorizing the use of Hindi in the high courts, when the appropriate state legislature so decides (and the president concurs), has been availed of in some of the high courts (e.g., in Uttar Pradesh, Rajasthan and Madhya Pradesh) where proceedings are now conducted both in English and in Hindi. However, in providing for the principal languages spoken in India, the constitutional draftsman apparently overlooked the innumerable 'mother tongues': languages spoken in homes in various parts of India.[56] In the census of 1961, 1652 'mother tongues' had been listed, but only 33 of them are still spoken by groups of people numbering more than 100,000! By a Constitutional Amendment in 1956, special obligations had been imposed on states and local authorities throughout India to provide adequate facilities for instruction in the 'mother tongue' at the primary stage of education for children belonging to linguistic minorities (Article 350-A).

* * *

Constitutional safeguards for linguistic groups are to be found in Article 29.

Any group of citizens having a distinct language, script or culture has a Fundamental Right to conserve it (Article 29[1]) and thus maintain its cultural identity. Likewise, no citizen can be denied admission on grounds of language, religion, race or caste into any educational institution maintained by the state or receiving aid out of state funds (Article 29[2]). Since language, script and culture can only be preserved and promoted through education, Article 30 guarantees to religious and linguistic minorities 'the right to establish and maintain educational institutions of their choice'. These rights are expressed in absolute terms and, like all other Fundamental Rights, are enforceable through writs and other directions issued by the high courts and by the Supreme Court of India.

In 1952, a small linguistic minority known as Anglo-Indians,[57] who managed many reputable schools in Bombay, were adversely affected when the state government passed an order forbidding state-aided schools that used English as a medium of instruction to admit pupils other than Anglo-Indians or citizens of non-Asian descent. Anglo-Indians could maintain and administer their schools and teach in English but only to Anglo-Indians. If they admitted other Indians, they forfeited state aid unless, of course, they switched to Hindi as the medium of instruction. The object was laudable: to encourage the use of the official language (itself a constitutional prescription under Article 351). Nonetheless, the order was struck down as violating Article 29(1) and (2) because Anglo-Indians had a distinct language (English), which they had the right to conserve, and because the direct effect of the order was to prevent Indians from entering Anglo-Indian schools, on grounds of race and language.[58]

The right of a 'section of citizens' to conserve its language (Article 29[1]) has been held to include the right to *agitate* for the protection of the language. Political agitation for conservation of the language of a section of the citizens could not be regarded as a 'corrupt practice' within the meaning of Section 123(3) of the Representation of People's Act 1951, since the right conferred upon a section of citizens residing in the territory of India or any part thereof to conserve its language, script or culture has been held to be absolute.[59] With the reorganization of states into linguistic units, a Constitutional Amendment in 1956 provided for the appointment of a special officer for linguistic minorities. His duty is to investigate all matters relating to constitutional safeguards for linguistic minorities and to report to Parliament and to the concerned state governments (Article 350-B).

***

Differing views have been expressed on the utility and effect of the regrouping of states on linguistic and cultural lines and on ensuring separate educational and cultural opportunities to linguistic groups.

Such regrouping has led to regional loyalties and, at times, even secessionist tendencies. To counteract them, the Constitution was amended in 1963 to introduce the overriding concept of the sovereignty and integrity of India.[60] Basic individual freedoms guaranteed under Article 19 (free speech, peaceful assembly, forming associations or unions, moving freely throughout India, residing and settling in any part of India and practising any profession, occupation, trade or business) are now subject to laws imposing reasonable restrictions on the exercise of these rights in the interests (inter alia) of 'the sovereignty and integrity of India'; in other words, in the wider interests of the unity of India. Then, in accordance with recommendations of the National Integration Council, amendments were introduced in the general penal law to make it an offence for anyone to promote or attempt to promote feelings of enmity or hatred among religious, social or language groups or communities.

The divisive force of language has been contained by the Supreme Court of India in its role as interpreter of the Constitution. Before 1976, the states had plenary power of legislation on the subject of 'education', which was then in List II – the State List – in the Seventh Schedule (of the Constitution of India). Yet, when the state of Gujarat enacted a law prescribing *Gujarati* as the exclusive language of instruction in the universities in the entire state, the Supreme Court struck it down as beyond the state's legislative competence.[61] This was because the 'coordination and determination of standards in institutions for higher learning' was also an exclusive head of legislation for Parliament – in the Union List (Entry 66) – and since this entry necessarily comprehended (in the view of the Supreme Court) the prescription of language, as a determinant of 'standards', the state law was held to be beyond the competence of the state legislature. The decision, although criticized in some circles, was largely welcomed, not merely in the wider interests of higher education, but in the larger interests of preserving the unity of India.

By the 42nd Constitution Amendment Act 1976, the subject of 'education' was removed from the exclusive State List and placed in the Concurrent List. Matters enumerated in the Concurrent List (List III – in the Seventh Schedule) can now be legislated upon both by Parliament as well as by state legislatures. In the event of a conflict, laws made by Parliament would prevail unless state laws have been enacted with the previous assent of the president of India. But even such state laws can be overridden by laws, inconsistent therewith, if and when made by Parliament.

* * *

Despite judicial and constitutional attempts at containment, linguistic factionalism has definitely fostered a spirit of regionalism.

Language differences are the most significant aspect of the diversity of India (a good thing); they have also contributed to the diversification of India (not such a good thing!). Differences in language are a part of regional identity, but they can and do promote (and perpetuate) regional distinctiveness. In earlier editions of the *State of the World Atlas*, 'India' had been described as 'a country with *a* significant linguistic conflict'. Even though this description has not been repeated in the latest (the eighth edition) of that book, India remains today 'a country with a significant linguistic conflict'. In the past two decades, regional political parties have become more vocal and more dominant in Indian politics. At the Centre, the traditionally national 'Congress Party', which in the British days fought hard for India's independence (and which, Mahatma Gandhi pleaded, should be disbanded after independence – a plea that fell on deaf ears!) has been reduced from being once the most formidable majority party in the country to being just one out of many political parties (earnestly looking for 'allies', whether like-minded or not!).

***

India is a religious – an overly religious – country!

Religious belief plays a dominant role in the lives of the people: it even permeates into officialdom. For instance, a purely secular activity like lodging a criminal case in a court of law is sometimes accompanied by religious ritual! A vernacular (Tamil) daily with a large circulation reported, in its issue of 22 January 2005, the following event:

> Kanchipuram:* Yesterday, police filed an 1873-page 'mega' charge sheet in the Sankararaman murder case** that has caused so much sensation over the last 4 months. Before presenting it to the court, SP [superintendent of police] Premkumar placed it at the altar of the Varadaraja Perumal Temple deity and performed a special puja

*Kanchipuram is a 'temple town' in Tamil Nadu located about 85 kilometres west of Madras (now Chennai).

**In 2004, an ex-employee (A. Sankararaman) of the Kanchi Math (monastic institution) was murdered. While investigating the case, the police charged Sri Jayendra Saraswati (the head of the Kanchi Math) and some of his associates with the murder.

> for winning the case. The chargesheet was prepared with the help of prominent legal advisors. The chargesheet was completed 2 days ago .... The other policemen who had been involved in investigating this case also took part in this special puja. They revealed [to us] that they prayed with all their hearts to win the case![62]

Not surprisingly, on a recent visit to India (in January 2012), America's talk-show host Oprah Winfrey was quoted as saying: 'People here don't just talk religion, *they live it*.'[63]

A majority of the population (81.8 per cent according to the census of 2001) of India profess the Hindu religion. Almost the same percentage did so when the Europeans (the French, the Portuguese and then the British) first came to India. Within its borders there are followers of all the major religions of the world. From the matrix of Hinduism have emerged three other great world religions: Jainism, Buddhism and Sikhism. Christianity came to India many centuries before it reached Europe. One of the twelve apostles of Jesus Christ – St Thomas – visited India in A.D. 56, converted a large number of its inhabitants, and was martyred at Mylapore. He lies buried in Madras. Judaism and its adherents (though now very few) had once found a home and refuge in India. The ancient and beautiful synagogue in Cochin (now Kochi), in the state of Kerala, built in 1568, bears testimony to the tolerance of Indian rulers to adherents of alien faiths.

Next to the several cults of Hinduism, however, the main religion has been Islam. It has been on Indian soil since A.D. 650, a few years after the Prophet's death, when Arab traders settled on the western seacoast of Malabar (now part of the state of Kerala). Their descendants are so Indianized that they speak the same language (Malayalam) as their Hindu brethren and read the Koran, not in Arabic, but in the Malayalam script!

Forced conversions in Europe and Central Asia in the Middle Ages effectively destroyed the identity of religious minorities. Not so in India. The Ismaili Khojas (followers of the Aga Khan), the Cutchi Memons and the Bohras (from western India) were originally Hindus. They had been converted to Islam about 800 to 900 years ago during the invasions of Mahmud of Ghazni (A.D. 997–1030) and his successors. They are today

Shia Muslims and practise the religion of Islam, but they have retained, for centuries, part of their original cultural identity. Until statutory law intervened in the late 1930s – with the passage of the Shariat Act 1937 and the Cutchi Memons Act 1938 – they were governed in matters of inheritance and succession by Hindu law.[64]

Religion in India not only means the profession of faith but also encompasses places – temples, gurudwaras, mosques, churches and synagogues. It includes idols and deities and offerings to them, bathing places, graves, tombs and properties attached to, and owned by, religious institutions. All this – faith, worship, ritual and the secular activities of religious groups – had to be provided for in the Constitution of India, in the chapter on Fundamental Rights, beyond the reach of legislative or executive interference.

In India, there is no provision similar to the First Amendment of the Constitution of the United States of America, which prohibits the US Congress from making any law respecting an *establishment* of religion. But in India, as in the USA, there is also no state religion (as there is in the United Kingdom). This was clarified by a Constitutional Amendment that added (in the year 1976 – for renewed emphasis) the word 'secular' in the Preamble to the Constitution.[65] In the 'Sovereign, Socialist, Secular Democratic Republic of India', no religious instruction can be provided in any educational institution wholly maintained out of state funds (Article 28[1]), nor can any person be compelled to pay taxes to be used for the promotion or maintenance of any particular religion or religious denomination (Article 27). Similarly, no person attending any educational institution recognized by the state or receiving aid out of state funds can be compelled to take part in any religious instruction imparted in that institution or to attend any religious worship conducted in it without his/her or his/her guardian's consent (Article 26[3]). At the same time, 'all persons' (not merely citizens) are equally entitled to freedom of conscience and the right to freely profess, practise and propagate their religion (Article 25). Every 'religious denomination' (there were 183 of them in the 2001 census), and even sections thereof, retain the Fundamental Right to establish and maintain institutions for religious and charitable purposes, to manage their own affairs in matters of religion and to own, acquire and administer property in accordance with law (Article 26).

The freedom to practise religion and the freedom to manage religious affairs are not absolute. They are subject to public order, morality and health. The clauses on freedom of religion have been modelled on Article 44 of the Constitution of Ireland 1937. The Supreme Court of India has repeatedly stressed the breadth (and the limits) of this freedom. Religion in India includes forms of worship and all religious practices that are (or are believed by the faithful to be) an integral part of the religion.[66] Even the right of the head of a religious denomination to excommunicate any of its members on religious grounds has been recognized and upheld.[67] In 1977, the Supreme Court of India held that the right to 'propagate' one's religion does not include the right of conversion to another faith, since Article 25 (it was said) guarantees freedom for *all* religions, not for any particular one![68] This decision – in *Stanislaus* (1977) – runs counter to the original intent of the draftsmen.[69] In the draft article approved by the Minorities Subcommittee (and later by the Constituent Assembly), the right to propagate religion was deliberately added so as to guarantee to proselytizing religions (such as Christianity and Islam) the right to preach religion with the object of conversion![70]

Although every religious denomination enjoys complete autonomy in deciding what rites and ceremonies are essential according to its tenets, the right to manage the properties of a religious institution has always been regarded as a secular matter that can only be regulated by law.[71]

* * *

Before the Constitution of India 1950, laws in British India responded to the dual function of law in a pluralist society: viz., enactments that reacted to social changes and those that initiated them.

In matters relating to customs governing various communities, the law responded to clearly formulated social sentiments. Thus the statutory prohibition against child marriages,[72] laws prohibiting bigamous marriages amongst Hindus,[73] the right of Hindu women to inherit and own property[74] and many other laws came to be introduced (and passed) in the wake of movements started by social reformers of the time, actively encouraged by means of penal sanctions imposed by the ruler. The practice of *suttee* (*sati*) among certain sections of the Hindu community – where a widowed woman, either voluntarily or by importunity or coercion, would immolate herself on her husband's funeral pyre – was made an offence punishable by death. When this law was rigorously implemented, a group of conservative Hindus from the then province of Sindh called on the British Army's commander-in-chief in India, protesting against what they considered to be an interference with their customary law. The response of the gruff General Charles James Napier was as follows: 'Gentlemen, you say it is your custom to burn widows. Very well, we also have a custom: when men burn a woman alive we tie a rope around their necks and hang them. You build your funeral pyre. Beside it my carpenters will build the gallows. You may follow your custom. We will follow ours.'[75]

The Indian Penal Code 1860 (principally, but not solely, the handiwork of Lord Macaulay[76]) virtually extended by legislation the English Common Law of Blasphemy to all religions practised in India. Under Section 298, 'any person who uttered any word or made any sound in the hearing of that person, or made any gesture in the sight of that person, or placed any object in the sight of that person, with deliberate intent of wounding the religious feelings of that person was to be punished with imprisonment or fine or both'. The framers of this section had two objects in view:

> We wish to allow all fair latitude to religious discussion and at the same time to prevent the professors of any religion from offering, under the pretext of such discussion, intentional insult to what is held sacred by others. We do not conceive that any person can be justified in wounding with deliberate intention religious feelings of his neighbour by word, gesture or exhibition. A warm expression dropped in the heat of controversy or an argument urged by a person not for the purpose of insulting and annoying the professors of a different creed, but in good faith for the purpose of vindicating his own, will not fall under the definition contained in this clause.[77]

By an amendment of the Penal Code in 1898, inciting enmity or hatred amongst different groups of His/Her Majesty's subjects on grounds of religion, race, language, caste or community was also made a separate offence (Section 153A). Despite this amendment, in 1927, a judge of the High Court of Lahore, then part of British India, held[78] that existing statutory provisions in the code prohibiting incitement of hatred and enmity between subjects of His Majesty were not meant to stop polemics, however scurrilous or in bad taste, against a particular religious leader, whether alive or dead. There were strong public protests and the legislature had to intervene. *Intentional insult* or attempts to *intentionally* insult any religion or outrage religious feelings of any class of His Majesty's subjects was then made a separate offence (Section 295A of the IPC) and freedom from vilification of one's religious beliefs and sentiments got restored.

But all this was before 1950, when India had no guaranteed Fundamental Rights. The Constitution of India 1950 guaranteed the right to freedom of speech and expression (Article 19 [1] [a]) as well as the right to freedom of religion and religious worship (Article 25). The enjoyment of each of these separate Fundamental Rights is subject to laws imposing reasonable restrictions in the interest of 'public order': (Article 19[2] and Article 25[1]). The constitutional validity of Section 295A of the Penal Code was challenged as an infringement of the Fundamental Right to freedom of expression. The challenge was repelled in a statesman-like decision of Chief Justice S. R. Das who spoke for a Constitution Bench of the Supreme Court of India.[79] He said that insults to religion offered unwittingly, and without deliberate or malicious intent, even though outraging the religious feelings of a class of citizens, did not come within the mischief of Section 295A. Section 295A only punished an aggravated form of insult to religion perpetrated with the deliberate or malicious intention of outraging religious feelings of a class, and it was the calculated tendency of this aggravated form of insult to disrupt public order that was prohibited by the section. The judgment preserved the delicate balance between two sets of rights, without losing the essence of either. It avoided a conflict between the Fundamental Right of free speech and the right of a person to be protected from blasphemy when exercising his/her equally Fundamental Right to profess and practise his/her own religion.

* * *

The conflict between the right to free speech and the law of blasphemy was differently resolved in the United Kingdom.

In 1979, the Judicial Committee of the House of Lords in England said[80] that the common law did not interfere with the expression of bona fide opinion. It prohibited, and rendered punishable as a misdemeanour, the use of coarse and scurrilous ridicule on subjects that were sacred to the majority of the people in the country. The true test was whether the words were calculated to outrage and insult the Christian's religious feelings; and in the modern law, the phrase 'a tendency to cause a breach of peace' was really a reference to that test. The law sought to safeguard public order and tranquillity. The English court said that in order to secure conviction for the offence of publishing a blasphemous libel (i.e., a scurrilous attack on Christ or Christianity), it was sufficient for the prosecution to prove the intent to publish material that was, *in fact*, blasphemous. It was then not at all necessary for the prosecution to prove (as in India) that the defendant also *intended to blaspheme*![81] The case arose out of a poem titled 'The Love that Dares to Speak Its Name', which appeared in the newspaper *Gay News*, edited and published by Denis Lemon. In the issue of June 1976, a Professor James Kirkup fantasized (in verse) explicit acts of sodomy with the body of Christ immediately after his death, ascribing to Jesus, during his lifetime, promiscuous homosexual practices with the Apostles and with others. A prosecution was launched, and Lemon and the publishing company, Gay News Limited, were found guilty and were convicted, and sentenced to nine months imprisonment (for the editor and publisher), the company being sentenced to pay a fine of £1000. In that case, the Crown (the prosecution) led no evidence to prove any intention other than the intention to publish the words complained of; and the judge directed the jury in effect that any such evidence would be irrelevant. The case was taken up to the final court of appeal in England – *first*, because for more that 50 years before the prosecution of *Gay News*, the offence of blasphemous libel had appeared to have become obsolete, the last trial for the offence of blasphemy having taken place in 1922, and *second*, because it involved an important question of law as to whether it was an essential ingredient of the common law offence of blasphemy that there should be an intent on the part of the publisher to hurt or injure the feelings of devout Christians, or whether it was sufficient merely to intend to publish what in the court's (or jury's) view was a blasphemous libel. The Judicial Committee of the House of Lords was sharply divided. By a majority of 3:2 the law lords upheld the conviction. Lord Leslie George Scarman – though a great liberal – endorsed the severity of the law of blasphemous libel, for reasons set out in his opinion. He recalled the speech of Lord Macaulay in the British Parliament way back in 1833 ('If I were a Judge in India I would have no scruple about punishing a Christian who should pollute a mosque') and added that 'when Macaulay became a legislator in India he saw to it that the law protected the religious feelings of all. In those days India was a plural society; today the United Kingdom is also'. Lord Scarman's criticism of the common law offence of blasphemy was not that it existed, but that it was not sufficiently comprehensive. 'It was' (as he said) 'shackled by the chains of history'. At the commencement of his opinion Scarman had explained as to why it was necessary in the UK to extend (by statute) the existing common law offence of blasphemy to all other religions:

> My Lords, I do not subscribe to the view that the common law offence of blasphemous libel serves no useful purpose in the modern law. On the contrary, I think there is a case for legislation extending it to protect the religious beliefs and feelings of non-Christians. The offence belongs to a group of criminal offences designed to safeguard the internal tranquillity of the kingdom. In an increasingly plural society such as that of modern Britain it is necessary not only to respect the differing religious beliefs, feelings and practices of all but also to protect them from scurrility, vilification, ridicule and contempt.[82]

But England's Parliament did not harken to Lord Scarman's view. A few years later, the Muslim community in the United Kingdom was inflamed by the publication (in 1988) of *The Satanic Verses* by Salman

Rushdie. To Muslims what was most offensive in the novel was that in the brothel of the City of Jahalia, the prostitutes were given the names of the Prophet's wives! It is an article of faith for the Muslims that the wives of the Prophet are the mothers of all Believers, held in the highest esteem, next only to the Prophet himself. Relying on the speech of Lord Scarman, the Muslims in the UK petitioned the authorities to extend the law of blasphemy to non-Christian religions, but the request was turned down. Despite the influx of millions of immigrants, England was – till recently – an *exclusively* Christian country!

But the Criminal Justice and Immigration Act 2008 has altered all this – it abolished the offence of blasphemy and blasphemous libel in the UK; the Racial and Religious Hatred Act 2006 had provided that if a publication stirred up religious hatred or caused a disturbance of public order then the criminal law would intervene. In the UK, Christianity is now treated no differently from other religions. In an article in the *Modern Law Review* (2008), it has been accurately said: 'The body of the blasphemy laws may be dead but its soul lives on in enacted criminal law.'[83] In the UK, it is the 2006 Act that now protects all religious beliefs and believers (as does the Penal Code in India); post-2006, the ultimate distinguishing feature both in the UK and in India between freedom of speech and vilification of religion is the intent of the author: if the vilification (blasphemy) is unintended, free speech prevails; if the vilification (blasphemy) is intentional, a criminal offence is committed!

* * *

The Objectives Resolution, moved by Jawaharlal Nehru at the first sitting of the Constituent Assembly on 13 December 1946, contained a pledge that 'in the Constitution adequate safeguards shall be provided for minorities, backward and tribal areas and other backward classes.'[84]

Accordingly, Article 30(1) of the Constitution had guaranteed to all minorities, whether based on religion or on language, the right to establish and administer educational institutions *of their choice.* The state was prohibited from discriminating against any educational institution on the ground that it was under the management of a religious or linguistic minority (Article 30[2]). When the right to acquire and hold property was deleted from the chapter on Fundamental Rights by a Constitutional Amendment in 1978, an exception was made for minority educational institutions. Under Article 30(1A) properties of minority educational institutions could be compulsorily acquired for public purposes *only if* the state ensured that the amount fixed or determined by law for the acquisition was such as would not restrict or abrogate the right guaranteed under Article 30(1).

When Sikkim became a part of India in 1975, special provision had to be made for the protection of its original inhabitants. With the waves of immigration of the Nepalese into Sikkim over the course of a hundred years, the Bhutia-Lepchas (the indigenous population) had become a minority in their own state. This ethnic group had to be ensured equal representation in the Sikkim Legislative Assembly, which was effected by the introduction of Article 371F by the 36th Constitution Amendment Act 1975.[85]

Despite declarations of constitutional rights, minorities in society cannot find adequate protection in the normal political process; they need the protection of courts. When dealing with minority rights, courts in India had initially conceptualized their role as that of a political party in opposition – until one of the political parties, the Bharatiya Janata Party (BJP), in the early 1990s characterized the policy of the Congress Party (the ruling party in power at the Centre) as an '*appeasement* of the minorities'; after which, I have noted (with much regret) that 'minority rights' have not been as fervently protected by the Supreme Court of India as they were before!

Minorities (religious minorities in particular), at all times and in all countries, have needed the protection of courts. What is probably the most renowned footnote in US Supreme Court history appeared in a case that would otherwise have been forgotten. In *United States* vs *Caroline Products* (1938),[86] the court applied the presumption of constitutionality to uphold a law passed by the US Congress regulating commerce, but included in its judgment 'Footnote Four', which contained three paragraphs: exceptions to this presumption. The footnote recommended the appropriateness of applying different degrees of judicial scrutiny to different types of legislation. The judgment in *US* vs *Caroline Products* appeared one year after the US Supreme Court had abandoned its previous position of judicial activism in defence of the economic rights of big business and employers.[87] In those cases, the court had rigidly scrutinized legislation affecting property rights to determine whether it served a legitimate public purpose and was reasonable in its terms. After 1937, the court embraced, instead, a posture of deference to the policy judgments of Congress and state legislatures, raising a presumption of the constitutionality of such laws, and declining to consider whether they were 'wise, necessary, or desirable'. Chief Justice Harlan Fiske Stone's footnote (in *US* vs *Caroline Products*) suggested that there might be situations in which this presumption of constitutionality should be less stringently applied, as, for instance, where laws affected 'discrete and insular minorities' – i.e., powerless groups hated or feared by the majority in society. This was because prejudice against religious national or racial minorities would distort the functioning of the political process. A more intensive judicial scrutiny was called for when laws were actually targeted at such minorities. Much legislation existed in the US at that time, particularly at the state level, that reflected white-majority prejudice against African-Americans, Asians (e.g., laws preventing aliens of Asian ancestry from owning land or pursuing certain occupations) and unpopular religious groups, such as Jehovah's Witnesses. Members of these groups, precisely because they were the victims of intense prejudice, were incapable of using the political process to protect themselves. The third paragraph of the footnote[88] reflected an awareness that an even-handed but pro forma application of the presumption of constitutionality would leave these groups at the mercy of an intolerant majority. The footnote provided a theoretical basis for future judicial activism in defence of powerless minorities. As mentioned in the *Oxford Companion to the Supreme Court of the United States*: 'recognition of the need for special judicial protection for such groups is the footnote's greatest strength and the principal reason for its continued vitality.'[89]

* * *

In India, the contest in courts over 'minority rights' had mainly turned on Article 30 – rights of minorities to establish and maintain minority educational institutions (MEIs) of their choice and the attempts of states to regulate and control them. The contest ended a few years ago with the Supreme Court's decision in *TMA Pai Foundation* vs *State of Karnataka* (2002) – a bench decision of 11 justices – that envisaged a regime of greater control over MEIs (which were in receipt of state aid) than that foreshadowed in some of the earlier cases decided by the court: e.g., in the *Presidential Reference: in re Kerala Education Act* (1959) by a bench of seven justices and in *Ahmedabad St Xavier's College Society* vs *State of Gujarat* (1974) by a bench of nine justices. Let me explain.

In 1958, the Supreme Court of India thwarted an attempt by the first communist-controlled government (which had come to power in Kerala in 1957) to take over the management of (private) Christian schools in the state. In an advisory opinion given on a Presidential Reference under Article 143 of the Constitution, a bench of seven justices of the Supreme Court – Chief Justice S. R. Das presiding – held that large parts of the Kerala Education Bill were unconstitutional.[90] Years later, some state governments complained that after the verdict they found it increasingly difficult to regulate educational standards. In a case concerning the St Xavier's College, Ahmedabad (before a Constitution Bench of five judges) counsel for the Teachers' Association (interveners) invited the court's attention to an opinion expressed by a former chief justice of India, Dr P. B. Gajendragadkar,[91] that prior decisions of the Supreme Court on Articles 29 and 30 required reconsideration. Chief Justice A. N. Ray who (in 1974) was then presiding over the bench directed that a larger bench be constituted to reconsider questions that had been raised in the Presidential Reference on the Kerala Education Bill. But the only consequence of the reconsideration was that what had been asserted by Chief Justice S. R. Das in his opinion in the Presidential Reference was emphatically reaffirmed (by majority) by an even larger bench of nine justices! In the case concerning the Ahmedabad St Xavier's College Society (1974), certain provisions of the Gujarat University Act of 1949 had laid down statutory conditions for affiliation of colleges in the state with the University of Gujarat. The law applied to all educational institutions, including those run by minorities, and they provided that teaching and training in all colleges affiliated with the university would be conducted and imparted by teachers appointed only by the university since the provisions interfered with the right of minorities 'to establish and administer educational institutions *of their choice*' – a guaranteed Fundamental Right under Article 30 – the provisions were challenged directly in the Supreme Court of India by the Ahmedabad St Xavier's College Society (managed by Jesuits). The court, sitting *en banc* (nine judges participating), struck down the offending provisions as inapplicable to colleges run by minorities.[92] The earlier advisory opinion of the Supreme Court of India in the *Kerala Education Bill* case (by a bench of seven justices) was reaffirmed. Secular education given in minority-established colleges was now looked upon as protected by the provisions of Article 30 in the same way as were minority-run schools in the earlier *Kerala Education Bill* case. Justice K. K. Mathew of the Supreme Court (a devout Christian) read into the article the right of parents to determine to which educational institution their children should be sent for study: 'The fundamental postulate of personal liberty excludes any power of the State to standardize and socialize its children by forcing them to attend public schools only.' Another member on the bench, Justice H. R. Khanna (a devout Hindu) gave the reason why minority interests were so zealously protected by the courts:

> The safeguarding of the interest of the minorities amongst sections of the population is as important as the protection of the interest amongst individuals of persons who are below the age of majority or are otherwise suffering from some kind of infirmity. The Constitution and the laws made by civilized nations, therefore, generally contain provisions for the protection of those interests. It can, indeed, be said to be an index of the level of civilization and catholicity of a nation as to how far their minorities feel secure and are not subject to any discrimination or suppression.[93]

The ambit of the constitutional protection for minorities had been extended by the judicial interpretation given to the term 'minorities'. Members of a reformed Hindu sect (Arya Samaj) were held to be entitled, under Article 30(1), to the Fundamental Right to establish and administer educational institutions of their choice in the state of Punjab (where Sikhs and not Hindus were in a majority).[94] In India, minority status is determined state-wise, not country-wise.[95]

* * *

State-aided MEIs, however, did not receive the same favourable reception from the apex court when Article 30 was invoked in the case of institutions of higher learning – in postgraduate courses in medicine, engineering and the like.

In these groups of cases (where I had been briefed and had appeared for some of the MEIs), different benches of the Supreme Court – at first – wavered as to how much, or how little, autonomy should be conceded to such minority educational institutions. The cases shuttled from a bench of two justices,[96] to a bench of five justices;[97] then from a bench of five justices to a bench of seven (on 18 March 1994[98]), and were ultimately referred to a bench of 11 justices (in *TMA Pai Foundation* vs *State of Karnataka*[99]). With the mandatory constitutional age of retirement of Supreme Court judges (at 65), the composition of the bench was entirely different from what it was in 1974! In 2002 the difficulty felt by the bench of 11 justices (in *TMA Pai*) was how to reconcile the provisions of Article 30 (1) and (2)[100] with the seemingly contrary provisions contained in Article 29(2).[101] In the *Kerala Education Bill* case (1958), an attempt had been made at reconciliation – but in somewhat cryptic terms: 'The real import of Article 29(2) and Article 30(1) seems to us to be that they clearly contemplate a minority (educational) institution with a *sprinkling of outsiders* admitted into it'; the expression 'sprinkling of outsiders' was later explained (in bench decisions of the court) as not restricting the number of outsiders so long as the minority character of the institution was not affected.[102]

The great Justice Holmes (Oliver Wendell Holmes) had once said: '*unconscious preferences* are often the basis of many court decisions!' In his famous dissent in *Lochner* vs *New York* (1905), he had written: 'General propositions do not decide concrete cases. The decision will depend on a judgment, *or intuition more subtle than any articulate major premise*.'[103] The inarticulate major premise underlying the decision of the justices who constituted the majority in the 11-judge bench in *TMA Pai Foundation* (2002)[104] was the strong suspicion that many of the MEIs, in receipt of state aid, were selling seats to the highest bidder and were thus disentitled to invoke the Fundamental Right to 'administer' the MEI in question. In the *Kerala Education Bill* case (1958), Chief Justice S. R. Das had warned that the Fundamental Right guaranteed by Article 30 to *administer* educational institutions would not include the right to 'maladminister' them. In the view of most of the judges on the bench (in *TMA Pai Foundation*), state-aided MEIs, which had established institutions for postgraduate courses in medicine, engineering and the like, were claiming a Fundamental Right to administer them almost solely with a view to profiteering in the matter of admissions and allotment of seats. It was money and not merit that mattered to them. 'Maladministration' therefore became a convenient stick with which to beat the MEIs – not unjustifiably, at times – but only at times: not every time!

I recall how Justice K. T. Thomas of the Supreme Court – who sat on one of the earlier benches in 1997 – related (from the bench) an incident of a particular minority educational institution in Kerala (of which he was personally aware) that had been guilty of such 'maladministration', and the example he mentioned (in some detail) did have an impact upon some of his colleagues on the bench (an impact adverse to MEIs!). But this is an occupational hazard for lawyers arguing all manner of cases before a bench of justices in any court. The accumulated experiences of a judge – what Justice Holmes used to call, 'his can't helps'![105] – contribute not a little to the shaping of the ultimate result in the case.

In my view, the ultimate majority decision in *TMA Pai Foundation* was not so much the result of a textual interpretation of the constitutional provisions as of the apprehension of the judges that treating the right of minorities under Article 30 as 'absolute' (as it had been described in the earlier cases) would totally negate the claim of the states to *regulate* MEIs – especially in higher education. My plea to the judges that not suspicion, but only concrete allegations and proof of such allegations in individual cases could deprive MEIs of their Fundamental Right to administer minority educational institutions established by them, was invariably met with stony silence!

I also recall one occasion when arguing on behalf of minority educational institutions, before the (initial) bench of seven judges

(6 February 1997), when the bench had reframed the questions and referred them for decision to a bench of 11 judges. On this occasion, Justice A. S. Anand (who was then on the bench presided over by the seniormost judge, Justice M. M. Punchhi) put to me the following question:

> Mr Nariman, was it ever contemplated by the framers of our Constitution that postgraduate education and specialty education should also fall within the provisions of Article 30?[106]

Obviously, he thought not. So when Justice Anand posed this question, I responded by saying that under Article 30 of the Constitution (in the Fundamental Rights chapter) all minorities whether based on religion or language had the right to establish and administer educational institutions *of their choice*, and that ever since the 1974 decision in the *Ahmedabad St Xavier's College Society* case,[107] in which a bench of nine judges had participated, even secular education in schools and colleges was regarded as covered by the provisions of Article 30. How then could it have been ever contemplated by the framers of the Constitution (I asked rhetorically with considerable heat and emphasis!) that postgraduate education would fall outside the provisions of Article 30?[108] But the judges on the bench politely ignored my interjection; the matter then proceeded and was later referred to a larger bench of 11 judges! On mature reflection, I am now convinced that my petulant reaction was overplayed. It ought to have been avoided. I do believe that all the complexity of current problems concerning minority educational institutions would have been obviated if we (on behalf of the petitioners – minority educational institutions (MEIs) – had argued, and the court in its final decision (in the bench of seven or even eleven judges) had simply said (as Justice Anand had tentatively suggested) that the provisions of Article 30 were meant to give MEIs complete protection, even in secular education, but only up to school and college (undergraduate) levels – not beyond. The decision of the seven-judge bench in the *Kerala Education Bill* (1958) and the further decision in 1974 of the nine-judge bench in *Ahmedabad St Xavier's College Society* had amply safeguarded the rights of MEIs under Article 30 as they were intended to be truly safeguarded. For us (MEIs) to have persisted in the plea that Article 30 also governed postgraduate and specialized studies – as was, in fact, upheld (by the majority) in the bench decision of 11 judges (presided over by Chief Justice B. N. Kirpal, 2002, 8 SCC 481) – was an unmitigated disaster: *for the minorities*! By insisting that Article 30 encompassed even postgraduate and specialty studies in medicine, engineering and the like, the minorities had reached out for something that was way beyond their grasp, and perhaps beyond the intendment of the Article, and had thereby subjected all educational institutions established and managed by minorities to state regulation as regards admission, courses of study, etc., to the same discipline as other non-minority educational institutions (in India statutory 'regulation' of almost every activity is apt to be heavy-handed!). As a result, it is the minorities that have lost out. The true content and ambit of minority rights under Article 30 (for state-aided MEIs) got diluted after the decision in the *TMA Pai Foundation* had approximated the Fundamental Right of minority educational institutions guaranteed under Article 30 to the Fundamental Right of all citizens to establish and maintain educational institutions as an 'occupation'. Under Article 19(1)(g) of the Constitution, the latter is always subject to reasonable restrictions that may be imposed by law in public interest;[109] Fundamental Rights of MEIs have got devalued, because approximating the provisions in Article 30 to the provisions contained in Article 19(1)(g) meant, that as a matter of perception, the 'reasonable restrictions' imposed by ordinary law on this Fundamental Right – permissible under Article 19(6) – had also got subsumed in what was an otherwise unrestricted Fundamental Right guaranteed under Article 30!

In the sphere of higher education, the only minority educational institutions that received what may be regarded as 'favourable' treatment from the courts were the *unaided* MEIs. It was Chief Justice R. C. Lahoti who steered a Supreme Court bench of seven judges to a unanimous conclusion in *P. A. Inamdar* vs *State of Maharashtra* (2005).[110] Speaking for the bench, he held:

- that for *unaided* minority educational institutions applying for affiliation or recognition, there could be no interference in day-to-day administration;

- that essential ingredients of management, of *unaided* minority educational institutions including admission of students, recruitment of staff and quantum of fee to be charged, could not be regulated;
- that there could be no inroad into the protection conferred by Article 30(1) of the Constitution by framing regulations whereby the essential character of the minority educational institutions was taken away;
- that the state could not insist on private educational institutions which received *no aid* from the state to implement the state's policy on reservation for granting admission on lesser percentage of marks, i.e., on any criterion except merit. Thus, imposition of quota of state seats or enforcing any reservation policy of the state on available seats in unaided professional institutions were [*sic*] acts constituting serious encroachment on the right and autonomy of minority educational institutions.

However, Chief Justice Lahoti steering the bench of seven judges (over which he presided) to a unanimous conclusion did not add up to much because, on 12 April 2012, a bench of three justices – after hearing arguments for several months – held by a majority (2:1) that the unanimous decision in *P. A. Inamdar*[111] stood overruled by a Constitutional Amendment, since:

- The Constitution 93rd Amendment Act 2005 (which added Clause 5 to Article 15) had decreed that there shall be reservations whereas *P. A. Inamdar* had stated that there shall be no reservations in private unaided colleges.
- *P. A. Inamdar* had said that there shall be no difference between the unaided minority and non-minority institutions and Article 15(5) had now decreed that *there shall be a difference.*[112]

Could two justices (in a bench of three judges) have legitimately said that a unanimous decision of a bench of seven justices was no longer good law? It is submitted that both as a matter of judicial discipline and propriety that they could not. The two judges in the three-judge bench (in *Society for Unaided Private Schools of Rajasthan*) overlooked the mandate of Article 145(3) of the Constitution of India, which categorically declares that 'the minimum number of judges who are to sit for the purpose of deciding any case involving a substantial question of law as to the interpretation of the Constitution ... *shall be five*'. What could have been a 'more substantial question of law as to the interpretation of the Constitution' than whether Article 15(5) of the Constitution had 'overruled' (*sub-silento*) a judgment of a Constitution Bench of seven judges? But it is not merely the transgression of Article 145(3) (by two justices in the later bench of three judges) that is the only disquieting aspect. Two justices out of three (in a bench decision of three justices) keep the law in an uncertain state: a bad thing for educational institutions, especially schools – when a new (and bold) experiment is being tried, viz., mandating unaided private schools in India to reserve 25 per cent seats for children of the poor: an otherwise meritorious measure. We have now to wait and watch how the majority decision unfolds. But one thing is certain – uncertainty in decision making in the highest court always clouds issues for years, sometimes for decades.[113]

As the composition of the apex court changes over time (as it must) and the correctness of the majority judgment (in *Society for Unaided Private Schools of Rajasthan* – 2:1) gets questioned before a larger bench (as it assuredly will), it is difficult to predict whether that larger bench will hold that the seven-judge bench decision in *P. A. Inamdar* (2005) is to be authoritatively treated as overruled by the insertion of Clause 5 in Article 15 of the Constitution (as two judges in a bench of three have said in the judgment dated 12 April 2012), or whether (as the third judge, Justice K. S. P. Radhakrishnan, has opined) the Right of Children to Free and Compulsory Education Act 2009 would not be applicable to unaided non-minority educational institutions even after Clause 5 has been added to Article 15![114]

All this points to the crying need – as a matter of sound judicial policy – that benches of two or three justices of the Supreme Court must studiously avoid rendering decisions on important constitutional questions and observe strictly the mandate of Article 145(3). This would make for greater finality in the law. Much court time (and expense) would be saved if cases on constitutional questions, particularly those arising from an interpretation of Articles 14, 15 and 16 (as they have been amended from time to time), are decided by a much larger complement of justices than three. If we have to choose between certainty and finality, in the scheme of things in which the higher judiciary operates, I would definitely choose finality – and in the highest court this could be better achieved by compelling decisions on constitutional questions being rendered only by benches of five justices or more, not by benches of two or three justices.

* * *

In the general elections of May-June 1991, one of the major political parties in India the BJP – the Bharatiya Janata Party – had included in its election manifesto the party's resolve, if and when it came into power, to amend Article 30 (to the disadvantage of the minorities).[115] Ultimately, it did come to power – not in 1991, but later, in 1999. When it did, after the elections of September-October 1999, and the BJP proceeded to form a coalition government at the Centre – it did not (to its credit) propose any change whatever in Article 30! Idealist that I am, I like to believe that this was because of the inherently secular character of Indian polity!

* * *

Sulak Sivaraksa,[116] the prominent Thai activist, who had been persecuted by many military dictatorships and had been forced into exile, when asked whether he felt that major world religions needed to reinvent themselves in order to be more effective, answered with an emphatic yes. He was then asked why there were great disparities in the way Buddhism was being practised. His answer was significant:

> I make a distinction between Buddhism with a Capital 'B' and buddhism with a small 'b'. Sri Lanka has the former, in which the state uses Buddhism as an instrument of power, so there are even Buddhist monks who say the Tamils should be eliminated. Thai Buddhist are not perfect either. Some Thai Buddhist monks have compromised: they possess cars and other luxuries. In many

Buddhist countries, the emphasis is on buddhism with a small 'b' which is non-violent, practical and aims to eliminate the cause of suffering ...[117] [Emphasis added.]

If I were to project myself into the mind of the founding fathers and review what they thought were the rights of minorities in the context of freedom of religion, I would lay great emphasis on the fact that whilst most of them started the business of Constitution making, by defining minorities with a big 'M', within a few years, they began to accept the fact that, in the vast Indian Union, the minorities had a great future if their sights were lowered – if they chose to accept minorities with a small 'm'. When we in India discuss the state of the nation, we should never forget the historical context: Minority with a *small 'm'* must be the watchword. Minority with a small 'm' helps to carry the majority with it. And I would respectfully suggest to my Hindu brethren that 'majority' with a small 'm' also helps to carry the minority along! The possibility of conflict arises when one or other of these groups stresses the big 'M' factor.

In 1984, at a conference in New Zealand to which I was invited, I heard its human rights commissioner (Justice John Wallace) say: 'the minority view is generally right, provided the minority can carry the majority with it.' His was the voice of mature experience, not of mere human-rights rhetoric.

***

The beneficiaries of preferential treatment had been indicated upfront in the Constitution of India (as originally promulgated) but there have been later amendments to the Constitution, to provide for exceptions to the paramount principle of equality so that we now have the following categories of preferential treatment:

1. '*Special provision for women and children*', notwithstanding the mandate of Article 15(1); Article 15(3) of the 1950 Constitution.
2. '*Special provision for the advancement of any socially and educationally backward classes of citizens, or for Scheduled Castes and Scheduled Tribes*' added by Article 15(4) by the Constitution First Amendment Act 1951.[118]

3. *'Provision for reservation of appointments to posts in favour of any backward class of citizens which in the opinion of the State is not adequately represented in the services under the State'* (Article 16(4).
4. *'Provision for reservation in matters of promotion with consequential seniority to any class or classes of posts in the services under the State in favour of the Scheduled Castes and the Scheduled Tribes which in the opinion of the State are not adequately represented in the services under the State'* added by the Constitution 85th Amendment Act 2001 (w.e.f. 17 June 1995).

Let me deal with each of them.

***

Preferential treatment for women and children is easily explained.

In every society, children are treated differently from adults. Women constitute nearly 50 per cent of India's total population and, as we all know, a large number of them continue to be oppressed and subjected to indignities. The personal and customary laws of the Hindus and Muslims in India have imposed constraints upon women. Manu, the ancient Hindu lawgiver, is said to have proclaimed: '*Na stree swatjamtramarhati*' (a woman does not deserve independence).[119] Under the Hindu Succession Act 1956, important changes were brought about in relation to the law of interstate succession amongst Hindus, but without affecting the special rights of the members of a Mitakshara (a school of Hindu law) coparcenary. The retention of the law of Mitakshara coparcenary meant that females (daughters, etc.) could not inherit ancestral property to an equal extent with their male counterparts (sons, etc.). To render 'social justice to women', several states (Andhra Pradesh, Tamil Nadu, Karnataka and Maharashtra) had made necessary changes in the law giving equal rights to daughters even in the Hindu Mitakshara coparcenary property. Central law then followed state laws. In September 2005, Parliament substituted a new section for Section 6 of the 1956 Hindu Succession Act, granting daughters equal rights with sons in the Hindu Mitakshara coparcenary property. But in some cases, where a preliminary partition decree had been passed before September 2005, which excluded daughters, the contention of the sons was that since a final partition decree had to follow the shares mentioned in the preliminary partition decree, even when the final partition decree was passed after September 2005, daughters would not be entitled to any share in the Mitakshara coparcenary property. The contention was upheld by some of the high courts. It was only in 2011 that this was finally settled by the Supreme Court of India by overruling the high courts.[120]

As for a divorced Muslim woman, her right to claim from her erstwhile Muslim husband even the monthly pittance of Rs 500 as maintenance (provided for under provisions of the Code of Criminal Procedure 1973), was denied simply because Parliament had enacted, in the wake of the *Shah Bano* case,[121] a new law (euphemistically) titled: 'The Muslim Women Protection of Rights on Divorce Act 1986': the new law gave no *protection whatsoever to women* on divorce! Instead, it provided for a deprivation of legal rights upon a unilateral divorce (talaaq) pronounced by the husband! Under the new law, the Muslim woman must now rest content with maintenance during the period of waiting (*iddat*): i.e., a sum stipulated by the husband at the time of marriage, to be paid for a limited period of three months after the customary divorce.

All this serves to illustrate how our laws (and our menfolk) continue to treat women! This prompts me to recall a story about the Mahabharata – not the well-known story, but a true story of modern times. A few years ago, Kartikeya Sarabhai (a dedicated environmentalist), son of the renowned scientist, Vikram Sarabhai,[122] witnessed in Avignon (in France) the performance of the great Indian epic the Mahabharata – a production by Peter Brook. It depicts the entire tale of how Yudhishtra lost all his wealth in playing dice with Duryodhana and continued with the game even whilst continuously losing and ultimately offering his wife Draupadi as a wager. The tale is familiar: after he loses, Draupadi is fetched by force to the victor's brother who starts removing her garments. And then a miracle occurs: fresh garments are seen to wrap her body, and good men praise God and weep!

After seeing the play, Kartikeya wrote a poem representing the thoughts of Draupadi and offered it to his sister Mallika who acted in the play. The poem 'I Draupadi' is not only inspired but is also poignant and expressive of the reality of conditions of women in modern India.

In the poem Draupadi says:

The Swayamvara was mine,
The decision my father's.
No garland was worn, the garland was me.
The prize myself, for the winner of the tournament
Not mine the decision whom to marry.
My heart was pledged to a bow and arrow …
My life an offering to the shooter of the fish

All rights belong to husbands, so says society,
But to be shared by five, a commodity in the market place?
Unknowingly Ma Kunti spoke: husband became husbands
In this the Pandava's kingdom of Dharma
All this I accepted, became the wife of five,
To each gave a son
Yet was the only wife of none.

And then the poem moves on:

Gambling they went, invited by Duryodhana,
Lost all they had, losing even themselves
I, unspared, was dragged into that court of men.
Which were these bounds of Dharma
That tied my husbands?
What kind of husbands [are] these,
That are tied by the Dharma of lies?

I asked, 'What of me?'
Bhishma said, 'Power is Truth, Dharma darkness'.
Robed limitlessly, I was saved by God.
The Kauravas stopped, exhausted, still not understanding.
Yes, Krishna gave me cloth, but where was the Gita's truth?
Was Arjuna not already in need of that counsel then?

The poem ends with a condemnation of the male gender for forsaking equality in practice:

Years went by; our lives we lived together,
Started on our journey's end towards the snow-clad Himalaya
I fell first; no Pandava stretched a hand.
Towards paradise they walked, not one stayed by my side,
Then I realised heaven too must be only for men ...
Better then, to rest in the warm embrace of this snow.[123]

The significance of the poem written with such spontaneity by an Indian male about Indian women highlights the difference between formal equality, professed by us all and, the actual inequality, which the fate of Draupadi has eternally symbolized – the inequality that women have had to bear, and continue to suffer, even in present-day India.

Towards the rather sad end of an otherwise remarkable career, Jawaharlal Nehru was asked what he regarded as his greatest achievement as the prime minister of independent India. He paused for a moment, and then said: '*Women's education*.' Women's education has been the catalyst for change in attitudes of men towards women. And we have come a long way. But we have a much longer way to go. It is not laws that oppress women; it is menfolk who do! And not in India alone! So exasperated have women become worldwide that only the other day one of our national newspapers reported a quote from a French woman (a journalist and a writer), Francoise Giroud, who, when asked how long she would fight for equality between the sexes, said: 'Until incompetent women can hold important jobs, like men do!' In India, even this will still be a long time coming! But we must make it happen. We must press on.

Preferential treatment for women and children, then, is not only easily explained – but also it is amply justified.

***

But why have special provisions and preferential treatment for 'Scheduled Castes', 'Scheduled Tribes' and 'Other Backward Classes'?

For treating adult citizens differently there must be a reason, because as Isaiah Berlin (noted philosopher and historian) said in a famous essay on the subject: 'The assumption is that equality needs no reason, only inequality does.'[124] *The reason – for preferential treatment for Scheduled Castes and Scheduled Tribes and Other Backward Classes – lies in India's history.*

In the past these groups had been disadvantaged for centuries, many of them beyond the pale of law, and Scheduled Castes and Scheduled Tribes even beyond human compassion. For more than 2000 years, 'untouchables' and 'tribals' were treated as if they were not human beings (most of them were dubbed by the British as 'criminal tribes' and so treated) – a treatment rationalized by the argument that they and their children were inherently inferior in ability to those born into superior stations in life. As Marc Galanter (law professor and writer) says in his treatise on the subject: 'India embraced equality as a cardinal value against a background of elaborate, and clearly perceived, inequalities.'[125] More poignantly, Mahatma Gandhi had said (and only he had the courage to say it) in a speech to the All India Congress Committee in Bombay way back in July 1946: 'Our sins have a strange way of coming home to roost. We turned a portion of ourselves into pariahs, and today the whites of South Africa are doing the same to our compatriots there!' Gandhi had no moral compunction in comparing caste discrimination in India with apartheid in South Africa. He was convinced that the consequences and effect of each of these evils were the same!

The Aryans were the first invaders of the land inhabited by the serpent-worshiping Nagas and other ancient tribes in the north and by the Dravidians in the south. The Aryans subjugated India without pretending to elevate it. They wanted land and pasture for their cattle. Slowly, they made their way eastward along the Indus and the Ganges until all Hindustan was under their control. Outnumbered by a subject people whom they considered inferior, the Vedic Aryans sought to preserve their racial identity. In a couple of centuries, however, they were assimilated and absorbed. The first caste division was not by status but by colour.[126] It separated the fair Aryans with long noses from the dark, broad-nosed Dravidians: 'It was' (as Will Durant reminded us) 'the marriage regulation of an endogamous group.'

As India, pictured in the Vedas (2000–1000 B.C.),[127] changed to the conditions described in the great Hindu epics, the Mahabharata and the Ramayana (1000–400 B.C.),[128] occupations became hereditary and more specialized, and caste divisions were more rigidly defined. First, there were the Kshatriyas (or fighters/warriors), who considered it a sin to die in bed. But as conditions of war gave way to peace and as religion and ritual (largely an aid to agriculture in the face of incalculable elements) grew in importance and complexity, requiring proficient intermediaries between men and the gods, the Brahmins consolidated their position. They alone knew the ancient Sanskrit (the oldest in the European group of languages) and could recite the Vedas. They were thus able to re-create the past and form the future in their own image, moulding each generation into one with greater reverence for the priests, building for their caste a prestige that, in later centuries, gave them a supreme place in the Hindu society!

Below the Brahmins and Kshatriyas were the Vaishyas – farmers and traders. These three castes (or varnas) were regarded as twice born, the second birth (or regeneration) consisting in the study of the Vedas and in the performance of sacraments. The twice-born status was denied to the fourth varna, the Shudras – or the working class – who made up most of the population. Over the years, a fifth category long unrecognized in theory, the outcastes, emerged – unconverted native tribes, captives of war and men and women reduced to slavery as punishment. This small group of the casteless formed the nucleus of what has become the world's largest minority: the 'untouchables' (now 'the Scheduled Castes').

It was not as if the caste principles on which Hindu society was organized was never questioned from within. The religious hegemony of the Brahmins was contested by the Kshatriya noblemen who founded Buddhism. This new religion rejected the predetermination of status by birth and the hierarchical ranking of castes. It became the religion of the kings who ruled India for nearly 900 years. Embraced by the Emperor Ashoka (273–232 B.C.) – grandson of the great Chandragupta Maurya – Buddhism gained a foothold in the subcontinent and for over 200 years posed a real threat to Hinduism. Then it became riddled with schisms and sects and was influenced by Hindu pantheistic beliefs. Generations of Hindu culture proved too much for this ascetic, non-theistic religion. Buddha was slowly absorbed into the Hindu pantheon as one of the incarnations of the God Vishnu.[129] During the reign of Harshvardhan (A.D. 606–648) – the last Buddhist king – the great casteless religion was stamped out in the land of its birth. The oriental scholar, Sir Charles Eliot, described the denouement in a chilling phrase: '*Brahmins killed Buddhism by a fraternal embrace.*'[130]

The Hinduism that replaced Buddhism was an amalgam of faiths and ceremonies that had four common characteristics: (1) it recognized the caste system; (2) it reaffirmed the leadership of the Brahmins; (3) it accepted the law of karma (destiny) and the transmigration of souls; and (4) it replaced with new Gods the deities of the Vedas. Caste came back into its own and with it the antithesis of 'pure' versus 'impure'. The untouchables – Hindu outcastes – grew in number, particularly with the introduction of new occupations. By the latter part of the Middle Ages, India was more advanced in agriculture, handicrafts and commerce than many other countries. To the traditional division of society into four main castes (Brahmins, Kshatriyas, Vaishyas and Shudras) were added an almost indefinite number of *occupational castes*. The criteria for the hierarchical status of high or low multiplied a hundredfold with new occupations. For each new activity, it was the Brahmins who determined which aspects were 'low' or 'impure', and the number of outcastes increased even further!

***

Muslim rule brought some changes into Indian society but neither the new language of the courts (Persian) nor the religion of the new rulers (Islam) made any difference to the traditional division of labour organized through specialized groups ranked in a hierarchical order. Thus, caste and untouchability continued to flourish during Muslim rule.

The first attempt made at emancipation was when the British came. The new economic order brought in by the conquerors from the West altered the design of a social system that had retained a remarkable continuity for centuries. Moreover, with English education more people became acquainted with modern European and American history, with their concepts of equality and fraternity. The beneficiaries of the British system of education, mainly the children of high-caste Hindu families, grew up questioning the principles on which their society was organized. A few cosmetic changes were introduced, such as the Caste Disabilities Removal Act of 1850, but this enactment was a dead letter from the start. Social consciousness had not yet been aroused.

Then, at the beginning of the last century, Mahatma Gandhi introduced into the independence movement two new concepts:

peaceful non-cooperation with the British (non-violent satyagraha) and a plea for a better deal for the outcastes. Gandhi lived among them and described them as 'Harijans' (children of God). In the liberal spirit of the age, the name stuck. It brought an increasing awareness to the Indian mind of the shame of untouchability. Among the more enlightened of the higher castes, a movement started to do something to relieve the lot of the depressed classes. To uplift them was regarded as an act of compassion, a voluntary righting of the wrongs of many years. But as the benefits of Western-style education permeated downward, the bright young men and women in the society of outcastes also spearheaded a movement that was based not on compassion but on *right*. The leader of this movement - and its most eloquent member - was Dr B. R. Ambedkar, a Harijan. (Nowadays, the word Dalit is used instead of Harijan.) Along with Jawaharlal Nehru, Dr Ambedkar was one of the principal architects of the Constitution of India.

* * *

This then was what we inherited with independence: this was the state of the nation when the Constitution was adopted in November 1949 and promulgated in January 1950.

* * *

Aware of the generations of accumulated and accentuated group inequalities, the Constituent Assembly adopted a constitutional policy of deliberate preferential treatment for the historically disadvantaged peoples.

First, untouchability was abolished and its practice in any form forbidden (Article 17).[131] The Untouchability Offences Act of 1955 (renamed in 1967 as the Civil Rights Act) adopted legal sanctions in aid of the constitutional prohibition. All temples and religious institutions were thrown open to 'all classes and Sections of Hindus' (Article 25[l][b]). A form of apartheid, long practised by the twice-born classes against the untouchables, was abolished, and all citizens became entitled to equal access to shops, public restaurants, hotels and places of entertainment and to the use of wells, tanks, bathing places, roads and places of public resort maintained out of state funds or dedicated to the use of the general public (Article 15[2]). Untouchability was not merely a stigma; it was an attitude of mind.

I recall what a correspondent of an English periodical said after a tour of India during the January 1980 general elections (I have misplaced the reference). He stated that the elections had witnessed several Harijans being shot, beaten and forcibly prevented from voting by higher caste groups; he spoke of a sort of kulak class born of the green revolution and hatred of landless labourers. He further added that 'hypocrisy is an English vice and that is how the Indians learnt it! The use of the term "Harijans" to describe untouchables is a prime example. Harijans means Children of God which makes people feel better about the way untouchables are treated by their fellow beings'!

Mere constitutional declarations are not enough. The Constitution therefore recognized, promoted and encouraged special treatment in educational institutions and employment opportunities for the socially less fortunate classes to any office under the state. It empowered Parliament and state legislatures to make special provisions through ordinary law for the advancement of Scheduled Castes, Scheduled Tribes and Other Backward Classes (OBCs) – those who by reason of their occupational background are socially and educationally backward. Provisions could be made for them, without infringing the equality clauses, in Articles 14 and 16, for reservation of seats in educational institutions and in posts in public services, at almost all levels.

The Constitution had also prescribed an agency and a method for designating Scheduled Castes and Scheduled Tribes. The president (that is, the Central Government, since all executive action of the Government of India is taken in the name of the president) was empowered to specify the castes, races or tribes that, for the purposes of the Constitution, would be deemed to be Scheduled Castes or Scheduled Tribes within any particular state or union territory (Articles 341 and 342). Once promulgated, these lists could be changed only by an Act of Parliament. The Scheduled Castes Order, promulgated by the president in 1950 (with amendments introduced over the years), proceeded primarily on the basis of 'untouchability', measured by the incidence of social disability combined with economic, occupational, educational, residential and religious criteria.[132] The Scheduled Tribes Order of 1950 – amended over the years – listed backward tribes in need of preferential treatment.

The scheme of Scheduled and Tribal Areas (under the Government of India Act of 1935) was adopted in the Constitution of India (in Part X, Articles 244 and 244[A], and in the Fifth and Sixth Schedules to the Constitution). These designated areas were to be administered as a special responsibility of the governor of the state in consultation with tribal committees and councils. The provisions for Scheduled Tribes in the Constitution were intended to preserve their separate identities. The aim was a balanced improvement of their condition with such a degree of assimilation as would preserve their distinctiveness and give them a measure of autonomy.

Primitive cultures react sharply to alien interference. Experience has shown that indigenous tribal communities are prepared to adapt themselves to change only on their own terms and in their own time. The constitutional policy for Scheduled Castes (and Scheduled Tribes) has been to overcome their disabilities and disadvantages by preferential treatment and to eliminate their distinctiveness by enabling them to share the advantages for lack of which they are still a class apart from other, more advantaged members of Hindu society.

***

While the categories of Scheduled Castes and Scheduled Tribes were constitutionally determined, the socially and educationally backward classes of citizens (also designated for preferential treatment) had been left undefined, even though specifically mentioned in Article 15(4) in 1951.[133]

The first Backward Classes Commission (the Kaka Kalelkar Commission) appointed by the Central Government submitted its report in 1955, listing 2399 castes as 'socially and educationally backward'. However, the report was not accepted by the government since no objective tests were laid down for identifying OBCs. At that time, the government was opposed to the adoption of caste as a criterion for backwardness; it would have preferred the application of an economic or means test.

These 'classes of citizens' were then left to be determined by the states and by the government agencies. But the states had been singularly remiss in not gathering data over the years to enable a realistic determination (at least in terms of percentages) of these classes of citizens as compared to the rest of the population in the state. Nor was there much progress in the amelioration of the lot of these classes of citizens. The absence of any constitutionally prescribed or judicially mandated method for identifying OBCs led to much speculative reasoning by different state governments. It also fostered bitterness and dissatisfaction amongst members of these classes as well as from those better-off, i.e., those not belonging to the class of OBCs, who objected to preferential treatment for the backward classes.

The state of Karnataka set up its own commission (in 1972) to investigate and report on backward classes in the state. The report of the Havanur Commission[134] (named after its chairman L. G. Havanur) ignored the principle of caste in the concept of social backwardness and devised a new test: that of *poverty coupled with isolation*. This test cut across the caste system and included as backward classes several groups of temple functionaries (who belonged to higher castes) as well as some Kshatriyas. At the same time, it excluded some groups in the traditionally low castes on the grounds of their economic advancement. The state of Karnataka accepted the report and proceeded to make reservations in accordance with it. As expected, the constitutional validity of the state action (order dated 22 February 1977 accepting the report) was challenged in the High Court of Karnataka by writ petitions (which were partially allowed). The case later reached the Supreme Court of India (in 1985 – *K. C. Vasanth Kumar* vs *State of Karnataka*).[135]

Called upon to frame guidelines for determining 'other backward classes' – for purposes of the Karnataka state's reservation policy[136] – each of the five justices in *K. C. Vasanth Kumar* (1985) spoke diffidently, and with different voices, without any unanimity on the vital points of contention, viz.: (1) whether a policy of reservation of more than 50 per cent for OBCs was permissible in law; (2) whether castes should form the basis – or at least an important element – for determining social and educational backwardness; and (3) whether in jobs in government requiring high expertise and skill, a policy of reservation, detracting from merit, was permissible.

On the first point of contention, after the decision of the Constitution Bench of the Supreme Court of India in *Nagaraj* vs *Union of India*

(2006),[137] the ceiling limit of 50 per cent for backward classes has been regarded – hopefully, finally regarded! – by the Supreme Court of India as 'a Constitutional mandate'. On the second point of contention, after the decision of the Constitution Bench of the Supreme Court of India, in *Ashoka Kumar Thakur* vs *Union of India and Ors.* (2008),[138] the court has made it (regrettably but abundantly) clear – by a majority of 4:1 – that *caste* does definitely constitute the basis for determining social and educational backwardness. But as to the third point of contention, this has not yet been authoritatively dealt with or answered by the highest court, although it needs to be. It has been left – by judicial diktat – to be decided by 'the government' – which, in the context of a non-majoritarian government, is today a euphemism for 'the politics of the day'!

Two of the judges on the Constitution Bench of five justices in *K. C. Vasanth Kumar* vs *State of Karnataka* (decided on 8 May 1985) said that they were in favour of a reservations policy having a time limit.[139] 'Otherwise', as one of them pointed out, 'concessions tend to become vested interests.'[140] However, the judges were all agreed (and alarmed) about a new trend, viz., that of privileged groups among underprivileged classes monopolizing for themselves the preferential benefits intended for the class. Justice Chinnappa Reddy dwelt on the degrading spectacle:

> The paradox of the system of reservation is that it has engendered a spirit of self-denigration among the people. Nowhere else in the world do castes, classes or communities queue up for the sake of gaining the backward status. Nowhere else in the world is there competition to assert backwardness and to claim 'we are more backward than you'. This is an unhappy and disquieting situation, but it is stark reality.

Justice D. A. Desai, who made a fervent plea for the recognition of poverty as a true criterion for backwardness, said that if a survey were made about the benefits of preferential treatment among the undefined economically and socially backward classes, 'it would unmistakably show that the benefits of reservations are snatched away by "the top creamy layer"[141] of the backward castes'.

This consideration prompted Chief Justice Yeshwant V. Chandrachud (who had delivered a separate order) to recommend that the test of economic backwardness be applied not only to the Other Backward Classes, but also to Scheduled Castes and Scheduled Tribes.[142] Chief Justice Chandrachud also suggested (a useful suggestion) that the policy of reservations in public employment, in education, and in legislative bodies should be reviewed once every five years, since it would help the state to rectify the distortions arising out of the implementation of the reservations policy. But since this was only a 'suggestion', it was not implemented by the states! Chief Justice Chandrachud also said (another useful recommendation that has been ignored) that an ongoing process of review would help the people (backward and others) to express their views 'in a continuing public debate on the practical effects of that policy'. But the 'continuing public debate' anticipated by Chief Justice Chandrachud got foreclosed with Prime Minister V. P. Singh's acceptance in totality of the recommendations of the second Backward Classes Commission – the Mandal Commission in August 1990 (see Notes 143 and 144). This is how it all happened.

* * *

In January 1979, the Government of India by an order issued (under Article 340 of the Constitution[143]) appointed a second Backward Classes Commission to investigate the conditions of socially and educationally backward classes within the territory of India. The commission was known (and will be long remembered – both by its protagonists and its antagonists as well!) as '*the Mandal Commission*', after its chairman B. P. Mandal, a former chief minister of Bihar. Its recommendations were to change the entire course of the social history of India. The terms of reference of the Mandal Commission were:

1. to determine the criteria for defining the socially and educationally backward classes;
2. to recommend steps to be taken for the advancement of the socially and educationally backward classes of citizens so identified;
3. to examine the desirability or otherwise of making provision

for the reservation of appointments or posts in favour of such backward classes of citizens which are not adequately represented in public services and posts in connection with the affairs of the Union or of any State; and

4. to present to the President a report setting out the facts as found by the Commission and making such recommendations as they thought fit.

The report of the Mandal Commission, which came in December 1980, said that the 'reservations' envisaged in Article 15(4) applied to socially and educationally backward classes, not to economically backward ones and concluded that in view of the permanent stratification of society in a hierarchical caste order, low-caste status had a direct bearing on a person's social backwardness. The report overlooked that Subclauses (3), (4) and (5) of Article 15 did not expressly provide for reservation. It envisaged '*any special provision*' for the advancement of socially and educationally backward classes of citizens or of Scheduled Castes and Scheduled Tribes, such as special wide-ranging scholarships and other ameliorative measures for improving standards, and any like provisions that the genius of lawmakers could devise for ensuring advancement amongst the 'classes of citizens' (including Scheduled Castes and Scheduled Tribes) mentioned in the three subclauses of Article 15. When *reservation* of posts was intended to be provided for by the framers of the Constitution that word was advisedly mentioned: only in Articles 16(4), (4A) and (4B).

The report of the Mandal Commission mentioned some startling data. It extrapolated from the census figures of 1931 (the last and only available decennial census that had recorded the caste status of Hindus) and concluded that the 'derived' percentage of population of Other Backward Classes (both Hindus and non-Hindus) was as high as 52 per cent of the total population of India), with the Scheduled Castes and Scheduled Tribes accounting for an additional 22.5 per cent.[144] The commission then recommended a 27 per cent reservation in favour of the OBCs (in addition to 22.5 per cent already existing in favour of SCs and STs) as also several measures for improving the conditions of backward classes. In its report, the commission stated that the representation of OBCs in government services and public employment was only 13 per cent and their representation in 'plum' jobs (Class I posts) a meagre 4.7 per cent to 6 per cent.[145] Statistics, when skilfully presented, dispel complacency. The OBCs were greatly agitated. But the Central Government looked the other way. With a characteristic lack of sensitivity, the government of the day took no action whatever although the report (1980) itself had been ritualistically laid before Parliament and discussed there – on one brief occasion in 1982 and again on another occasion in 1983.

It was some years later, in August 1990, when under the government of V. P. Singh, an office memorandum dated 13 August 1990[146] was sprung upon the nation (to the surprise of all and to the delight of the steadily increasing members belonging to the OBCs[147]); it lit the match that started a conflagration that many believed would lead to *real* 'social justice'. The prime minister himself added fuel to the fire when he spoke in Parliament on 25 September 1991, somewhat deprecatingly, about merit:

> We talk about merit. What is the merit of the system itself? That the section which has 52% of the population gets 12.55% in Government employment. What is the merit of the system? That in Class I employees of the Government it gets only 4.69% for 52% of the population in decision-making at the top echelons ... it is not even one-tenth of the population of the country; in the power structure it is hardly 4.69%. I want to challenge first the merit of the system itself before we come and question ... whether on merit to reject this individual or that. *And we want to change the structure basically, consciously, with open eyes. And I know when changing the structures, there will be resistance...*[148] [emphasis added].

* * *

From this time on, the structural matrix of 'social justice' got radically changed! And, as expected, there was resistance.

There is always resistance to change! There were widespread protests in certain northern states and a serious disturbance to law and order involving damage to private and public property. Some people lost their lives by self-immolation. Petitions were filed in the Supreme Court, the leading Writ Petition No. 930 of 1990 (under Article 32 of the Constitution) titled *Indira Sawhney* vs *Union of India and Ors* questioning the constitutional validity of the office memorandum. The writ petition was admitted, and (with a view not to aggravate matters further), the operation of the memorandum was temporarily stayed by an interim order of the court, reflecting a truism attributed to Justice Benjamin N. Cardozo (a noted US jurist): 'The great tides and currents which engulf the rest of men do not turn aside in their course and pass the judges by.'

Soon after the general elections held in May-June 1991, there was a change of government at the Centre, and a second office memorandum was issued on 25 September 1991 (modifying the earlier one), which gave some weightage to economic factors and to poverty – though only in name. This office memorandum (which was stated to come into force with immediate effect) declared:

1. Within the 27% of the vacancies in civil posts and services under the Government of India reserved for SEBCs (socially and educationally backward classes), preference shall be given to candidates belonging to the poorer sections of the SEBCs. In case sufficient number of such candidates are not available, unfilled vacancies shall be filled by the other SEBC candidates.
2. 10% of the vacancies in civil posts and services under the Government of India shall be reserved for other economically backward sections of the people who are not covered by any of the existing schemes of reservation.
3. The criteria for determining the poorer sections of the SEBCs or the other economically backward sections of the people who are not covered by any of the existing schemes of reservations are being issued separately.

The office memorandum of even number, dated 13 August 1990, was deemed to have been amended to the extent specified by the one of 25 September 1991. [The criteria mentioned in (iii) above have not been listed, issued or published at any time!]

The group of writ petitions was first heard by a Constitution Bench presided over by Chief Justice Ranganath Misra. After sometime, the petitions were referred to a 'special bench' of nine justices 'to finally settle the legal position relating to reservations'. The reason given was that 'several judgments of this Court have not spoken in the same voice on this issue and a final look by a larger Bench in our opinion should *settle the law in an authoritative way*'. But expectations raised in the referral order were dashed by the decision subsequently rendered, by a majority, in the bench of nine justices!

In the course of judgments running into more than 500 closely printed pages, 'the law', regarding reservation for backward classes, was adverted to in the *Indira Sawhney* case but not expounded in any 'authoritative way' as had been initially intended in the order of reference, save in one particular, viz., that Article 16 – as framed – did not include reservation at promotion levels. But treating this as a lacuna and not as a deliberate constitutional impediment, India's Parliament (in its constituent role) promptly added Clause (4A) to Article 16, by the Constitution 81st Amendment Act 2000, expressly permitting the state to prescribe reservations for OBCs even after the initial stage of appointment to posts under the Union or the state!

On the vital points raised in *Indira Sawhney*, there did emerge a majority view (6:3), but the opinion of the majority was not expressed firmly nor in peremptory language. This is what the majority said:[149]

- that neither the Constitution nor the law prescribes the procedure or method of identification of backward classes; *nor was it possible or advisable for the Court to lay down any such procedure or method*;
- *that it must be left to the appointed authorities to identify backward classes*, and so long as the identification (by a survey) covered the entire populace no objection could be taken to it;
- that it was not necessary for a class to be designated as a backward class [and] that it was similarly situated to the Scheduled Castes and Scheduled Tribes; *backward classes of citizens could not be identified only and exclusively with reference to economic criteria*;

- that the distinction made in the office memorandum of 25 September 1991 between 'poorer sections' and others among the backward classes was not invalid 'if the classification is understood and operated as based upon *relative backwardness* among the several classes identified as 'Other Backward Classes';
- that the adequacy of representation of a particular class in the services under the State was a matter within the *subjective satisfaction of the appropriate Government: not to be ordinarily interfered with by Courts on judicial review.*[150]

In the Constituent Assembly itself Dr Ambedkar had indicated what he perceived as the court's role in the determination of reservations for OBCs.[151] He had said that the rule of equality of opportunity must not get destroyed by the magnitude of the reservation prescribed by the executive authorities. This is how he put it:

> My honourable friend Mr T. T. Krishnamachari [a member of the Constituent Assembly who went on to become the Union finance minister in 1957] asked me whether this rule (viz., that a backward community is that which is backward in the opinion of the Government) will be justiciable. It is rather difficult to give a dogmatic answer. *Personally I think it would be a justiciable matter* [emphasis added]. If the local Government included in this category of reservations such a large number of seats; I think one could very well go to the Federal Court and the Supreme Court and say that the reservation is of such a magnitude that the rule regarding equality of opportunity has been destroyed and the court will then come to the conclusion whether the local Government or the State Government has acted in a reasonable and prudent manner.

In the majority judgment of Justice Jeevan Reddy – in *Indira Sawhney* – concurred in by separate judgments of Justices S. R. Pandian and P. B. Sawant, only the first part of Dr Ambedkar's speech was quoted, which read:

> Somebody asked me: 'What is a backward community?' Well, I think anyone who reads the language of the draft itself will find that we

> have left it to be determined by each local Government. A backward community is a community which is backward in the opinion of the Government …

But the latter part of Dr Ambedkar's speech (already set out earlier) – the more pertinent, the more relevant part – where the architect of the Constitution had opined that it was a *justiciable matter*, was not even mentioned in the principal judgment of Justice Jeevan Reddy, or in the concurring judgments of Justices Pandian and Sawant!

* * *

In Indira Sawhney, *a great opportunity to lay down the limits beyond which the government could not go was passed over.*

Where the court could have, and should have, spoken authoritatively it refrained from doing so, particularly in that portion of its judgment dealing with '*whether reservations are anti-meritarian*'? Whilst correctly holding that 'it may not be said that reservations (per se) are anti-meritarian', the court (majority) did say that there were certain services and positions where, whether on account of the nature of the duties attached to them or the level (in the hierarchy) at which they obtain, '*merit alone counts*'. But then the court went on to simply caution that 'in such situations it *may not* be advisable to provide for reservations'; it was for the Government of India (the court said) to consider and specify the service and posts to which the rule of reservation shall not apply.

Again, even after enumerating in detail the services and posts where (in the opinion of the majority) '*there should be no rule of reservation*' *in certain services* (mentioned in detail in the judgment of Justice Jeevan Reddy), viz.:

> in defence services, in technical posts in establishments engaged in Research and Development including those connected with atomic energy and space, in teaching posts of Professors, in posts in super-specialities in medicine, engineering and other scientific and technical subjects, in posts of pilots and co-pilots in Indian Airlines and Air India,

the court (majority) went out of its way to add:

> The list given above is merely illustrative and not exhaustive. It is for the Government of India to consider and specify the service and posts to which the rule of reservation shall not apply, but on that account the implementation of the impugned Office Memorandum dated 13 August 1990 cannot be stayed or withheld.

The passages quoted above – in my view – indicate an almost deliberate abdication by the majority of its solemn duty of upholding the constitutional guarantee of Equality before the Law and the Equal Protection of the Law.

The concept of equality in our Constitution has two distinct dimensions. First, it embodies the principle of non-discrimination [Articles 14, 15(1), (2) and 16(2)], and second, at the same time, it obligates the state to take affirmative action for ensuring that unequals (the downtrodden, the oppressed and the *have-nots*) in society are brought at a level where they can compete with others (the *haves* of society) [Articles 15(3) (4) (5), 16(4), (4-A), (4-B), 39, 39-A and 41].[152] But as to which 'dimension' is the more important in a given case, and as to what should be the balancing factor in the broad conspectus of the Equality Provisions, are *only* for the Supreme Court to say. It could not – it cannot – be left for the government to provide or for a commission appointed by the government to determine!

Marc Galanter has offered a philosophical justification for the lack of a strong consistent judicial approach in the field of (what he describes as) 'compensatory discrimination':[153]

> *Compensatory discrimination offers a way to leaven our formalism without entirely abandoning its comforts.* The Indian example is instructive: India has managed to pursue a commitment to substantive justice without allowing that commitment to dissolve competing commitments to formal equality that make law viable in a diverse society with limited consensus. The Indian experience displays a principled eclecticism that avoids suppressing the altruistic

> fraternal impulse that animates compensatory policies, but that also avoids being enslaved by it. *From afar* it reflects to us a *tempered legalism* – one which we find more congenial in practice than in theory [emphasis added].

But whatever the view 'from afar' (sometimes, distance does, lend enchantment to the view!), the experience of others, within India, has been far more pragmatic and realistic; it has been expressed in the following terms:

> From being an instrument of egalitarianism, the reservation policy is now seen as the most blatant expression of what has come to be known as 'vote-bank politics'. This is particularly so in regard to reservations for the OBCs in the post-Mandal scenario, where the most contentious controversies are centred. It is precisely here that affirmative action seems to be falling short. *Addressing one injustice or inequality at the cost of causing others will only politicise society further, not make it more equitable or egalitarian.* Both Parliament and the Court must *critique* reservation policies and legislation from a constitutional understanding of inclusive and integral justice [emphasis added].[154]

What is sorely lacking in India is *the critique* of the country's highest court!

It is precisely because Indian society is so diverse and there is little or no consensus (as Galanter says) that an effective judicial pronouncement by the Supreme Court would have provided a very helpful guide, and, more importantly, it would have served as a most useful check. The court, when called upon to lay down the 'law', unfortunately, yielded to the temptation of not firmly saying either yea or nay. If only the majority in *Indira Sawhney* (and it was a learned, experienced and distinguished majority) had set the goalposts and had specified what could or could not be done in the matter of 'reservations', its exposition in its judgment would then have been regarded as 'law', binding on us all under Articles 141 and 144 of the Constitution.[155] Instead, there have been only bits of advice and recommendations from the court, which, since they were not expressed in authoritative terms, have been largely ignored!

***

In *Indira Sawhney* (1992), in para 861 of the majority judgment, the following directions were given:

1. that the Government of India and each of the State Governments and the Administrations of Union Territories would within four months constitute a permanent body for entertaining, examining and recommending upon requests for inclusion and complaints of over-inclusion and under-inclusion in the lists of other backward classes of citizens – the advice tendered by such body being ordinarily binding upon the Government; and
2. within four months the Government of India would specify the bases, apply the relevant and requisite socio-economic criteria to exclude socially advanced persons/sections ('creamy layer') from Other Backward Classes and the implementation of the impugned Office Memorandum of 13 August 1990 would be subject to exclusion of such socially advanced persons ('creamy layer').

The directions were complied with. Pursuant to these directions, Parliament then passed the National Commission for Backward Classes Act 1993,[156] in which the term 'backward classes' was defined exhaustively as meaning such backward classes of citizens other than the Scheduled Castes and the Scheduled Tribes, as may be specified by the Central Government in the list, i.e., the list prepared by the Government of India from time to time for purposes of making provisions for the reservation of appointments or posts in favour of backward classes of citizens which, in the opinion of that government, are not adequately represented in the services under the Government of India and any local or other authority within the territory of India or under the control of the Government of India. The list is an ongoing one to be revised (with inclusions or exclusions) every 10 years based on the advice of the Backward Classes Commission. But the 'advice' of the commission is declared to be 'ordinarily binding upon the Central Government' (Sections 9 and 11).[157]

There is no guidance either from Parliament or the Supreme Court as to the governing legal principles. The Central Government is now empowered (under Section 11) to include in the list 'new backward classes', but on what criteria is not stipulated. The National Commission for Backward Classes Act 1993 has conferred far-reaching powers on the commission. Parliament has also viewed Articles 15 and 16 as distinct and separate provisions, independent even of the main equality clause (Article 14), overlooking prior Constitution Bench decisions rendered by the Supreme Court,[158] which have held that the '*three* provisions (Articles 14, 15 and 16) form part of the same constitutional role of guarantees and supplement each other'.

* * *

By the 1992 judgment in *Indira Sawhney* and since the enactment of the National Commission for Backward Classes Act 1993, the highest court has denied itself its constitutional function as the guardian of Equal Protection under the Law – a right solemnly guaranteed by Article 14 of the Constitution of India.

In balancing 'equal treatment' and 'compensatory discrimination', *Indira Sawhney* (followed in subsequent decisions) has left it to politicians and administrators as to how far they could go. It is only in *Nagaraj* vs *Union of India* (2007)[159] that a Constitution Bench of the Supreme Court of India has said (for once, boldly not timidly), though only in respect of one aspect of 'reservations', viz., that the ceiling limit of 50 per cent reservation for backward classes, was, and is '*a constitutional mandate*'.

* * *

After a debate in Parliament that ultimately resulted in the passing of the Constitution 93rd Amendment Act 2005, another lingering doubt has been cleared: in the criteria for determining OBCs, economic backwardness is OUT.

In 2005 the newly added Article 15(5) has reproduced the language previously used in Article 15(4) in 1951; Parliament has reaffirmed that it is the advancement of socially and educationally backward classes of citizens (not economically backward classes of citizens) that is the ultimate aim and goal of our Constitution.

After the Constitution 93rd Amendment Act 2005, Parliament passed the Central Education Institutions (Reservation in Admission) Act 2006 (assented to by the president in 2007 and described as Act 5 of 2007). Section 3 provides for reservation of 15 per cent seats for Scheduled Castes, 7.5 per cent per cent for Scheduled Tribes and 27 per cent for Other Backward Classes[160] in Central educational institutions, i.e. (1) universities established or incorporated by or under Central Acts, (2) institutions of national importance set up by Acts of Parliament, (3) deemed universities under Section 3 of the University Grants Commission Act, (4) institutions maintained or receiving aid from the Central Government and (5) educational institutions set up by the Central Government under the Societies Registration Act 1860. (Act 5 of 2007, however, is not to apply to minority educational institutions.)

***

In Ashoka Kumar Thakur *vs* Union of India and Ors. (2008), *the constitutional validity of Article 15(5) – added by the Constitution 93rd Amendment Act 2005 – was challenged before a bench of five justices of the Supreme Court on the ground that it was contrary to the 'basic structure of the Constitution', because the thrust of our Constitution was to establish a casteless society. However, the challenge was negatived (4:1).*[161]

The court held that Article 15(5) was valid to the extent that it has permitted reservation for socially and educationally backward classes in state (or state-aided) educational institutions with the exclusion of the 'creamy layer' from amongst the OBCs. However, the mode or method to be adopted for such exclusion was not prescribed either by Parliament or by the judges. Justice R. V. Raveendran (in a separate judgment, concurring with the majority) went on to add:

> Failure to exclude the 'creamy layer' from the benefits of reservation would render the reservation for other backward classes under Act 5 of 2007 unconstitutional.[162]

In other words, failure to exclude 'the creamy layer' would violate the *basic structure of the Constitution*.[163] Lacteal phraseology is increasingly in vogue! In a recently published book,[164] the author refers to a black union leader who described the economy of South Africa as 'cappuccino economy' with 'white cream over the large black mass, sprinkled with some black chocolate on top'! The remark may or may not have been appropriate. But in the context of OBCs, the expression 'creamy layer' is inappropriate. When milk is boiled, the 'creamy layer' readily floats up to the top and is easily skimmed off, but alas not when determining who, or how many OBCs, have become economically better off by having 'floated to the top' (and to be henceforth skimmed off and so excluded from the general class of OBCs)!

***

Ashoka Kumar Thakur vs *Union of India* (2008) was not a unanimous judgment of the Constitution Bench of five justices. The judge who dissented was in a (brave) minority of one. At the very commencement of his separate judgment, Justice Dalveer Bhandari posed what he rightly described as 'the fundamental question':

> 361. The fundamental question that arises in these writ petitions is: Whether Article 15(5), inserted by the Ninety-third Amendment, is consistent with the other provisions of the Constitution or whether its impact runs contrary to the constitutional aim of achieving a *casteless and classless society* [emphasis added].
>
> 362. On behalf of the petitioners, Senior Advocate, Mr F. S. Nariman, eloquently argued that if Article 15(5) is permitted to remain in force, then, instead of achieving the goal of a casteless and classless society, India would be converted into a caste-ridden society. The country would forever remain divided on caste lines. The Government has sought to repudiate this argument. The petitioners' argument, however, echoes the grave concern of our Constitution's original Framers.
>
> 363. On careful analysis of the Constituent Assembly and the Parliamentary Debates, one thing is crystal clear: our leaders have

> always, and unanimously, proclaimed with one voice that our constitutional goal is to establish a casteless and classless society.

He then dealt with the question posed in para 361 in succeeding paragraphs (537–560) of his judgment and concluded as follows:

> 605. In conclusion, the First Parliament, by enacting Article 15(4), deviated from the original Framers' intent. They passed an amendment that strengthens rather than weakens casteism. If caste-based quotas in education are to stay, they should adhere to a basic tenet of secularism: they should not take caste into account. Instead, exclusively economic criteria should be used. For a period of 10 years, other factors such as income, occupation and property holdings, etc., including caste, may be taken into consideration and thereafter only economic criteria should prevail. [But] *Indira Sawhney* (1992) has tied our hands. I nevertheless believe that caste matters and will continue to matter as long as we divide society along caste lines. Caste-based discrimination remains. Violence between castes occurs. Caste politics rages on. Where casteism is present, the goal of achieving a casteless society must never be forgotten. Any legislation to the contrary should be discarded.

Justice Bhandari's regret that 'caste-based discrimination remains' is a cry of distress – albeit in the wilderness – and a courageous appeal (as in the case of all dissents) to 'the brooding spirit of the future'! But after the majority decision (4:1) in *Ashoka Kumar Thakur* (2008), whatever the Preamble may say, the vision of a secular society can no longer be said to be the true aim of our written Constitution. A great opportunity has been missed by the court to steer the ship of state into casteless waters. It is the Supreme Court of India itself that has helped to perpetuate the division of Indian society along caste-based lines. Alas, who *will* – who *can* – guide the guardians?

* * *

After more than 60 years of the Constitution, how can one accurately define Equality in the context of educational and job opportunities?

This is one of the more difficult – as yet unanswered – questions in the life of a 65-year-old nation. Even in 2012, no one is quite sure as to what Equality of educational and job opportunities truly means. Here's why:

1. It can hardly be argued that once a backward class, always a backward class as this would defeat the very purpose of special provisions made in the Constitution for the advancement of the backward classes, and for enabling them to come to the level of, and to compete with, the 'forward' classes, as equal citizens.
2. To continue to confer upon 'advanced sections' of the backward classes (designated as the 'creamy layer') the special benefits amounts to treating equals unequally. It undoubtedly violates the provisions of the Constitution (Article 14 read with Article 16).
3. Since there is no judicially recommended criteria evolved of these 'advanced sections' amongst the OBCs, there is room for 'executive change of opinion' (a euphemism, for 'administrative manipulation for political purposes'). And it is happening. The game of 'moving the goalposts' is in play! 'Advanced sections' of backward classes are now sought to be placed on an 'upward sliding' scale! For instance, the existing ceiling for 'creamy layer' – a mere administrative determination – has been fixed at an annual income of Rs 4.5 lakh per annum, but (if news reports are to be believed – and there are a proliferation of them[165]), the Congress-led government at the Centre is trying to 'reach out' to OBCs by drastically relaxing the figure placed by the executive on the judge-invented concept of 'creamy layer'. It is no longer to be at Rs 4.5 lakh per annum, but is proposed to be fixed (in the metros) at Rs 12 lakh per annum! This means that OBCs with an income of Rs 1 lakh per month would become eligible for job reservation in the public sector; and there is also expected to be a corresponding upward revision for OBCs in the non-metros to Rs 9 lakh per annum.

4. To rank 'advanced sections' of the backward classes with the rest of the backward classes would equally violate the right to equality of the rest in those classes. It would amount to treating unequals equally! This will lead to perverting the objectives of the special constitutional provisions, since the 'forwards' among the backward classes will be thereby facilitated to 'gobble up' (or appropriate) all the *special benefits*, to the exclusion and at the cost of the rest in their own class – keeping the rest of the really backward classes (e.g., at present, those earning below Rs 4.5 lakh per annum) in a state of 'perpetual backwardness'! But a state of perpetual backwardness is certainly not envisaged in our Constitution.
5. Taking out or weeding out the 'forwards' from among the backward classes is therefore mandated (by dicta of the Supreme Court) as obligatory under the Constitution, but unfortunately as to how and within what time this has to be ensured has not been indicated. Only the Supreme Court can devise a realistic and practicable scheme and time frame, which would then have to be enforced by agencies of the state as law declared by the Supreme Court, binding on all! The American courts have said that a time frame is vital because it affects the equal-protection principle, and they have even legislated (judicially) about it: Justice Sandra O'Connor – expressed the view of the majority of the US Supreme Court – when she wrote (in the case of the Michigan Law School's admission policy – *Grutter* vs *Bollinger*, 2003 539, US 306 =* 156 L. Ed. 2d 304, 341) as follows:

> Race-conscious admissions policies must be limited in time. This requirement reflects that racial classifications, however compelling their goals, are potentially so dangerous that they may be employed no more broadly than the interest demands. Enshrining a permanent justification for racial preferences would offend this fundamental equal-protection principle. We see no reason to exempt race-conscious admissions programs from the requirement that all governmental use of race must have a logical end point.

*'=' denotes 'as reported in'.

But the Supreme Court of India has not said a word about the time frame for weeding out the 'forwards' from among the backward classes. It needs to.

6. A possible solution to the vexed problem of 'reservations' had been suggested many years ago (by Justice Krishna Iyer in *State of Kerala* vs *N. M. Thomas*, AIR 1976, SC 490, p. 531, para 149, in a bench decision of seven judges), viz.: by improvement of the social environment; by added educational facilities; and by cross-fertilization of castes by intercaste and interclass marriages sponsored by a massive state programme. But there is a hidden danger in these suggestions (as pointed out by the great judge himself): 'the danger is that this solution is calculatedly hidden from view by the higher "backward" groups with a vested interest in the *plums of backwardism*!'[166] It is the enemy within – not the detractors without – that has become the main problem with *quotas* for the OBCs.
7. There has been thus far too much dithering on this subject. What will help, I believe, is a constant and assiduous gathering of data, a continuous process of objective re-evaluation of progress registered by the 'underdog' categories, a more focused preferential treatment for the disadvantaged and vulnerable and (above all) a broader constitutional vision (on the part of India's Supreme Court and India's Parliament) of a more inclusive and egalitarian society – together with a firm articulation of this – lest an otherwise deserving policy of 'reservations' (for OBCs) be degraded into a vote-catching exercise leading ultimately to 'reverse discrimination'.

***

As I see it – in the context of the provisions of our Constitution – this then is the current State of the Nation in the social, religious, cultural and educational spheres.

Notes and References

1. The old Sanskrit name was Himalaya – the abode of snow. The Himalayas are not a mountain chain in the ordinary acceptation of the term. They stretch across a large part of Asia, immediately to the north of India, in the form of 'great protuberances above the general level of the earth's surface'. The whole of its southern border is usually called by the name Himalaya, and its northern border, in a much less definite way, is called Kunlun-Shan (or the Kunlun mountains), one of the longest mountain chains in Asia extending more than 3000 kilometres. Between the Himalayas and the Kunlun mountains lies the mountainous tableland of Tibet, with an average elevation of 4500 metres above sea level. Neither the Himalayas nor Kunlun-Shan nor the Tibetan tableland has any separate existence, the whole constituting 'one huge agglomeration of mountains'. See Sir John Strachey: *India* (new and revised edition, 1903, pp. 18-19); originally published in 1888, Kegan Paul, Trench, Trubner & Co., London.
2. It is not the inhabitants of Hindustan who are Hindus, but only those who profess the *Hindu* religion. Etymologically, the word 'Hindu' is derived from Sindhu (literally, large mass of water, used to describe the mighty Indus). The Persian invaders described all northern India as Hindustan, the land of the rivers. It is out of this derived Persian term 'Hindu' that the invading Greeks coined 'India'. See Will Durant: *The Story of Civilization*, Vol. I, Simon and Schuster, New York, 1954, pp. 392-93.
3. The Great Rann of Kutch comprises about 30,000 square kilometres between the Gulf of Kutch and the mouth of the Indus River in what is now southern Pakistan.
4. But the 'impossible' is never far from the 'probable', and is only a shade away from the 'the possible'. Almost a century later, a Union 'of the various nations of Europe' did get formally established when the Maastricht Treaty came into force on 1 November 1993!
5. Jawaharlal Nehru: *The Discovery of India*, Signet Press, Calcutta, 1946, pp. 55-57.
6. Eight times: in 1929, 1930, 1936, 1937, 1951, 1952, 1953 and 1954.
7. In 1934, the Indian National Congress, whilst rejecting the White Paper on Proposals for Constitutional Reforms, 1933 (Cmd. 4268), first made its demand for a Constituent Assembly to draw up India's Constitution. (Cmd.: Command Paper.)
8. Mohammad Ali Jinnah (the founder of Pakistan) had finally left the Congress in September 1920 and switched his loyalties entirely to the Muslim League, which he had already joined in 1913. In those days, it was possible to be a member of both the Congress and the Muslim League!
9. Published statement of the viceroy, 3 June 1947, Cmd. 7136. Nicholas Mansergh and Penderel Moon (eds.): *The Transfer of Power 1942–47*, Volume XI, Her Majesty's Stationery Office (HMSO), 1976 London, p. 89.

10. From the Mountbatten Papers (at the Hartley Library in Southampton) as mentioned by Narendra Singh Sarila in *The Shadow of the Great Game: The Untold Story of India's Partition*, HarperCollins India, New Delhi, 2005. Sarila was, at one time, ADC to Lord Mountbatten.
11. George Nathaniel Curzon, viceroy of India (January 1899 to November 1905), quoted in Denis Judd: *The Lion and the Tiger – The Rise and Fall of the British Raj: 1600 to 1947*, Oxford University Press, New York, 2010, p. 138.
12. Maulana Abul Kalam Azad: *India Wins Freedom – The Complete Version*, Orient and Black Swan, New Delhi, 2009.
13. In March 1971, East Bengal (known as East Pakistan) broke away from Pakistan and formed the separate state of Bangladesh. The imposition of Urdu in the Arabic script proved the breaking point as the majority of the people of East Bengal spoke and wrote in Bengali (an Indo-Aryan language).
14. Many parts of British India were initially governed by the East India Company (founded in 1600), which nominally acted as the agent of the Mughal Emperor. In 1773, the British Government assumed partial control over the governance of India with the passage of the Regulating Act. A governor-general and council were appointed to rule over the Presidency of Fort William in Bengal and the first governor-general and council was named in the Act; their successors were to be elected by the East India Company's Court of Directors. The Act provided for a five-year term for the governor-general and council, but the Crown had the power to remove any of them. The Charter Act 1833 replaced the governor-general and council of Fort William with the governor-general and council of India. The power to elect the governor-general was retained by the Court of Directors, but the choice was subject to the Crown's approval.

    After the Indian Mutiny of 1857, the East India Company was abolished and the territories it controlled in India were placed under the direct control of the Crown. The Government of India Act 1858 vested the power to appoint the governor-general in the Crown. The governor-general, in turn, had the power to appoint all lieutenant governors in India, subject to the approval of the Crown.

    After 1858, the governor-general (henceforth usually known as the viceroy) functioned as the chief administrator of India and as the Sovereign's representative. India was divided into numerous provinces, each under the head of a governor, lieutenant governor or chief commissioner or administrator. Governors were appointed by the British Government, to whom they were directly responsible; lieutenant governors, chief commissioners, and administrators, however, were appointed by, and were subordinate to, the viceroy. The viceroy was the plenipotentiary of the most powerful princely rulers: the Nizam of Hyderabad, the Maharaja of Mysore, the Maharaja (Scindia) of Gwalior, the Maharaja of Jammu and Kashmir and the Maharaja (Gaekwar) of Baroda. The remaining princely rulers were under the suzerainty of either the Rajputana Agency or the Central India Agency (headed by representatives of the viceroy); or they were under provincial authorities. After independence in August 1947, the title of viceroy was abolished. The representative of the British Sovereign became known once again as the governor-general. C. Rajagopalachari was the first and the only Indian to be governor-general.

15. Literally, the word 'paramountcy' conveys supremacy or suzerainty. But it does not adequately describe the relationship between the Crown and the rulers of Indian states. When His Exalted Highness the Nizam of Hyderabad, on whom the British conferred the title of 'Faithful Ally', claimed (in September 1925) that in respect of the internal affairs of Hyderabad, he, the Nizam as ruler of the Indian state of Hyderabad, stood on the same footing as the British Government in India in respect of the internal affairs of British India, Lord Reading (viceroy and governor general, aka Rufus Issacs) responded in a now-famous letter of 27 March 1926 that rejected the Nizam's assertion as 'a complete misconception'! This is how the viceroy described the doctrine of paramountcy:

    > The Sovereignty of the British Crown is supreme in India and therefore no Ruler of an Indian State can justifiably claim to negotiate with the British Government on an equal footing. Its supremacy is not based only upon treaties and engagements, but exists independently of them; and quite apart from its prerogative in matters relating to foreign powers and policies, it is the right and duty of the British Government, whilst scrupulously respecting all treaties and engagements with the Indian States, to preserve peace and good order throughout India.
    >
    > The right of the British Government to intervene in the internal affairs of the Indian States is another instance of the consequences necessarily involved in the supremacy of the British Government.

    The Nizam's claim to an 'exalted' status – different from rulers of other Indian States – was dealt with deftly but firmly:

    > I merely add that the title 'Faithful Ally' which Your Exalted Highness enjoys has not the effect of putting your Government in a category separate from that of other States under Paramountcy of the British Crown. (!)

    Lord Reading's letter of 27 March 1926 is quoted in full in the First Appendix to the Government of India's White Paper on Indian States, 1950, pp. 149-51.

16. Editor of *Punch*, the British weekly magazine of humour and satire published from the year 1841 up to the year 2002. *Punch* was responsible for the modern use of the word 'cartoon' to describe a comic drawing!
17. A few acceded to Pakistan such as the state of Junagadh and the smaller state of Bantva Manavadar (both now in Gujarat).
18. The state of Hyderabad, located over most of the Deccan Plateau in southern India, was established in 1724 by Nizam-ul-Mulk Asaf Jah after the collapse of

the Mughal Indian Empire. As was the case in several Indian royal states, the Nizam was a Muslim, while a majority of the subject population was Hindu. In 1798, Hyderabad became the first Indian State to accede to British protection under the policy of Subsidiary Alliance instituted by Arthur Wellesley. When the British finally departed from the Indian subcontinent in 1947, they offered the various princely states in the subcontinent the option of acceding to either India or Pakistan, or staying on as an independent state. The State of Hyderabad under the leadership of its seventh Nizam, Mir Usman Ali, was the largest and most prosperous of all princely states in India. It covered 82,698 square miles (214,190 km^2) of fairly homogeneous territory and comprised a population of roughly 16.34 million people (as per the 1941 census), of which a majority (85 per cent) was Hindu. Hyderabad State had its own army, airline, telecommunication system, railway network, postal system, currency and radio broadcasting service.

The Nizam decided to keep Hyderabad independent. The leaders of the new Union of India, however, were wary of having an independent – and possibly hostile – state in the heart of a new country and were determined to assimilate Hyderabad into the Indian Union, even if it was by compulsion, unlike the other 565 Princely States, which had already voluntarily acceded either to India or to Pakistan. (Source: Wikipedia.)

19. For a fuller account of the Indian states, see Shiva Rao: *The Framing of India's Constitution*, Indian Institute of Public Administration, New Delhi, 1967, Chapter 18, and the White Paper on Indian States issued by the Government of India in July 1948.
20. The British Indian State of Sikkim was under a hereditary ruler called the Chogyal. With the lapse of paramountcy, Sikkim became a protectorate of India. In 1974 the Sikkim Assembly passed the Government of Sikkim Act, establishing a fully responsible government and seeking representation for the people of Sikkim in India's parliamentary system. By a Constitutional Amendment (1974), Sikkim was given the status of an 'associate state', entitled to send two representatives to each of the two Houses of Parliament. The Chogyal resented this and sought international intervention, which prompted the Sikkim Assembly to pass a resolution abolishing the institution of Chogyal and expressing a desire to become part of India. The decision was approved in a referendum by an overwhelming majority of the Sikkimese people and Sikkim was admitted to the Union by the Constitution 36th Amendment Act 1975.
21. Oinam Sunil, 'The Battle for Imphal', *The Times of India*, Crest Edition, Saturday, 14 January 2012.
22. The Objectives Resolution was passed by the Constituent Assembly. Constituent Assembly Debates (CAD), Vol. I, reprinted by the Lok Sabha Secretariat, New Delhi, pp. 5 and 59.
23. The Constituent Assembly formally approved the draft Constitution on 26 November 1947 and the Constitution took effect on and from 26 January

1950 (Republic Day). At this point, the Constituent Assembly became the Provisional Parliament of India continuing its existence until after the first elections held under the Constitution in 1952.

24. 'Social, Economic and Educational Status of the Muslim Community of India – A Report', November 2006, published by the Government of India, New Delhi.

    Since there was a lack of authentic information about the social, economic and educational status of the Muslim community of India, which came in the way of planning, formulating and implementing specific policies and programmes to address issues relating to the socio-economic backwardness of this community, the Government of India constituted a high-level committee on 9 March 2005 under the chairmanship of Justice Rajinder Sachar (a former chief justice of the Delhi High Court) to prepare a comprehensive report covering these aspects.

    In one of its comments, the Sachar Committee report has concluded that the Muslim OBCs (Other Backward Classes) constitute 40.7 per cent of the total Muslim population and are a sizeable component (15.7 per cent) of the total OBC population in the country. The report noted: 'While Hindu OBCs continue to be relatively deprived in terms of all India data, the Muslim community as a whole is lagging behind Hindu OBCs. The abysmally low representation of Muslim OBCs suggests that the benefits of entitlement meant for the backward classes are yet to reach them.'

25. Granville Austin: *The Indian Constitution: A Cornerstone of a Nation*, Oxford University Press, Bombay, 1966.

26. So said by an illustrious group of justices of the Supreme Court of India (Justice B. P. Jeevan Reddy, speaking for himself, and for Chief Justice M. H. Kania, Justice M. N. Venkatachaliah and Justice A. M. Ahmadi) in *Indra Sawhney and Ors.* vs *Union of India*, 1992, Supp. 3, SCC 217, pp. 631-32.

27. Percival Spear: 'Bentinck and Education', in *Cambridge Historical Journal*, **6**, 1938/40, p. 78. (Lord William Bentinck was the governor-general of India from 1833 to 1835.)

28. Jawaharlal Nehru: *Glimpses of World History*, Oxford University Press, London, 1942, p. 434.

29. Malcolm Muggeridge: 'Twilight of Empire', *The Listener*, Vol. LXXII, 1964, p. 966.

30. James Dunlop-Smith and Martin Gilbert: *Servant of India: A Study of Imperial Rule from 1905 to 1910 as Told through the Correspondence and Diaries of Sir James Dunlop-Smith*, Longman, London, 1966 edition, p. 132.

31. The historian Lawrence James has written that, in 1947, Mountbatten was left with no option but 'to cut and run'. See *Rise and Fall of the British Empire*, Abacus, London, 2008.

32. Shriman Narayan Agarwal: *Gandhian Constitution for Free India*, Khanna Publishers, New Delhi, 1997 reprint. Mahatma Gandhi wrote in the Foreword:

    Perhaps the expression 'Gandhian Constitution' is not a fitting title for

Principal Agarwal's pages. It may be acceptable as a convenient and compact title. The framework is really Principal Agarwal's, based on his study of my writings. He has been interpreting them for a number of years. And as he is anxious not to misinterpret them in any way he would publish nothing without my seeing it. This is both an advantage and a disadvantage. The advantage is obvious. The disadvantage lies in the reader mistaking the particular writing being my view in every detail. Let me then warn him against making any such mistake. If I were to commit myself to every word appearing in these pages, I might as well write the thing myself. Though I have endeavoured to read the constitution twice, with as much attention as I was able to bestow on it during my other engagements, I could not undertake to check every thought and every word of it. Nor would my sense of propriety and individual freedom permit me to commit any such atrocity. All therefore I am able to say is that the brochure contains ample evidence of the care bestowed upon it by the author to make it as accurate as he could. There is nothing in it which has jarred on me as inconsistent with what I would like to stand for. The author was good enough to make such alterations as I thought were necessary.

33. Sir Ivor Jennings: *Some Characteristics of the Indian Constitution*, Oxford University Press, London, 1953, pp. 1, 9-16. Sir Ivor Jennings drafted some of the constitutions of the new nations that emerged (post-World War II) after the break-up of the British Empire.
34. Constituent Assembly Debates, reprinted by Lok Sabha Secretariat, New Delhi, Vol. XI, p. 975.
35. In Western classical literature, linguistic Sanskrit occupies a pre-eminent position along with Greek and Latin in Indo-European studies. Rig Vedic Sanskrit is one of the earliest of the Indo-European group of languages, which includes English and most European languages. Spoken Sanskrit was and is in use at some traditional institutions in India, and since 1950 there have been many attempts at its revival: for example, after the formation of the state of Uttarakhand (in 2000), its Legislative Assembly has adopted Sanskrit as its second official language!
36. The six major religions are: Hinduism, Islam, Christianity, Sikhism, Buddhism and Jainism. According to the census of 2001, the Hindus constitute 81.4 per cent of the population, Muslims: 12.4 per cent, Christians: 2.34 per cent, Sikhs: 1.9 per cent, Buddhists: 0.8 per cent and Jains: 0.4 per cent. Those having no stated religion constitute only 0.07 per cent of the population. The census lists 183 'other religions and persuasions', from Abutani, a small religious cult in the north-eastern state of Arunachal Pradesh, to one of the world's oldest monotheistic religions, Zoroastrianism, whose adherents in India (the Parsis) number only 69,600. Results of the decennial census of 2010-11 are awaited.
37. All those Indians, past and present, traditionally regarded as outcastes and untouchable are labelled 'Dalits'. A commission charged with reviewing the National Council of Educational Research and Training (NCERT) school-level textbooks on political science has recommended that the word 'Dalit' should be replaced with 'Scheduled Caste' (SC). But the director, Centre for

Modern Indian Studies, University of Goettingen, Germany, writes that the SC category was first created in 1931 to specify a subcategory of the 'depressed classes' – a portmanteau term that referred to 'untouchables', which, in British colonial usage, included those who were then called 'hill tribes' and 'criminal tribes' – listed or 'scheduled' as the beneficiaries of more welfare provisions to be made by the state. The British had made welfare provisions for all castes traditionally treated as 'untouchables', irrespective of whether those castes chose to call themselves Hindu or to follow Buddhism, Christianity or Islam. It was only under Congress rule in 1950 that the Presidential Order redefined SCs on the basis solely of religious criteria – Dalits who had converted from Hinduism to other religions lost not only reservation but also (after 1989) protection under the Prevention of Atrocities Act. Rupa Viswanath (a well-known columnist) writes that discrimination against Dalits spans all religious communities – it is not a Hindu problem, but an Indian problem, and she concludes: '... by adopting language that excludes Christian and Muslim Dalits, the proposed textbook [commission] recommendation whitewashes this reality'. See her article entitled 'A Textbook Case of Exclusion', *The Indian Express*, 13 July 2012.

38. The Preamble of the Constitution resolved to constitute India into a sovereign democratic Republic, to secure to all its citizens justice, liberty and equality, to promote fraternity and to ensure 'the dignity of the individual and the unity of the Nation'.
39. Under the Citizenship Act of 1955 (which supplements Part II of the Constitution), Indian citizenship is acquired by birth, descent, registration or naturalization.
40. There are also two minor language groups. The tribes in India's central hill regions (in Bihar, Chota Nagpur, Orissa and Central India) speak Mundu, a language belonging to the Austro-Asiatic family. The other branch language of the family (Mon Khmer or Khasi) is spoken by the Khasis in north-eastern India and by the Nicobarese in the Andaman and Nicobar islands stretching across Bay of Bengal and the Indian Ocean in the south. The inhabitants of the north-eastern mountain areas, who have had a longstanding connection with the people of Tibet and South-east Asia, have developed their own language dialects, which are Sino-Tibetan. The Sino-Tibetan family is represented in India by two branches: Thai-Chinese and Tibeto-Burman. The latter includes Manipuri, the regional language of the state of Manipur.
41. It was with the Sultanate of Delhi in A.D. 1206 that Muslim (or Afghan) rule took hold in India; after which a large part of India was dominated by a succession of Muslim dynasties, the longest being the Mughal. The Mughal Empire was tottering by 1750 but lingered on for a hundred years more and was ultimately wiped out by the British soon after the suppression of the Indian Mutiny of 1857, which finally put an end to Mughal rule in India. The Parliament in Great Britain then passed the Government of India Act 1858, which authorized the British Crown to take over the administration of all

Indian territories from the East India Company. A unified legal system with a tiered pattern of civil and criminal courts was established, which remains unchanged to this day.

42. The Federal Court of India was the highest court in British India. It was established in 1937 under the Government of India Act 1935 (passed by the British Parliament). Appeals from the Federal Court of India lay to His Majesty's Privy Council. The Federal Court stood abolished with the coming into force of India's Constitution. The Privy Council jurisdiction was abolished with the Abolition of Privy Council Act 1949, which came into effect upon the establishment of the Supreme Court of India in January 1950 (Article 395 of the Constitution).
43. A detailed and well-documented account of the forces at play is given in Granville Austin: Chapter 12, 'Language and the Constitution: The Half-Hearted Compromise', *The Indian Constitution: A Cornerstone of a Nation*, Oxford University Press, Bombay, 1966, pp. 265-307.
44. Among the various dialects of Hindi, the dialect chosen as official Hindi was the standard Khariboli, originally spoken in Delhi and in western Uttar Pradesh.
45. Telangana has remained a festering problem. In its report (the Justice B. N. Sri Krishna Committee Report of December 2010), the 'Committee for Consultations on the Situation in Andhra Pradesh' observed that the formation of the state of Andhra in 1956 was itself 'somewhat conditional', 'brought about through the "Gentleman's Agreement", the objective of which was to bring the less developed region of Telangana on par with the rest of the state. This goal, which looked achievable at the time was not fully realized'. Disaffection on both the Telangana and the Andhra sides came to a head in the late 1960s and early 1970s with both sides, at one point, wishing to go their separate ways. At that time, the Six-Point Formula ushered in by Prime Minister Indira Gandhi, and agreed to by both sides, served to dissolve the tension and keep the state united. Subsequently, the state saw significant economic and social progress over three decades. As a result, Andhra Pradesh today is one of the progressive states in the country. This very progress has led the people of Telangana to revive their demand for a separate state in order to gain greater political space and to bridge more rapidly the remaining, though diminishing, disparities. The resulting agitation, which posed a serious law and order problem in the state in late 2009 and early 2010, eventually led to the setting up of the aforementioned Committee for Consultations on the Situation in Andhra Pradesh. Its report has done little to assuage the desire for a separate state!
46. The First States Reorganization Commission (December 1953) was chaired by Senior Justice Fazl Ali, a judge of the Supreme Court of India from 1951 to 1952. His son Murtaza Fazl Ali was also a judge of the Supreme Court from 1975 to 1985.
47. Nari Rustumjee: *Imperilled Frontiers*, Oxford University Press, London, 1983.

48. In 1952, it was the imposition of Urdu by the Government of Pakistan in the Bengali-speaking East Pakistan that ultimately led to the break-up of that country and the formation of the independent state of Bangladesh in 1971.
49. Including the new states of Chhattisgarh (carved out of the state of Madhya Pradesh); Uttarakhand (carved out of India's most populous state of Uttar Pradesh); and Jharkhand (carved out of the state of Bihar). All three states came into existence in November 2000.
50. Till the year 2000, when out of three of the five northern states were created three more states: Jharkhand, Chhattisgarh and Uttarakhand. They are predominantly Hindi-speaking states, but Uttrakhand has adopted Sanskrit as the second official (regional) language.
51. BIMARU (a variant of BIMAR, sick) was the uncomplimentary acronym coined for the four north Indian states Bihar, Madhya Pradesh, Rajasthan and Uttar Pradesh. Later Orissa (now Odisha) was included. But BIMAROU is now a discredited term in view of economic and social progress in these states in recent times. (Source: Wikipedia.)
52. Urdu and Hindi have the same grammar and the same basic vocabulary. They differ mainly in the script: Urdu is written in the Persian-Arabic script (right to left) and Hindi in the Nagari (or Devnagari) script. Urdu has a large admixture of Persian and Arabic words; Hindi (particularly official Hindi) is enriched (some would say 'burdened') with Sanskrit words!
53. The Mizos are a distinct linguistic ethnic and cultural unit of hill tribes. They came under the influence of British missionaries in the nineteenth century, and many of them were converted to Christianity, with which came the English language and English education. The missionaries introduced the Roman script for the indigenous Mizo language.
54. Even amongst the Telugu-speaking inhabitants of Andhra Pradesh, there are differences: Telugu as spoken in coastal Andhra is different from Telugu spoken in Telangana! Reportedly, the grievance of the Telangana region is that people from coastal Andhra look upon Telangana Telugu (which has an admixture of Urdu words) as 'inferior'. The language of coastal Andhra is considered 'standard' Telugu, whereas that spoken in Telangana is condemned as a 'dialect' – the complaint is that the Telangana 'dialect' is ridiculed in government offices, universities and colleges! (See para 7.14.06, p. 394 of the report of the Justice Sri Krishna Committee of December 2010.)
55. 'Originally an English transplant with Anglo-Saxon roots, the legal system in India has grown over the years, nourished in Indian soil; what was intended to be an English oak has turned into a large, sprawling Indian banyan whose serial roots have descended to the ground to become new trunks.' Fali S. Nariman: *India's Legal System: Can It Be Saved?* Penguin, New Delhi, 2006, p. v.
56. Almost half of the world's 6700 languages could become extinct by the end of the twenty-first century, according to an estimate made by the United Nations. 'If those languages die, a unique view of the world will expire with them. People who live close to their land and rely upon its resources for their existence, use their own language ("mother tongue") to describe their environment with

a precision and nuance that other languages cannot approach.' Currently, experts estimate that some 470 languages are on the critical list, 182 of them in the Western hemisphere, 152 in the Pacific and the remainder divided among other regions. Ben Block: *World Watch,* Vol. 23, No. 4, July/August 2010, pp. 24-28.

57. The Anglo-Indians were a group of people who could trace their ancestry in 1950 to an English parent or grandparent. They were a preferred class during the British rule. Since they were a minority, the reservations for them in posts (railway, customs and postal and telegraph services) and the facilities of state educational grants were continued for a decade (Articles 336 and 337). In addition, they have two reserved seats in the House of the People (Lok Sabha) and in assemblies in states that have sizable Anglo-Indian communities (Articles 331 and 333). They quickly lost their identity as a separate group. Some of them migrated (e.g., to Australia) and others assimilated into Indian society and are now indistinguishable from other Indians.
58. *State of Bombay* vs *Bombay Education Society*, AIR 1954, SC 561.
59. *Jagdev Singh* vs *Pratap Singh*, AIR 1965, SC 183.
60. By the Constitution (16th Amendment) Act 1963: Objects and Reasons:

    The Committee on National Integration and Regionalism, appointed by the National Integration Council, had recommended that Article 19 be so amended that adequate powers become available for the preservation and maintenance of the integrity and sovereignty of the Union. The Committee was further of the view [that] every candidate for the membership of a State Legislature or Parliament, and every aspirant to, and incumbent of, public office should pledge himself to uphold the Constitution and to preserve the integrity and sovereignty of the Union and, towards that end in view, desired that forms of oath in the Third Schedule to the Constitution should be suitably amended.
61. *Gujarat University vs Shri Krishna*, AIR 1963, SC 703 (seven judges).
62. *Dinamalar*'s account of the charge sheet ceremony!
63. *The Hindu*, Sunday, 22 January 2012.
64. However, the Bohras (Dawoodi Bohras and Sulaimani Bohras) – also original converts from Hinduism – were, from the time of their conversion, always governed by Shia Mohammedan law.
65. That secularism was a basic feature of the Constitution of India had already been stated in *Kesvananda Bharati* vs *State of Kerala* (AIR 1973, SC 1461 – a bench of 13 judges) by Justice H. R. Khanna, whose judgment is now regarded by all as the decisive and authoritative majority opinion in the case.
66. *Commissioner of Hindu Endowments* vs *L. T. Swamine*, AIR 1954, SC 853. The court refused to follow *Davis* vs *Beason*, 133 US 333, 342, 1890, where the Supreme Court of the United States had held that cults and forms of worship of a particular sect were not matters of religion. In holding that matters of religion included acts done in pursuance thereof, the Supreme Court of India preferred the views of the High Court of Australia whilst interpreting Section

116 (the religious freedom clause) of the Australian Constitution (Chief Justice John Latham in *Adelaide* vs *Commonwealth*, 66 Commonwealth Law Reports, 127).

67. In *Saifuddin Saheb* vs *State of Bombay*, AIR 1962, SC 853 (by a majority – 4:1).
68. *Reverend Stanislaus* vs *State of Madhya Pradesh*, AIR 1977, SC 908 (a decision not acceptable to the Christian minority).
69. It is also a standing repudiation (by India's Supreme Court) of what in the USA is called the Doctrine of Original Intent.
70. See Shiva Rao: *Framing of India's Constitution: A Study*, Indian Institute of Public Administration, New Delhi, 1967, p. 261.
71. *Durgah Committee Ajmer* vs *Syed Husain Ali*, AIR 1961, SC 1402. *Shri Govindlalji Maharaj* vs *State of Rajasthan* (Nathdwara Temple case), AIR 1963, SC 1638.
72. The Child Marriage Restraint Act of 1929.
73. The Hindu Marriage Act 1955.
74. The Hindu Women's Rights to Property Act 1937.
75. S. M. Stirling: *Island in the Sea of Time*, Penguin, New York, 1998, p. 526.
76. Lord Macaulay was appointed member of the Viceroy's Council and the first subject taken up by the council after he joined was the preparation of a penal code. The draft (mainly of Lord Macaulay) was completed by him while he was in India, between 1834 and 1838. The code remained as a mere draft for 22 years, and it was not until 1860 that it became law. During this interval, it was revised from time to time by Lord Macaulay's successors, and especially by Sir Barnes Peacock, the last chief justice of the Supreme Court of Calcutta. 'The long delay in the enactment of the Penal Code,' writes Sir James Fitzjames Stephen (author of the Indian Evidence Act 1872), 'had thus the singular but most beneficial result of reserving a work which had been drawn up by the most distinguished author of the day for a minutely careful revision by a professional lawyer, possessed of as great experience and as much technical knowledge as any man of his time. *An ideal code ought to be – drawn by a Bacon and settled by a Coke.*' (Sir James Fitzjames Stephen: *History of the Criminal Law*, Vol. III, p. 300: passage reproduced from Sir John Strachey: *India*, Kegan Paul, Trench, Trubner & Co., London, 1903, p. 75.) The allusion in the italicized sentence of the above quote is to Sir Francis Bacon (1561–1626), a renowned English philosopher, statesman, jurist and author, and to Sir Edward Coke (1552–1634) who was a wise and fiercely independent chief justice of England in the reign of James I: Coke declared the king to be subject to the law and the laws of Parliament were void if in violation of '*common right and reason*'. These actions led at first to Coke's transfer to the lesser chief justiceship of the King's Bench and then, in another judgment, he restricted the definition of treason and declared a letter of the king as illegal, which led to his dismissal from the bench on 14 November 1616!
77. Report dated 14 October 1837 of the Indian Law Commission on the Penal Code, Note J.

78. *Raj Paul* vs *Emperor*, AIR 1927, Lahore 590: Whilst reluctantly accepting the revision application of the petitioner who had been convicted under Section 153A of the Indian Penal Code (IPC) and sentenced to six months rigorous imprisonment in default, and when acquitting him, the judge did say that '*a clause might well have been added to S.* [Section] *297 by which the publication of pamphlets published with the intention of wounding the religious feeling of any person or of insulting the religion [of] any person might be made criminal. I can only say that speaking for myself I regret the absence of such a clause but I am unable to hold that this particular case comes within the purview of Section 153A* [emphasis added]'.
79. *Ramji Lal Modi* vs *State of UP*, AIR 1957, SC 620 (bench of five judges). The case itself concerned an article published with deliberate and malicious intent of outraging religious feelings of Muslims. The Constitution Bench opined that this fell within the mischief of Section 295A of the Penal Code; that the Section 295A so read was valid and constitutional and fell within the protection of Article 19(2), being a law imposing reasonable restrictions on the exercise of the Fundamental Right of freedom of speech and expression guaranteed by Article 19(1)(a) of the Constitution.
80. In *R* vs *Lemon* (*R* vs *Gay News Ltd*), 1979 (1), All England Reports 898 (HL).
81. The reason why the law in England considered that the publication of a blasphemous libel was an offence was that the law considered that such publication should not take place. And if it did take place, and the publication was deliberate, there was justification for holding that there was an offence even though there was no intent to hurt the feelings of devout Christians. According to English law, guilt of the offence of publishing a blasphemous libel depended not on the accused having an intent to blaspheme but on proof that the publication was intentional and that the matter published was blasphemous. This was far stricter than the provisions of the Indian Penal Code.
82. 1979(1), All England Reports 898 (House of Lords or HL), p. 921.
83. See Russell Sandberg and Norman Doe's article entitled 'The Strange Death of Blasphemy', *Modern Law Review*, 2008 (71), pp. 971-86.
84. Constituent Assembly Debates, official series, Vol. I, reprinted by the Lok Sabha Secretariat, New Delhi, pp. 58-60.
85. Clause (f) of Article 371F (Special Provisions with respect to the State of Sikkim) reads as follows:

    371F. Special Provisions with respect with respect to the State of Sikkim – Notwithstanding anything in this Constitution –

    (f) Parliament may, for the purpose of protecting the rights and interests of the different sections of the population of Sikkim make provision for the number of seats in the Legislative Assembly of the State of Sikkim which may be filled by candidates belonging to such sections and for the delimitation of the Assembly Constituencies from which candidates belonging to such sections alone may stand for election to the Legislative Assembly of the State of Sikkim.

86. 304 US 144 (1938).
87. In February 1937 President Franklin D. Roosevelt sent to the US Congress a bill to change the composition of the federal judiciary restricted constitutionally to only nine justices. This 'court-packing bill', as it was promptly dubbed, was FDR's attempt to expand the membership of the Supreme Court (beyond nine justices) so that he could nominate justices who would uphold the constitutionality of the New Deal legislation. The court-packing struggle constituted a critical episode in Roosevelt's presidency and witnessed a bitter clash between the judiciary and the executive. However, in March 1937 a 5-to-4 majority of the court upheld a Washington minimum wage law that was almost identical to the one struck down the previous year, and upheld the constitutionality of the National Labor Relations Board (*NLRB* vs *Jones & Laughlin Steel Corp.*). Justice Owen Roberts' shift, which journalists called the 'switch in time that saved nine', doomed the president's court-packing legislation because Americans believed that FDR had already achieved his goals without tampering with tradition. FDR lost the legislative battle, but won the war. His reforms were thereafter upheld by the US Supreme Court!
88. 'Nor need we enquire whether similar considerations enter into the review of statutes directed at particular religions, or national or racial minorities ... whether prejudice against discrete and insular minorities may be a special condition, which tends seriously to curtail the operation of those political processes ordinarily to be relied upon to protect minorities, and which may call for a correspondingly more searching judicial inquiry ...'
89. Kermit L. Hall (ed.): *Oxford Companion to the Supreme Court of the United States*, Oxford University Press, New York, 1992, pp. 306-07.
90. Re: Kerala Education Bill, 1957, AIR 1958, SC 956 (bench of seven judges). In a significant and eloquent passage in the opinion of the court, Chief Justice S. R. Das had said (pp. 986-87): 'There can be no manner of doubt that our Constitution has guaranteed certain cherished rights of the minorities concerning their language, culture and religion. These concessions must have been made to them for good and valid reasons. Article 45, no doubt, requires the State to provide for free and compulsory education for all children, but there is nothing to prevent the State from discharging that solemn obligation through Government and aided schools and Article 45 does not require that obligation to be discharged at the expense of the minority communities. So long as the Constitution stands as it is and not altered, it is, we conceive, the duty of this Court to uphold the fundamental rights and thereby honour our sacred obligation to the minority communities who are of our own. Throughout the ages endless inundations of men of diverse creeds, cultures and races – Aryans and non-Aryans, Dravidians and Chinese, Scythians, Huns, Pathans and Mughals – have come to this ancient land from distant regions and climes. India has welcomed them all. They have met and gathered, given and taken and got mingled, merged and lost in one body. India's tradition has thus been epitomised in the following noble lines:

None shall be turned away from the shore of this vast sea of humanity that is India.

Indeed India has sent out to the world her message of goodwill enshrined and proclaimed in our National Anthem:

Day and night, the voice goes out from land to land, calling Hindus, Buddhists, Sikhs and Jains round thy throne, and Parsees, Mussalmans and Christians. Offerings are brought to thy shrine by the East and the West to be woven in a garland of love. Thou bringest the hearts of all peoples into the harmony of one life, Thou Dispenser of India's destiny, Victory, Victory, Victory to thee.

It is thus that the genius of India has been able to find *unity in diversity by assimilating the best of all creeds and cultures. Our Constitution accordingly recognises our sacred obligations to the minorities* [emphasis added].'

91. In the Tagore Law Lectures, included in P. B. Gajendragadkar, *Indian Parliament and Fundamental Rights*, Eastern Law House, Calcutta (now Kolkata), 1972, pp. 54-57.
92. *The Ahmedabad St Xavier's College Society* vs *State of Gujarat*, AIR 1974, SC 1389: Writ petition filed directly in the Supreme Court of India under Article 32.
93. Ibid., para 89, SC 1421.
94. *DAV College Jalandhar* vs *State of Punjab*, AIR 1971, SC 1737.
95. So held authoritatively a bench of 11 justices in *TMA Pai Foundation* vs *State of Karnataka*, 2002 (8), SC, 481, p. 587: 'since reorganization of States in India has been on linguistic lines, therefore for the purposes of determining the minority, the unit will be the State and not the whole of India.'
96. Order dated 14 May 1993 (two judges) unreported.
97. *Shahal Musaliar* vs *State of Kerala*, 1993 (4), SCC 112 (five judges); *TMA Pai Foundation and Others (I)* vs *State of Karnataka*, 1993 (4), SCC 276 (five judges); and *TMA Pai Foundation and Others (II)* vs *State of Karnataka*, 1993 (4), SCC 286 (five judges).
98. This Order dated 18 March 1994 has been quoted in *TMA Pai Foundation*, 1995 (5), SCC 220, para 6 (seven judges).
99. *TMA Pai Foundation* vs *State of Karnataka*, 2002 (8), SCC 481 (eleven judges).
100. Article 30 – Right of minorities to establish and administer educational institutions:

    (1) All minorities, whether based on religion or language, shall have the right to establish and administer educational institutions of their choice.

    (1-A) In making any law providing for the compulsory acquisition of any property of an educational institution established and administered by a minority, referred to in clause (1), the State shall ensure that the amount fixed by or determined under such law for the acquisition of such property is such as would not restrict or abrogate the right guaranteed under that clause.

(2) The State shall not, in granting aid to educational institutions, discriminate against any educational institution on the ground that it is under the management of a minority, whether based on religion or language.

101. Article 29 (2) – No citizen shall be denied admission into any educational institution maintained by the State or receiving aid out of State funds on grounds only of religion, race, caste, language or any of them.

102. *Rev. Sidhajbhai Sabhai* vs *State of Bombay* 1963 (3), SCR 837; *Father Proost* vs *State of Bihar* 1969 (2), SCR 73 at 81 and 82; *and St Stephen's College* vs *University of Delhi* 1992 (1), SCC 558.

103. *Lochner vs New York*, 198 US 45, 76 (1905) – Justice Holmes (dissenting). In a book of reminiscences, *Five Chiefs*, by the recently retired US Supreme Court, Justice John Paul Stevens (Little Brown and Company, New York, 2011), the author says: 'the case (*Lochner* vs *New York*) is famous because there is universal agreement among judges and scholars that it was incorrectly decided. It is the case in which Justice Oliver Wendell Holmes wrote the most influential dissenting opinion in the Court's history.' Holmes believed that the word 'liberty' in the Fourteenth Amendment to the US Constitution – the Due Process Clause – (like in Article 21 of India's Constitution as interpreted by a Supreme Court bench of seven justices in Maneka Gandhi's case 1978) protected at least some substantive rights (not only procedural rights) that the justices must identify in individual cases.

104. 2002 (8), SCC 481 at 588.

105. Although Justice Holmes' phrase 'his can't helps' is not in any of his published works, it has been attributed to him. See Anthony A. D'Amato: *Jurisprudence: A Descriptive and Normative Analysis of Law*, Martinus Nijhoff Publishers, Leiden, The Netherlands, 1984, p. 62.

106. Article 30 (1) of our Constitution reads as follows:

All minorities, whether based on religion or language, shall have the right to establish and administer educational institutions of their choice.

107. 1974 (1), SCC 717.

108. I have briefly adverted to this incident in my memoirs: *Before Memory Fades ...*, Hay House Publishers India, New Delhi, fourth reprint, 2010, p. 100.

109. Article 19: Protection of certain rights regarding freedom of speech, etc. (1) All citizens shall have the right:

(a) to freedom of speech and expression;
(b) to assemble peaceably and without arms;
(c) to form associations or unions (or co-operative societies);
(d) to move freely throughout the territory of India;

(e) to reside and settle in any part of the territory of India;

.

.

.

(g) *to practise any profession, or to carry on any occupation, trade or business* [emphasis added].

19 (2) ...

19 (3) ...

19(4) ...

19(5) ...

19(6): Nothing in subclause (g) of the said clause shall affect the operation of any existing law in so far as it imposes [on], or prevents the State from making any law imposing, in the interests of the general public, reasonable restrictions on the exercise of the right conferred by the said subclause ...

110. 2005 (6), SCC 537: All these were the same group of cases that came up for determination, at different times, before smaller benches though under different names!

111. 2005 (6), SCC 537.

112. Judgment dated 12 April 2012 by Chief Justice S. H. Kapadia (joined by Justice Swatanter Kumar) in Writ Petition No. 95 of 2010, *Society for Unaided Private Schools of Rajasthan* vs *Union of India & Another*. The third judge, Justice K. S. P. Radhakrishnan, dissented, holding that although Article 21A casts an obligation on 'the State to *provide free and compulsory to all children of the age of 6 to 14 years in such manner as the State may by law determine*' – this cannot be in *unaided* educational institutions, even if they were non-minority schools.

113. A balanced comment by Pratap Bhanu Mehta, president, Centre for Policy Research, Delhi, reads:

> The serious problem with the RTE (Right to Education) is not 25% reservation. There is no expropriation as schools are being compensated to some degree. But the Court's vague homilies on burden sharing skirt a fundamental issue of fairness .... Everyone pronouncing on the RTE is very confident in their answers: they range from revolution to disaster. But my honest answer is the three words that policy analysts hate using, but should use more often, 'I don't know'. (*The Indian Express*, 18 April 2012, editorial page.)

114. All the three judges in *Society for Unaided Private Schools of Rajasthan* vs *Union of India & Another* concurred in holding that the provisions of the Right of Children to Free and Compulsory Education Act 2009 would not apply to unaided minority schools.

115. The BJP election manifesto (1991): '8. Article 30 permits minorities to run their own schools. It will be rationalized and suitably amended to ensure justice & equality to all irrespective of religions.'

116. Sulak Sivaraksa presents his view of Buddhism in his autobiography, *Loyalty Demands Dissent* (Parallax Publishers, Berkeley, California, 1998), wherein along with a first-hand account of his life, he also includes information about his views on the relationship among religion, society and politics. Sivaraksa is known in the West as one of the fathers of the International Network of Engaged Buddhists (INEB), which was established in 1989. When awarded the Alternative Nobel Prize (Right Livelihood Award, given by Sweden) in 1995, he became known to a wider public in Europe and the USA. Sivaraksa was chair of the Asian Cultural Forum on Development and has been a visiting professor at American universities including Berkeley and Cornell.
117. Source: Sulak Sivaraksa in an interview (with Meenakshi Shedde in Mumbai) en route to the New York Summit (Millennium World Peace Summit), 'Don't Treat Gandhi, Buddha as Idols, Imbibe Their Teachings', *The Times of India*, 1 September 2000.
118. Passed by the first Parliament, which consisted of members of the Constituent Assembly that had debated and passed the Constitution of India 1950.
119. Experts are unable to agree as to the exact year in which the Laws of Manu were promulgated, but 200 B.C. appears to be the commonly accepted date.

    The Laws of Manu endorsed and gave recognition to the continued existence of the caste system and the unfair treatment of women!

    Ironically, 'the Laws of Manu' do give India the standing of having one of the oldest written legal codes, although the legal tradition from which they emanated avoided written law as long as possible so as to accommodate adaptability (in the law) and so as to not limit the discretion exercised by the uppermost class, the Brahmins!
120. See *Prema* vs *Nanje Gowda and Others*, 2011(6), SCC 462 (Justices G. S. Singhvi and K. S. P. Radhakrishnan); more recently followed in *Ganduri Koteshwaramma and Anr.* vs *Chakiri and Anr.*, Civil Appeal No: 8538 of 2011. Judgment dated 12 October 2011 (unreported).
121. *Mohd. Ahmed Khan* vs *Shah Bano Begum*, AIR 1985, SC 945. It was held in *Shah Bano Begum* that the statutory right to maintenance available to a divorced Muslim woman under Section 125 of the Code of Criminal Procedure 1973 remained unaffected by the provisions of Muslim Personal Law. The bench decision caused a furore amongst conservative sections of Muslims, which prompted the passing of the Muslim Women Protection of Rights on Divorce Act 1986.
122. I have known Kartikeya Sarabhai for many years and he has inherited many of the traits of his father Vikram Sarabhai (whom I did not have the privilege of knowing). I was once travelling with my wife – it must have been more than 40 years ago – on a plane from Bombay to Delhi. Almost all the passengers had boarded and were seated waiting for the door to close in preparation for takeoff. But there was one high government official who stood just outside the front door of the plane and there was much consternation amongst the purser and staff of Indian Airlines who were toing and froing up and down the

plane not knowing what to do. Apparently, this high official had insisted on a front seat and felt insulted that he was given a seat in the second row! Whilst this was being sorted out, a gentleman on the front seat asked the purser why the plane was not taking off and when he was told (in whispers) about this important government official, he himself said: 'I will sit in the second row, let this gentleman occupy my seat in the front row.' That was Vikram Sarabhai, whom I did not know, but whom as a fellow passenger I congratulated. This is the quintessential humility of the good and the great!

123. Published in *Mainstream*, Vol. XXVII, No. 34, 20 May 1989. The poem is reproduced by kind permission of the author.

124. Isaiah Berlin: *Two Concepts of Liberty*, Oxford University Press, London, 1958.

125. Marc Galanter: *Competing Equalities: Law and the Backward Classes in India*, University of California Press, Los Angeles, 1984. See also Louis Dumont: *Homo Hierarchius: An Essay on the Caste System*, University of Chicago Press, Chicago, 1970.

126. Will Durant: *Story of Civilization*, Vol. I, Simon and Schuster, New York, 1935, p. 398. The early Hindu word for caste was *varna* (colour). The Portuguese later translated it as *casta*, from the Latin *castus*: pure.

127. The word 'Veda' means knowledge: literally, a book of knowledge. Of the many Vedas that existed, only four have survived: the Rig Veda, or knowledge of the hymns of praise; the Sama Veda, or knowledge of the melodies; the Yajur Veda, or knowledge of the sacrificial formulas; and the Atharva Veda, or knowledge of the magic formula. Each of these is divided into four sections: (1) the hymns; (2) the Brahmanas, or manuals of ritual, prayer and incantation for the priests; (3) the Aranyakas, or 'forest texts' for hermit saints; and (4) the Upanishads, which describe the mysteries of the unintelligible world. They are the oldest extant commentaries on the philosophy and psychology of the human race.

128. These great epics are the most famous and best-loved of ancient Hindu literature. The Mahabharata resembles the *Iliad*, being the story of a great war fought by gods and men and occasioned partly by the loss of a beautiful woman by one nation to another. The Ramayana resembles the *Odyssey* and tells of the hero's hardships and wanderings and his wife's patient waiting for reunion with him.

129. Brahmins even adopted Buddhist practices as their own; under pressure of the ethics of renunciation preached by Buddhism (and Jainism), a majority of the Brahmins changed to a vegetarian diet and 'renounced' all forms of meat. Since then they have regarded caste Brahmins who ate meat as impure. The caste system conceptualized 'purity'. (See Louis Dumont: *Homo Hierarchius: An Essay on the Caste System*, University of Chicago Press, Chicago, 1970, pp. 55-56.)

130. Sir Charles Eliot: *Hinduism and Buddhism: An Historical Sketch*, Vol. 3, Routledge & Kegan Paul, London, 1921, p. 147.

131. This article and others – Article 15(2), free access to public places; Article 23(1), prohibition of forced or bonded labour; and Article 24, prohibition of

employment of children in factories, mines or hazardous occupations – are primarily directed against individual groups and citizens and accordingly are enforceable against them.

132. The Scheduled Castes Order applies only to Hindus and a part of the Sikhs. In 1950, Dalit Sikh castes (Mazhabis, Ramdasias, Kabirpanthis and Sikligars) were placed in the Schedule Castes Order; the remaining Dalit Sikh castes were added in 1956. Those among the traditionally depressed classes of India (Hindu outcastes) who have embraced Buddhism, Jainism, Islam or Christianity and members of other non-Hindu religious groups do not qualify for preferential treatment as Scheduled Castes, although they may qualify under the other constitutionally recognized (but undefined) category, viz., OBCs. Although the Supreme Court has rejected the inclusion of Buddhists in the meaning of 'Hindu' (AIR 1965, SC 1179), in 1990, neo-Buddhists were included. But Muslim and Christian Dalits are still struggling for their inclusion in a Scheduled Castes Order.

133. Added by the Constitution 1st Amendment Act 1951 by India's first Parliament – the same body (Constituent Assembly) that framed the Constitution of India 1950.

134. Report dated 19 November 1975.

135. Meanwhile, the Rane Commission (headed by C. V. Rane), in the state of Gujarat, appointed (in 1981) to recommend identifying tests for the socially and educationally backward classes in the state, had also submitted its report to the state government. It also ignored castes and subcastes in listing the socially and educationally backward classes and concluded that, for an initial period of 10 years, it should be assumed that those who belonged to the lower castes or subcastes but who were individually and financially well off did not suffer from any social and educational backwardness. The financial criterion adopted was an annual family income of over Rs 10,000. Those with family incomes less than that figure would become beneficiaries of Articles 15(4) and 16(4) of the Constitution. The state government's acceptance of this recommendation and its decision to increase the percentage of reservations from about 30 per cent to nearly 50 per cent sparked a series of riots in the state in the summer of 1985, threatening to spread even beyond Gujarat.

136. During the hearing of *Vasanth Kumar*, the state of Karnataka agreed to appoint a commission afresh and therefore requested the justices on the Supreme Court Bench to frame guidelines. This was so stated by Chief Justice Yeshwant V. Chandrachud at the beginning of his judgment:

> My learned Brethren have expressed their respective points of view on the policy of reservations which, alas, is even figuratively, a burning issue today. We were invited by the counsel not so much as to deliver judgments but to express our opinion on the issue of reservations, which may serve as a guideline to the Commission which the Government of Karnataka proposes to appoint, for examining the question of affording better employment and educational opportunities to Scheduled Castes, Scheduled Tribes and other backward classes. A somewhat unusual exercise is being undertaken by the

Court in giving expression to its views without reference to specific facts. But institutions profit by well-meaning innovations.

137. 2006 (8), SCC 212.

138. 2008 (6), SCC 1.

139. See 1985, Supp. SCC 714, p. 723, para 2, Chief Justice Chandrachud.

140. Ibid., p. 736, para 31, Justice D. A. Desai.

141. In *State of Kerala* vs *N. M. Thomas*, AIR 1976, SC 490 (bench of seven judges), Justice Krishna Iyer had first used this expression ('the top creamy layer').

142. *K. C. Vasanth Kumar* vs *State of Karnataka*, 1985 (Supp.), SCC 714, para 2, p. 723. But this suggestion was later categorically rejected both in *Indira Sawhney* vs *Union of India and Ors*,1992, Supp. 3, SCC 684 (by a bench of nine judges) and again in *Ashoka Kumar Thakur* 2008, 6, SCC 1, p. 511 (by a bench of five judges).

143. Appointment of a Commission to investigate the conditions of backward classes:

> (1) The president may by order appoint a Commission consisting of such persons as he thinks fit to investigate the conditions of socially and educationally backward classes within the territory of India and the difficulties under which they labour and to make recommendations as to the steps that should be taken by the Union or any State to remove such difficulties and to improve their condition and as to the grants that should be made for the purposes by the Union or any State and the conditions subject to which such grants should be made, and the order appointing such Commission shall define the procedure to be followed by the Commission.
>
> (2) A Commission so appointed shall investigate the matters referred to them and present to the president a report setting out the facts as found by them and making such recommendations as they think proper.
>
> (3) The president shall cause a copy of the report so presented together with a memorandum explaining the action taken thereon to be laid before each House of Parliament.

144. Paragraph 12.19 of the Mandal Commission report reads:

> Systematic caste-wise enumeration of population was introduced by the Registrar General of India in 1881 and discontinued in 1931. In view of this, figures of caste-wise population beyond 1931 are not available. But assuming that the inter se rate of growth of population of various castes, communities and religious groups over the last half a century has remained more or less the same, it is possible to work out the percentage that all these groups constitute of the total population of the country.

145. Marc Galanter in the Preface to the paperback edition (1991) of *Competing Equalities: Law and the Backward Classes in India*, Oxford University Press, New Delhi (originally published in 1984 by the University of California Press, Los Angeles), has criticized the Mandal Commission report of 1980:

> The appearance of precision in applying the Commission's criteria is undermined by a serious methodological flaw. These caste groups have not been counted in the census since 1931; the extrapolation of community population figures for half a century on the assumption that all communities experienced equal growth rates renders suspect many of the Commission's findings about relative conditions.

However, according to an uncorroborated report published in the *Times of India* (31 August 2010), it is stated that regardless of the recommendations of the Mandal Commission of a 27 per cent reservation in posts in the services under the state, only 7 per cent of the seats had been filled by OBCs till the year 2010.

146. OFFICE MEMORANDUM:

Subject: Recommendations of the Second Backward Classes Commission (Mandal Report) Reservation for Socially and Educationally Backward Classes [SEBC] *in services under the Government of India.*

1. In a multiple undulating society like ours, early achievement of the objective of social justice as enshrined in the Constitution is a must. The Second Backward Classes Commission called the Mandal Commission was established by the then Government with this purpose in view, which submitted its report to the Government of India on 31.12.1980.
2. Government have carefully considered the report and the recommendations of the Commission in the present context regarding the benefits to be extended to the *socially and educationally backward classes* as opined by the Commission and are of the clear view that at the outset certain weightage has to be provided to such classes in the services of the Union and their Public Undertakings. Accordingly orders are issued as follows:

(i) 27% of the vacancies in civil posts and services under the Government of India shall be reserved for SEBC.
(ii) The aforesaid reservation shall apply to vacancies to be filled by direct recruitment. Detailed instructions relating to the procedures to be followed for enforcing reservation will be issued separately.
(iii) Candidates belonging to SEBC recruited on the basis of merit in an open competition on the same standards prescribed for the general candidates shall not be adjusted against the reservation quota of 27%.
(iv) The SEBC would comprise in the first phase the castes and communities which are common to both the list in the report of the Mandal Commission and the State Governments' lists, a list of such castes/communities is being issued separately.
(v) The aforesaid reservation shall take effect from 7.8.1990. However, this will not apply to vacancies where the recruitment process has already been initiated prior to the issue of these orders.

3. Similar instructions in respect of public sector undertakings and financial

institutions including public sector banks will be issued by the Department of Public Enterprises and Ministry of Finance, respectively.

Sd/- (Smt. Krishna Singh) Joint Secretary to the Govt. of India

147. The population growth in India has been quite staggering and with it the corresponding swelling numbers of the Backward Classes. According to the latest census, India's population rose from 533 million in 1971 to 665 million in 1981, to 838 million in 1991, to 1025 million in 2001 and to over 1200 million in 2011!

148. Quoted in the Order of the Supreme Court of India in the case of *Indira Sawhney* vs *Union of India and Ors*, AIR 1993, SC 477, para 21, p. 514.

149. Justice B. P. Jeevan Reddy on behalf of himself and Chief Justice M. H. Kania, Justice M. N. Venkatachaliah and Justice A. M. Ahmadi, concurred in by Justices S. R. Pandian and P. B. Sawant, each of whom delivered separate judgments. The dissenting justices – Justices T. K. Thommen, Kuldip Singh and R. M. Sahai – did not agree that the office memorandum of 13 August 1990, which had been upheld by the majority, was valid. They were in favour of declaring it to be unenforceable; according to them reservation was a remedy only for *historical discrimination* and its continuing ill-effects whilst other affirmative action programmes were intended to redress discrimination of all kinds whether current or historical.

150. Foreclosing judicial review is a perilous step. One of America's longest serving justices in the history of the US Supreme Court, Justice William Douglas – his term lasted 36 years and 209 days – had wisely observed that '*judicial review gives time for the sober second thought*'.

151. Constituent Assembly Debates, 8 November 1948, Vol. 7, p. 702.

152. See *Union of India* vs *Pushpa Rani*, 2008 (9), SCC 242, para 39, p. 271 (Justice B. N. Agrawal and Justice G. S. Singhvi).

153. Marc Galanter: *Competing Equalities, Law and the Backward Classes in India*, University of California Press, Los Angeles, 1984, p. 567. The same passage is repeated in the paperback Indian edition, Oxford University Press, New Delhi, 1991.

154. Rudolf C. Heredia: 'Quotas and Minority Rights: Recapturing the Constitutional Vision', *Economic and Political Weekly*, 23 July 2011, Vol. XLVI, pp. 66-67.

155. Articles 141 and 144 of the Constitution read as follows:

> 141. Law declared by Supreme Court to be binding on all courts. The law declared by the Supreme Court shall be binding on all courts within the territory of India.
>
> 144. Civil and judicial authorities to act in aid of the Supreme Court: All authorities, civil and judicial, in the territory of India shall act in aid of the Supreme Court.

156. A permanent body was to be set up known as the National Commission of Backward Classes.

157. 9. Functions of the Commission:

(1) The Commission shall examine requests for inclusion of any class of citizens as a backward class in the lists and hear complaints of over-inclusion or under-inclusion of any backward class in such lists and tender such advice to the Central Government as it deems appropriate.
(2) The advice of the Commission shall ordinarily be binding upon the Central Government.

11. Periodic revision of lists by the Central Government:

(1) The Central Government may at any time, and shall, at the expiration of 10 years from the coming into force of this Act and every succeeding period of 10 years thereafter, undertake revision of the lists with a view to excluding from such lists those classes who have ceased to be backward classes or for including in such lists new backward classes.
(2) The Central Government shall, while undertaking any revision referred to in subsection (1), consult the Commission.

158. See AIR 1962, SC 34 (five judges), p. 41, para 16, and AIR 1968, SC 349 (five judges), p. 351.
159. AIR 2007, SC 71.
160. 'Other Backward Classes' are defined in the Act (Act 5 of 2007) as meaning 'a class or classes of citizens who are socially and educationally backward and are so determined by the Central Government'.
161. 2008 (6), SCC 1.
162. 2008 (6), SCC 1, para 650, p. 711.
163. The court also held, in keeping with the unanimous decision of a bench of seven judges in *P. A. Inamdar* vs *State of Maharashtra* (2005), that the exclusion of minority educational institutions from the purview of Article 15(5) was valid, but the question of validity (i.e., the constitutional validity) of the inclusion of private unaided institutions within the purview of Article 15(5) was 'left open': soon to be 'closed' by the decision of two justices (in a bench of three) in *Society for Unaided Private Schools of Rajasthan* vs *Union of India and Anr*. The judgment, dated 12 April 2012, held that it was constitutionally permissible to include private unaided educational institutions within the purview of Article 15!
164. Ruchir Sharma: *Breakout Nations,* Allen Lane, London, 2012.
165. For instance:

(1) 'OBC Creamy Layer Ceiling Raised', *The Economic Times,* 17 November 2011, p. 2;
(2) 'Cutoff for OBC "Creamy Layer" May Be Raised to Rs 7 Lakh/Year', *The Times of India*, 11 June 2012;
(3) 'OBC Creamy Layer Ceiling May Go Up to Rs 6 Lakh/Yr', *Hindustan Times,* 13 June 2012;
(4) 'Cabinet to Consider Raising Creamy Layer Ceiling to Rs 6 Lakh a Year, *The Hindu,* 14 June 2012;

(5) 'Proposal for Raising Income Ceiling of OBC Creamy Layer Deferred', *The Economic Times*, 14 June 2012;

(6) 'Will "Creamy Layer" Ceiling Be Raised?' *The Asian Age*, 14 June 2012;

(7) 'Congress OBC Lobby Blocks Govt Move to Raise Bar for "Creamy Layer" Reservations', *The Times of India*, 15 June 2012.

166. When Justice Krishna Iyer was at a loss for words, he invented them!

Chapter II

The State of the Nation and India's Constitution

After all, for whose benefit was the Constitution enacted; what is the point of making all this pother about fundamental rights? I am clear that the Constitution is not for the exclusive benefit of governments and States; it is not only for lawyers, politicians and officials, and those highly placed. It also exists for the common man, for the poor and the humble for those who have businesses at stake, for 'the butcher, the baker, and the candlestick maker'. It lays down for this land a rule of law as understood in the free democracies of the world.[1]

CAMPAIGN SPEECHES OF THE FUTURE...
HE IS A CHEAT!..
HE IS A GANGSTER!...
HE ROBBED A BANK...
RASCAL...
GANGSTER!
MURDERER
THIEF..
CHEAT!
FRAUD
ROGUE
PICK-POCKET!
...THEREFORE KINDLY GIVE YOUR VALUABLE VOTE TO ME! I'LL FULFIL ALL MY PROMISES.

The State of the Nation is invariably conditioned by the provisions and purposes laid down in its Constitution.

The survival of India as a nation depends on how *We the People* implement the provisions of our Constitution. Therefore, all citizens need to have a closer look at, and understand, its broad features, because the law of the Constitution is not only for those who govern – or for the intellectual and scholarly – but also for the bulk of the people, especially for the common man, for whose benefit and safeguard the document of governance has been written and enacted. The people are influenced by what the judges in the country's highest court think and by what they say. One must never underestimate the power of the judiciary under a written Constitution.

***

India boasts of a parliamentary system of government, which, though British-inspired, is not a model imposed upon us; it has 'swadeshi (indigenous) origins'. The first non-official attempt at drafting a constitution for (a free) India was made way back in 1895 under the inspiration of the scholar, mathematician and great freedom fighter Lokmanya Balgangadhar Tilak. It was called 'The Constitution of India Bill 1895' and its first chapter made provision for a 'Parliament of India'. Thirty years later another attempt was made under the inspiration of the eminent lawyer and statesman, Sir Tej Bahadur Sapru. India's political leaders sent a draft Bill for self-government to England ('A Bill to constitute within the British Empire a Commonwealth for India'), which found support with Britain's Labour Party, then in power. 'The Commonwealth of India Bill 1925' was introduced in Britain's Parliament. This Bill provided that 'there shall be a Parliament which shall consist of the Viceroy as the King's representative, a Senate and a

Legislative Assembly'. It also included a clause conferring fundamental rights on all citizens: of personal liberty; of security; of property; of freedom of expression; of conscience; of equality before law; of equality between sexes; and of free elementary education. The Bill also provided that every literate citizen – 'literate in the language of the *taluka*' – over 21 years of age and owning some property or having some income was to have a vote. After the Bill passed its first reading in the House of Commons, it was ordered to be printed, in anticipation of it being enacted into law. But soon thereafter, the Labour Party lost its majority in the House of Commons, and Indian expectations faced a setback for 20 long years!

* * *

Under our 1950 Constitution, the principle of one-citizen-one-vote (without restrictions or qualifications) flows, indirectly, from the equality clause (Article 14), but it is reiterated with specificity in Article 326 ('Elections to the House of People and to the Legislative Assemblies of States to be on the basis of adult suffrage').

In the USA, the world's oldest democracy, adult suffrage has been regarded as basic to the concept of a 'Government-of-laws-and-not-of-men', a phrase initially coined by John Adams and adopted in Article XXX of the Constitution of the State of Massachusetts (1780), a document that predates the US Constitution (1789). One of the founding fathers and a leading champion of US independence in 1776, John Adams was the second president of the United States of America (1797 to 1801). He wrote the Massachusetts State Constitution in 1780, which ended slavery in that state. But he became better known as a judge of character, because, in 1775, he nominated George Washington to be commander-in-chief and 25 years later (as president) he nominated John Marshall to be the chief justice of the United States! Marshall remained, as the head of the judiciary from 1801 to 1835, since when he has been known by generations of lawyers and judges in the US as the Great Chief Justice.

* * *

An elected parliament is the only political expedient by which any degree of self-government can be combined with the organization of a nation-state. Though not the most efficient system, parliamentary democracy is certainly better than all others. Malcolm Muggeridge[2] once said, in a light-hearted moment, that the '*best* form of government is despotism, tempered with assassination', adding that since this form of government would be impossible to replicate, we would be well advised to remain content with the *next best*!

***

India's 1950 Constitution, embodying a parliamentary form of government, had its roots in the past.

Shaken and divided by the 'earthquake' of partition, our written Constitution was also a compelling accident of history. In 1947, the British decided to call it a day and leave the subcontinent, and, for many years after independence, it was believed that this was because of Mahatma Gandhi's call to the British in August 1942 to Quit India. But a recent revelation points to a different reason. In 1956, Chief Justice P. V. Chuckraborty, of the Calcutta High Court, was acting governor of West Bengal; while playing host to former British Prime Minister Clement Attlee, he records:

> I put it straight to him like this: 'The Quit India Movement of Gandhi practically died out long before 1947 and there was nothing in the Indian situation at that time which made it necessary for the British to leave India in a hurry. Why then did they do so?'

In response, Attlee said that the most important reason was the Royal Indian Navy mutiny in Bombay (from 18 to 23 February 1946), which made the British realize that the Indian armed forces could no longer be trusted to protect the British in India! Justice Chuckraborty then pointedly inquired as to the extent to which the decision to quit India was influenced by Gandhi's call in 1942, at which

> Attlee's lips widened in a smile of disdain and he uttered, slowly, 'minimal'.[3]

***

It was the hasty retreat of the British, amidst the trauma of partition, which prompted members of India's Constituent Assembly – inspired by the need to preserve the political and cultural unity of the rest of the subcontinent – to rise to the occasion, and to draft what became known as the Constitution of India 1950.

In December 1946, India's Constituent Assembly (an ad hoc body constituted of persons elected in 1947 by members of legislative assemblies in India's various provinces) declared

> its firm and solemn resolve to proclaim India as an Independent Sovereign Republic and to draw up for her future governance a Constitution …
>
> > (4) wherein all power and authority of the Sovereign Independent India, its constituent parts and organs of government, are derived from the people; and
> > (5) wherein shall be guaranteed and secured to all the people of India justice, social, economic and political; equality of status, of opportunity, and before the law; freedom of thought, expression, belief, faith, worship, vocation, association and action, subject to law and public morality; and
> > (6) wherein adequate safeguards shall be provided for minorities, backward and tribal areas, and depressed and other backward classes; and
> > (7) whereby shall be maintained the integrity of the territory of the Republic and its sovereign rights on land, sea and air according to justice and the law of civilized nations, and
> > (8) [whereby] this ancient land attains its rightful and honoured place in the world and makes its full and willing contribution to the promotion of world peace and the welfare of mankind.[4]

The Indian Constitution is a highly centralized document with the expression '*unity and integrity of the Nation*' mentioned in the Preamble, and with the very first Article describing its structure. India (it says) is a 'Union of States'. The Constitution was drafted for the survival of the nation as a whole – in good times and in bad times. In other words, times not affected by proclamations of emergency, which last for limited periods, and which, after the Constitution 44th Amendment Act 1978, are compulsorily reviewable by Parliament.

* * *

The Preamble to the Constitution, when adopted by the Constituent Assembly, stated upfront its grand purpose: to secure to all citizens (in capital letters!) JUSTICE, LIBERTY, EQUALITY and FRATERNITY – an aspiration too ambitious to be realized in the first 65 years after independence!

In the preamble, JUSTICE, is not just an abstract concept. It conveys (as one of the purposes of the Constitution) the removal of injustices to the extent possible, a theme projected by the Nobel Laureate, Professor Amartya Sen, in his *The Idea of Justice*:

> … the strong perception of manifest injustice applies to adult human beings. What moves us, reasonably enough, is not the realization that the world falls short of being completely just – which few of us expect – but that there are clearly *remediable injustices around us which we want to eliminate.*
>
> This is evident enough in our day-to-day life, with inequalities or subjugations from which we may suffer and which we have good reason to resent, but it also applies to more widespread diagnoses of injustice in the wider world in which we live. It is fair to assume that Parisians would not have stormed the Bastille, Gandhi would not have challenged the empire on which the sun used not to set, Martin Luther King would not have fought white supremacy in 'the land of the free and the home of the brave', without their sense of manifest injustices that could be overcome. They were not trying to achieve a perfectly just world (even if there were any agreement on what that would be like), but they did want to remove clear injustices to the extent they could.[5]

In our constitutional scheme, the social and economic aspects of JUSTICE are left primarily to the lawmakers (Parliament and state legislatures). Under Article 37 of the Constitution, the principles laid down in Part IV (Directive Principles of State Policy) are fundamental in the governance of the country and it is the duty of the state to apply these principles in making laws. At the time of the framing of our Constitution, it was a given postulate that the entire legislative process was influenced by considerations of JUSTICE and REASON: because of the general legal principle that the law should be just and court decisions should further the ends of justice. It is on this principle that the courts in England (where there are no entrenched fundamental rights) have always presumed that Parliament, in its law-making function, at all times intends to act justly and reasonably.

In India, judges too have accepted this *conceptual* aspect of justice-in-the-law.

In *Budhan Singh* vs *Babi Bux* (AIR 1970, SC 1880) – a case otherwise insignificant except for the parties to it – a principle of law of seminal importance was laid down.

Babi Bux (and his family) were ryots[6] (peasant cultivators) under the appellants (Budhan Singh and his family) in an inconspicuous village called Machara, near Meerut, in Uttar Pradesh. The site in dispute had been taken over by the father of Babi Bux from Budhan Singh's ancestors some years ago; thereafter Babi Bux had put up buildings on that site for residential purposes. During the communal disturbances of 1947, Babi Bux and his family left the village as a measure of safety and took shelter with some of their relatives in another district in Uttar Pradesh. When conditions had improved, they returned to Machara, in 1949, and Babi Bux found Budhan Singh in occupation of the site; the latter had put up a cowshed on the site on which Babi Bux's residential buildings stood. The residential buildings had been demolished and the site in question had been included as part of the dwelling house of Budhan Singh. Since Budhan Singh refused to deliver possession of the site and the dwelling house on it, Babi Bux filed a suit for possession on 9 January 1951. On 26 January 1951, the UP Zamindari Abolition and Land Reforms Act 1950 came into force. It prescribed that after the commencement of the Act, the State Government was empowered by notification to declare that, as from a date to be specified, all estates situated in Uttar Pradesh shall vest in the state and, as from the date so specified, all such estates shall stand transferred to and vest (except as otherwise provided in the Act) in the state free from all encumbrances. But in respect of lands or buildings (mentioned in Section 9) it was provided that they were to be treated as 'settled on the persons who *held* such lands and buildings'. The controversy between the parties in the appeal before the Supreme Court was as to the meaning to be attached to the word '*held*' in Section 9 of the Act. Was the holding contemplated therein a *lawful holding* or a *mere holding, lawful or otherwise*? On behalf of the appellants, it was contended that the dictionary meaning of the word 'held' merely meant 'to have possession of', and so Section 9 merely contemplated physical possession and nothing more. On the date of the vesting, it was persons who were in physical possession of the site as well as the building thereon who were protected from being evicted by the state – the building must be deemed to have been settled with them: i.e., in the instant case, with Budhan Singh and his family. On the other hand, it was contended on behalf of the respondent (Babi Bux) that the word 'held' in Section 9 meant 'lawfully held' and that the section did not and could not have been intended to confer any benefit on a trespasser. Upholding the respondent's contention, the Supreme Court of India rationalized its decision as follows:

> It is necessary to mention that it is proper to assume that the lawmakers who are the representatives of the people enact laws which the society considers as honest, fair and equitable. The object of every legislation is to advance public welfare .... Justice and reason constitute the great general legislative intent in every piece of legislation. Consequently where the suggested construction operates harshly, ridiculously or in any other manner contrary to prevailing conceptions of justice and reasons ... it would seem that the apparent or suggested meaning of the statute (suggested by Budhan Singh) was not the one intended by the lawmakers. In the absence of some other indications that the harsh or ridiculous effect was actually intended by the Legislature, there is little reason to believe that it represents the legislative intent.

The Supreme Court judges therefore said that they were unable to persuade themselves to believe that the legislature intended to ignore rightful persons having legal title to possession and wanted to make a gift of the building to a trespasser, howsoever recently that trespasser might have been there if only he happened to be in physical possession of the building on the date of vesting. As they put it: '*we are unable to discern any legislative policy in support of that construction.*' It was true, the court said,

> *that according to the dictionary meaning the word 'held' can mean either a lawful holding or even a holding without any semblance of right, such as a holding by a trespasser. But the real question was as to what was the legislative intent. Did the Legislature intend to settle the concerned building with a person who was lawfully holding or with any person holding lawfully or otherwise.*

The principle that was upheld was one of law, viz., that where the suggested construction of the statute operated harshly, courts in India would assume that the apparent or suggested meaning of the statute was not the one intended by the lawmakers – the reason being that it was contrary to JUSTICE.

But how is JUSTICE to be administered in courts of law? In 1954, one of the first judges of the Supreme Court (Justice Vivian Bose) described, in elegant prose, what the constitutional provisions meant (and should mean) to the justices:

> We have upon us the whole armour of the Constitution and walk henceforth in its enlightened ways, wearing the breast plate of its protecting provisions and flashing the *flaming sword* of its inspiration [emphasis added].[7]

I like to believe that the 'flaming sword', about which Justice Bose had written, is located in Article 142(1)! In implementing the idea of JUSTICE mentioned in the Constitution's Preamble, judges of the Supreme Court of India have been empowered by Article 142(1) 'to pass such decree or make such order as is necessary for doing *complete justice* in any cause or matter pending before it'.

In my view, the title of a recent *New York Times* bestseller – *Justice: What's the Right Thing to Do?*[8] – encapsulates the best definition of the concept embodied in Article 142(1) that stresses 'the right thing to do', when, on some rare occasion, it is found by the highest court that enacted law, if applied, would divert the true course of justice; power is conferred on the Supreme Court (and on this court alone) to make such orders as may be necessary for doing *complete justice* – in any cause or matter pending before it. This is the trust that the founding fathers had placed in the highest court and this is how the justices of the Supreme Court of India had interpreted Article 142(1) during the first 40 years of the court's existence. In 1991, in a bench decision of three justices, the Supreme Court had said:[9]

> This Court's power under Article 142(1) to do 'complete justice' is entirely of [a] different level and of a different quality. Any prohibition or restriction contained in ordinary laws cannot act as a limitation on the constitutional power of this Court. Once this Court has seisin of a cause or matter before it, it has power to issue any order or direction to do 'complete justice' in the matter. This constitutional power of the Apex Court cannot be limited or restricted by provisions contained in statutory law.

But soon after this decision, larger benches (of five justices) of the Supreme Court had second thoughts. Taking shelter under enacted law, they asserted that nothing could be done even by the highest court by way of JUSTICE when enacted law stood in the way![10] A pity! Lord Alfred Denning, the most celebrated English judge of the twentieth century, would have characterized these justices as 'timorous souls'![11]

The only reason power was reserved, to justices of the highest court, was because it was they who were to be trusted more than any other judges in the country 'for doing complete justice'. They were expected – at all times – to do what was right. This was the faith that the Constitution placed in the justices of the Supreme Court – a faith unfortunately not shared or reciprocated by later justices of the court in themselves!

* * *

The next word in the Preamble - LIBERTY - is of equal importance. It is also reflected in the text of the Constitution (in Article 21), which provides that no person shall be deprived of his life or *personal liberty* except according to procedure established by law. There is a historical background to Article 21. Geographically, India and the United States are miles apart, while in politics and in social thought and aspirations, the two countries are (both literally and figuratively) continents apart. What initially brought India nearer to the United States was a shared common-law tradition, which both the countries inherited from what was at one time called Great Britain. British India was the first country outside the United States where decisions of US State and Federal Courts were referred to in court decisions, not because lawyers in India cited them, but because a few Indian judges took a global view of the legal universe. Sir Ashutosh Mookerjee, the first Indian judge to be appointed to the High Court of Calcutta in the early years of the last century and who later became the first Indian acting chief justice of that court,[12] was one of them. His private library was stocked with American State and Federal Court reports (to which he regularly subscribed) and he frequently made use of them, in his decisions. The influence of US judges increased considerably after the end of the Second World War and they were frequently consulted by constitution makers from newly emerging nation-states. I recall that on a visit to Jerusalem (in 1993) I had called on Israel's former chief justice, Haim Cohn, a great judge and a friend of both India and the United States. He had been Israel's very first attorney general. He told me that he had been instructed by his prime minister, David Ben-Gurion, to draft a constitution for the new state of Israel, which had come into existence in May 1948. On his constitutional pilgrimage to Washington, he met Justice Hugo Black (of the US Supreme Court) who told Cohn to ensure that the provisions of the Constitution of Israel were sufficiently stringent to control the executive. Cohn then met Felix Frankfurter (another judge of the US Supreme Court) who advised him to draft for Israel a constitution that would severely limit the powers of the judiciary! With such a sharp cleavage of views amongst America's leading justices, Cohn came back and told his prime minister that it was best that Israel stopped experimenting with a written constitution - only Basic Laws (as they came to be known later) should be passed by the Knesset (Israel's Parliament) amendable by a specified majority of its members! And so it was (and so it has remained).

About the same time, India's constitutional adviser, Sir Benegal Rau, had been entrusted with the task of drafting a constitution for independent India. Benegal Rau visited Washington where he showed to Justice Frankfurter the draft of our life-and-liberty clause, which then read: 'no person shall be deprived of his life or liberty except according to due process of law.' Frankfurter was appalled; he told Rau that 'due process' had been one of the major headaches for successive generations of judges of the US Supreme Court! He suggested that India should take as a model the then-recent Constitution of post-war Japan and redraft the clause guaranteeing life and liberty in accordance with this document. On his return home, Rau conveyed to the Constitution Committee (set up by the Constituent Assembly) the advice of Justice Frankfurter; and pursuant, to this advice, the draft of Article 21 was altered to read: 'No person shall be deprived of his life or liberty *except in accordance with procedure established by law*.' The Article was ultimately passed by the Constituent Assembly and, for more than 25 years, that was how Article 21 in our Fundamental Rights chapter was read and understood by justices of our Supreme Court.[13] According to this view *enacted law* was sufficient justification for deprivation of a person's life or liberty; this is what a majority of four judges in a bench of five justices (popularly described as a Constitution Bench) said in *A. K. Gopalan* (1950): a case concerning preventive detention; a decision followed in later cases.

But the hydraulic pressure of great events exercises its influence on judicial thinking – and helps to shape better decision making. During the internal Emergency (imposed on 25 June 1975, which lasted till 21 March 1977), personal liberties were taken away by enacted law, resulting in excessive harassment and oppression of innocent citizens who were left with no legal recourse. When Fundamental Rights under Article 21 were 'suspended' – under the provisions of Article 359(1) as it then stood[14] – a majority of four justices in a bench of five expressed the following opinion about 'liberty' (as a concept):[15]

> Liberty is confined and controlled by law, whether common law or statute. It is in the words of [Edmund] Burke a regulated freedom. It is not an abstract or absolute freedom. The safeguard of liberty is in the good sense of the people and in the system of representative and responsible government which has been evolved.

Guided by the majority opinion in a decision of England's House of Lords in *Liversidge* (1942)[16] – a wartime decision, which in England itself had been long since discredited – Chief Justice A. N. Ray (who delivered the majority judgment) went on to say:

> Liberty is itself the gift of the law and may by the law be forfeited or abridged.[17]

However, Justice H. R. Khanna (the seniormost judge on the bench next to Chief Justice A. N. Ray) dissented. This was how he looked upon the concept of LIBERTY:

> Men born to freedom are naturally alert to repel invasion of their liberty by evil-minded persons. [The] greatest danger to liberty lies in insidious encroachment by men of zeal, well-meaning but lacking in due deference for the rule of law.
>
> Even in the absence of Article 21 in the Constitution, the State has got no power to deprive a person of his life or liberty without the authority of law. This is the essential postulate and basic assumption of the rule-of-law-and-not-of-men in all civilised nations. Without such sanctity of life and liberty, the distinction between a lawless society and one governed by laws would cease to have any meaning. The principle that no one shall be deprived of his life or liberty without the authority of law is rooted in the consideration that life and liberty are priceless possessions which cannot be made the plaything of individual whim and caprice and that any act which has the effect of tampering with life and liberty must receive sustenance from and sanction of the laws of the land. Article 21 incorporates an essential aspect of that principle and makes it part of the fundamental rights guaranteed in Part III of the Constitution.

It does not, however, follow from the above that if Article 21 had not been drafted and inserted in Part III, in that event, it would have been permissible for the State to deprive a person of his life or liberty without the authority of law.

The majority view of the Supreme Court (4:1) in *ADM Jabalpur* (1976) was the low watermark in Indian human-rights jurisprudence. It can be compared with the decision of the US Supreme Court in *Dred Scott,*[18] where Chief Justice Roger Taney speaking (in 1857) for a majority in the court over which he presided (7:2) said that a 'Negro' (a term now considered offensive), whose ancestors were imported into the US and sold as slaves, could never become a member of the political community formed and brought into existence by the Constitution of the United States: He could never be a 'citizen' of the United States of America! Of *Dred Scott*, John Paul Stevens (a long-serving, now retired, judge of the US Supreme Court) has recently written:

> … the only good thing which can be said about that case is Abraham Lincoln's criticism of it, which, in his famous debates with Stephen Douglas [Lincoln's opponent in the 1860 US presidential elections] received nationalist attention, and helped get him elected President of the United States![19]

However, there is one thing in common between the decisions in *Dred Scott* (1857) and in *ADM Jabalpur* (1976) given more than a hundred years apart. In each of them, there were powerful dissents: testimony to the independent thinking of individual justices in the highest courts of two of the largest democracies in the world!

After the internal Emergency was lifted in late March 1977, judges in the Supreme Court of India took a second, closer (and more mature) look at Article 21. Recalling to themselves the excesses of the Emergency era, they then said that the words 'procedure established by law' could not possibly mean *any* procedure whatever established by enacted law. Such procedure had to be one which was not arbitrary or discriminatory. It had to meet the test of reasonableness.[20] This fresh approach to Article 21 gave a new dimension to human rights guaranteed by the Constitution of India. The term 'due process', which had been deliberately excluded by the framers of the Constitution, got reintroduced by a more informed judicial interpretation! In jurisprudence, necessity is sometimes the mother of innovation!

All of which only serves to illustrate what Edmund Burke[21] used to say – that judges are trained to augur misgovernment and can sniff the approach of tyranny in every political breeze. It was the memory of the 'political breeze' of the June 1975 Emergency that prompted the need for a further check on unrestrained executive power. To us in India, it is heartening to know that, on almost similar grounds, the US president's claim to executive privilege was emphatically denied by the US Supreme Court in Richard Nixon's case.[22]

In each of our countries, there is the realization that all power corrupts and absolute power corrupts absolutely. Hence, absolute power must be controlled. And the only organ that is entrusted with this task both under the Constitution of the US and under the Constitution of India is the country's highest court.

* * *

Maneka Gandhi (1978),[23] a decision of a bench of seven justices – rendered after the end of the internal Emergency (25 June 1975 to 21 March 1977) – authoritatively established that the word 'law' in Article 21 (in the phrase '*except according to procedure established by law*') meant not *any enacted law*, but a law made in conformity with Article 14 (the right to equality) and Article 19 (the right to freedom of speech and expression, the right of assembly, the right to form associations, the right to move freely throughout the country and reside and settle in any part of India and the right to practise any occupation, trade or business or profession). In *Maneka Gandhi,* Justice Krishna Iyer handed down the court's unanimous interpretation of Article 21:

> To sum up, 'procedure' in Article 21 means fair not formal procedure. 'Law' is reasonable law, not any 'enacted piece' (para 120).

The judge then went on to say:

> What is law? Anything formal, legislatively proceeded, albeit absurd or arbitrary? Reverence for life and liberty must overpower this *reductio ad absurdum*. Legal interpretation, in the last analysis, is a value judgment. The high seriousness of the subject matter – life and liberty – desiderates the need for law, not fiat. Law is law when it is legitimated by the conscience and consent of the community generally. Not any capricious command but reasonable mode ordinarily regarded as dharma or law, approximating broadly to other standard measures regulating criminal or like procedure in the country. It is a legislative act, *but it must be functional, not fatuous* [emphasis added].[24]

Justice John Paul Stevens of the US Supreme Court has written[25] (in retirement) that it was in *Lockner* vs *New York* (1905)[26] that Justice Oliver Wendell Holmes had handed down 'the most influential dissenting opinion in the Court's history'.[27] Holmes had said (in *Lockner*) that the 'liberty' (mentioned in the Fourteenth Amendment to the US Constitution[28]) would be infringed where 'a rational and fair man would admit that the statute proposed would infringe fundamental principles as they have been understood by the traditions of our people and the law'. Simply put, in words that can be easily understood by all. I believe that Article 21 embodies the same enlightened idea.

But then, does this not make judges (of the highest court) 'superlegislators'? The answer is: if it does, then *that* is the role the Constitution of India has written for them. And, if it is believed that it does not, then again that is the (limited) role the judges of the Supreme Court (for the time being) have (erroneously in my view) chosen for themselves! 'Erroneously' because, in Article 19, our written Constitution has empowered the higher judiciary (the high courts and the Supreme Court of India) to determine whether 'restrictions' imposed by law on Fundamental Rights guaranteed under Article 19 (right to freedom) are or are not 'reasonable', or, are or are not 'in the interest of the general public' (Article 19[2] to [6]). In this determination, courts invariably do defer to legislative wisdom, but not always; in the end, it is the individual justices' perception of 'the law' that ultimately prevails!

***

The great question is *how must judges decide*? In the latest edition of his treatise on American constitutional law,[29] Professor Emeritus Laurence H. Tribe of Harvard University suggests that the judge's duty is

> first, not to be pigheaded, to avoid becoming too certain of one's premises ... and, second, to connect his decision in the case to an intelligible view of the Constitution.

Tribe assimilates the judge's role when interpreting the Constitution to that of an artist drawing a picture: 'The picture's frame [and] the artist's tools must be drawn from the Constitution's text, structure and history; but there can be no escape from the need to supply at least some measure of the artist's own vision and understanding.' But beyond that? Well, beyond that (says Tribe):

> One can offer no advice calculated to take judges off the hook nor should one try – for that is where, sometimes for better, and sometimes for worse, our constitutional system has put them!

However, judges have to be well-equipped – every judge must at all times perform like a true 'artist'; never like a mere artisan. This is what the Constitution expects from justices of the highest court.

* * *

Amongst the Fundamental Rights enumerated in Part III of the Constitution is *the right to EQUALITY*: 'the State shall not deny to any person equality before the law or the equal protection of laws within the territory of India' (Article 14).

Equality before the law is universally recognized. It has become an integral part of the written constitutions of nation-states around the world. Nearly 75 per cent of these Constitutions contain clauses about EQUALITY: a fundamental principle of modern democracy and of government based on the rule of law. In a book published in 1945 (then, the first of its kind), Sir Hersch Lauterpacht,[30] renowned jurist and president of the International Court of Justice, wrote about the pre-eminence of Equality in the governance of states:

> The claim to equality before the law is in a substantial sense the most fundamental of the rights of man. It occupies the first place in most written Constitutions. It is the starting point of all other liberties.[31]

The interpretation of Article 14 of our Constitution by the Supreme Court had initially raised some problems as to the approach to be adopted by courts when considering whether a statute (or some of its provisions) enacted by Parliament or state legislatures was void on account of violating the 'equality clause'. But by the end of the first two decades of our constitutional history, it was assumed that these problems had been judicially settled. In the early years of the Supreme Court, the interpretation and application of Article 14 were considered in a group of leading cases relating to state statutes, enacted both after and before the 1950 Constitution. For instance: statutes that had set up special courts to try certain criminal cases. In *State of West Bengal* vs *Anwar Ali Sarkar* (1952)[32] and in the companion case, *Kathi Rani Rawat* vs *State of Saurashtra* (1952),[33] a Constitution Bench of the Supreme Court (consisting of seven judges) heard arguments on the scope and applicability of Article 14: (i) to the West Bengal Special Courts Act 1950 and (ii) to the Saurashtra State Public Safety Third Amendment Ordinance 1949. The question in each of these two cases was whether the special courts set up under the 1950 Act and the 1949 Ordinance to try certain cases violated the provisions of Article 14. A majority of the court (6:1) held (in the *West Bengal* case) that they had. Five of the judges, applied what was by then taken to be the acknowledged test for cases arising under Article 14, that is, the 'classification test' (derived from American case law).[34] On the application of this test, the West Bengal Act was struck down as violating Article 14. But in the companion case, the Saurashtra Ordinance (a pre-Constitution law) was upheld (by a majority) as not being in violation of Article 14.

One of our most distinguished judges of the past – Justice Vivian Bose – was in the majority in the first case and in the minority in the second! He struck a different note from his fellow-justices. His was an individualistic approach. And it has been influential! He did not agree with his brethren about the 'classification test':

> What, after all, is classification? It is merely a systematic arrangement of things into groups or classes, usually in accordance with some definite scheme. But the scheme can be anything and the laws which are laid down to govern the grouping must necessarily be arbitrarily selected; also granted the right to select, the classification can be as broad based as one pleases, or it can be broken down and down until finally just one solitary unit is divided off from the rest. Even those who propound this theory are driven to making qualifications. Thus, it is not enough merely to classify but the classification must not be 'discriminatory', it must not amount to 'hostile action', there must be 'reasonable grounds for distinction', it must be 'rational' and there must be no 'substantial discrimination'. But what then becomes of the classification? And who are to be the judges of the reasonableness and the substantiality or otherwise of the discrimination? And, much more important, whose standards of reasonableness are to be applied? The judges'? The government's? Or that of the mythical ordinary reasonable man of law which is no single man but a composite of many men whose reasonableness can be measured and gauged even though he can neither be seen nor heard nor felt? With the utmost respect I cannot see how these vague generalizations serve to clarify the position. *To my mind they do not carry us one whit beyond the original words and are no more satisfactory than saying that all men are equal before the law and that all shall be equally treated and be given equal protection. The problem is not solved by substituting one generalization for another* [emphasis added].

Justice Bose preferred *the common man's test – unequal simply because it is not fair or just*. This is what he said:

> I can conceive of cases where there is the utmost good faith and where the *classification is* scientific and rational and yet which would offend this law. Let us take an imaginary case in which a State Legislature considers that all accused persons whose skull measurements are below a certain standard, or who cannot pass a given series of intelligence tests, shall be tried summarily whatever

> the offence on the ground that the less complicated the trial the fairer it is to their substandard of intelligence. Here is classification. It is scientific and systematic. The intention and motives are good. There is no question of favouritism, and yet I can hardly believe that such a law would be allowed to stand. But what would be the true basis of the decision? Simply, that the judges would not consider that fair and proper. However much the real ground of decision may be hidden behind a screen of words 'reasonable', 'substantial', 'rational' and 'arbitrary' and [the] fact would remain the judges are substituting their own judgment of what is right and proper and reasonable and just for that of the legislature; and up to a point that, I think, is inevitable when a judge is called upon to crystallise a vague generality like Article 14 into a concrete concept …

Bose J. went on to give expression to his view that the laws of liberty, of freedom and of protection under the Constitution must be left to assume shape slowly as decision was added to decision: 'They cannot be enunciated in static form by hide-bound rules and arbitrarily applied standards or tests.' He held that the entire West Bengal Special Courts Act 1950 offended Article 14 – *but not because it fell afoul of the 'classification test'.* He reasoned, in felicitous prose, as follows:

> When the froth and the foam of discussion [are] cleared away and learned dialectics placed on one side, we reach at last the human element which to my mind is the most important of all. We find men accused of heinous crimes called upon to answer for their lives and liberties. We find them picked out from their fellows, and however much the new procedure may give them a few crumbs of advantage, in the bulk they are deprived of substantial and valuable privileges of defence which others, similarly charged, are able to claim. It matters not to me, nor indeed to them and their families and their friends, whether this be done in good faith, whether it be done for the convenience of government, whether the process can be scientifically classified and labelled or whether it is an experiment in speedier trials made for the good of society at large. It matters not how lofty and laudable the motives are. The question with which I

> charge myself is, can fair-minded, reasonable unbiased and resolute men, who are not swayed by emotion or prejudice, regard this with equanimity and call it reasonable, just and fair, regard it as that equal treatment and protection in the defence of liberties which is expected of a sovereign democratic republic in the conditions which obtain in India today? I have but one answer to that. *On that short and simple ground I would decide this case and hold the Act bad.*

In the companion case (*Kathi Rani Rawat*) – in which judgments were handed down a month later – Justice Bose said that in his opinion the Saurashtra Ordinance 1949 was also unconstitutional. But here he was in a minority. He wrote:

> I agree with my brothers [Meher Chand] Mahajan and Chandrasekhara Aiyar/[Iyer] [also in the minority] that the Saurashtra State Public Safety Measure (Third Amendment) Ordinance, 1949, offends Article 14. As I explained in my judgment in the *State of West Bengal* vs *Anwar Ali Sarkar* (case no. 297 of 1951: AIR 1952, SC 75), *I prefer not to base my decision on the classification test* [emphasis added]. For the reasons given there I am of opinion that the differentiation here travels beyond bounds which are legitimate. It is true the points of differentiation are not as numerous here as in the other cases but the ones which remain are, in my judgment, of a substantial character and cut deep enough to attract the equality clauses in Article 14. I would hold the Ordinance invalid.

According to Justice Bose, Article 14 could not be restricted within the narrow confines of the classification test, or for that matter any other test. The only test (he said) was *the conscience of the court.* But the judicial-conscience test first adopted by this judge was (at the time) a plaintive cry in the judicial wilderness.

His colleagues, and those who came after him, preferred the objective test of *reasonable classification*. Justice S. R. Das, speaking for a bench of five justices in *Ram Krishan Dalmia* (1958),[35] had formulated this test in a series of six propositions, which soon became a classical (though extremely constricted) statement of the law on Article 14![36]

The bench in *Dalmia*'s case cautioned future judges that these six principles would have to be constantly borne in mind by the courts when called upon to adjudge the constitutionality of any particular law attacked as discriminatory and violative of the equal protection of the laws. The prior decisions of the court were then encapsulated and summarized as falling into five classes or categories.[37] In the third class of cases, where the statute provided for delegation of arbitrary and uncontrolled power to the government so as to enable it to discriminate between persons or things similarly situated – and such discrimination was inherent in the statute itself – the court said that it would strike down both the law and executive action taken under such law, as it did in *State of West Bengal* vs *Anwar Ali Sarkar*. But where guidelines were laid down in the statute for classifying persons or things to whom its provisions were to be applicable the court would uphold the law as constitutional as it did in *Kathi Rani Rawat* vs *State of Saurashtra* (fifth class of cases). After the erudite formulation by Chief Justice S. R. Das, it was assumed that the detractors of the 'classification theory' had been finally worsted! And in 1960, in *Kangshari Haldar's* case,[38] the Supreme Court of India said, with an almost supreme sense of satisfaction, that the propositions applicable to cases arising out of Article 14 had been repeated so many times that 'they now sound platitudinous'. But the court spoke too soon!

* * *

Only a few years later, Justice K. Subba Rao, another of our great judges, who had been chafing under the burden of a straitjacket formula adopted by the preponderating majority of his colleagues, expressed agreement with Justice Bose. In his dissent in *Lachmandas* vs *State of Punjab* (1963),[39] he reminded his colleagues of the danger of rendering the equality clause 'a mere rope of sand'[40] and warned that an overemphasis on the doctrine of classification, or an anxious attempt to discover *some* basis of valid classification, would deprive Article 14 of all its content. 'The court would end up', he said, 'by substituting the Doctrine of Classification for the Doctrine of Equality!' But Justice Subba Rao's voice, like that of Justice Bose eight years before, was also a voice in the judicial wilderness. No judge responded to it – not till almost a generation later. After *Ram Krishan Dalmia* (1958), all judges of the Supreme Court dutifully followed Chief Justice S. R. Das's careful analysis of cases and principles when determining the applicability of Article 14, with the result, that, until 1995, very few challenges to enacted laws (Central or state) were successful on the touchstone of Article 14.

Then came *Royappa* (1974),[41] where what is now, sometimes disparagingly called the *New Doctrine*,[42] was first enunciated. This was the handiwork of two judges (Justice P. N. Bhagwati and Justice Krishna Iyer) who have left their mark on the jurisprudence of the Supreme Court. The New Doctrine was formulated as follows:

> The basic principle which, therefore, informs both Articles 14 and 16 is equality and inhibition against discrimination. Now, what is the content and reach of this great equalizing principle? It is a founding faith, to use the words of [Vivian] Bose, J., 'a way of life', and it must not be subjected to a narrow pedantic or lexicographic approach. We cannot countenance any attempt to truncate its all-embracing scope and meaning, for to do so would be to violate its activist magnitude. Equality is a dynamic concept with many aspects and dimensions and it cannot be '*cribbed, cabined and confined*' [emphasis added] within traditional and doctrinaire limits. From a positivistic point of view, *equality is antithetic to arbitrariness* [emphasis added]. In fact, equality and arbitrariness are sworn enemies; one belongs to the rule of law in a republic while the other, to the whim and caprice of an absolute monarch. Where an act is arbitrary, it is implicit in it that it is unequal both according to political logic and constitutional law and is therefore violative of Article 14 – and if it affects any matter relating to public employment, it is also violative of Article 16. Articles 14 and 16 strike at arbitrariness in State action and ensure fairness and equality of treatment.

But this conclusion in *Royappa* was virtually no more than an aside, since the ratio (or reasoning) in that case did not reflect any conscious or critical application of 'the new approach' to Article 14. The two judges concurred with the remaining three on the bench in holding (on the facts of the case before them) that the displacement from his post of the chief secretary of Tamil Nadu (E. P. Royappa) did not attract even the expanded interpretation of Article 14.

It was only in *Maneka Gandhi*[43] (1978) – a case in which the daughter-in-law of Mrs Indira Gandhi (after the latter had ceased to be prime minister) had been refused a passport to travel abroad by a government that had ousted Mrs Gandhi from power – a refusal that was not accompanied by any reason. It was in this case that, for the first time after the lifting of the internal Emergency (in March 1977), six judges in a bench of seven (which included Justice Bhagwati and Justice Krishna Iyer) applied the *Royappa* test to the procedure prescribed by law under the Passport Act 1967, and held that *law* for purposes of Article 21 must answer the test of reasonableness in order to be in conformity with Article 14. The court said (that for purpose of Article 21) the *'law must be right, just and fair, and not arbitrary, fanciful and oppressive – otherwise such a law would not satisfy the requirements of Article 14* [emphasis added]'. This was a conscious departure from the traditional time-honoured classification test. The old rule was that a law was invalid under Article 14 only if there was discrimination – i.e., only if the classification of persons and things under it was arbitrary and unreasonable. Unreasonableness and arbitrariness of the law per se could not result in the court striking down the law for two reasons: first, because there was a presumption of constitutionality of laws enacted by a competent legislature and, second, because courts would pay due deference to the will of the legislature and its collective wisdom as to circumstances requiring differential treatment. But after *Royappa,* as affirmed in *Maneka Gandhi,* the law itself, or at least the procedural part of the law, had to be justified before the court as just and fair and not arbitrary, fanciful or oppressive.

* * *

In 1979, when a proposed law (Bill) was questioned (in a Presidential Reference) as violating Article 14, the apex court tested its validity on the touchstone of 'fairness' and 'justness'. In a Special Courts Bill, a Special Constitution Bench (of seven justices) of the Supreme

Court, while handing down its opinion whether the Special Courts Bill, when enacted, would be constitutionally valid or not held – after applying the tests of classification and (after reformulating them in a set of 13 propositions) – that, by the application of these tests, the conclusion was irresistible that the classification provided for by the Special Courts Bill was valid and no objection could be taken to it. But the court did not stop there. It then went on to state (on the basis of *Royappa* and *Maneka Gandhi*, without specific reference to either of these cases) that the provisions in the Bill (a Bill that was to be enacted by Parliament as law) 'appeared' to the judges to be 'unfair' and 'unjust' in three important respects: First, regarding the absence of a provision for the transfer of cases from one special court to another; second, that it enabled retired high court judges to be appointed to the special courts; third, the only obligation of the Central Government in nominating a person to preside over the court was only to consult the chief justice of India – not obtain his concurrence. *And the reference to the president was answered accordingly*. What Justice Bose had said (in 1952) was revived and brought back to life in the answer of the Constitution Bench of seven judges in the Presidential Reference on the Special Courts Bill.[44] The Bill was then altered by the government of the day in accordance with the opinion of the court, and only then was it passed by Parliament!

Later that year, in a challenge (on this occasion) to an administrative action in *International Airports Authority* (1979),[45] the dictum that arbitrariness was the antithesis of Article 14 was reaffirmed. When, after seven years, in the (second) *Express Newspapers* case,[46] the former solicitor general of India, Lal Narayan Sinha (appearing for the Union of India) criticized the observations in *Royappa*, *Maneka Gandhi* and *International Airports Authority* and suggested that this would mean that all governmental Acts not supportable by law were per se violative of Article 14, the response of the court (speaking through Justice A. P. Sen) was:[47]

> I am afraid, it is rather late in the day to question the correctness of the landmark decision in the *Maneka Gandhi* (AIR 1978, SC 579)

and the innovative construction placed by Bhagwati, J. on Article 14 in the three cases of *Royappa* (AIR 1974, SCR 555), *Maneka Gandhi* and *International Airport Authority* (AIR 1978, SC 597, and 1979, SC 1628), which have evolved new dimensions in the judicial process.

In the realm of Article 14, the trend of the court was now towards 'new dimensions in the judicial process'. In later cases, the words 'arbitrariness in State Action' (first used in *Royappa*) were interpreted as applying to legislation as well as to executive action, although *Royappa* was not concerned with statute law but administrative action.[48]

Two later judgments of the Supreme Court – each by a bench of three justices – handed down, respectively, in November 1995 and January 1996, harkened back to the 'shocked-judicial conscience' test (the Vivian Bose test) when considering challenges under Article 14 to substantive provisions of statute law.

In the first case,[49] a section of the Tamil Nadu Acquisition of Law for Harijan Welfare Schemes Act 1978, providing payment of the compensation amount in instalments and not in one lumpsum, was struck down with the following observation:

> In our view the provision in regard to the payment of compensation amount by instalments in this manner is *wholly unreasonable* [emphasis added]. The owner of the land or another person interested therein would require compensation in lieu of the land forthwith to re-establish himself whether in a new residence or another piece of agricultural land or otherwise ... to the extent that Section 11 provides for payment of compensation by instalments it is ultra vires Article 14.

There is no discussion in the judgment of the court about the conclusion reached – no 'motivation' for the decision as lawyers trained in the civil law are used to saying! But to my mind, it is obvious that the court was conscious of the leading judgment of Justice K. K. Mathew in *Godhra Electricity Co.* vs *State of Gujarat* (AIR 1975, SC 32), in which the Supreme Court had said that it was per se 'unreasonable' to ask the owner of an electricity undertaking to deliver it to government without payment to him of the entire price or, if price was deferred, by compensating him with payment of interest. The acceptability of the decision in *Ananthi Ammal* (see Note 49) is not in its reasoning, but in its approach, an approach that had commended itself to Justice Vivien Bose: *would reasonable minded people consider the provision fair or just*?

The second case directly concerned a state law: the Madras Race Club Acquisition and Transfer of Undertaking Act 1986.[50] In this case, by a series of prior enactments, the Madras State Legislature had disclosed its consistent policy to declare and prohibit horse racing as 'gambling', and when the operation of these Acts was stayed by the Supreme Court and horse races were continued under interim orders of the court, the state enacted, in 1986, the impugned Act declaring horse racing as being for a public purpose and in the interest of the general public! It then served acquisition notices for transfer of the undertaking of the Madras Race Club to the state government. There was the inevitable challenge. The apex court's response to the challenge was brief but pointed:

> The policy of the State Government as projected in all the enactments on the subject prior to 1986 shows that the State Government considered horse racing as gambling and as such prohibited under the law. The 1986 Act on the other hand declares horse racing as a public purpose and in the interest of the general public .... We fail to understand how the State Government can acquire and take over the functioning of the race club when it has already enacted the 1974 Act with the avowed object of declaring horse racing as gambling .... Having enacted a law to abolish betting on horse racing and stoutly defending the same before this Court in the name of public good and public morality, it is not open to the State Government to acquire the undertaking of horse racing again in the name of public good and public purpose. It is ex facie irrational to invoke 'public good and public purpose' for declaring horse racing as gambling and as such prohibited under law and at the same time speak of 'public purpose and public good' for acquiring the race club and conducting the

> horse racing by the Government itself. *Arbitrariness is writ large on the face of the provisions of the 1986 Act* [emphasis added].[51]

And it was on that ground alone (viz., *gross inconsistency of legislative policy*) that the entire Act was struck down as it was 'arbitrary', in the opinion of the court, and, as such, violated the right to equality guaranteed under the Constitution!

***

Textbook writers[52] have been critical of the doctrine enunciated in *Royappa* and later applied by the apex court in cases concerning statute law as a 'naked judicial usurpation of legislative power'(!), and there have been some ardent proponents of this view on the bench as well. In *State of Andhra Pradesh* vs *McDowell & Co.* (1996),[53] it was observed by Justice Jeevan Reddy (speaking for a bench of three judges) that no enactment can be struck down 'by just saying that it is unreasonable or arbitrary – an expression used widely and rather indiscriminately, an expression of inherently imprecise import'; an enactment could not be declared void only on the ground that 'the Court thinks it unjustified'. But after the Constitution Bench decision of nine judges in *I. R. Coelho's* case,[54] expressly following and approving the dictum in *Maneka Gandhi*'s case (1978) – a bench of seven judges – it appears that the view of the Supreme Court (as of now) is that *Maneka Gandhi* holds the field. The word 'law' in Article 21 means:

> Law that is not arbitrary or unreasonable in the opinion of the Justices of the Supreme Court of India.

***

We must not run away with the idea that it is only an overactive judiciary in this country that holds exalted and exaggerated views of the court's supervisory powers over legislation under the equality clause of our Constitution.

Similar views have been expressed by distinguished judges abroad. In the Annual F. A. Mann Lecture delivered in the UK in November 1994, Lord Harry Woolf (then Lord of Appeal in Ordinary) said, whilst accepting the absolute supremacy of the British Parliament, that there was need to make a distinction between legislation and 'that which sought to undermine in a fundamental way the rule of law on which the unwritten British Constitution depended'. He was addressing the question as to the validity of a law removing or substantially impairing the entire reviewing role of the high court on judicial review, 'a role which in its origin is as ancient as the Common Law and pre-dates our present form of Parliamentary sovereignty and the Bill of Rights'. Lord Woolf didn't then say that he would (as judge) strike down a statutory provision made by Parliament excluding all or, substantially all, judicial review, but this is what he did say:

> However if Parliament did the *unthinkable* then I would say that the courts be also required to act in a manner which would be without precedent. Some judges might choose to do so by saying that it was an unrebuttable presumption that Parliament could never intend such a result. I myself would consider there were advantages in making it clear that ultimately there are even limits on the supremacy of Parliament which it is the courts' inalienable responsibility to identify and uphold. They are limits of the most modest dimensions which I believe any democrat would accept. They are no more than are necessary to enable the rule of law to be preserved.[55]

In 1997, as Master of the Rolls (i.e., as president of the Court of Appeal in the UK), Lord Woolf went a step further by saying (again extra-judicially, in a speech off the bench) that in 'extreme circumstances', English judges could 'disapply' Acts of Parliament by reference to some higher norm of justice (in a substantive, not procedural sense) – a doctrine dormant in the English law since the heyday of Chief Justice Sir Edward Coke in seventeenth-century England![56] (Do read Note 56 to appreciate how that chief justice, quite literally, kept his head!) Lord Woolf mentioned two examples of such 'extreme circumstances': viz., an infinite perpetuation by Parliament of its own life or the enactment of racially discriminatory laws on the Nazi model.

***

In the United States of America, despite claims to the contrary, its Supreme Court has actively enforced 'values', which a majority of the justices felt were essential in American society, even though these 'values' had no specific textual basis in the Constitution. Courts in the United States control the substance of legislation under the due process clause (the Fifth Amendment)[57] simply on the ground that certain types of lawmaking go beyond 'any proper sphere of governmental activity'. The basic judicial premise for this position is that the taking or deprivation of life, liberty or property by such a law is unconstitutional simply because 'the Constitution never granted the government the ability to pass such a law'.[58] A manifestation of this recognized exercise of judicial power (in the USA) is the opinion of Supreme Court Justice David Souter in the case of *Washington* vs *Glucksberg* (1997).[59] The question presented in this case was whether the State of Washington's prohibitory law on causing and aiding suicide offended the XIV Amendment to the US Constitution.[60] The court held that it did not, because an examination of the nation's history, legal traditions and practices revealed that the asserted right to assistance in committing suicide was not 'a fundamental-liberty-interest' protected by the 'due process' clause. In concurring with the majority, Justice Souter referred to the concept of *ordered liberty* – 'comprising a continuum of rights to be freed from arbitrary impositions and purposeless restraints'.[61] Justice Souter described the substantive due process guarantees against arbitrary legislative deprivation of liberties as the court's *duty* of giving strict scrutiny to 'a legislative resolution (perhaps unconscious) of clashing principles, each quite possibly worthy in and of itself, but each to be weighed within the history of our values as a people'.[62]

* * *

As to the width of the equality clause in our Constitution, I would say:

(1) Article 14 deals primarily, but not wholly, with discrimination. The validity of any alleged discriminatory law is to be tested on the time-honoured touchstone of 'classification'.

(2) Even where laws so enacted pass the classification test, the procedure prescribed by such laws may be so unfair, and

unreasonable, that the procedural provisions may be struck down as 'wholly unjust'. Such a course of action would be warranted not only on the basis of the decision in *Royappa* (1974), but also more directly on the basis of the ratio of separate Constitution Benches (of seven judges) in *Maneka Gandhi* (1978) and in the opinion in the President's Reference of the Special Courts Bill (1979): the dicta in the former case has been expressly approved in *I. R. Coelho* (2007) by a bench of nine justices.[63]

(3) Substantive laws cannot and ought not to be struck down merely because the courts think they are 'unjustified' or 'unreasonable'.[64] But there are cases that demand (what Professor Laurence Tribe has called) 'heightened scrutiny'; and there is always an ultimate residual discretion in the highest court (to be exercised sparingly of course) to invalidate substantive provisions of statutes where such provisions are 'wholly unjust' or 'arbitrary, beyond the bounds of reason'. In other words, where they shock the judicial conscience of the court: (i) as they did in the *Madras Race Club* case (1996) ('arbitrariness is writ large on the face of the provisions of the 1986 Act') and (ii) as they also did still earlier in *Mithu* vs *State of Punjab* (1983),[65] where a provision in the Indian Penal Code (Section 303), which mandated the sentence of death for the offence of murder committed by a person already under sentence of life imprisonment, was challenged on the ground of invalid discrimination and a bench of five justices of the Supreme Court struck down Section 303 as violating Article 14 because (as four of the judges said) it was '*arbitrary beyond the bounds of reason*' and also (as the fifth judge added) because it '*excluded all judicial discretion*'.

* * *

The word FRATERNITY in the Preamble to the Constitution had its origin in Article 1 of the UN Declaration of Human Rights (UDHR 1948) to which the sovereign Republic of India had subscribed and to which it was also a signatory. This Article reads as follows:

> All human beings are born free and equal in dignity and rights. They are endowed with reason and conscience and *should act towards one another in a spirit of brotherhood.*

But, unfortunately, the word 'fraternity' is mentioned only in the Preamble to our Constitution, not in any enacting part. It needs to be more widely practised – but it is not.

* * *

There are some other provisions of the Constitution of India about which citizens need to be familiar.

First, the Constitution's Fundamental Rights chapter (Part III) is addressed only to the state and its agencies, and infringement of these rights either by executive orders or by enacted laws is visited with a declaration of voidness by the superior courts, with the grant of some consequential relief in individual cases. But no part of the chapter prohibits citizens, individually or collectively, from violating the civil and human rights of other citizens, nor are penalties prescribed by law, nor remedies guaranteed, for such violations. That is why living in peace and justice still eludes a large number of people in India: too large a number for comfort!

Some years ago, when high-profile American judges visited India in an exchange programme initiated by our Supreme Court (known as the Indo–US Legal Forum), some of us lawyers acquainted our guests about the advantages of *our* Bill of Rights (Part III of the Constitution). The American judges listened, but one of them, Justice Antonin Scalia – a judge of the US Supreme Court not known for polite reticence[66] – told us that he was not impressed! He said that what the US Civil Rights Act 1964 had granted to US citizens (responding to the pressures of the civil rights movement) was not part of India's constitutional framework or of its laws. I am afraid that in this instance the justice was *right* – not just *forthright*! We do have a Civil Rights Act, but it only prohibits the practice of 'untouchability' in all its forms.

* * *

The second set of constitutional provisions relates to members of the armed forces (Articles 33 and 34).

Under the Constitution, members of the armed forces, though citizens, may have their rights curtailed in the wider national interest (Article 33). And even qua all other citizens, there is hidden, within the provisions of Article 34,[67] the possibility of a declaration of martial law in any particular part of the country and that of indemnifying any person in respect of any acts done in connection with the maintenance of restoration of order in any area within the territory of India where such martial law was in force. Despite many provocations, and thanks to the wisdom of successive governments, at the Centre, 'martial law' has not been resorted to in any part of India.

* * *

The third set of provisions relates to criticism of our Constitution – and a comment about its centrist bias.

After the Constitution was promulgated, there was criticism of some of its provisions. A former chief minister of Karnataka, and a down-to-earth politician, K. Hanumanthaiya, was disappointed with the work of the Constituent Assembly. 'We wanted the sweet notes of the *veena*', he complained, 'but we were given the music of an English band.' The parliamentary system of government is based on a neat division of governmental functions: executive, legislative and judicial, but not in watertight compartments.

Since 1950, the lurking fear of a Balkanized and fragmented subcontinent has been the inarticulate major premise in the process of adjudication by the highest court in all Centre–state disputes. Consequently, a centrist bias has dominated judicial thinking. Such a bias in my view is a laudable one – to uphold and preserve the Union.

* * *

The fourth set of provisions relates to the balance (if any) among the three organs of the state: the executive, the legislature (Parliament) and the judiciary.

If one browses through India's document of governance, one may be misled into thinking that there is a delicate balance among the three organs of state by the very neat arrangement of the topics in Part V of the Constitution. In it there are separate chapters containing provisions relating to: (1) the executive (Articles 52 to 78); (2) the legislature (Articles 79 to 122); and (3) the Union judiciary (Articles 124 to 147).

The executive consists of the president, the vice-president, and the Council of Ministers, with the prime minister at the head, to aid and advise the president.

The Union legislature (Parliament) comprises the head of state (president) along with two Houses of Parliament, known as the Council of States (Rajya Sabha) and the House of the People (Lok Sabha). The Council of States (presided over by the vice-president, in his role as chairman of the Rajya Sabha) consists of 238[68] representatives from the states and the union territories, elected by the elected members of the Legislative Assembly of each state. The House of the People comprises 530 members,[69] chosen by direct election from the territorial constituencies in the states. The superintendence, direction and control of elections are vested in a constitutional body known as the Election Commission of India: Part XV – Articles 324–329A. Elections to the House of the People (Lok Sabha and to the Legislative Assembles of the states) is to be on the basis of adult suffrage (Article 326), and Parliament and state legislatures are empowered to make special provisions with respect to elections: Articles 327 and 328.

Then there is the third leg of what is an integral part of the Union: the Union judiciary. It comprises the high courts in the states and the Supreme Court of India at New Delhi. The Supreme Court is the final interpreter of the Constitution and the laws – the final appellate authority with respect to all decisions of high courts and tribunals. It is also the exclusive forum for deciding all disputes between states and between any state and the Union.

There is a similar division of functions with regard to the states in Part VI of the Constitution (The States). The executive in each state consists of the governor and a Council of Ministers, with the chief minister at the head, to aid and advise the governor. There are also the state legislatures and the high courts in the states. However, the imbalance that exists in functions, at least as between the legislature and the executive, is in the detail.

***

The fifth set of provisions relates to the president and the governor.

The words 'president' and 'governor' are euphemisms. They do not, in reality, mean the president acting at his (or her) own absolute discretion.

The president, in the exercise of his/her functions, is required to act with the aid and advice of his/her Council of Ministers (with the prime minister at the head): Article 74(1). Similarly, the governors in the states are required to act on the aid and advice of their Council of Ministers (with the chief minister at the head) – except in so far as the governor is by, or under, the Constitution required to exercise his/her functions or any of them in his/her discretion: Article 163.

The supreme command of the defence forces of the Union is vested in the president under Article 53(2) and, for this reason, the president of India is often looked upon as the head of all the defence forces. But the description is only titular, since, under the Constitution, the exercise of supreme command of the defence forces is to be 'regulated by law'. And the law on the subject – the Commander-in-Chiefs Act 1955 – provides that reference by whatever form of words in any law to the commander-in-chief of the regular Indian Army, the commander-in-chief of the Indian Navy and the commander-in-chief of the Indian Air Force is to be construed as a reference to the chief of the Army Staff, the chief of the Naval Staff and the chief of the Air Staff (not to the president!). The 'supreme command' of the defence forces is in reality with the defence minister, who along with other members of the Council of Ministers, is 'collectively responsible' to the House of the People (Lok Sabha): Article 75 (3).

***

The sixth set of provisions covers the power of the president and the governor to promulgate Ordinances (Articles 123 and 213).

In India, the power to promulgate Ordinances (a law-making power) has been deliberately conferred on the executive (Article 123 in Part V – The Union and Article 213 in Part VI – The States). This power is to be exercised when Parliament or state legislatures are not in session so as to ensure continuity of governance since these bodies are not continuously in session. In England the executive has no such power to legislate (or to make laws) by Ordinance (when Parliament is not in session) except when a state of emergency is declared. The executive has no independent power of legislation in any other country in the Commonwealth, not even in Ireland, under the Irish Constitution, from which many provisions of the Indian Constitution have been drawn.

Even the president of the United States of America does not possess this power. In 1952, during the Korean war, defence contractors in the US needed enormous quantities of steel, which they apprehended they would not get because workers in private steel mills had threatened a country-wide strike. President Harry S. Truman was approached, and acting in exercise of the executive power vested in him under Article II of the US Constitution, he issued an order authorizing government officials to seize control of all privately owned steel mills and to work them,[70] the president bona fide believing that a strike would jeopardize US efforts in the Korean war. The steel companies sued, and the US Supreme Court held that Article II (the executive power) did not authorize a seizure! The court said (6:3) that the rule of law implied that the president could not, under the Constitution, take the property of the steel companies, *however good his reasons*, without authorization from an act of Congress. In the court's majority opinion (in what is now known as the Steel Seizure Case) Justice Hugo L. Black wrote:

> In the framework of our Constitution, the President's power is to see that the laws are faithfully executed. The Founders of this Nation entrusted the law-making power to the Congress alone in both good and bad times. It would do no good to recall the historical events, the fears of power and the hopes for freedom that lay behind their choice. Such a review would but confirm our holding that this seizure order cannot stand.

The judgment of the district court (granting an injunction against the US secretary of commerce from executing the order of the president) was upheld and affirmed.[71]

In recent times, however, American presidents have again resorted to Executive Orders – and what are known as 'recess appointments' (appointments made by the president that cannot go to the Senate for confirmation because the Senate is in recess). An article in the *New York Times* has commented on this phenomenon:

> Last fall [i.e., 2011], after the summer's debt-deal negotiations, [President Barack] Obama told aides they needed to be more aggressive about executive power and coined the slogan 'We can't wait'. Since then Obama has pushed through dozens of new policies aimed at things like jobs for veterans, preventing drug shortages, and easing the terms on student loans. Obama is set to unveil another such executive order – aimed at foreign nationals' use of cellphone tracking and Internet monitoring to carry out human-rights abuses. But the strategy opens Obama up to charges that he's concentrating too much power in the executive branch which deprives him of the ability to blame Congress when he issues an order unpopular with his base, like overruling the EPA's [Environmental Protection Agency] anti-smog rules![72]

In India the unique power conferred on the executive to pass laws temporarily by means of Ordinances (till the legislative bodies are called into session and approve or disapprove of them) was borrowed from British India's first Constitution Act, viz., the Government of India Act 1935 enacted by England's Parliament. The Constituent Assembly lifted this provision from the 1935 Act and introduced it into the Indian Constitution. The Ordinance-making provisions establish – at the very start – a tilt in the balance of powers and functions in our Constitution. They emphasize that it is the executive branch that is in the driving seat of governance.

But governance, almost perpetually, by Ordinance is something frowned upon by the Supreme Court. In *D. C. Wadhwa* vs *State of Bihar* (1987),[73] a Constitution Bench of the court had said that repromulgation of Ordinances by the governor of a state without getting them replaced by an Act of the state legislature was a 'flagrant violation of the constitutional provisions and hence void'. To quote:

> The executive cannot, by taking resort to an emergency power exercisable by it only when the legislature is not in session, take over the law-making function of the legislature. That would be clearly subverting the democratic process which lies at the core of our constitutional scheme, for then the people would be governed not

by the laws made by the legislature as provided in the Constitution but by laws made by the executive. The government cannot bypass the legislature and, without enacting the provisions of the ordinance into an Act of the legislature, repromulgate the ordinance as soon as the legislature is prorogued.

* * *

The seventh set of provisions deals with the duration of sessions of the legislature.

As if to stress the dominance of the executive, there is no period prescribed in our Constitution for the duration of sessions of Parliament and of state legislatures. It is left entirely to the governments (both at the Centre and in the states) as to when the Houses of Parliament and the state legislatures are to be summoned, and for how long. In fact, the Lok Sabha sits on an average of about 75 days in a year[74] and many state legislatures sit for an even lesser number of days.

* * *

The eighth set of provisions again relates to the executive.

Our Constitution thus envisages both at the Centre and in the states an all-powerful executive, which sets the agenda for all legislative business. When the elected bodies are not in session, it is the Council of Ministers (at the Centre and in the states) that is empowered to make laws (by promulgating Ordinances) and to take all executive action pertaining to subjects within the legislative competence of Parliament and of state legislatures, respectively. But under our Constitution, the executive can be likened to an air-filled balloon that is dependent for a continuous supply of oxygen on elected legislatures. The executive remains omnipotent only so long as the Council of Ministers retains the confidence of the elected representatives. Once that is lost, it becomes impotent. The 'air-filled balloon' gets deflated, and the government of the day has to resign and call fresh elections. This is the essence of ministerial responsibility, which is at the heart of a parliamentary form of government.

* * *

The ninth set of provisions relates to the doctrine of separation of powers.

Subject to ministerial responsibility to the elected bodies (Parliament and state legislatures), the executive can do all that the legislature can do (although it cannot undo what the legislature has already done – in the form of enacted law). In 1955, the publishing, printing and selling of textbooks prescribed in schools in Punjab had been taken over exclusively by the state government, not by enacted law but by an executive order ousting private publishers from the business; the ouster was challenged in court. Article 298 of the Constitution expressly empowers the Union and the states to engage in any trade or business activity. The contention of the petitioners was that this could only be done by a law enacted by the state legislature, not otherwise. The contention was negatived. In *Rai Sahib Ram Jawaya Kapur's* case (1955),[75] it was pointed out by a Constitution Bench of the Supreme Court that Articles 73 and 162 of our Constitution expressly declare that the executive power of the Union extends to matters with respect to which Parliament has the power to make laws, and that the executive power of the state extends to matters with respect to which the state legislature has power to make laws. Hence, there is no necessity for an enacted law to support executive action: either at the Centre or in the states.

It was in this context that Justice Bijan Kumar Mukherjea – speaking for the apex court (in *Ram Jawaya Kapur*'s case, 1955) – had said that the Indian Constitution *did not* recognize the doctrine of separation of powers in its absolute rigidity.[76] He went on to say that the Council of Ministers in India enjoying (as does the cabinet in the UK) a majority in Parliament concentrates in itself (and to itself) the virtual control of both legislative and executive functions.

The theory of separation of powers is a synthesis of a number of distinct ideas: the distinction between law creation and law application, the independence of the judiciary and the desirability of a balance of power between different constitutional institutions. In the UK, it has been stated that the doctrine is 'no longer, if it ever was, absolute' (Lord David Hope: in 2006, 1 AC 262). I believe that in India it is a doctrine invoked by judges (supported by lawyers) to retain hold on 'judicial power' – an expression not separately defined in our Constitution. Judges of the Supreme Court have enthusiastically endorsed the doctrine according to their own understanding of it, which is that of the supremacy of judicial power and they have given it recognition as part of the basic structure of the Constitution.[77] However, amongst lawmakers (members of Parliament and of state legislatures), the understanding of the doctrine is that it is meant to uphold 'legislative supremacy', and they invoke it in propounding the view that there should be no judicial interference with laws enacted by legislative bodies! Conflicting approaches! Which then is the correct view? Neither. The correct view is: the Constitution is supreme – not courts, not legislatures, and that the final interpreters of the Constitution are the justices (for the time being) of the Supreme Court of India!

* * *

An aside: In the Supreme Court of India, it is for good reason that Justice Bijan Kumar Mukherjea's portrait hangs in Court No. 1, opposite to that of India's first chief justice, Sir Harilal Kania. Mukherjea was a scholar-judge. He was appointed chief justice of India on 23 December 1954 on the retirement of his predecessor in office, Justice Mehr Chand Mahajan. But he (Mukherjea) could have been chief justice longer if he had responded to Prime Minister Jawaharlal Nehru's call to assume the office of CJI immediately after the retirement of India's second CJI, Patanjali Sastri, on 3 January 1954. But by constitutional convention, it was the turn of Justice Mehr Chand Mahajan (as the next seniormost judge), whom Nehru was reluctant to have.[78] But Mukherjea was a stickler for doing the right thing and said he would sooner resign than 'usurp' the highest office before his turn! Accordingly, Mehr Chand Mahajan was appointed chief justice of India on 4 January 1954, and it was only after he had retired (at age 65), in December 1954, that Mukherjea assumed office as CJI.[79] Mukherjea was a judge long before my time, but amongst the first judges of the Supreme Court, he was (in the reckoning of all with whom I have spoken) perhaps the noblest.

* * *

The tenth set of provisions has to do with Appropriation Bills – control by legislatures over the executive.

Howsoever powerful the executive – and it is extraordinarily powerful at the Centre – the purse strings are controlled by the legislature and not by the executive. There the balance gets restored. All revenues received by the Government of India and all other public monies collected by and on its behalf must go into the Consolidated Fund of India (Article 266) – and likewise in the states. No monies can be withdrawn from this fund *except* under appropriation made by enacted law. Such withdrawal must be by Appropriation Bills (Article 114), which ensures the continuance of a parliamentary system of government. The expenses of the government can only be met by means of a Bill introduced in the elected House of the People (Lok Sabha) and in the elected Legislative Assembly in the state, and such a Bill must provide for appropriation out of the Consolidated Fund of India (or the consolidated fund of the state) and the Bill must be passed by the people's elected representatives.

The true reason why Parliament meets and conducts Union Government business and state legislatures conduct state government business is primarily because the control of the purse strings is with the elected representatives of the people, and not with the executive. That is one of the hallmarks of a parliamentary system of government. It is a safeguard against the executive transforming itself into a dictatorship.

* * *

The eleventh set of provisions relates to important constitutional functionaries: they shape the NATION.

The Election Commission of India[80]

In an article (entitled 'On My Mind: The World of India') in the *New York Times* (1 December 1989), its former chief editor, A. M. Rosenthal, made the following ecstatic comment on India's parliamentary elections of November 1989:

> When India voted, a whole world voted.
>
> A whole world – hundreds of millions of people, speaking in a great orchestra of different languages, praying to different gods,

living in a continental hugeness that not long ago was divided into hundreds of principalities, people driven to centuries of war against each other by rulers seeking conquest, foreigners seeking booty, religious zealots seeking blood, educated people by the millions, illiterate peasants by the scores of millions, from mountains through great stretches of plains to southern seas.

Once again this whole world voted as one nation in a countrywide election, nine times now.

The February-March 2012 Assembly elections[81] were commented on by Gopalkrishna Gandhi (former administrator, diplomat and governor) in the following terms:

Let us be proud.
Five states went to the polls last month.
The voter turnout was extraordinary. That of women voters, specially so.
All these facts are not only well-known by now; they are axioms …
We can be proud.
The voters have won, voting has won.
But the 'man-of-the-match' is the Election Commission (EC) of India …

Elections now do not mean the spending of crores, but of multiples of crores.

When I read those figures, I was reminded of an election episode in UP[82] of 75 years ago. It has been recounted by Lal Bahadur Shastri[83] in a 1959 tribute to Jawaharlal Nehru:

> The general elections under the new Government of India Act took place in 1937; they were of great significance. In these elections Nehru played a very important role. I remember his visit to the district of Allahabad. It was about 8.30 p.m. when he finished his speech … Nehru had taken no tea in the afternoon and … he was feeling very hungry. He asked me whether there was any restaurant in the city … I remembered

> the railway station where some tea could be got. He said: 'Let us go there.'
>
> We motored to the railway station and went to the railway restaurant .... After having ... the tea we were asked to pay the bill. Every one of us searched his [or her] pockets and found that none of us carried sufficient money. Between us we could collect about Rs 2.50. Nehru had about Rs 1.25. Purnima Banerjee [a dedicated freedom fighter, who later became a member of the Constituent Assembly] another rupee and I gave the few annas to complete the full amount required. How awkward would it have been if we had failed to make up the amount among ourselves!

Seventy-five years is not all that long ago. That is, we are not talking of the 1800s. And we are talking of people whose names are invoked in today's election campaigns.

Money played a part in elections even then, but by and large it was licit money, modest money. *It was money, not the monster called black money.*[84]

The Election Commission of India has now become one of the most significant constitutional institutions in our democracy. It is greatly respected because it acts independently and not in accordance with the wishes of the government for the time being. It also assists emerging democracies around the world in the conduct of free and fair elections.

The Comptroller and Auditor General of India (CAG)[85]

The constitutional authority that supervises all financial matters is the CAG who is appointed by the president, by warrant, under his (or her) hand and seal, and can only be removed from office in a like manner and on like grounds as a judge of the Supreme Court: i.e., on a motion passed by a two-thirds majority in Parliament for 'proved misbehaviour', not otherwise. The CAG is required to submit reports to the president who must place them before each House of Parliament. A large number of questions in Parliament arise because of the reports of the CAG, who, next only to the Supreme Court, exercises a restraining influence on the all-powerful executive under our Constitution. The fact that the government of the day at the Centre, and some of its supporters, are nowadays seen criticizing the CAG and his functioning – both in Parliament and outside – points to a dangerous trend: viz., of scant regard for constitutional functionaries and non-observance of constitutional norms.

In a timely editorial in the *Hindu*,[86] the importance of the institution of the CAG was (rightly) emphasized:

> As auditor to a nation whose institutions of oversight are weak and underdeveloped, the Comptroller and Auditor General of India is more than just the keeper of our national accounts. It is, in many ways, a conscience keeper and a watchdog, which may not bite but can bark and warn ordinary citizens that something is amiss in the wider affairs of state. Like the Election Commission and the Supreme Court, the CAG has managed to protect its integrity and independence despite pressure from various arms of the state. If conducted freely and fairly, a robust audit can serve as a catalyst for corrective action. The CAG's report on Bofors in 1989 had major political consequences. Its explosive 2010 report on the allocation of 2G spectrum led to the filing of criminal charges against politicians, bureaucrats and businessmen. Other reports may have been equally useful. The CAG's observations may be politically embarrassing to the government but they clearly contribute to the public good. Democratic India must ensure that the government takes the work of this constitutionally sanctioned institution very seriously and removes the obstacles placed in the path of a more effective and efficient audit process.

The officials in the CAG's office were (and are) absolute sticklers for rules, about which there is an amusing story told by John Masters in his autobiography *Bugles and a Tiger* (1956).[87] Way back in the 1940s, a certain Lieutenant Dishington stationed in Multan (in the Punjab, now in Pakistan) fell in love with an Anglo-Indian girl. He robbed the battalion chest of its money and eloped with her, by taking the train to Lahore (which was then in British India). His superior, a major, followed him by train, and found Dishington outside Falettis Hotel (in Lahore). But the lieutenant with his girl gave him the slip by jumping into a taxi! The major got into another taxi and chased him all round town. Ultimately, poor Dishington was caught and made to part with the balance of the battalion's money. The major then returned to Multan, and claimed reimbursement for train and taxi fare from the office of the comptroller of accounts. The claim was resisted all down the line by fatuous queries from the clerks in the comptroller's office. The first query was: as the major was entitled under FR (Fundamental Rule) 1097 to a charger, why did he not apprehend Dishington by using his horse? The major kept his temper in check and responded by pointing out that he didn't have the time to load his horse on to the train to Lahore, and even if he had, he could not have used his horse in Lahore since Dishington was in a vehicle with an internal combustion engine that ran faster than his horse! Undeterred, another official in the comptroller's office fired a second query: '... It is further noted that the alleged culprit – i.e. Lt. Dishington is an Adjutant. Adjutants are also entitled to government charger (vide FR 1097). Kindly state why Government Charger was not used by Lieutenant Dishington in alleged flight and oblige!'

When, many years ago, I related this story to one of India's most distinguished CAGs, S. Ranganathan – Rangi (as he was affectionately known to his friends) – smiled indulgently and said: 'My dear Nariman, if the babus in the Auditor General's Office didn't stick to the book, this country would have become bankrupt soon after independence!' He was right. The CAG had been described by Dr B. R. Ambedkar as the 'most important officer in the Constitution'.[88] He still is. Those holding the reins of power are always respectful towards the CAG – sometimes a little scared of him – as they rightly should be! His findings have been the subject of 'storms' in Parliament. For instance, in the 'Performance Audit Report on the Issue of Licences and Allocation of 2G Spectrum' submitted to Parliament in 2010 and laid before both the Houses of Parliament, the CAG had pointed out that, based on values determined through various indicators, the estimate of loss to the exchequer of India on account of grant of new UAS (unified access service) licences and 2G spectrum during the period 2007 to 2010 appeared to be over

Rs 1 lakh crore (pp. 56-57 of the CAG Report of March 2010). The furore created in the two Houses of Parliament over this report has not yet subsided, especially since the Supreme Court of India on a PIL filed before it, based on the CAG's finding, has issued a spate of directions to various bodies and institutions, including the Central Bureau of Investigation (CBI). The CAG Report is still awaiting consideration by the PAC (Public Accounts Committee), after whose recommendations, it will be adopted (or not adopted) by Parliament.

***

The twelfth set of provisions relates to the 'executature' – which shows that real legislative power lies with ministers.

Purse strings apart, the power of the executive to determine most of what Parliament enacts is a fact of modern political history – true not only in India but also in parliamentary systems of government elsewhere. Lord Hailsham of St Marylebone,[89] England's Lord Chancellor for many years, after he had retired from his high office, coined a new word for the English Parliament: 'executature', i.e., a legislative body under the control of the executive. This would not be an exaggerated description of India's Parliament, especially when the government of the day used to consist of members of only one political party – during the first three decades of our Republic.

But ministerial power even in coalition governments is parliamentary power. In other words, *real parliamentary power lies with the ministers*. Even in this day and age, during the average 70-75-day sessions of Parliament each year, Mondays to Thursdays, and the first half of Friday, are taken up only with government business, Friday afternoons being reserved for private members' Bills. But hardly any Bill introduced by a private member is ever passed. The motions are gone through, as a sort of debating exercise, in order to draw the attention of the government of the day to some glaring inadequacies in existing laws.

A rare exception has been the latest episode in the controversy over the Lokpal Bill. In early April 2011, under pressure from a mass movement inspired by social activist and crusader-against-corruption, Anna Hazare, who had gone on a fast-unto-death unless an effective

Lokpal Bill was passed in Parliament, the government of the day (for the first – and only time) agreed to the active participation by named representatives of civil society in the drafting of a new Bill.[90] But this was an aberration.

In the future, Bills will continue to be drafted (as in the past) by bureaucrats (trained in drafting skills) in accordance with the wishes of the ministers, who will then introduce and shepherd the Bills through Parliament. Not too much happens in their passage through Parliament except when Bills are referred to committees, at which time a more detailed scrutiny is made. Substantive amendments are rare exceptions and passed only because the minister accepts them, or when the amendment represents a compromise across the political spectrum.

The assumption that governments put into execution what legislatures have confided to them is correct, but only in theory. In practice, it is the government that makes laws, and, through its majority, requires the Houses of Parliament to consent to them! Long ago, in 1867, Walter Bagehot, a shrewd political analyst of his time, wrote that the 'efficient secret of the English Constitution' (an unwritten one) was that of 'the close union with nearly complete fusion of all executive and legislative powers.'[91] It is a correct description of India's Constitution – both in theory and in practice.

That Parliament has wishes to which it requires governments (even coalition governments) to conform is a myth and not justified by the working experience of a parliamentary system of government. It is *governments* that have wishes and policies to which, through their majority, they require Parliament to conform! Then again, by authorization under statute, ministers and executives and bureaucrats frequently legislate – by proxy. The Latin maxim *delegatus non potest delegare* (a delegated authority cannot again delegate to others) remains only in the books. Courts generally find sufficient reasons to uphold nearly all forms of delegated legislation!

* * *

There is another balancing feature in the state of the nation – seldom realized, and even less appreciated. It is the office of the country's president.

In the USA, there is what is called a-growing-better-with-age theory of presidential history! This is so in India as well, although the extent of powers exercised by heads of state in each country is varied and dependent on the country's written constitution. In India, the president is neither a cipher nor a rubber stamp, but more appropriately a 'quiescent volcano'.[92]

India's head of state has been compared to the constitutional position of the Crown in England, stated in elegant terms some one hundred and fifty years ago by Walter Bagehot:

> To state the matter shortly, the Sovereign has, under a constitutional monarchy, three rights – *the right to be consulted, the right to encourage and the right to warn* [emphasis added]. And a king of great sense and sagacity would want no others. He would find that his having no other would enable him to use these with singular effect. He would say to his (First) Minister: 'The responsibility of these measures is upon you. Whatever you think best must be done. Whatever you think best shall have my full and effectual support. But you will observe that for this reason and that reason what you propose to do is bad; for this reason and that reason what you do not propose is better. I do not oppose, it is my duty not to oppose; but observe what I warn.' Supposing the king to be right, and to have what kings often have, the gift of effectual expression, he could not help moving his Ministers. He might not always turn his course, but he would always trouble his mind.[93]

K. M. Munshi, a brilliant lawyer and a prominent member of India's Constituent Assembly (one who took a leading role in the drafting of our Constitution) held views different from Bagehot:

> The President's position essentially differs from that of the British Crown as to (i) the oath; (ii) the election; (iii) the basis of allegiance of people; (iv) impeachability; and (v) the powers specifically conferred necessarily involving personal discretion.[94]

But it was the architect of our Constitution, Dr B. R. Ambedkar, who made it clear as to how the role of India's president was to be viewed when, at a late stage of the debate in the Constituent Assembly, he said that, like the English king, 'our President will have not only Bagehot's three rights (the right to advise, to warn and to be consulted), but also the prerogative powers of appointing the prime minister and the dissolution of the House'.[95]

***

In India's quasi-federal polity with a parliamentary system of government, there is a head of state at the Centre whose job it is to keep the 'ship of state' (the Union) on an even keel. There is also a governor at the head of each state. The head of state at the Centre has hardly ever 'rocked the boat',[96] except during some periods of the first presidency. In the states, however, there have been several occasions when governors have 'played politics', sometimes on their own, but more often at the behest of the Central Government that appointed them.

In the life of almost every president of India over the past 60 years and more, there have been occasions when he/she has exercised his/her individual powers of persuasion – and his/her 'right to warn'. It is only in critical times – in crisis situations – that the true mettle and personality of the person occupying the highest office in the land get revealed.

Amongst all our presidents, the role of Dr Rajendra Prasad, India's first head of state (in office from 26 January 1950 to 13 May 1962), has been unique. He did not respond to crisis situations. He was responsible for creating them! During a full decade in office as president – India's only head of state to be elected for two successive terms – he maintained strong views about the role of a president. Having the 'gift of effective expression' (as Bagehot would have said) his views did frequently 'trouble the mind' of India's first prime minister, Jawaharlal Nehru! In private, Prasad often complained to Minoo Masani, his friend and a compatriot in the Constituent Assembly, that Nehru did not allow him to exercise the powers which he was sure he had under the document they together had got passed in the Constituent Assembly. Years later, Masani was to say that Rajendrababu did not have the force of Nehru's personality, gave in too readily, and yet went on grumbling (as he gave in) saying: 'this is not the way we framed the Constitution.' Masani added: 'when people [ask] what is wrong with this Constitution, I say nothing is wrong; what is wrong is us, we have destroyed the Constitution because people in Delhi love power too much to tolerate either a *strong president* or a *strong State* [emphasis added]!'[97]

Within two months of being elected, Dr Rajendra Prasad wrote a three-page paper titled 'Questions Relating to the Powers of the President under the Constitution of India'. One of questions was: 'Does the Constitution contemplate any situation where the President "has to act independently" of the ministers?' The queries were addressed to Nehru, who passed them on to India's first attorney general, M. C. Setalvad.[98]

Setalvad responded firmly and authoritatively – as he was invariably accustomed to doing – opining that the position of the king in England and that of India's president were analogous. Whilst India's president did have discretion in selecting the prime minister and in deciding when to dissolve Parliament, either at the instance of the prime minister or when he personally felt the overarching force of public opinion, he, the president, had to always follow the 'advice' of his Council of Ministers. But even into his second term in office, Dr Rajendra Prasad was not convinced that he was simply a constitutional head of state! In 1960, in a speech to the Indian Law Institute, New Delhi, he said that our Constitution contained no provision 'which in so many words lays down that the President is bound to act on ministerial advice'. This assertion created a stir. In Granville Austin's view: 'it set the presidential fox among the constitutional geese!' But the reaction in the press to Rajendra Prasad's statement favoured the president's position![99]

When Dr Sarvepalli Radhakrishnan was elected to succeed Rajendra Prasad on 13 May 1962, the storm over 'presidential powers' had abated. If we are to accept, what H. N. Pandit says in his book (on the years in office of Dr Radhakrishnan), acquaintances who called on India's second president at Rashtrapati Bhavan were invariably treated to a worm's eye view of the presidency. 'What is a President after all?' Radhakrishnan would (reportedly) ask. 'Anyone nearing 75 and who has lost his will power is fit enough to be President of India!' Nearing 75 himself, India's second president, however never lost *his* will power during *his* term of office! For instance, presidential 'pressure' was clearly perceived after India's defeat in the war with China in late 1962. There was then growing clamour for the resignation of V. K. Krishna Menon, minister of defence and a very close friend of Nehru. Menon had been blamed for India's defeat, but Nehru, in failing health, would not drop him. It was then that President Radhakrishnan diplomatically wrote to the prime minister: '*As you have said* we have to accept Menon's resignation.' (Nehru had said nothing of the sort!) It was a tactful exhibition of presidential pressure in relation to sustained public opinion. The comment of Radhakrishnan's biographer to this incident was: 'the recognized procedure of the President acting on the advice of the Prime Minister was reversed!'[100]

Soon after President Radhakrishnan took office, it was reported that he had told the United States ambassador to India, Chester Bowles, that upon Nehru's departure from office, he, the president, might take temporary charge of government, set policy and administration right and then step aside for a democratically chosen prime minister. There was a storm of protest by the 'constitutionalists'! In retirement, Radhakrishnan angrily told his biographer that the report of the Chester Bowles incident was 'a tissue of lies'![101]

Dr Zakir Hussain – the scholar-president who succeeded Dr Radhakrishnan (on 13 May 1967) but died in office just under two years later (on 3 May 1969) – had said that the presidency was a 'unique institution'. His biographer (D. Sheikh Ali) says that Zakir Hussain believed that, in theory, the Indian presidency was 'more powerful than that of the President of the United States where Woodrow Wilson [March 1913 to March 1921] reduced his Cabinet to office boys, but in India, he (the President of India) could not write his own speech to Parliament; like the British Monarch, he was to read what is written for him.'[102] Years later, President A. P. J. Abdul Kalam (25 July 2002 to 24 July 2007) was skilfully able to circumvent this particular constraint of high office! On 25 February 2005, I was witness to an innovative bit of constitutional statesmanship by President Kalam, who delivered the customary address to both Houses of Parliament to herald in the new session. The Constitution provides for a presidential address at the beginning of each session. It does not say who is to prepare it. Since the president acts only on the advice of his Council of Ministers, the address, by convention, is prepared by the government of the day. But on the morning of 25 February 2005, President Kalam made a studied departure. He had with him the full text of the written speech prepared by the government. But he chose to begin with a poem in Tamil, composed not by the government of the day, but by himself the previous night! It was titled: 'Where Are We?' (composed and translated by India's head of state):

Where are we?
Where are we now, dear friends,
In the Maha Sabha that shapes history,
The call of heartbeats of Indian people,
People ask us, people ask us;
Oh! Parliamentarians, the sculptors of Mother India,
Lead us unto light, enrich our lives.
Your righteous toil is our guiding light,
If you work hard, we all can prosper.
Like King, so the people,
Nurture great thoughts, rise up in action,
May righteous methods be your guide;
May you all prosper ever with Almighty's grace.

It was a criticism of parliamentarians and their erstwhile manner of functioning – firmly, but politely, expressed in verse. It was meant as a gentle exhortation from the people's president to the country's representatives not to walk out of legislative chambers, but to work hard and do their job. And since the president could not alter the text of his address to both Houses of Parliament, he devised a new way of saying (what he had to say) in verse – and it was well received! An instance of an enlightened head of state taking advantage of one of the great silences in the Constitution – to slightly amend a constitutional convention – and exhort the people's representatives to perform their task as parliamentarians with honesty of purpose and with dedication. No one could fault him on expressing the sentiments of the vast majority of India's thinking millions.

Dr Zakir Hussain died in office (on 3 May 1969) before completing his term, creating a vacancy. Vice-president V. V. Giri assumed charge as acting president. Giri, however, wanted to contest for the president's office, which necessitated his resignation from the office of vice-president. The (double) constitutional void brought in the then chief justice of India, Mohammed Hidayatullah, for a brief period, as acting president.[103] In his scintillating memoir,[104] Justice Hidayatullah devotes an entire chapter to this fortuitous event beginning with a quote from William Shakespeare's *Macbeth*:

> If chance will have me King, chance may crown me, without [my] stir!

He methodically relates how, in cloak-and-dagger-fashion, he was first informed about the acting president, Giri, wanting to resign and stand for election as president; how he got news of it only on the afternoon of 15 July 1969 when the Constitution Bench of the Supreme Court (over which he presided as chief justice of India) had adjourned for lunch and he ('Haddi') received an urgent message that he, should come and see Giri post-haste; how he could not (or would not) go to Rashtrapati Bhavan in his own car but in the court registrar's car to avoid publicity; and how after driving straight to meet the acting president, the awkward manner in which the conversation between the two proceeded!

> I was taken immediately to the [acting] President who was pacing his chambers. The ADC left and after the door closed the President hugged me (this seemed to be his *forte*) and the conversation proceeded something like this:
>
> President: I have decided to make you the President.
> Chief Justice: Kindly explain yourself.
> President: I have decided to resign and contest the Presidential election … you will be the Acting President.
> Chief Justice: You don't have to resign to contest the election.
> President: I know that. But I cannot effectively conduct my campaign from this palace. I have to visit the States for canvassing.
> Chief Justice: Well, that is your concern. If you resign, the law will take its course.

PRESIDENT: Now tell me to whom do I address the letter of resignation? I am going to write to you as you will succeed me. Will that be sufficient?

CHIEF JUSTICE: I am afraid I cannot give you advice as I am a Judge.

PRESIDENT: Then whom do I consult?

CHIEF JUSTICE: Speak to the Prime Minister [Mrs Indira Gandhi].

PRESIDENT: I do not want to speak to her.

CHIEF JUSTICE: Then ask the Attorney General.

PRESIDENT: At least tell me [from] which office do I resign – Acting President or Vice-President?

CHIEF JUSTICE: That should be obvious. You hold only one elected office and that is the office of the Vice-President. The other office is by virtue of the original office. You are not an elected President.

PRESIDENT: Thank you. I now understand this. How glad, my friend, your father would have been to see you as President. I am glad that I shall be instrumental in your becoming a President, even for a short time. You have my good wishes.

CHIEF JUSTICE: Thank you, Sir, and I hope the risk you are taking will be worth something.[105]

The parting shot was fortuitous.

As events turned out (for Giri), it *was* definitely a risk worth taking!

Giri was 'the dark horse' backed by Mrs Indira Gandhi – then head of the newly formed Indira-inspired political party: Congress (I) – to contest against N. Sanjeeva Reddy, the nominee of the traditional Congress Party: now called Congress (O) (Organization Congress comprising members of the old guard). The old guard consisted of veterans such as Morarji Desai (a former Union minister), S. K. Patil (another former Union minister) and K. Kamaraj (the Congress president). Kamaraj later became the president of the Congress (O) after the party split in late 1969. Reddy was roundly defeated, and Giri was elected as India's fourth president and began his term on 24 August 1969.

During Giri's presidentship, his own election to the office of president was challenged directly before India's Supreme Court in accordance with the provisions of the Presidential and Vice-Presidential Elections Act 1952. After a prolonged hearing, and much oral evidence (the president himself, appearing for the first – and only – time in court and giving his version of events), a bench of five judges of the Supreme Court (presided over by Chief Justice S. M. Sikri) upheld the election.[106]

After Giri, the gravest crisis that had been faced by any president in India was that to which Dr Fakhruddin Ali Ahmed was exposed. He was elected president in August 1974 but died in office (11 February 1977) before completing his term. The 'crisis' was when he was asked to sign the Proclamation of internal Emergency of 25 June 1975, the direct and inevitable consequence of which was the rounding-up of his own (the president's) erstwhile friends and compatriots; they were all preventively detained overnight in jails spread across the country! One of the lessons of the internal Emergency (which lasted till 21 March 1977) has been not to place excessive reliance on constitutional functionaries. They failed us – the president, ministers of the government, most of the Members of Parliament and even senior judges of our Supreme Court: the latter for their majority judgment (4:1) delivered in April 1976 in *ADM Jabalpur*[107] – upholding the Proclamation of internal Emergency. Nine high courts in the country had struck down the Proclamation but all their judgments were overturned in *ADM Jabalpur*.

It was because President Fakhruddin Ali Ahmed so readily agreed to sign the Proclamation of Emergency on the night of 25 June 1975, even before the cabinet knew anything about it, that three years later (after revocation of the Emergency in March 1977), a Constitutional Amendment was enacted by the newly elected Parliament – the Constitution (44th Amendment) Act 1978 – which declared that in the future, a president was not empowered to sign a Proclamation of Emergency unless the decision of the Council of Ministers was communicated to him *in writing*! (Article 352 [3].)

* * *

The signing of the Emergency Proclamation in June 1975 by the president at the behest of the government of the day was not an aberration occasioned by the Emergency. Constitutional functionaries have failed us not only when times were bad, but at other times as well! In the general elections of March 1977, the Janata Government was swept into power, on a tidal wave of protest against the 'internal Emergency'. And promptly, a circular was issued in May 1977 by Charan Singh, then home minister in the government of Morarji Desai; he also addressed letters to chief ministers of nine states asking them to recommend dissolution of state assemblies, even though in respect of legislatures of some of the states, their constitutionally prescribed term of five years had not yet expired! It was a pressure tactic, by the Centre not warranted by any of the provisions of the Constitution. But as with some pressure tactics, it worked! When the validity and propriety of the circular were challenged by the state of Rajasthan, the Supreme Court of India (regrettably) upheld it as a direction that had to be complied with (by a majority of 6:1).[108] It was only 17 years later that the Supreme Court had second thoughts. In *S. R. Bommai* (1994),[109] a nine-judge bench of the same court (now differently composed), which had previously put its imprimatur on undemocratic and unconstitutional executive action, differed from its own prior decision (of a seven-judge bench) in the *State of Rajasthan* – too late for it to make any difference whatever, the prior decision having already worked itself out!

In early 1980, when the Janata Party wave had petered out, Indira Gandhi was voted back to power. What was sauce for the goose was made sauce for the gander![110] Relying on the Supreme Court judgment in the *State of Rajasthan* vs *Union of India* (of May 1977) – which was then still good law – Prime Minister Indira Gandhi instructed her home minister, Zail Singh, to draft a proclamation under Article 356 for dissolution of nine state assemblies and imposing president's rule in each of the states. N. Sanjeeva Reddy[111] (who had been elected president in July 1977 and continued in office till July 1982 – in succession to President Fakhruddin Ali Ahmed) dutifully signed the proclamation, '*with hesitation*' (as he told Granville Austin!).[112] Sanjeeva Reddy's excuse was: 'given the precedent how could I say no. I told Indira that Morarji had been wrong in principle and to dissolve again was still wrong.' But right or wrong, Reddy did put his signature to the proclamation – like that ill-fated Duchess of Kent in the limerick of old, 'who said she would not go but she went'!

During the Emergency, when many Members of Parliament belonging to opposition parties were placed under preventive detention, the government of the day rushed through Parliament the Constitution (42nd Amendment) Bill 1976. One of its provisions, which became law, substituted a new clause for Article 74(1). It read:

> There shall be a Council of Ministers with the Prime Minister at the head to aid and advise the President who shall, in the exercise of his functions, act in accordance with such advice.

What was previously left to constitutional convention was incorporated as a constitutional mandate in the written text. After the 1976 Amendment, the role of India's head of state was intended to be confined to that of a titular functionary: he/she must have no 'elbow room'; he/she must act according to the wishes of his/her ministers. When the Janata Government came to power in the wake of the end of the Emergency, after the March 1977 elections, it moved a Constitutional Amendment in 1978, adding a proviso to the substituted provision (which was like a breath of fresh air). It read:

> Provided that the President may require the Council of Ministers to reconsider such advice, either generally or otherwise, and the President shall act in accordance with the advice tendered after such reconsideration.

Even after the Constitutional Amendment obliging the president to act in accordance with the reconsidered advice given by his/her Council of Ministers, there is no constitutional prescription as to the time when he/she should so act. This omission in our Constitution was exploited to the full by Zail Singh, India's next president from July 1982 to July 1987. During the tenure of Rajiv Gandhi (Indira Gandhi's elder son) as prime minister, when the Post Office Bill 1987 was submitted to him for assent, there was much criticism of its provisions, particularly the one which permitted an interception of all communications through the mail by the government of the day. Although the Bill was passed by both Houses of Parliament and submitted to Zail Singh for assent, the president paused. He did not assent. He paid heed to the groundswell of public opinion.

The British Constitution is not written. But it recognizes that the British monarch, on rare but important occasions, is entitled to intervene in public affairs in a way that may be decisive. As the constitutional historian of England, Walter Bagehot, used to say, 'the greatest wisdom of a constitutional King would show itself in *well-considered inaction*'. Zail Singh may have been untutored about what went on in Westminster, but he had an astute political sense. He could sense that people were behind him when he delayed (and so withheld) assent to the Post Office Bill (under the Constitution unless the president assents to a Bill passed by both Houses of Parliament it does not become 'law'). In politics, nothing succeeds like success. The public outcry against the Bill gathered greater momentum, and the Bill lay unsigned even on the desk of Zail Singh's successor, R. Venkataraman. The latter expressed his own displeasure at the Bill before returning it, in January 1990, to the prime minister of the day, V. P. Singh (who had succeeded Rajiv Gandhi).[113] (V. P. Singh eventually withdrew the Bill.)

* * *

The sudden and cruel assassination of Prime Minister Indira Gandhi (on 31 October 1984) was a great shock to the nation. But the spontaneous reaction to this event proved to be President Zail Singh's finest hour! He could think on his feet – and he did. The burning question was who should be asked to become prime minister. Zail Singh did not vacillate. He firmly told two senior Union ministers – Pranab Mukherjee and P. V. Narasimha Rao, possible aspirants to the top post – about his decision to place the mantle of prime ministership on Rajiv Gandhi.[114]

As to how presidents function in times of acute crises, we have the version of President R. Venkataraman, who penned a memoir of his years in office.[115] He has written about the crisis occasioned by the resignation of Chandrashekhar as prime minister in March 1991. (Chandrashekhar had succeeded V. P. Singh as prime minister in November 1990.) The first question was whether the prime minister, after acceptance of his resignation by the president, and asked to continue in office, was competent to pilot any legislation in the Lok Sabha, and the second was what could the president do to carry on the administration of the government in the event of Parliament not passing the Finance Bill, which, at the time, was a distinct possibility. Slightly departing from his position as constitutional head ('a textbook president' as he liked to describe himself), Venkataraman wrote a letter to Speaker Rabi Ray, as well as to the prime minister, expressing his own view based on British precedents, viz., that the prime minister did have the power to function in legislative and administrative matters, even after the acceptance of the resignation of a prime minister. It worked like magic. After these letters, the menacing cloud on the political horizon lifted with the Lok Sabha approving all financial business and the president endorsing the same. As necessary budgetary and other legislative measures had been passed by both Houses of Parliament and as the Union Council of Ministers headed by Chandrashekhar had already resigned and recommended a fresh poll and no political party had staked a claim to form an alternative government, a Presidential Order under Article 85 of the Constitution dissolving the Lok Sabha was issued, with a direction for the constitution of the new Lok Sabha on or before 5 June 1991.

Dr Shankar Dayal Sharma was elected to the highest office after the expiry of the (full) term of President Venkataraman. Dr Sharma became the president on 25 July 1992. He was presented by the government of the day with the Representation of Peoples Amendment Ordinance 1996, recommended to him by the entire cabinet. This Ordinance was aimed at shortening the period of the poll campaign, after announcement of elections, from three weeks to two weeks. Also approved by the cabinet, the draft Constitutional Schedule Castes (Amendment) Ordinance, intended to extend reservations in public employment to a large number of 'dalit Christians', was submitted to him for promulgation. President Sharma returned both the Ordinances, refusing to promulgate them, since they were recommended by the government of the day on the eve of elections, and according to him this would not pass the test of 'constitutional propriety'.[116]

During the presidentship of K. R. Narayanan (25 July 1997 to 25 July 2002) – who succeeded President Shankar Dayal Sharma – Prime Minister I. K. Gujral and his Council of Ministers sent to the president, in October 1997, for promulgation a proclamation, under Article 356 of the Constitution, for the imposition of president's rule in the state of Uttar Pradesh. Acting under the proviso to Article 74(1) of the Constitution, the president returned the proclamation for reconsideration by the Council of Ministers giving elaborate reasons (as he invariably did) for his decision. This became widely known, and the Union Government refrained from sending back the proclamation to him a second time.[117] If it had, President Narayanan would have had to sign it, but the public ('We the People') would have been against it. In politics, as in life, discretion is often the better part of valour.

The next president, Dr A. P. J. Abdul Kalam (in office from 25 July 2002 to 25 July 2007), had his share of crises. The Bihar Dissolution Bill, which he had signed in haste when he was on a state visit to Moscow in May 2005, was struck down by a Constitution Bench of the Supreme Court of India in *Rameshwar Prasad* vs *Union of India* (AIR 2006, SC 980) though by a narrow majority (3:2). But his role in what was popularly known as the Office of Profit Bill (2006) was exemplary. Dr Kalam's biographer, his secretary P. M. Nair, says in his book:[118]

> The President's position is very clear in the Constitution. Article 111 gives three options to him: give assent, withhold assent or return the Bill to the Houses with a message for reconsideration – the latter two applicable only in the case of non-money Bills. The Article which gives such a right to the President also vests the Parliament with a right to resubmit that Bill after reconsideration to the President with or without amendments. When that happens, he 'shall not withhold assent therefrom'. The phrasing of the Article takes into account the need to do so without delay.

Exercising this right, the president decided to send a message to Parliament:

I received, on 25 May 2006, the Parliament (Prevention of Disqualification) Amendment Bill, 2006, duly passed by both Houses of Parliament for my assent under Article 111 of the Constitution of India.

2. While having the highest regard for the sagacity and mature wisdom of my fellow Parliamentarians and with due deference to the Parliament, I would like the Parliament to reconsider the proposed Bill:

(a) in the context of the settled interpretation of the expression 'Office of Profit' in Article 102 of the Constitution, and
(b) the underlying Constitutional principles therein.

3. While reconsidering, among other things, the following may be specifically addressed:

(i) evolution of generic and comprehensive criteria which are just, fair and reasonable and can be applied across all States and Union Territories in a clear and transparent manner,
(ii) the implication of including for exemption the names of offices the holding of which is alleged to disqualify a member and in relation to which petitions for disqualification are already under process by the competent authority, and
(iii) soundness and propriety of law in making the applicability of the amendment retrospectively.

4. As provided under Article 111 of the Constitution, I, therefore, hereby return the Bill to the Houses for reconsideration with this message.

– (signed) A. P. J. Abdul Kalam
30 May 2006

Parliament reconsidered the Bill, and as thought fit by that body, passed it again without any amendment. However, out of politeness and regard for the president, Parliament also resolved to refer the entire matter to a Parliamentary Committee to evolve 'suitable norms'. The Bill was reconsidered along with the president's 'message' and promptly repassed, and sent back to the president for assent on 1 August 2006. Having exercised, and exhausted, his constitutional right under Article 111 of the Constitution, the president was duty-bound to discharge his constitutional responsibility under the same Article by assenting to it, which President Kalam duly did on 18 August 2006, thus establishing a healthy precedent of presidential conformity with the provisions of the Constitution.

***

The president of India, as its first citizen, has the constitutional right, and correspondingly, the duty to interpose in public affairs of great moment, giving of his wisdom – privately, never publicly; quietly, never with fanfare. An elected president notionally represents the collective will of the people – he can use his constitutional right (and must use it) to temper the occasional excesses of its elected representatives.

I believe that on those very rare occasions when Parliament (or the government) chooses to do something that the president believes to be unconstitutional, or even morally wrong or improper, it is his function, right and duty to intervene and to make known his views. An illustrative instance in point would be an excessive prolongation (by a proposed constitutional amendment) of the life of an existing Parliament, which would keep in office a government whose normal term has run out, and which is anxious to avoid elections!

But then, how must a president, as a constitutional head of state, express his/her disapproval? It was a former chief justice of Pakistan who provided the answer! Many years ago, Chief Justice Muhammad Munir[119] was asked by his country's president (during Pakistan's initial experiment with parliamentary democracy) whether he could constitutionally refuse to give his assent to a Bill passed by the National Assembly (Pakistan's first Constitution after independence was like ours – fashioned on the Westminster model). His answer was:

> If you think it is a matter of the gravest importance, and you cannot in all conscience accept the measure presented to you, you can, and

> you must (if you are true to your oath) refuse assent – but having refused assent you must then resign; the system must go on; people will know why you resigned, and will sort things out with their Governments.

Pearly words of wisdom. They show how important, and how potentially effective, is the great office of the president in a parliamentary democracy. But they also show that the words of the Constitution, though important, are never decisive, because 'the silences in our constitutional law' speak louder than words![120] Harvard Professor Emeritus Laurence H. Tribe has said that a true understanding of a written Constitution must always reflect its '*invisible dark matter*'![121] Many years before – more eloquently (and more expansively) – Justice Felix Frankfurter had written in his judgment in the Steel Seizure Case:

> Deeply embedded traditional ways of conducting government cannot supplant the Constitution but they give meaning to the words of the text or supply them. It is an inadmissible narrow conception of American Constitutional Law to confine it to the words of the Constitution and to disregard the gloss which life has written upon them ...[122]

* * *

The Union judiciary, particularly India's highest court, contributes much to the State of the Nation – especially when governments at the Centre are weak and shaky!

The judiciary is where the 'executature' (to use Hailsham's evocative phrase, mentioned earlier in this chapter) is called to account and asked to justify its action under law before the courts – including the Supreme Court of India. The imbalance in the power equation gets righted – even if only on a case-to-case basis – by the excesses of administrative action being controlled, and executive inaction being corrected, by judicial diktat; where, occasionally (and sometimes not-so-occasionally) even lawmaking gets faulted!

The most significant feature of the Constitution of India is the area, extent and nature of the jurisdiction of India's Supreme Court. It is all-pervasive. Laws enacted by India's Parliament and by state legislatures, in fact, all executive action taken in the name of the president at the Centre, and in the name of the governors in the states, are authoritatively (and finally) interpreted and corrected by the courts. The law declared by the Supreme Court is binding (under the Constitution) on all courts and authorities in the country, though not on the Supreme Court itself (Article 141). There is virtually no area of legislative or executive activity that is beyond the highest court's scrutiny. It is the ultimate court of appeal in all civil and criminal cases. Its writ now extends to more than 3 million square kilometres of Indian territory and to its (now) over one billion inhabitants – 1.23 billion to be more accurate. India was much more manageable to govern in 1950 with only 330 million people!

High courts in the states (there are 22 high courts for the 28 states and seven union territories) are empowered under the Constitution to issue all manner of writs, orders and directions not only for enforcement of the wide range of Fundamental Rights guaranteed under Part III of the Constitution, but also for 'any other purpose' (Article 226). This great 'searchlight' provision of our Constitution was attempted to be dimmed during the dark days of the internal Emergency (25 June 1975 to 21 March 1977). A Constitution Committee, which included three prominent lawyers, was set up by the Centre to clip the wings of the high courts by proposing drastic changes in Article 226: Power of high courts to issue certain writs 'to any person or authority' for the enforcement of Fundamental Rights or for any other purpose. The committee chairman, Swaran Singh (a minister in Indira Gandhi's government), told his colleagues that when he was himself a minister in Punjab, he found that, as minister, it was just not possible to render justice in individual cases because of the pressures and pulls of party politics, and that it was far better that courts were left to do the job, and that was why Article 226 was best left to remain in the Constitution. Swaran Singh[123] was the one person – a non-practising lawyer – who set his face against the abolition of Article 226, not when times were good, but when times were bad! And we should all be grateful to him for having saved the writ jurisdiction of the high courts. It is a sad commentary of our times that it was the practising lawyer-politicians on the Constitution Committee who so fervently wanted not just to amend, but to scrap, Article 226 in obedience to the wishes of the high command. The moral of the story is that we should avoid relying on high-profile lawyers (who have political interests or ambitions), to guide our destinies, because it is they (with their argumentative skills) who are able to rationalize anything – including all forms of tyranny!

The Supreme Court of India supervises the decisions rendered by high courts (and tribunals) in the states through powers conferred on it, by Article 136, of granting special leave to appeal against any decision or order of any court (or tribunal) in the country. The Supreme Court is also vested with original jurisdiction under Article 32 for the direct enforcement of Fundamental Rights. The Supreme Court is also invested with a special advisory jurisdiction (Article 143) to answer questions of law or of fact of 'public importance' that may be referred to it by the president of India,[124] i.e., by the Central Government – a jurisdiction not infrequently invoked, especially when the government is keen to pass on to the judges a 'political hot potato'.[125] But the court is aware of this too. It is not bound to answer a Presidential Reference. It may respectfully decline to do so, as it did in the Presidential Reference on 'the Ayodhya dispute'.[126] On 6 December 1992, the structure known as Ramjanambhumi*-Babri Masjid (initially erected as a mosque by Mir Baqi Tashqandi[127] in Ayodhya in A.D. 1528) was deliberately and systematically demolished by some Hindu fanatics and became the focal point of the dispute. This dastardly event marked a turning point in India's political history – from a non-violent Indian nation it had become, at one bound, a fractious and turbulent one! In a white paper issued by the Government of India, the destruction was described as a

> *... most reprehensible act. The perpetrators of this deed struck not only against a place of worship but also at the principles of secularism, democracy and the rule of law ...*

In the Presidential Reference of 7 January 1993 framed under the provisions of Article 143 of the Constitution,[128] it was acknowledged that the demolition had

---

*Ramjanambhumi means the birthplace of Lord Ram.

> *... affected the maintenance of public order and harmony between different communities in the country and that the Government proposed to settle the dispute after obtaining the opinion of the Supreme Court of India and in terms of the said opinion.*

The question of public importance posed for the opinion of the Supreme Court was:

> Whether a Hindu temple or any Hindu religious structure existed prior to the construction of the Ramjanambhumi-Babri Masjid (including the premises of the inner and outer courtyards of such structure) in the area on which the structure stood?

Simultaneously with the Presidential Reference, the Government of India promulgated (in the name of the president) an Ordinance titled 'Acquisition of Certain Area at Ayodhya Ordinance 1993' for the acquisition of 67.703 acres of land in the Ramjanambhumi-Babri Masjid complex. The Ordinance was later replaced by an Act whose constitutional validity was challenged. Both the Presidential Reference and challenge to the constitutional validity of the Ordinance/Act were heard together by a Constitution Bench of five judges.[129] The bench was divided – regrettably (and most noticeably) – along communal lines! Two justices belonging to the minority communities in India – the largest (Muslim) and the smallest (Parsi) – joined in striking down the entire Central Act known as the Acquisition of Certain Area at Ayodhya Act 1993 (the Act that had replaced the Ordinance). They struck it down as unconstitutional because it 'offended the principles of secularism which was a part of the basic structure of the Constitution, being slanted in favour of one religious community as against another'. The other three justices – who did not belong to any minority community – rejected the challenge to the constitutional validity of the Act except one provision which had declared, as abated, all pending suits and proceedings.

On one point, however, the Constitution Bench was unanimous – it declined to answer the Presidential Reference. The 'political hot potato' issue was left to be decided in substantive suits then pending between the parties, which were in adversarial positions. The suits were decided (in September 2010) to the general dissatisfaction of all parties to the litigation(!) by a special three-judge bench of the Allahabad High Court. Appeals vis-à-vis the decision of the Allahabad High Court were admitted by the Supreme Court of India (on 9 May 2011), and still await a final hearing.

But anyone who thinks that a final adjudication of the civil dispute will assuage the resentment (on both sides of the divide) is obviously not aware of what an English judge (familiar with the workings of courts) had once said: 'litigation is an activity that does not markedly contribute to the happiness of mankind.'[130] It never has; it never will. The solution lies in assuaging justifiable resentment, and in respecting religious sentiment, by one group stretching its proverbial hand of friendship in the hope and expectation that it is firmly grasped (by the other group) as a goodwill gesture! As for myself, I have said this publicly before, and I say it again: 'If I were a Muslim, I would tell my brethren: a certain group believes, and genuinely believes, that their God was born at this particular spot. I may not agree with that belief. If no saint of mine, nor my God was born at this spot, I would say give the land to them.' This would not be an act of surrender, but an act of statesmanship – for the greater good of the greater number.

* * *

One comment, not out of place in a book concerning the State of the Nation: For centuries, Hinduism has been the most tolerant of all religions.

But one cannot say the same after 6 December 1992. The Hindu tradition of tolerance is showing signs of strain, the strain of religious tension, fanned by fanaticism. This 'great orchestra of different languages praying to different Gods'[131] that we love, and call 'India', is now seen and heard playing out of tune!

Is Hinduism then changing its face? I hope not – but I fear it is and it is as well to express this fear openly. Secular India versus militant Hinduism is reminiscent of observations made by Ambassador George F. Kennan about democracy:[132]

... I sometimes wonder whether a democracy is not uncomfortably

> similar to one of those prehistoric monsters (dinosaurs) with a body as long as a large room and a brain the size of a pin; he lies there in his comfortable primeval mud and pays little attention to his environment; he is slow to wrath – in fact, you practically have to whack his tail off to make him aware that his interests are being disturbed; but, once he grasps this, he lays about him with such blind determination that he not only destroys his adversary but largely wrecks his native habitat. You wonder whether it would not have been wiser for him to have taken a little more interest in what was going on at an earlier date and to have seen whether he could have prevented some of these situations from arising instead of proceeding from an undiscriminating indifference to a holy wrath equally undiscriminating.

We in India must take heed not to let the 'dinosaur' destroy our habitat!

***

In the early years of the working of India's Constitution, the Supreme Court had consistently held that whatever was intended by the framers of the Constitution was expressed in the language used in its provisions; there was no scope for any intendment. The court eschewed a positivist approach when interpreting constitutional provisions. No attempt was made to probe into the crevices of the Constitution and to plumb the depths of its silences so as to ascertain a meaning revealed only to the judges!

That was to come in later years, when the confidence of the court in the wisdom of legislatures had been consistently weakened and when the presumption of executive acts being regularly performed had worn thin.[133] The mid to late 1970s and early 1980s marked the turning point in the way the courts *looked at, and read*, the Constitution. Consistent legislative and executive encroachments on judicial power ultimately alerted the court to its true role – that of the conscience keeper of the nation. It was only after this realization that the judges in the highest court embarked on a 'broadly expansive' interpretation of the Constitution's provisions.

The most notable example was the one concerning the judicial review of constitutional amendments.

Under the Constitution, courts are empowered to invalidate not only executive orders but also legislative enactments that violate any part of the Fundamental Rights guaranteed in Part III of the Constitution (Bill of Rights). But are they empowered to adjudicate on the validity of constitutional amendments passed with the requisite special majority and following the procedure prescribed in Article 368? (Article 368 is the provision dealing with amendments to the Constitution.) On this crucial question, the Constitution is silent.

With one single political party almost consistently returned to power at each election since 1951-52 – and returned with a two-thirds majority (at least up to 1989; except in 1977) – the judges had for long plumbed the depths of silence in one of the world's longest constitutions searching for some limitations on the amending power.

Early in our constitutional history, the Constitution 1st Amendment Act 1951 was enacted by India's provisional Parliament (which had been India's erstwhile Constituent Assembly) taking away some of the Fundamental Rights already granted and guaranteed in Part III of the Constitution.[134] The provisions (Article 31A and Article 31B) – which had no place at all in the chapter on Fundamental Rights! – were challenged as being ultra vires and unconstitutional. The background was that the Congress Party, commanding as it did a majority of votes both in Parliament and in several state legislatures, had carried out certain measures of agrarian reforms in the states by enacting legislation in the form of Zamindari Abolition Acts. The validity of these Acts was challenged in the high courts on the ground that they contravened the Fundamental Rights conferred by Part III of the Constitution, including the Fundamental Right to own and hold property granted by Article 19 (1)(f), subject only to restrictions imposed by law, which had to be reasonable. There was also Article 19(5) as well as the substantive Fundamental Right to property (Article 31 – i.e., the right to insist that property acquired by the state could only be so acquired for a public purpose and only on payment of just compensation).[135] The High Court of Patna had held that the Bihar (Abolition of Zamindari) Act was unconstitutional, but the High Courts of Allahabad and Nagpur had upheld the validity of the corresponding laws enacted by the states of Uttar Pradesh and Madhya Pradesh, respectively. Appeals from each of those decisions were pending in the Supreme Court. To put an end to all this litigation and to remedy what the Union Government considered to be 'certain defects brought to light in the working of the Constitution', the Constitution 1st Amendment Bill was introduced and passed in Parliament. Reacting to this move the zamindars (landlords of vast tracts of land)[136] filed petitions in the Supreme Court under Article 32 challenging the constitutional validity of the Constitution 1st Amendment Act itself as 'unconstitutional and void'. The (first) justices of the Supreme Court (Chief Justice Harilal Kania, Patanjali Sastri, B. K. Mukherjea, S. R. Das, and Chandrashekhara Iyer), sitting in a Constitution Bench, heard the petitions. They found little difficulty in deciding the matter. In a short but unanimous judgment,[137] the court held that 'to make a law which contravenes the constitution constitutionally valid is a matter of constitutional amendment and as such falls within the exclusive power of Parliament.' The petitions filed by the zamindars were dismissed.

But, as written constitutions get older, those whose duty it is to interpret them get wise – and more circumspect! Fourteen years after *Sankari Prasad* (1951), several writ petitions (for instance: *Sajjan Singh* vs *State of Rajasthan,* 1965) were filed challenging the constitutional validity (on this occasion) of the Constitution 17th Amendment Act 1965. This Act, inter alia, placed (pursuant to the enabling provisions of Article 31B) several state enactments in the Ninth Schedule – in order to make them valid even if they contravened the provisions of the Fundamental Rights chapter, including the Fundamental Right to own and hold property (Article 19[1][g]) and the right not to be deprived of property except for a public purpose and on payment of 'just' compensation (Article 31). A Constitution Bench of five justices (Chief Justice P. B. Gajendragadkar and Justices K. N. Wanchoo, Mohammed Hidayatullah, Raghubar Dayal and J. R. Mudholkar) dismissed all these writ petitions. Three of the judges on the bench (the chief justice and Justices Wanchoo and Dayal) held that the power of amendment was plenary and included the power to take away or amend all or any of the Fundamental Rights guaranteed in Part III of the Constitution.[138] Two of the remaining justices were not so sure, although they agreed that the petitions deserved to be dismissed (on the basis of the earlier Constitution Bench decision of the court in *Sankari Prasad*, 1951). They gave expression to their doubts. Justice Hidayatullah said that Article 368 did not give power to amend *any* provision of the Constitution and that 'the Constitution gives so many assurances in Part III that it would be difficult to think that they were the playthings of a special majority'. He concluded:

> As at present advised I can only say that the power to make amendments ought not ordinarily to be a means of escape from absolute constitutional restrictions.
>
> For these reasons though I agree with the order proposed, I would not like to be understood to have expressed a final opinion on the aspect of the case outlined above.[139]

In his autobiography (*My Own Boswell – Memoirs*) written many years later, Justice Hidayatullah revealed that he had requested the presiding judge in *Sajjan Singh* (Chief Justice Gajendragadkar) to refer the matter to a larger bench, a request that was not accepted.

The other judge-in-doubt, Justice Mudholkar, also agreed that the writ petitions should be dismissed, but said he would prefer to reserve his opinion as to whether the previous decision in *Sankari Prasad* (1951) was right: 'I do not regard what this Court has held in that case as the last word.' He went on to say that so long as the Preamble of the Constitution stood unamended, it would have to be considered whether the power to amend could be exercised 'with respect to any of the basic features of the Constitution'. It is clear from paragraph 59 of the judgment of Justice Mudholkar that he was greatly impressed by the judgment of Chief Justice A. R. Cornelius of Pakistan in a case dealt with by the Supreme Court of Pakistan just a couple of years before:

> 59. The Constitution has enjoined on every member of Parliament before entering upon his office to take an oath or make an affirmation to the effect that he will bear true faith and allegiance to the Constitution. On the other hand, under Article 368 a procedure is prescribed for amending the Constitution. If upon a literal

> interpretation of this provision an amendment even of the basic features of the Constitution would be possible it will be a question for consideration as to how to harmonize the duty of allegiance to the Constitution with the power to make an amendment to it. Could the two be harmonized by excluding from the procedure for amendment alteration of a basic feature of the Constitution? It would be of interest to mention that the Supreme Court of Pakistan has, in *Fazlul Quader Chowdhry* vs *Mohd. Abdul Haque*, 1963, PLD 486 (SC), held that franchise and form of government are fundamental features of a Constitution and the power conferred upon the President by the Constitution of Pakistan to remove difficulties does not extend to making an alteration in a fundamental feature of the Constitution. For striking down the action of the President under, what he calls 'subconstitutional power', Cornelius CJ, relied on the Judges' oath of office.

By taking a cue from the judgment of the Supreme Court of Pakistan about 'basic features', Justice Mudholkar doubted whether the basic features of India's Constitution could be at all amended despite the provisions of Article 368.

* * *

After K. Subba Rao became the chief justice of India in 1966 (and probably because of it!) people were emboldened to file writ petitions once again challenging the validity of constitutional amendments:[140] viz., the Constitution 1st Amendment Act 1951 (which had introduced Article 31A and 31B in the Constitution), the Constitution 4th Amendment Act 1955 and the provisions of the Constitution 17th Amendment Act 1964.[141] Chief Justice Subba Rao had strong views on Fundamental Rights. He firmly believed that it was an oxymoron to say that Fundamental Rights could ever be taken away or abridged: how could anything described as 'fundamental' in the Constitution itself be ever taken away or abridged by an amendment to it? The principal writ petition filed under Article 32 was titled *Golak Nath* vs *State of Punjab*, and when presented by counsel, M. K. Nambiar, to a bench presided over by Chief Justice Subba Rao, the petition (along with several others) were straightaway admitted and referred to a larger bench of 11 justices for final disposal!

In *Golak Nath* (1967), I had the good fortune to be briefed as junior to A. K. Sen and Nani A. Palkhivala (both senior advocates), each of whom, along with senior advocate M. K. Nambiar (who made the lead argument), addressed the court at the final hearing of the case. The bench decision in *Golak Nath*[142] held that there was nothing in the Constitution that prevented the Supreme Court from departing from a previous decision of its own if it was satisfied of its error and its baneful effect on the general interest of the public. It also held (by a narrow majority of 6:5) that even an amendment of the Constitution was 'law' within the meaning of Article 13 of the Constitution, and that if a 'law', including an amendment to the Constitution, took away or abridged the rights conferred by Part III, or any part thereof, it was void under Article 13(2) of the Constitution.[143] I remember that it was Mohan Kumaramanglam, then advocate general for the state of Madras (later, he became cabinet minister in Indira Gandhi's Government) who, in the course of a powerful and somewhat intemperate address, 'warned' Chief Justice Subba Rao of 'grave consequences' if the writ petitions were allowed! I heard him say that if the provisions of the Constitution could not be amended '... it will lead to a revolution'! But Chief Justice Subba Rao took the remark in his stride, smiling nonchalantly, and shaking his head from side to side, but saying nothing! However, in his judgment he wrote:

> We have not said that the provisions of the Constitution cannot be amended but what we have said is that they cannot be amended so as to take away or abridge the fundamental rights. Nor can we appreciate the argument that all the agrarian reforms which the Parliament in power wants to effectuate cannot be brought about without amending the fundamental rights. It was exactly to prevent this attitude and to protect the rights of the people that the fundamental rights were inserted in the Constitution. If it is the duty of the Parliament to enforce the directive principles, it is equally its duty to enforce them without infringing [on] the fundamental rights.

Whilst the majority of six justices denied to Parliament the right to take away or abridge any of the Fundamental Rights in Part III of the Constitution, all the justices upheld the constitutional validity of the Constitution 1st Amendment Act 1951, the Constitution 4th Amendment Act 1955 and the Constitution 17th Amendment Act 1964, even though, according to the majority of the justices (6:5), these enactments abridged Fundamental Rights. This was because Justice Hidayatullah, who was also a party to the earlier Constitution Bench decision in *Sajjan Singh* (1965), had said that even if the court decided that the amending Acts challenged were held to be unconstitutional and void, 'we will not bring back the zamindars'. It was this sentiment that moved Chief Justice Subba Rao to formulate a new theory – a theory antithetical to the traditional Blackstonian doctrine[144] – borrowed from decisions of American courts: the 'doctrine of prospective overruling'.[145] In *Golak Nath*, Chief Justice Subba Rao, who spoke for the majority of the court, said 'that the prior operation of these constitutional amendments and its consequences could no longer be challenged on the basis of this doctrine since the earlier decisions of the Supreme Court in *Sankari Prasad* (1951) and *Sajjan Singh* (1965) had specifically upheld the validity of these amendments'.

At first, the reaction in Parliament to the majority decision in *Golak Nath* (1967) was one of stunned silence. Later, after the famous decision in the *Privy Purse* case (1970), Indira Gandhi's Government characterized it as 'infamous' when the Supreme Court in a bench decision of 11 justices struck down (10:1) as invalid a Presidential Ordinance abolishing the titles of erstwhile princes of the former Indian states together with their privy purses.[146] Mrs Gandhi advised the president (somewhat in pique) to dissolve the fourth Lok Sabha and call for elections. In the ensuing elections in March 1971, she romped back to power with a large majority. The mood of the newly constituted Parliament changed – from one of stunned silence to one of open defiance!

In a somewhat delayed response to the Supreme Court's majority decision in *Golak Nath* (1967), the newly elected Parliament passed, in quick succession, the following enactments amending the Constitution:

- The Constitution 24th Amendment Act 1971: an Act to enable Parliament in its constituent power to amend all and any part of the Constitution including the chapter relating to Fundamental Rights.
- The Constitution 25th Amendment Act 1971 introducing Article 31C: an Act to provide in the Constitution that no law giving effect to the policy of the State towards securing the principles specified in Clause (b) or Clause (c) of Article 39[147] shall be deemed to be void on the ground that it is inconsistent with or takes away or abridges any of the rights conferred by Articles 14, 19 or 31.[148]
- The Constitution 29th Amendment Act, 1972: an Act to include two State enactments in the Ninth Schedule, parts of which had been previously struck down by the High Court of Kerala and the striking down had been upheld by the Supreme Court of India.

The Supreme Court's response to this fresh crop of constitutional amendments was to refer the challenges (to it) to a bench of justices even larger than 11 judges, viz., to a bench of 13 judges! The great question before this bench was the true nature, extent and ambit of the amending power in Article 368 of the Constitution. As Justice Yeshwant V. Chandrachud said:[149]

> The largest Bench sat for the longest time[150] to decide issues of grave moment not only to the future of this country but to the future of democracy itself.

He might also have added there was that much ill-will and bickering generated amongst the 13 justices, both on and off the bench, about which one member on that bench (Justice Jaganmohan Reddy) has written in some detail, long after his retirement from the court.[151]

In the course of their separate judgments (there were eleven such judgments), ten of the justices held that *Golak Nath* (1967) was wrongly decided, since Article 13(2) did not place any limitation on the power of

Parliament to amend the Fundamental Rights under Article 368. *Golak Nath* thus stood overruled by a near unanimity of all the justices. But the 'doctrine of prospective overruling' – subsequent to *Golak Nath* – has remained part of Indian jurisprudence.[152] The judges also said that the first part of Section 3 of the Constitution (25th) Amendment Act 1971 (adding Article 31C) was valid, with a majority of seven justices (out of 13) holding that the second part of Article 31C was invalid:

> ... and no law containing a declaration that it is for giving effect to such policy shall be called in question in any Court on the ground that it does not give effect to such policy.

A summary of the judgment of the Special Bench of 13 justices in *Keshavanand Bharati* was issued after the judgment had been delivered:[153]

> The view by the majority in these writ petitions is as follows:
>
> 1. Golak Nath's case is overruled;
> 2. Art. 368 does not enable Parliament to alter the basic structure or framework of the Constitution;
> 3. The Constitution (Twenty-fourth Amendment) Act 1971 is valid;
> 4. Section 2(a) and (b) of the Constitution (Twenty-fifth Amendment) Act 1971 is valid;
> 5. The first part of Section 3 of the Constitution (Twenty-fifth Amendment) Act 1971 is valid. The second part, namely, 'and no law containing a declaration that it is for giving effect to such policy shall be called in question in any court on the ground that it does not give effect to such policy', is invalid;
> 6. The Constitution (Twenty-ninth Amendment) Act 1971 is valid.
>
> The Constitution Bench will determine the validity of the Constitution (Twenty-sixth Amendment) Act 1971 in accordance with law.

The cases are remitted to the Constitution Bench for disposal in accordance with law. There will be no order as to costs incurred up to this stage.

S. M. Sikri CJ
J. M. Shelat J
K. S. Hegde J
A. N. Grover J
P. Jaganmohan Reddy J
D. G. Palekar J
H. R. Khanna J
A. K. Mukherjea J
Y. V. Chandrachud J
Date: 24 April 1973

Two justices (Palekar and Chandrachud) who did not agree with the views of the majority of seven judges (viz., Sikri, Shelat, Grover, Hegde, Mukherjea, Reddy and Khanna) also signed the summary acknowledging that it was in fact the majority view. Justices A. N. Ray, K. K. Mathew, M. H. Beg and S. N. Dwivedi refused to put their signature to the summary – a refusal that has prompted distinguished lawyers like H. M. Seervai, and distinguished academics like Upendra Baxi, to opine that the summary did not and could not truly reflect the majority decision. But neither Ray or the other judges – Mathew, Beg and Dwivedi – said at any time after the judgment (in or out of court) as to why they did not sign the summary of conclusions, nor did they ever write or say that the summary did not accurately reflect the views of the majority! It has been stated in Justice Jaganmohan Reddy's memoirs (1999)[154] that the summary of conclusions

> … indicated that nine of them (of the 13 judges) including the two of them who did not agree with the other seven (i.e., Palekar and Chandrachud) *clearly perceived what the seven had held* [emphasis added].[155]

The 'summary of conclusions' has been regarded, in subsequent decisions of the Supreme Court of India, as embodying accurately the conclusions arrived at by the majority – as, for instance, in *Raghunath Ganpat Rao* vs *Union of India* (1993) in a five-judge bench decision – a judgment that was unanimous. The entire summary of conclusions is quoted verbatim, as accurately recording what was decided in *Keshavanand Bharati* (1973)![156]

In *Keshavanand*, six of the justices, viz., Justices Ray, Palekar, Mathew, Dwivedi, Beg and Chandrachud, held that the power of amendment of the Constitution conferred by Article 368 was wide and unfettered and that it reached every part and provision of the Constitution including the chapter on Fundamental Rights. Six others, viz., Chief Justice Sikri and Justices Shelat, Grover, Hegde, Mukherjea and Reddy, held that the power of amendment was limited, but were not all agreed as to the extent of such limitation. It could therefore be said that the court was evenly divided. The judgment that tilted the 6:6 view was the opinion of Justice H. R. Khanna – the same Justice Khanna whose portrait hangs in Court No.2, where he sat till he was superseded in January 1977 by not being appointed chief justice of India although, by convention (as the next seniormost member on the bench), he was entitled to occupy that post! That was the desire of the appointing authority, viz., the government of the day. Besides, A. N. Ray on his retirement as chief justice of India on 28 January 1977 did not recommend the name of Khanna only because of the latter's judgment delivered during the internal Emergency – in *ADM Jabalpur* vs *Shivkant Shukla* (1976) – where he alone amongst five justices on the bench refused to countenance the facile view that 'liberty was itself the gift of the law' (Ray's words) and hence could be taken away by law! Before he retired at age 65, Ray had recommended that Justice M. H. Beg (judge number 3 in the hierarchy) be appointed as chief justice – a controversial appointment; the event becoming known (unpopularly) as the 'Second Supersession'.[157]

In *Keshavanand*, when construing Article 368 (the power of amendment) Justice Khanna had clearly said:

> … although it is permissible under the power of amendment to effect changes, howsoever important, and to re-adapt the system to the requirement of changing conditions, it is not permissible to touch

the *foundations or to alter the basic institutional pattern* [emphasis added].

It was this judgment that tilted the balance against the primacy of Parliament even when that body had enacted (or amended) 'constitutional law'. In his judgment Justice Khanna had also said: 'Subject to the retention of the basic structure or framework of the Constitution, I have no doubt that the power of amendment is plenary and would include within itself the power to add, alter or repeal the various articles including those relating to fundamental rights' (AIR 1973, SC 1461, para 1445). This quote has been authoritatively regarded by the Supreme Court itself as the majority view rendered in the bench decision of 13 judges.[158]

* * *

With which judge or lawyer did the phrase 'basic structure' originate? At a function held on 14 November 1980 in Abhinav Theatre, Cultural Academy (Jammu), a few years after he demitted office, Justice H. R. Khanna was feted. A group of university students including Ghulam Mohammad Bhat (now professor), along with my own junior, Subhash Sharma, asked the great judge where he got the idea of 'basic structure'. Justice Khanna's prompt and frank reply was: 'Sajjan Singh's case.' He meant (of course) Justice J. R. Mudholkar's judgment in the 1965 decision of the Supreme Court.

Long after he had retired, Chief Justice Hidayatullah, when confronted with the doctrine of 'basic structure' evolved by the judges in *Keshavanand*, publicly said that the seed of this doctrine of basic structure was embodied in Article 32 of the Constitution.[159]

Dr Ambedkar had said much the same thing in the Constituent Assembly when the Constitution was being framed. He described Article 32 as 'the very soul of the Constitution' and the very heart of it and called it the most important Article without which 'this Constitution would be a nullity'.[160]

* * *

A great American judge once said that the power to declare the law carries with it the power, and within limits, the duty to *make* law where none exists:[161] he explained this cryptic assertion in a passage that is both eloquent and revealing (quoted in extenso in Note 162).[162]

In *Keshavanand*, in reading implied limitations in the amending power, the Supreme Court had certainly 'made' new law. The majority view (7:6) in that case was criticized as an unwarranted assertion of naked political power in the guise of judicial interpretation! Frankly, it was. It upset the balance-of-powers in the Constitution. By propounding 'the basic structure theory', the guardians *of* the Constitution (it was said) had at one bound become guardians *over* the Constitution. Constitutional adjudicators had assumed the role of constitutional governors. The criticism was valid.

After the 1971 general elections, with the Congress Party having an overwhelming majority in Parliament, we might have moved into a state of grave constitutional crisis. But then fate intervened in the form of a fortuitous event. The hand of fate even keeps a written Constitution in place! On 12 June 1975, Mrs Indira Gandhi lost the election petition filed against her by Raj Narain (who had contested against her in the 1971 elections from Rae Bareilly in Uttar Pradesh) in the Allahabad High Court. The extraordinary had happened. A prime minister in office had been unseated. Whilst her appeal in the Supreme Court was pending, on 25 June, internal Emergency (with ominous consequences) was imposed. Then, the Constitution 39th Amendment Bill 1975 was hastily drafted – by a band of lawyers, 'more loyal than the King', as the saying goes. It was, even more hastily, passed by Parliament: all in three days in August of that fateful year when Mrs Gandhi's appeal was scheduled to be heard by the court! The power to amend the Constitution was invoked virtually to strike out an item listed for hearing (on 12 August 1975) before the Supreme Court: viz., the election appeal of Mrs Gandhi. The Constitution 39th Amendment Act 1975 provided that notwithstanding any judgment or order of any court the election of a prime minister could never, and would never, be deemed to be invalid or void. The judgment (dated 12 June 1975) of Justice Jagmohan Lal Sinha of the Allahabad High Court holding Mrs Gandhi guilty of 'corrupt practice' under the election laws was attempted to be reversed by a Constitutional Amendment – in order to pre-empt the Supreme Court deciding Mrs Gandhi's election appeal! Fortunately, the court resisted this crude attempt, relying for the first time after *Keshavanand* (1973) on the basic structure theory of the Constitution. It was this decision (in *Indira Gandhi* vs *Raj Narain*, 1975) that helped to cement the 'basic structure theory'[163] and give it constitutional validity. (I believe that the theory has been kept in place by not being too often successfully invoked since then![164])

In *Indira Gandhi* vs *Raj Narain* (1975), a Constitution Bench of the Supreme Court held – under compulsion of a monstrous law – that free and fair elections were a fundamental part of the Constitution, so fundamental as to be beyond the reach of the amending power. This decision constitutes the high watermark in the assertion of the court's judicial power in the teeth of a very determined majoritarian regime. If all the pernicious clauses of the 39th Constitutional Amendment 1975 had been upheld, Indian democracy would not have survived for long. The 'basic structure theory' stresses the superiority not of the Union judiciary but of the Constitution itself. It has now come to stay, more because of political compulsions than parliamentary acquiescence. For a period of more that 35 years since March 1977, no single political party[165] in India has secured (nor does a single political party have, in the foreseeable future, the remotest prospect of securing) a two-thirds representation in Parliament!

* * *

In the March 1977 Lok Sabha elections, the Congress was voted out. In fact, even Prime Minister Indira Gandhi was defeated by her archrival Raj Narain. The Janata Government under Prime Minister Morarji Desai (which lasted from 23 March 1977 to 28 July 1979) endeavoured to recast Article 368 (the Amending Clause) and introduced in Parliament provisions for a referendum for effecting changes in what the government of the day considered to be 'basic features of the Constitution'.[166] But the 45th Constitution Amendment Bill 1978 could not secure the requisite two-thirds majority in the Rajya Sabha owing to the opposition of members belonging to the Congress (I)! Parliament would not pass an amending Bill that enumerated basic features of the Constitution, and it would not permit an amendment of the Constitution by a way of a referendum defining basic features! Besides, Parliament did not choose to re-enact afresh a Constitutional Amendment containing an ouster of the jurisdiction clause in Article 368 after an earlier attempt at such an enactment (the Constitution 42nd Amendment Act 1976) had been struck down by the court in 1980.[167] As a matter of fact, five years after the basic structure theory was first propounded in the *Fundamental Rights* case, Parliament gave implicit recognition to it in the Constitution (44th Amendment) Act 1978 by virtually declaring that the Fundamental Right of life and liberty guaranteed by Article 21 of the Constitution could not be suspended even during an emergency because the right to life and liberty was basic to the constitutional framework![168]

* * *

In July 1986, just before his premature retirement from the office of chief justice of the United States, Justice Warren Burger, during a television interview by Bill Moyers, said:

> 'Congress can review us and change us when we decide a statutory question, and frequently do. But when we decide a constitutional issue, right or wrong, that's it until we change it, or, the people change it. Don't forget that. The people made it, and the people can change it. The people could abolish the Supreme Court entirely.'
>
> 'How?' asked Bill Moyers.
>
> 'By a constitutional amendment.'[169]

He was right. If the people really willed it, they could. But no one in the United States is going to abolish the Supreme Court, and one can predict with equal confidence that judicial review over constitutional amendments will remain a vital and integral part of Indian constitutional law. Undoubtedly, primary control on governmental activity in this as in any other democratic country is with the people. The power that the Supreme Court of India exercises rests, ultimately, upon their tacit approval. But experience has taught us to take (what James Madison, the fourth president of the USA, once described as) 'auxiliary precautions'.[170]

The basic structure theory was the response of an anxious and activist court to the experience of the working of India's Constitution during the nation's first 25 years. It remains today as an 'auxiliary precaution' against the somewhat remote (though not impossible) return to majoritarian rule!

Notes and References

1. A quote from the judgment of the learned and eloquent Justice Vivian Bose (a former judge of the Supreme Court of India) reported in AIR 1956, SC 479, p. 487. 'The butcher, the baker and the candlestick maker' are remnants of an old English nursery rhyme to describe the 'man-in-the-street'.
2. Malcolm Muggeridge was the editor (from 1953 to 1957) of the English weekly *Punch* – the magazine of humour and satire – that ran almost continuously since 1841, eventually closing down in 2002!
3. Mentioned by former Chief Justice P. V. Chuckraborty in a letter dated 30 March 1976. Quoted by Dhananjay Bhat in an article entitled 'RIN Mutiny Gave a Jolt to the British', *The Tribune*, Chandigarh, Sunday, 12 February 2006 (Spectrum Supplement).
4. Objectives Resolution: See Shiva Rao: *The Framing of India's Constitution: Select Documents*, Indian Institute of Public Administration, New Delhi, 1967, pp. 3 and 4.
5. In the Preface to *The Idea of Justice*, Penguin Books, New Delhi, 2009.
6. Ryot (alternative: raiyat) is a general economic term used throughout India for peasant cultivators but with variations in different provinces. While zamindars were landlords, raiyats were tenants and cultivators, and served as hired labour. A raiyat was primarily defined as someone who had acquired a right to hold land for the purpose of cultivating it, whether alone or by members of his family, hired servants or partners.
7. *Virendra Singh and Others* vs *State of UP*, AIR 1954, SC 447, p. 454, para 34.
8. Michael Sandel: *Justice: What's the Right Thing to Do*? Farrar, Straus and Giroux, New York, 2009. Sandel has been teaching political philosophy at Harvard University since 1980.
9. In *Delhi Judicial Service* vs *State of Gujarat*, AIR 1991, SC 2176.
10. *Union Carbide Corporation* vs *Union of India*, AIR 1992, SC 248 (bench decision of five justices); affirmed in *Supreme Court Bar Association* vs *Union of India*, AIR 1998, SC 1895.
11. Wielding a straight bat as in cricket, Denning (then Lord Justice of the Court of Appeal) met the argument made by counsel in the case before him that 'no action had ever been allowed for negligent statements, and urged that

this want of authority was a reason against it being allowed now', to which Denning responded:

> This argument about the novelty of the action does not appeal to me in the least. It has been put forward in all the great cases which have been milestones of progress in our law, and it has always or nearly always, been rejected .... On the one side there were the *timorous souls* who were fearful of allowing a new cause of action. On the other side there were the bold spirits who were ready to allow it if justice so required. It was fortunate for the common law that the progressive view prevailed (*Candler* vs *Crane*, 1951, 2 KB, 164, p. 178).

But in *Candler* vs *Crane*, then Lord Justice Denning was in a minority of one. Lord Justice Cyril Asquith, speaking for the majority, said:

> I am not concerned with defending the existing state of the law or contending that it is strictly logical – it clearly is not. I am merely recording what I think it is. If this relegates me to the company of 'timorous souls', I must face that consequence with such fortitude as I can command! (Ibid., p. 195.)

12. Sir Ashutosh Mookerjee was a judge from 1904 to 1923 and the acting chief justice in 1920 for six months.
13. Initially in *A. K. Gopalan* vs *State of Madras*, AIR 1950, SC 27 (majority of 4:1): a case concerning preventive detention (provided for in Article 22). But one judge, Justice Fazl Ali, had dissented with the majority view in *A. K. Gopalan*.
14. Article 359: Suspension of the enforcement of the rights conferred by Part III during emergencies:

    > (1) Where a Proclamation of Emergency is in operation, the President may by order declare that the right to move any court for the enforcement of such of the rights conferred by Part III as may be mentioned in the order and all proceedings pending in any court for the enforcement of the rights so mentioned shall remain suspended for the period during which the Proclamation is in force or for such shorter period as may be specified in the order.

15. *ADM* (additional district magistrate) *Jabalpur* vs *Shivkant Shukla*, AIR 1976, SC 1207.
16. *Liversidge* vs *Anderson*, 1942, Appeal Cases, 206.
17. Chief Justice A. N. Ray (speaking for the majority) in *ADM Jabalpur*, AIR 1976, SC 1207, p. 1223, para 27.
18. 60 US, 393, 404-406, 419-420 (1857).
19. John Paul Stevens: *Five Chief Justices*, Little Brown and Company, New York, 2011, p. 20.
20. The majority view in *A. K. Gopalan* (1950) was overruled in *Maneka Gandhi* vs *Union of India*, AIR 1978, SC 597, p. 659, para 120: the unanimous opinion of a bench of seven justices. This view has been more recently reaffirmed by a bench of nine justices in *I. R. Coelho* vs *State of Tamil Nadu*, AIR 2007, SC 861-874 and 875, paras 58 and 59.

21. Edmund Burke (1729–97) was a renowned author, political theorist and philosopher.
22. *United States* vs *Nixon*, 418 US 683 (1974).
23. *Maneka Gandhi* vs *Union of India*, AIR 1978, SC 597.
24. Ibid., p. 659, para 120 (bench of seven justices). As mentioned in Note 20, this view has been reaffirmed by a bench of nine justices in *I. R. Coelho* vs *State of Tamil Nadu*.
25. John Paul Stevens: *Five Chief Justices*, Little Brown and Company, New York, 2011.
26. 198 US 145 (1905).
27. John Paul Stevens: *Five Chief Justices*, Little Brown and Company, New York, 2011, p. 25. Justice Stevens characterized the majority decision in *Lockner* as 'notorious'!
28. 'No State shall deprive any person of life, liberty or property without due process of law; nor deny to any person within its jurisdiction the equal protection of the law.'
29. Laurence H. Tribe: *American Constitutional Law*, Vol. I, third edition, Foundation Press, New York, 2000, pp. 1370-71.
30. Sir Hersch Lauterpacht was a scholar-judge who expanded the frontiers of law. It was he who expounded for the first time what came to be known as 'the modern view' of international law, which was that states, though primarily the subject of international law, were not exclusively so – a view that he introduced into the eighth edition of *Oppenheim's International Law* (Cambridge Univeristy Press, Cambridge, 1945), which was edited by him. [Lassa Francis Lawrence Oppenheim (1858–1919) was a respected German jurist.]
31. Sir Hersch Lauterpacht: *International Bill of the Rights of Man*, Columbia University Press, New York, 1945.
32. AIR 1952, SC 75 (decided on 11 January 1952) by a bench of seven judges (6:1).
33. AIR 1952, SC 253 (decided on 27 February 1952) by a bench of seven judges (4:3).
34. Article 14 forbade class legislation but did not forbid reasonable classification. The central test for permissible classification had to satisfy two conditions. It had to be founded on an intelligible differentia, which distinguished persons or premises that were grouped together from others left out of the groups and the differentia had to have a rational relation to the object sought to be achieved by the Act in question. A law based on a permissible classification was held to fulfil the guarantee of equal protection of the laws and was valid, whereas a law based on an impermissible classification violated the guarantee and was void. Equality is violated, it was said, by treating persons *similarly situated* differently; but they had to be 'similarly situated'.
35. *Ram Krishan Dalmia* vs *S. R. Tendolkar*, AIR 1958, SC 53: 'It is now well established that while Article 14 forbids class legislation, it does not forbid

reasonable classification for the purposes of legislation. In order, however, to pass the test of permissible classification two conditions must be fulfilled, namely (i) that the classification must be founded on an intelligible differentia which distinguishes persons or things that are grouped together from others left out of the group and (ii) that that differentia must have a rational relation to the object sought to be achieved by the statute in question. The classification may be founded on different bases, namely, geographical, or according to objects or occupations or the like. What is necessary is that there must be a nexus between the basis of classification and the object of the Act under consideration.'

36. The statement is as follows:

(a) that a law may be constitutional even though it relates to a single individual if, on account of some special circumstances or reasons applicable to him and not applicable to others, that single individual may be treated as a class by himself;
(b) that there is always a presumption in favour of the constitutionality of an enactment and the burden is upon him who attacks it to show that there has been a clear transgression of the constitutional principles;
(c) that it must be presumed that the Legislature understands and correctly appreciates the need of its own people, that its laws are directed to problems made manifest by experience and that its discriminations are based on adequate grounds;
(d) that the Legislature is free to recognize degrees of harm and may confine its restrictions to those cases where the need is deemed to be the clearest;
(e) that in order to sustain the presumption of constitutionality the Court may take into consideration maters of common knowledge, matters of common report, the history of the times and may assume every state of facts which can be conceived existing at the time of legislation; and
(f) that while good faith and knowledge of the existing conditions on the part of a Legislature are to be presumed, if there is nothing on the face of the law or the surrounding circumstances brought to the notice of the Court on which the classification may reasonably be regarded as based, the presumption of constitutionality cannot be carried to the extent of always holding that there must be some undisclosed and unknown reasons for subjecting certain individuals or corporations to hostile or discriminating legislation.

The above principles will have to be constantly borne in mind by the Court when it is called upon to adjudge the constitutionality of any particular law attacked as discriminatory and violative of the equal protection of the laws.

37. A close perusal of the decisions of the Court in which the above principles have been enunciated and applied by this Court will also show that a statute which may come up for consideration on a question of its validity under Article 14

of the Constitution may be placed in one or other of the following five classes:

(i) A statute may itself indicate the persons or things to whom its provisions are intended to apply and the basis of the classification of such persons or things may appear on the face of the statute or may be gathered from the surrounding circumstances known to or brought to the notice of the Court. In determining the validity or otherwise or such a statute the Court has to examine whether such classification is or can be reasonably regarded as based upon some differentia which distinguishes such persons or things grouped together from those left out of the group and whether such differentia has a reasonable relation to the object sought to be achieved by the statute, no matter whether the provisions of the statute are intended to apply only to a particular person or thing or only to a certain class of persons or things. Where the Court finds that the classification satisfies the tests, the Court will uphold the validity of the law, as it did in *Chiranjitlal* vs *Union of India*, AIR 1951, SC 41; *State of Bombay* vs *F. N. Balsara*, AIR 1951, SC 318; *Kedar Nath Bajoria* vs *State of West Bengal*, AIR 1953, SC 404 (I); *V. M. Syed Mohammad & Company* vs *State of Andhra Pradesh*, AIR 1954, SC 314 (J); and *Budhan Choudhry* vs *State of Bihar*, AIR 1955, SC 191.

(ii) A statute may direct its provisions against one individual person or thing or to several individual persons or things but no reasonable basis of classification may appear on the face of it or be deducible from the surrounding circumstances, or matter or common knowledge. In such a case the Court will strike down the law as an instance of naked discrimination, as it did in *Ameerunnissa Begum* vs *Mahboob Begum*, AIR 1953, SC 91 and *Ramprasad Narain Sahi* vs *State of Bihar*, AIR 1953, SC 215.

(iii) A statute may not make any classification of the persons or things for the purpose of applying its provisions but may leave it to the discretion of the Government to select and classify persons or things to whom its provisions are to apply. In determining the question of the validity or otherwise of such statute the Court will not strike down the law out of hand only because no classification appears on its face or because a discretion is given to the Government to make the selection or classification but will go on to examine and ascertain if the statute has laid down any principle or policy for the guidance of the exercise of discretion by the Government in the matter of the selection or classification. After such scrutiny the Court will strike down the statute if it does not lay down any principle or policy for guiding the exercise of discretion by the Government in the matter of selection or classification, on the ground that the statute provides for the delegation of arbitrary and uncontrolled power to the Government so as to enable it to discriminate between persons or things similarly situated and that, therefore, the discrimination is inherent in the statute itself. In such a case the Court will strike down both the law as well the executive action taken under such law, as it did in *State of West Bengal* vs *Anwar Ali Sarkar*,

AIR 1952, SC 75; *Dwarka Prasad* vs *State of Uttar Pradesh*, AIR 1954, SC 224; and *Dhirendra Kumar Mandal* vs *Superintendent and Remembrancer of Legal Affairs*, AIR 1954, SC 424.

(iv) A statute may not make a classification of the persons or things for the purpose of applying its provisions and may leave it to the discretion of the Government to select and classify the persons or things to whom its provisions are to apply but may at the same time lay down a policy or principle for the guidance or the exercise or discretion by the Government in the matter of such selection or classification; the Court will uphold the law as constitutional, as it did in *Kathi Rani Rawat* vs *State of Saurashtra*, AIR 1952, SC 123.

(v) A statute may not make a classification of the persons or things to whom [its] provisions are intended to apply and leave it to the discretion of the Government to select or classify the persons or things for applying those provisions according to the policy or the principle laid down by the statute itself for guidance of the exercise of discretion by the Government in the matter of such selection or classification. If the Government in making the selection or classification does not proceed on or follow such policy or principle, it has been held by this Court, e.g., in *Kathi Rani Rawat* vs *State of Saurashtra*, AIR 1952, SC 123, that in such a case the executive action but not the statute should be condemned as unconstitutional.

In the light of the foregoing discussions the question at once arises: In what category does the Act or the notification impugned in these appeals fall?

38. *Kangshari Haldar* vs *State of West Bengal*, AIR 1960, SC 457.
39. *Lachmandas* vs *State of Punjab*, AIR 1963, SC 222, p. 240.
40. An expression used by Justice David Brewer in the US case of *Gulf Colorado* vs *Sante Fe*, 1897, 165 US 150.
41. *Royappa* vs *State of Tamil Nadu*, AIR 1974, SC 555.
42. See H. M. Seervai: *Constitutional Law of India*, fourth edition, Universal Law Publishers, Delhi, 1996, pp. 436 ff.
43. *Maneka Gandhi* vs *Union of India*, AIR 1978, SC 597 (bench of seven judges).
44. AIR 1979, SC 478, and 1979 (1), SCC 380.
45. In re: Special Courts Bill 1979, AIR 1979, SC 478 (bench of seven judges).
46. *Express Newspapers (Pvt). Ltd* vs *Union of India*, AIR 1986, SC 872, and 1986 (1), SCC 133, p. 192.
47. AIR 1986, SC 872-907, para 71, and 1986 (1), SCC 133, para 70, p. 192 (bench of three judges).
48. See Justice K. Ramaswamy in *Delhi Transport Corporation* case (AIR 1991, SC 1001) (bench of five judges). See also Justice K. J. Shetty in *Neelima Misra* vs *H. K. Paintal*, AIR 1990, SC 1402-1411, and 1990(2), SCC 746, p. 761 (bench of two judges). However, in a Constitution Bench decision of nine judges in *I. R. Coelho*'s case, AIR 2007, SC 861, the dictum of the majority in *Maneka Gandhi's* case has been followed.

49. *State of Tamil Nadu* vs *Ananthi Ammal*, AIR 1995, SC 2114 (bench of three judges).
50. *Dr K. R. Lakshmanan* vs *State of Tamil Nadu*, AIR 1996, SC 1153, and 1996 (2), SCC 226 (bench of three judges).
51. Ibid.
52. H. M. Seervai: *Constitutional Law of India*, fourth edition, Vol. 1, Universal Law Publishers, Delhi, 1996, pp. 436-42.
53. AIR 1996, SC 1627, and 1996 (3), SCC 709 (bench of three judges).
54. *I. R. Coelho* vs *State of Tamil Nadu*, AIR 2007, SC 861, and 2007 (2), SCC 1, pp. 83-84.
55. The lecture is reported in 'Droit Public – English Style', *Public Law*, 1995, pp. 57-71.
56. OF HOW, IN THE SEVENTEENTH CENTURY, ENGLAND'S CHIEF JUSTICE (QUITE LITERALLY) KEPT HIS HEAD! On Sunday morning, 10 November 1607, there was a remarkable interview in Whitehall between Sir Edward Coke, Chief Justice of the Common Pleas, and King James I of England. We have only Coke's account of the interview and not the King's, but there is no reason to doubt its essential authenticity. The question between them was whether the King, in his own person might take what causes (or cases) he pleased. In the words of Chief Justice Coke: 'Then the King said that he thought the law was founded upon reason as well as the Judges; to which it was answered by me, that true it was that God had endowed His majesty with excellent science and great endowments of nature, but His majesty was not learned, in the laws of his realm of England, and causes which concern the life, or inheritance, or goods, or fortunes of his subjects (which) are not to be decided by *natural reason* but by the *artificial reason and judgment of law*, which law is an act which requires long study and experience before that a man can attain to the cognisance of it; and that the law was the golden metwand and measure to try the causes of the subjects; and which protected His Majesty in safety and peace: with which the King was greatly offended, and said, that then he should be under the law, which it was treason to affirm (as he said): to which I said that [Henri de] Bracton saith, *quod Rex non debt esse sub-homine sed Deo at lege*. "The King ought not to be under man, but under God and the law."' R. F. V. Heuston: *Essays in Constitutional Law*, second edition, Stevens & Sons, London, 1964, pp. 32-33. While referring to Coke's account of his interview with the King, Heuston says 'that it would be hard to find a single paragraph in which more of the essence of English constitutional law and history can be found'!
57. The Fifth Amendment provides inter alia that no person shall be deprived 'of life, liberty or property without due process of law …'
58. John E. Nowak and Ronald D. Rotunda: *Constitutional Law*, Hornbook Series, fourth edition, West Publishing Company, Eagan (Minnesota, USA), 1991, p. 340.
59. 521 US 702, 1997.
60. Quoted in Note 28 supra.

61. *Washington* vs *Glucksberg*, 521 US 702, 1997, pp. 765-66 = 138 Lawyers Edition 2d 772 (816).
62. 521 US 702, 1997, p. 764.
63. AIR 2007, SC 861, 874-875 and 2007 (2), SCC 1, pp. 83 and 84.
64. It was argued before a bench of three judges – in *State of Andhra Pradesh* vs *McDowell & Co.*, AIR 1996, SC 1627, 1641-1642 and 1996 (3), SCC 709, 738 – that the total prohibition of manufacture and production of intoxicating liquors was 'arbitrary' and the amending Act was liable to be struck down on this ground alone. But Justice Jeevan Reddy, speaking for the court, said: 'no enactment can be struck down by just saying that it is arbitrary or unreasonable. Some other constitutional infirmity has to be found before invalidating an Act. An enactment cannot be struck down on the ground that the court *thinks* it unjustified.' But this bench decision of three judges appears to run counter to two other bench decisions (also of three justices), viz., AIR 1998, SC 602, and AIR 2004, SC, p. 2371, and for this reason the question as to whether manifest arbitrariness and unreasonableness is a ground to invalidate enacted laws has been referred to a larger bench in *Subramanium Swamy* vs *Director CBI*, 2005 (2), SCC 317, p. 321, para 8 (reported in Supreme Court Cases and not in the All India Reporter Series).
65. AIR 1983, SC 473 (bench of five justices).
66. Not even whilst sitting on the bench! In *Charles Dickerson* vs *United States* (2000), Justice Scalia dissented from the opinion of the court, an opinion written by the chief justice, in which the court had concluded that *Miranda* vs *Arizona*, 521 US 702, 1997 (which held that certain warnings must be given before a suspect's statement made during custodial interrogation could be admitted in evidence) had announced a constitutional rule that even Congress could not legislatively supersede! Hence, in the opinion of the court, *Miranda* was good law and simply could not be overruled. In the dissenting opinion of Justice Scalia in *Dickerson*, he criticized Chief Justice William Rehnquist's opinion (the majority opinion) in the following words:

    > Today's judgment converts *Miranda* from a milestone of judicial overreaching into the very Cheops' Pyramid (or perhaps the Sphinx would be a better analogue) of judicial arrogance. In imposing its Court-made code upon the States, the original opinion at least *asserted* that it was demanded by the Constitution. Today's decision does not pretend that it is – and yet *still* asserts the right to impose it against the will of the people's representatives in Congress. Far from believing that *stare decisis* compels this result, I believe we cannot allow [it] to remain on the books even a celebrated decision – *especially* a celebrated decision – that has come to stand for the proposition that the Supreme Court has power to impose extraconstitutional constraints upon Congress and the States. This is not the system that was established by the Framers, or that would be established by any sane supporter of government by the people.

67. Article 33 reads as follows:

> Power of Parliament to modify the rights conferred by this Part in their application, etc.: Parliament may, by law, determine to what extent any of the rights conferred by this Part shall, in their application to,
> (a) the members of the Armed Forces; or
> (b) the members of the Forces charged with the maintenance of public order; or
> (c) persons employed in any bureau or other organization established by the State for purposes of intelligence or counterintelligence; or
> (d) persons employed in, or in connection with, the telecommunication systems set up for the purposes of any Force, bureau or organization referred to in clauses (a) to (c), be restricted or abrogated so as to ensure the proper discharge of their duties and the maintenance of discipline among them.

Article 34 reads as follows:

> Restriction on rights conferred by this part (i.e., Part III): 'Notwithstanding anything in the foregoing provisions of this Part, Parliament may by law indemnify any person in the service of the Union or of a State or any other person in respect of any act done by him in connection with the maintenance or restoration or order in any area within the territory of India where martial law was in force or validate any sentence passed, punishment inflicted, forfeiture ordered or other act done under martial law in such area.'

Article 34 is primarily concerned with granting indemnity by law in respect of acts done during periods of martial law. The Constitution does not have a provision expressly authorizing proclamation of martial law. Declaration of martial law does not ipso facto result in suspension of the writ of habeas corpus. That can only be achieved by the suspension of Article 21 (*ADM Jabalpur* vs *Shivkant Shukla*, AIR 1976, SC 1207, para 535, per Justice P. N. Bhagwati). But by the Constitution 44th Amendment Act 1978, Article 21 can no longer be suspended by a presidential order even in times of emergency.

68. Article 80(1)(b): 238 representatives and Article 80(1)(a): 12 nominated by the president. Total: 250 members in the Rajya Sabha.
69. Article 81(1)(a): 530 representatives from states. Article 81(1)(b): 20 representatives from the union territories. Article 331: two seats for Anglo-Indians. Total: 552 members in the Lok Sabha.
70. Article II: Section 1 provides that the executive power shall be vested in a president of the United States of America and Section 3 provides that the president 'shall take care that the laws be faithfully executed'.
71. In *Youngstown Sheet and Tube Company* vs *Charles Sawyer*, secretary of commerce, 343 US, 579 (1952).

72. *New York Times*, 23 April 2012.
73. AIR 1987, SC 579.
74. Lok Sabha sittings from 2000 onwards were as under: 2000 – 85 days; 2001 – 81 days; 2002 – 84 days; 2003 – 74 days; 2004 – 53 days; 2005 – 85 days; 2006 – 77 days; 2007 – 66 days; 2008 – 46 days; 2009 – 64 days; 2010 – 81 days; and 2011 – 73 days.
75. *Rai Sahib Ram Jawaya Kapur & Others* vs *State of Punjab*, AIR 1955, SC 549.
76. In the USA, a pithy and eloquent account of the doctrine of separation of powers under the US Constitution is given in Laurence H. Tribe: *The Invisible Constitution*, Oxford University Press, New York, 2008, p. 83:

    Ours is a 'government of laws, not men.' But where is that principle to be located in our constitutional canon? In the Supreme Court's landmark 1958 ruling in *Cooper* vs *Aaron* (1958), leaving no doubt that it meant to enforce the holding of *Brown* vs *Board of Education* (1954) even against recalcitrant state governors who had not been parties to the *Brown* litigation. Justice Felix Frankfurter wrote: 'From their own experience and their deep reading in history, the Founders knew that Law alone saves a society from being rent by internecine strife or ruled by mere brute power however disguised.' Justice Frankfurter then quoted from Roscoe Pound's [a leading US legal scholar] article 'The Future of Law': 'Civilization involves subjection of force to reason, and the agency of this subjection is law ...'

77. See *I. R. Coelho* vs *State of Tamil Nadu*, AIR 2007, SC 861 (bench of nine justices) and *Union of India* vs *R. Gandhi*, president, Madras Bar Association, 2010, 11 SCC, 1, pp. 38-39 (bench of five justices): citation given of Supreme Court Cases as the case is not reported in the All India Reporter Series.
78. Mehr Chand Mahajan, prior to his being one of the first judges of the Federal Court of India from October 1948, and then one of the first judges of the Supreme Court of independent India (26 January 1950), had a political past – he was prime minister of Jammu and Kashmir during the reign of Maharaja Hari Singh and during the crucial period of Indian independence (August 1947). He played a role in the accession of the maharaja of the princely state of Jammu and Kashmir to India. He had a brilliant mind and had authored many leading judgments of the Supreme Court.
79. This story was related to me by a friend, P. K. Chatterjee, senior advocate, who had practised in the Supreme Court since its inception and who was very close to Justice Bijan Kumar Mukherjea.
80. Elections: Articles 324 to 329 (Part XV).
81. Elections were held in the states of Goa, Punjab, Uttarakhand, Uttar Pradesh and Manipur.
82. The state of Uttar Pradesh then known as United Provinces.
83. Shastri was India's second prime minister (9 June 1964 to 11 January 1966), who, like Nehru, died in office.

84. 'A Blot on Democracy', an article in the editorial page of the *Hindustan Times*, Saturday, 10 March 2012.
85. Articles 148 to 151: Chapter V in Part V of the Constitution.
86. Wednesday, 29 June 2011.
87. Cassell Military Paperbacks (republished by Cassell Military, London, June 2002). John Masters was commissioned into the Gurkha Rifles on the eve of the Second World War and rose to command one of the Chindit columns fighting behind the lines against the Japanese in Burma. He left the army after the war to pursue a very profitable career as a novelist. Khushwant Singh, a renowned Indian writer, has remarked that 'while [Rudyard] Kipling understood India, John Masters understood Indians'. (John Masters, *Pilgrim Son*, G. B. Putnam and Sons, New York, 1971 edition, p. 348.)
88. Constituent Assembly Debates, Vol. 8, pp. 407-08. The Supreme Court itself has described the CAG of India as a high-ranking constitutional authority and as constitutional head of one of the most important departments of the state: *Accountant General & Another* vs *S. Doraiswamy & Others*, AIR 1981, SC 783, pp. 788-89.
89. Before being ennobled, he was plain Quintin Hogg, barrister at law.
90. *The Gazette of India* dated 8 April 2011 (Union Ministry of Law and Justice), Resolution No. 1 (42/2004): 'Joint Drafting Committee to prepare a draft of the Lokpal Bill'. Ultimately, the Bill introduced by the government in Parliament – after it underwent some changes – was passed by a majority of the members in the Lok Sabha (on 26 December 2011), but in the Rajya Sabha, the Bill was debated and then 'talked out'; the Bill now stands adjourned; in all probability, it will be taken up in the budget session of Parliament (in 2013).
91. 'The efficient secret of the English Constitution may be described as the close union, the nearly complete fusion, of the executive and legislative powers. No doubt, by the traditional theory, as it exists in all the books, the goodness of our Constitution consists in the entire separation of the legislative and executive authorities, but in truth its merit consists in their singular approximation. The connecting link is the cabinet. By that new word, we mean a committee of the legislative body selected to be the executive body. The legislature has many committees, but this (the cabinet) is its greatest.' Walter Bagehot, *The English Constitution*, D. Appleton & Company, New York, 1911 edition, p. 10.
92. So described in H. N. Pandit: *The PM's President – A New Concept on Trial*, S. Chand & Co., New Delhi, 1974, p. 3.
93. Walter Bagehot: *The English Constitution*, republished by Fontana Press, London, 1991, p. 113.
94. K. M. Munshi: *The President under the Indian Constitution*, Bharatiya Vidya Bhawan, Bombay, 1963.
95. Constituent Assembly Debates, Vol. VII, p. 1158, November 1948 to January 1949.
96. Figuratively: 'to cause trouble when none is welcome'; 'to disturb a situation that is otherwise stable and satisfactory'.

97. Minoo Masani: *Of Four Real Leaders: Some Reminiscences*, written in 1994 but only published posthumously by the Indian Committee for Cultural Freedom, Bombay, in 2011. Masani (who passed away on 27 May 1998) said about his friend and comrade:

> Some time in the late forties, I had an unpleasant argument with Jawaharlal about Stalin whom I criticized. Jawaharlal banged his breakfast table and said: 'You are perverse.' I told him that this attitude of his made personal conversation with him impossible. I did not blame him but I blamed his sycophants in Delhi. '*Panditji, Panditji, Panditji*, they have been saying to you and it is going to your head. You think you are God Almighty and I do not propose to treat you as such. You are just a nice chap so it is better we do not talk to each other privately. We shall talk to each other across the floor of Parliament.'
>
> The result was that we did not talk to each other for 15 years. Early in 1963 I visited Taiwan. On my return to India, the New China News Agency in Peking [as Beijing was then spelt] charged Nehru with sending me to Taiwan. This, of course, was not at all true. So I issued a press statement in Bombay absolving Nehru of the charge. I sent Jawaharlal a copy of my statement saying 'I have let you off the hook'.
>
> I got a very nice letter in reply asking me to see him on my return to Delhi. When I did this, Jawaharlal was having a cup of tea. 'Come and have a cup of tea with me, Masani,' he said with great charm. 'Thank you', I said, somewhat coldly. 'What's wrong with my tea?' he asked. 'Nothing', I said, 'it is not the tea I object to.' Anyway, I had a cup of tea with him and reported to him on my visit to Taiwan. Jawaharlal made a note of my report. When he asked me whether President Chiang Kai Shek referred to him, I said, yes, but that he would not like what he said. 'Never mind,' said Jawaharlal. He (Chiang Kai Shek) said: 'In spite of Nehru's base ingratitude, I have never said a bitter word against him.' Next day, when Nehru turned over my report to his officials in the Ministry of External Affairs, they told me that he had repeated this remark with a straight face I said ... I would like to take my hat off to him. He did not have to do that.
>
> In many ways, Jawaharlal was a schizophrenic. Half British gentleman, half Communist. I often reminded him of Lenin's remark – you cannot make an omelette without breaking eggs. Nehru wanted to take India to Communism by democratic methods. What a hope.

98. H. N. Pandit: *The PM's President – A New Concept on Trial*, S. Chand & Co., New Delhi, 1974, Appendix I, p. 91. See also Granville Austin: *Working a Democratic Constitution – The Indian Experience*, Oxford University Press, New Delhi, 1999, p. 21.
99. Granville Austin, op. cit., p. 25.
100. Sarvepalli Gopal: *Radhakrishnan – A Biography*, Oxford University Press, New Delhi, 1989, p. 315.

101. See C. L. Datta: *With Two Presidents*, Vikas Publishing House, New Delhi, 1971.
102. D. Sheikh Ali: *Zakir Hussain: Life and Times*, Vikas Publishing House, New Delhi, 1991, p. 291.
103. Under the President (Discharge of Functions) Act.
104. Mohammed Hidayatullah: *My Own Boswell – Memoirs*, Arnold-Heinemann, New Delhi, 1980, pp. 228-36.
105. Ibid., pp. 229-30.
106. *Shri Kirpal Singh* vs *V. V. Giri*, AIR 1970, SC 2092 (Constitution Bench).
107. *ADM Jabalpur* vs *Shivkant Shukla*, AIR 1976, SC 1207.
108. *State of Rajasthan* vs *Union of India*, AIR 1977, SC 1361 (bench of seven judges – 6:1).
109. *S. R. Bommai* vs *Union of India*, AIR 1994, SC 1918, 2072-2073 (bench of nine judges: interpreting Article 356).
110. This is an old saying, which, in a nutshell, means that if some kind of behaviour is wrong, it is wrong for both sides, not just one: In other words: 'don't do it yourself either'! (Wikipedia.)
111. Granville Austin: *Working a Democratic Constitution – The Indian Experience*, Oxford University Press, New Delhi, 1999, p. 536.
112. Ibid.
113. R. Venkataraman: *My Presidential Years*, HarperCollins India, 1994, p. 84.
114. Manohar Singh Batra: *Memoirs of Giani Zail Singh*, Har Anand Publications, New Delhi, 1997, p. 205. The author says that both Pranab Mukherjee and P. V. Narasimha Rao had agreed with Zail Singh's decision.
115. R. Venkataraman: *My Presidential Years*, HarperCollins India, New Delhi, 1994.
116. The heading in the *Times of India*, 28 March 1996 was: 'The President Sends Back Ordinances: Constitutional Propriety in Question.'
117. Granville Austin: *Working a Democratic Constitution – The Indian Experience*, Oxford University Press, New Delhi, 1999, p. 582.
118. P. M. Nair: *The Kalam Effect – My Years with the President*, HarperCollins India, New Delhi, 2008, pp. 110-13.
119. Muhammad Munir (1895–1979) was chief justice of Pakistan from 1954 to 1960. He first introduced the concept of 'the doctrine of necessity', validating the dismissal of Khwaja Nazimuddin's government by Governor-General Ghulam Mohammed in 1953. With the passage of time the 'doctrine of necessity' had been used by the superior judiciary in Pakistan to validate military coups (Wikipedia).
120. Fali S. Nariman: 'Silences in Our Constitutional Law', the First Durga Das Basu Endowment Lecture, published in *Supreme Court Cases* (journal), 2006 (2), p. 15.
121. Laurence H. Tribe: *The Invisible Constitution*, Oxford University Press, New York, 2008, p. 115.

122. In *Youngstown Sheet and Tube Company* vs *Charles Sawyer*, secretary of state for commerce – the Steel Seizure Case – 343 US 579, p. 610, 96, Lawyers Edition 1153 (1952).
123. Swaran Singh was one of India's longest serving Union cabinet ministers. In 1952 he joined the cabinet during the prime ministership of Jawaharlal Nehru and remained in successive governments as cabinet minister till 1975, when he resigned!
124. In the USA, its Supreme Court has no such power. John Jay, who served as the first chief justice of the US Supreme Court from 1789 to 1795, was one of the authors of the Federalist Papers – the pamphlets that advocated ratification of the Constitution – when they were written and that still provide guidance to judges interpreting the US Constitution. Under Jay's leadership the court rejected a request made by President George Washington that it provide the executive branch with advisory opinions about the meanings of treaties, the laws of nations and federal rules of law. 'In the Court's view, the Constitution drew lines separating the three departments of government, and that argued against having judges of the national court of last resort giving any advice to the executive. Jay's determination that advisory opinions would exceed the limits of the power to decide "cases and controversies" conferred on federal judges by Article III of the Constitution has been steadfastly followed throughout our history.' See John Paul Stevens: *Five Chiefs – A Supreme Court Memoir*, Little Brown and Company, New York, 2011, pp. 11-12.
125. 'Hot potato': A problem so controversial and sensitive that it is risky to deal with: *American Heritage Dictionary of Idioms*.
126. *Dr M. Ismail Faruqui* vs *Union of India and Others*, AIR 1995, SC 605. This case was decided by a bench of five judges comprising Chief Justice M. N. Venkatachaliah, Justice A. M. Ahmadi, Justice J. S. Verma, Justice G. N. Ray and Justice S. P. Bharucha. Justices Ahmadi and Bharucha were of the view that the entire Act (the Acquisition of Certain Area at Ayodhya Act 1993) was anti-minority and violated the secular character of the Constitution; the rest of the judges upheld its main provisions.
127. Mir Baqi Tashqandi also known as Mir Banki was a Mughal nobleman of medieval India during the reign of the first Mughal emperor, Babur. He was the governor of the then province of Awadh. In A.D. 1528, he had the Babri Mosque constructed in Ayodhya (Wikipedia).
128. Article 143: Power of President to consult Supreme Court: (1) If at any time it appears to the President that a *question of law or fact* has arisen, or is likely to arise, which is of such a nature and of such public importance that it is expedient to obtain the opinion of the Supreme Court upon it, he may refer the question to that Court for consideration and the Court may, after such hearing as it think fit, report to the President its opinion thereon.
129. The judges in the Constitution Bench comprised the following: Chief Justice M. N. Venkatachaliah and Justices A. M. Ahmadi, J. S. Verma, G. N. Ray and S. P. Bharucha.

130. *Gallie* vs *Lee*, 1969 (1), All England Reports, 1062 CA, p. 1076 (per Thomas Patrick Russell, Lord Justice).
131. A. M. Rosenthal: 'On My Mind: The World of India', *New York Times*, 1 December 1989 (quoted earlier in this chapter).
132. George F. Kennan: *American Diplomacy – World War I*, http://en.wikiquote.org/wiki/George.
133. This presumption had been statutorily enacted in the Evidence Act, 1872, Section 114: 'Court may presume existence of certain facts. The Court may presume the existence of any fact which it thinks likely to have happened [*sic*], regard being had to the Common Course of natural events, human conduct and public and private business in their relation to the facts of the particular case. The Court may presume that the common course of official business has been followed in particular cases [illustration (f) to Section 114].
134. By enacting Article 31A (saving of laws providing for acquisition of estates, etc.) and Article 31B (validating of certain Acts and Regulations): None of the Acts specified in the Ninth Schedule could be deemed ever to become void or be declared void even if inconsistent with the provisions of Part III.
135. Article 19(1)(f) was omitted for the Constitution by the Constitution 44th Amendment Act 1978 (w.e.f. 20 June 1979); Article 31 had been earlier omitted by the Constitution 25th Amendment Act 1971 (w.e.f. 20 April 1972).
136. Zamindars were typically hereditary, who held enormous tracts of land and control over the peasantry from whom they were empowered to collect taxes. The zamindari system had been operated for centuries. Before the Mughals, Indian aristocracy was used to collecting and retaining revenue from lands. The Mughals introduced a new brand of officials and courtiers (zamindars) to divert the revenue back to the imperial capital at Delhi. Under the Mughals, all categories of zamindars were required to perform various police, judicial and military duties and were, in fact, more public functionaries than revenue-collecting agents. Later, under the British, some of the formerly independent states were given the status of zamindari and some of these zamindars held titles to vast tracts of lands for which they were required to pay annual rents to the Government of British India (from Wikiepedia).
137. In *Sankari Prasad* vs *Union of India* (1951), AIR 1951, SC 458.
138. *Sajjan Singh* vs *State of Rajasthan*, AIR 1965, SC 845.
139. Mohammed Hidayatullah: *My Own Boswell – Memoirs*, Arnold-Heinemann, New Delhi, 1980, p. 214.
140. The Constitution 4th Amendment Act 1955, inter alia, extended the scope of Article 31A to 'protect' from challenge essential welfare legislation by the Centre and states against violation of Fundamental Rights (under Article 19[1][f] and Article 31); the Constitution 17th Amendment Act 1964 added 43 laws passed in different states (effectuating land reforms) in the Ninth Schedule, which in terms of Article 31B prevented such Acts from being challenged in courts for violating any of the Fundamental Rights including property rights (Article 19[1][f] and Article 31).

141. In a 2011 (posthumous) publication (of the Indian Committee for Cultural Freedom, Bombay), Minoo Masani: *Of Four Real Leaders: Some Reminiscences*, there is an interesting – and somewhat tragic – anecdote about the Constitution 17th Amendment Act 1964:

> A few weeks before he died, Jawaharlal [Nehru] moved the 17th Amendment to the Constitution which would have permitted the Government to expropriate land without compensation, from peasants who owned more than the land permitted by ceiling laws. When I demanded a division of the House before lunch break, on noticing that the Congress Party was not there in adequate numbers, the Speaker put the Amendment to the vote and declared it lost on the ground that the majority of the Members of Parliament were not present in the House at that time. Jawaharlal appeared very angry and banged his fist on the desk when he was told that I was responsible for this mishap. Rather than bow to this decision of Parliament, Jawaharlal called a special one-day session of Parliament at great cost to pass this amendment and to prove who was the boss. Well, this was not to be. The Amendment was to come up on Monday for discussion. Jawaharlal died [the previous week].

142. *Golak Nath* vs *State of Punjab*, AIR 1967, SC 1643 (decided by a bench of 11 judges).

143. Article 13: Laws inconsistent with or in derogation of the fundamental rights: (2) The State shall not make any law which takes away or abridges the rights conferred by this Part and any law made in contravention of this clause shall, to the extent of the contravention, be void.

144. The orthodox Blackstonian view (its proponent: Sir William Blackstone 1723–80) was that judges do not *make* law but only declare it. This view was criticized by later English jurists. John Austin (1790–1859) called it 'the childish fiction employed by our judges that law is not *made* by them but is a miraculous something made by nobody, existing I suppose from eternity and merely, *declared* from time to time by the judges'. John Austin: *Lectures on Jurisprudence*, Vol. II, J. Murray, London, 1885, p. 634.

145. A canon of interpretation: The basic meaning of prospective overruling is to construe an earlier decision in a way so as to suit the present-day needs, but in such a way that it does not create a binding effect upon the parties to the original case or other parties bound by the precedent. The use of this doctrine overrules an earlier laid down precedent with its effect limited to future cases and all the events that occurred before it are bound by the old precedent itself. In simpler terms, it means that the court is laying down new law for the future.

146. *Madhav Rao Scindia* vs *Union of India*, reported in AIR 1971, SC 530 (bench of 11 judges). In this case, Justice Hidayatullah wrote his last judgment before his retirement; as CJI it should have been the lead judgment. But it was not – since it was delayed, the other justices joined in agreeing with the judgment of

Justice Hidayatullah's successor, Justice J. C. Shah! In *My Own Boswell*, Justice Hidayatullah muses:

> The last case I presided over was the well-known *Privy Purse* case of the ex-Rulers of Indian States. Unfortunately I had to go away to Venice for a very important international conference. The lawyers also wanted a break and I returned to the Court after five or six days. The case went on almost to the end of my term as a judge. Shah in anticipation of the shortness of time had already prepared a judgment although I had undertaken to write the leading judgment. Learning this I prepared my own judgment in 24 hours. This was the last judgment in my career of almost 25 years as a Judge. When I described the orders of the President as 'midnight orders' some people criticised me. I was alluding to President [John] Adams' 'midnight appointments' and 'midnight judges' in the United States and the famous painting by Lisa Biganzoli, showing Adams making 'midnight appointments'.
>
> Thus ended on 16 December 1970 my career as a Judge which began on 24 June 1946. It pleases me that it is the longest in the history of Indian High Courts, the Federal Court and Supreme Court till today.

147. Article 39(b) and (c): Directive Principles of State Policy read as follows: Certain principles of policy to be followed by the State – The State shall, in particular, direct its policy towards securing:

    (a)…
    (b) That the ownership and control of the material resources of the community are so distributed as best to subserve the common good.
    (c) That the operation of the economic system does not result in the concentration of wealth and means of production to the common detriment.

148. Article 31C: Saving of laws giving effect to certain directive principles. Notwithstanding anything contained in Article 13, no law giving effect to the policy of the State towards securing the principles specified in Clause (b) or Clause (c) of Article 39 shall be deemed to be void on the ground that it is inconsistent with, or takes away or abridges, any of the rights conferred by Article 14, Article 19 or Article 31 (and no law containing a declaration that it is for giving effect to such policy shall be called in question in any court on the ground that it does not give effect to such policy: Provided that where such law is made by the Legislature of a State, the provisions of this article shall not apply thereto unless such law, having been reserved for the consideration of the President, has received his assent).

149. In *Keshavanand Bharati* vs *State of Kerala*, AIR 1973, SC 1461, pp. 2011 to 2020. The bench of 13 justices consisted of Chief Justice S. M. Sikri and Justices J. M. Shelat, K. S. Hegde, A. N. Grover, A. N. Ray, P. Jaganmohan Reddy, D. G. Palekar, H. R. Khanna, K. K. Mathew, M. H. Beg, S. N. Dwivedi, A. K. Mukherjea and Y. V. Chandrachud.

150. The case was heard from 31 October 1972 to 23 March 1973, with arguments extending over 66 days.
151. Jaganmohan Reddy: *The Judiciary I Served*, Orient Longman, New Delhi, 1999, pp. 226-34.
152. The doctrine of prospective overruling has been resorted to by the Supreme Court of India when striking down statutes that offend one or more provisions of the Constitution: e.g., the judgment of a bench of seven justices in *Synthetics and Chemicals and Others* vs *State of UP and Others*, AIR 1990, SC 1927.
153. It is reproduced in the official law report 1973 (Supp.) Supreme Court Reports, pp. 1001-02.
154. Jaganmohan Reddy: *The Judiciary I Served*, Orient Longman, New Delhi, 1999.
155. Ibid., p. 242.
156. *Raghunath Ganpat Rao* vs *Union of India*, AIR 1993, SC 1267, p. 1280.
157. The 'First Supersession' was on 25 April 1973, when A. N. Ray himself was appointed chief justice of India on the retirement of S. M. Sikri, 'superseding' Justices J. M. Shelat, K. S. Hegde and A. N. Grover who were 'senior' on the bench to him (Ray).
158. See *I. R. Coelho* vs *State of Tamil Nadu*, AIR 2007, SC 861, at 879-882 (bench of nine judges).
159. Article 32: Remedies for enforcement of rights conferred by this Part:

    (1) The right to move the Supreme Court by appropriate proceedings for the enforcement of the rights conferred by this Part is guaranteed.
    (2) The Supreme Court shall have power to issue directions or orders or writs, including writs in the nature of habeas corpus, mandamus, prohibition, quo warranto and certiorari, whichever may be appropriate, for the enforcement of any of the rights conferred by this Part.
160. Constituent Assembly Debates, Vol. 7, p. 953.
161. Benjamin N. Cardozo: 'Lecture III – The Judge as a Legislator', *The Nature of the Judicial Process*, Yale University Press, New Haven, Connecticut, USA, 1921, p. 124.
162. Ibid. 'In thus recognizing, as I do, that the power to declare the law carries with it the power, and within limits, the duty, to make law when none exists, I do not mean to range myself with the jurists who seem to hold that in reality there is no law except the decisions of the courts. I think the truth is midway between the extremes that are represented at one end by [Edward] Coke and [Matthew] Hale and [William] Blackstone [all three English judges] and at the other by such authors as [John] Austin and [T. E.] Holland and [J. C.] Gray and Jethro Brown. The theory of the older writers was that judges did not legislate at all. A pre-existing rule was there, imbedded, if concealed, in the body of the customary law. All that the judges did was to throw off the wrappings, and expose the statue to our view. Since the days of [Jeremy] Bentham and Austin [late eighteenth century to mid-nineteenth century], no one, it is believed, has accepted this theory without deduction or reserve, though even in modern decisions we find traces of its lingering influence.

'Today there is rather danger of another though an opposite error. From holding that the law is never made by judges, the votaries of the Austinian analysis have been led at times to the conclusion that it is never made by anyone else! Customs, no matter how firmly established, are not law, they say, until adopted by the courts. Even statutes are not law because the courts must fix their meaning. That is the view of Gray in his *Nature and Sources of the Law*. The true view, as I submit, is that the Law is what the Judges declare; that statutes, precedents, the opinions of learned experts, customs and morality are the sources of the Law. So, Jethro Brown, in a paper on "Law and Evolution," tells us that a statute, till construed, is not real law. It is only "ostensible" law. Real law, he says, is not found anywhere except in the judgment of a court. In that view, even past decisions are not law. The courts may overrule them. For the same reason present decisions are not law, except for the parties litigant. Men go about their business from day to day, and govern their conduct by an *ignis fatuus*. The rules to which they yield obedience are in truth not law at all. Law never is, but is always about to be. It is realized only when embodied in a judgment, and in being realized, expires. There are no such things as rules or principles: there are only isolated dooms.'

163. It was fortified by the decision of a bench of five judges in the *Minerva Mills* vs *Union of India* case (AIR 1980, SC 1789) and later by a bench of nine justices in *I. R. Coelho* vs *State of Tamil Nadu*, AIR 2007, SC 861.

164. It is only in three other cases, apart from *Indira Gandhi* vs *Raj Narain*, in which a challenge to a Constitutional Amendment on the ground of violation of the 'basic structure' has been upheld:

(a) *Minerva Mills* vs *Union of India* (AIR 1980, SC 1789), which declared that 'there shall be no limitation on the constituent power of Parliament to amend by way of addition, variation or repeal the provisions of this Constitution under this Article', and which stipulated that 'no amendment of this Constitution shall be called in question in any court on any ground'. It was unanimously held that Article 368(4) and (5) violated the basic structure of the Constitution.

(b) *Kihoto Hollohan* vs *Zachillhu and Ors* (AIR 1993, SC 412; five judges) declared para 7 of the Tenth Schedule to the Constitution added by the Constitution 52nd Amendment Act 1985 as violative of the basic structure of the Constitution. This para declared that 'notwithstanding anything in this Constitution no court shall have any jurisdiction in respect of any matter connected with the disqualification of a member of a House under this [Tenth] Schedule'.

(c) In *L. Chandrakumar* vs *Union of India* (AIR 1997, SC 1125), a bench of seven judges held unanimously that Clause 2(d) of Article 323A and Clause 3(d) of Article 323B, to the extent that they excluded the jurisdiction of the high courts and the Supreme Court under Articles 226 and 227 and Article 32 of the Constitution (in respect of decisions given by Administrative

Tribunals constituted under Article 323A), were unconstitutional since they violated the basic structure of the Constitution.

It is now well settled that only constitutional amendments can be subjected to the test of the basic feature structure: not legislative measures. Legislations (Centre or state) can be declared unconstitutional or invalid only on two grounds, viz.: (i) lack of legislative competence and (ii) violation of any fundamental right or of any provision of the Constitution: see *Union of India* vs *Madras Bar Association*, 2010 (11), SCC 1, p. 54, para 99 (bench of five judges).

165. Except for a flash in the pan – in the December 1984 elections, when the Congress won more than 400 seats in the Lok Sabha.

166. The Constitution 45th Amendment Bill 1978 (Clause 45) provided that in Article 368 of the Constitution in Clause 2 after the existing proviso, the following proviso shall be inserted:

Provided further that if such amendment –

(a) seeks to make any change which, if made, would have the effect of –
  (i) impairing the secular or democratic character of this Constitution; or
  (ii) abridging or taking away the rights of citizens under Part III; or
  (iii) prejudicing or impeding free and fair elections to the House of the People or the Legislative Assemblies of States on the basis of adult suffrage; or
  (iv) compromising the independence of the judiciary; or

(b) seeks to amend this proviso, the amendment shall also require to be approved by the people of India at a referendum under Clause (4).

167. In *Minerva Mills* vs *Union of India*, AIR 1980, SC 1789.

168. This was done by resorting to an amendment in Article 359 of the Constitution (suspension of the enforcement of the rights conferred by Part III during emergencies) to provide that Fundamental Rights under Articles 20 and 21 could never be suspended during the period of the proclamation of emergency.

169. In the course of a 11-part mini-series documentary celebrating the bicentennial of the signing of the US Constitution, Bill Moyers interviewed sitting Supreme Court justices, including Chief Justice Warren Burger.

170. James Madison, 'The Federalist No. 51', *Independent Journal*, 6 February 1788, para 4.

Chapter III

Federalism in India: 'Our Federalism'

Personally, I do not attach any importance to the label which may be attached to it – whether you call it a Federal Constitution or a Unitary Constitution or by any other name. It makes no difference so long as the Constitution serves our purpose.[1]

– Dr Rajendra Prasad, India's first and only president who was elected for two successive terms of office (1950–1962)

CHIEF MINISTER
GOVERNOR

There is no set theory of FEDERALISM. Its concept and practice vary in different democratic political systems and also within the same political system at different times. Perhaps this is why, in the USA – the world's oldest democracy – one of the associate justices of its Supreme Court (Justice Hugo Black; in office from 1937 to 1971) invariably emphasized in his judgments on federal questions that it was '*our federalism*' about which he was speaking!

Around the world, strange are the ways of federalism. In an enabling act providing for the admission of Oklahoma to statehood, the US Congress had stipulated that Guthrie would be its temporary capital until 1913. Accepting this provision, Oklahoma was admitted to the Union on an equal footing with the original states in 1907. But just three years later, the Oklahoma Legislature passed a law for the removal of the state's capital to Oklahoma City. When a suit challenging the action was instituted, courts in Oklahoma upheld the act of the State Legislature. On an appeal filed in the Supreme Court, the question raised was whether the Congress, in its acknowledged discretion to admit new states, could impose conditions that would bind the state after its admission. The majority of the justices (7:2) held it could not – that the restrictions that the Congress had placed on Oklahoma were invalid. The Supreme Court upheld the state's rights to locate its capital wherever it chose to. Although the majority of the justices could find no constitutional language imposing any check on Congressional power, they did not hesitate to read into the Constitution the unwritten understanding of state equality: 'The constitutional equality of the states is essential to the harmonious operation of the scheme upon which the Republic was organized. When that equality disappears we may remain a free people, but the Union will not be the Union of the Constitution.'[2]

US President Woodrow Wilson had written in 1911 that 'the proper balance of state and national powers in the American federal system is not a matter that can be settled "by the opinion of any one generation". Changes in the social and economic condition of the society, in the electorate's perception of issues needing to be addressed by government and in the prevailing political values, Wilson declared, required each successive generation to treat federal–state relationships as *a new question*, subject to full and searching reappraisal.[3*]

* * *

In the writing of India's Constitution, the fear of a Balkanized and fragmented subcontinent (as well as the need for a strong and united India) was 'an inarticulate major premise'. In this bulky document of governance, the word 'federal' – or any variant of it – was not even once mentioned! The framers consciously refused to adhere to any professed theory of federalism. They refashioned traditional forms of federal government by an alteration in the scheme of relations between the federal government at the Centre and its constituent units, the states: this is why Indian federalism has been popularly regarded as 'asymmetric'[4] (i.e., lacking in symmetry).

During the debates in the Constituent Assembly, Gopalaswami Ayyangar, a prominent member, had said that India faced unique problems that had not confronted other confederations elsewhere; such problems (he added) could not be solved by recourse to theory. As the draft document of governance emerged in November 1949, it visualized a new kind of federation to meet India's needs and to help solve new problems in the post-independence era.

* * *

'Federalism' in India has characteristics that are associated both with unitary and non-unitary forms of government. At the start, the Constitution proclaims that 'India, that is Bharat, shall be a union of States' (Article 1) – i.e., states and union territories specified in the First Schedule. But then, almost immediately thereafter (in Article 3), it goes on to provide that Parliament has the power, by law, to diminish the area of any state, alter its boundaries and change its name! The

---

*Read more at: http://www.answers.com/topic/federalism#ixzz27MffIdYa.

proviso to Article 3 mentions two preconditions (originally intended as safeguards):

1. that no Bill for the purpose of increasing the area of a state or diminishing its area, or altering its boundaries or altering its name could be introduced in either House of Parliament except on the recommendations of the president and
2. that the proposal contained in the Bill must first be referred by the president to the legislature of that state 'for expressing its views thereon'.

In practice, however, these preconditions have had only a prophylactic effect: references to 'the president' in our Constitution mean the president acting with the aid and advice of his/her Council of Ministers: i.e., in effect, the Central Government. The second precondition has proved to be no 'safeguard' at all – not since the Supreme Court of India held in 1960 (in *Babulal Parate's* case)[5] that the proviso to Article 3 does not require the *consent* of the state to its area being diminished or its boundaries being altered. In fact (the court went on to say), this change could be lawfully made despite the opposition of the state and its inhabitants! As now authoritatively interpreted, Article 3 stands as a textual refutation of the assumption that India's Constitution is 'federal'!

* * *

Under our constitutional scheme, there is a clear distribution of legislative and executive powers between the Union and the states, but the powers of the states are so hedged in by restrictions that they have no independent 'political sovereignty'. This was affirmed, way back in 1963, by a majority of judges (5:1) in a Constitution Bench decision of the Supreme Court (in the case of the *State of West Bengal* vs *the Union of India*):[6] the crucial question there was whether or not the Centre, in exercise of its powers of *eminent domain*,[7] could acquire properties owned by a state. Chief Justice B. P. Sinha speaking for himself and four other justices held that it could: 'It would be difficult to hold', he noted, 'that Parliament which is competent to destroy a State, is, on account of some assumption as to sovereignty of the State, incompetent effectively to acquire by legislation property owned by the State for governmental purposes.'

The dissent was by Justice K. Subba Rao, who pleaded for 'adherence to federal principles' – an appeal not heeded by any of his colleagues on the bench! According to Justice Subba Rao, the legal theory on which the Constitution was based was that *political* sovereignty lay with the people of India and *legal* sovereignty was divided between the Union and the states. He described the states as 'juristic personalities possessing properties and functioning through instrumentalities created through the Constitution' and went on to say that our Constitution had adopted a federal structure with a strong bias towards the Centre, that, under such a structure, while the Centre remains strong (to prevent the development of fissiparous tendencies), the states are made practically autonomous, within the spheres allotted to them. But over the years, Subba Rao's dissent has remained a lone voice in the judicial wilderness.

* * *

Professor K. C. Wheare, noted constitutional expert, has written:

> What makes one doubt that the Constitution of India is strictly and fully federal, however, are the powers of intervention in the affairs of the States given by the Constitution to the Central Government and Parliament.[8]

He was referring to Article 356, which finds its place in our Constitution to safeguard the oneness of India.

Article 356 provides that where the government of a state cannot be carried on in accordance with the provisions of the Constitution, the Central Government can step in, by means of a presidential proclamation, to impose what is popularly called 'president's rule'. It was meant to be used only in times of grave constitutional crises. But it was the first invocation of Article 356, in the year 1951, that set the tone for its subsequent misuse! It was Jawaharlal Nehru (India's first prime minister) who pressurized the Congress Parliamentary Board to compel Punjab Chief Minister Gopichand Bhargava to resign even though he enjoyed majority support in the State Legislature! C. Rajagopalachari, India's home minister, then glibly informed the president that:

> . . . after Bhargava resigns, no new Ministry will be constituted in the State and then the Governor *will submit a report that it is not possible to run the administration under the Constitution and the President would then have to take over the administration*!

This is the way the Article was worked in 1951, and, this is the way the Article has been frequently invoked since then – not once, not twice, but (up to the present) more than 120 times.[9]

It was only a Constitution Bench decision of the Supreme Court of India in the *Bihar Assembly Dissolution* case (2006)[10] that attempted to put an end to the unhealthy trend of the Centre calling to its aid Article 356 whenever it felt it expedient so to do! But the judgment in the *Bihar Assembly Dissolution* case was a close call, with two justices in a bench of five voting in favour of upholding Governor Buta Singh's proclamation.

The important features of Article 356 are as follows:

1. The chief executive authority of the state, the governor, owes his tenure of office solely to the Centre. Though appointed for five years, he holds office (according to Article 156) at 'the pleasure of the president': a constitutional euphemism meaning, in practice, at the pleasure of the Council of Ministers at the Centre.[11]
2. The governor (of a state) is required, by Article 163, to act in accordance with the advice given to him by the state's Council of Ministers. But, at the same time, the governor is also the 'eyes and ears' of the Centre – the Centre's representative in the state to determine whether or not the government (in the state) can or cannot function 'in accordance with the provisions of the Constitution'.
3. In case the governor is of the opinion that there is a failure of the 'constitutional machinery' in the state – an opinion, more often than not, prompted by the Centre – a report to that effect is sent directly by the governor to the president.

4. On receipt of such a report, the president, who is also required (by Article 74) to act in accordance with the aid and advice of his/her Council of Ministers, forwards it to the appropriate minister (normally, the Union home minister in the Ministry of Home Affairs). The cabinet (Council of Ministers) at the Centre (with the prime minister at its head) then takes a decision whether or not to resort to the provisions of Article 356.
5. Even if there is no report from the governor, the Centre is empowered by Article 356 to invoke president's rule in a state. ('If the President on receipt of a report from the Governor of a State *or otherwise* ...')
6. When Article 356 is invoked, the Central Government arrogates to itself in the name of the president of India all the functions of the government of the state and declares that all the legislative powers of the state would be henceforth exercisable by, and under the authority of, Parliament.

* * *

At one time, action taken under Article 356 was thought to be beyond the purview of courts.[12] But not any more. Innovative judicial power grows by what it feeds on. In December 1992, a proclamation under Article 356 of the Constitution was issued shortly after the wanton destruction of the Ramjanambhumi-Babri Masjid structure at Ayodhya. The Central Government then assumed to itself all the functions of the government of the state of Madhya Pradesh, dissolved the State Assembly and declared that the powers of the Madhya Pradesh State Legislature would be exercisable by, or under the authority of, Parliament. The proclamation was challenged in a writ petition filed in the High Court of Madhya Pradesh under Article 226 of the Constitution and was struck down by a full bench (of three judges) of that court on 2 April 1993: though in a split verdict (2:1).[13] This decision, along with decisions rendered in other like cases from other states, was taken in appeal to the Supreme Court of India.

Meanwhile, elections had been held in various states (including the state of Madhya Pradesh) and effective relief (for restoration of the dissolved State Assembly) could not be granted by the court; the appeals in the Supreme Court of India would have had to be dismissed as infructuous. But the parties in several cases (from the states of Karnataka, Madhya Pradesh, Nagaland, Himachal Pradesh and Rajasthan) requested the highest court to express its views on the important issues arising so that the principles laid down by it may serve as guidelines for the future. Accordingly, a bench of nine judges was constituted to hear all these cases – the title under which the decision in these cases have been reported is *S. R. Bommai* vs *Union of India*[14] (the lead case from the state of Karnataka). In this group of cases, the Supreme Court held that judicial review was available, but, as to the area of justiciablity, there were differences: a majority (of five justices[15]) laid down the extent of judicial review permissible in respect of proclamations issued under Article 356. Such review was limited to (i) examining whether there was any material at all for the issue of the proclamation, (ii) whether such material was relevant and (iii) whether it was tainted by mala fides or by perverse or irrational exercise of power.[16]

A majority of the justices in the nine-judge bench also held that if the proclamation was held invalid by the courts, then, notwithstanding its approval by Parliament, the status quo ante could be restored in the court's discretion: in other words, the court could lawfully revive the dissolved Legislative Assembly and bring back to power the erstwhile Council of Ministers! Whilst restoring the status quo ante, the court was also empowered to validate the president's action taken till that date and grant other necessary relief. In appropriate cases (in the interim), the court would also have the power to issue an order restraining fresh elections till the validity of the proclamation was decided finally by it (the court). However, the issuance of a proclamation, or the exercise of any power under it, could not be interdicted pending final hearing of the writ petition challenging it.

The bench of nine justices (by a majority of 7:2) then held that the presidential proclamation dissolving the Legislative Assembly of Madhya Pradesh had been wrongly struck down by the state high court (and set aside its judgment) since the satisfaction of the president in issuing the proclamation was because of violation of the secular features of Constitution, 'which itself is sufficient ground to hold that a situation has arisen in which the Government of the State concerned [Madhya

Pradesh] cannot be carried on in accordance with the provisions of the Constitution.'[17]

***

The governor of a state (except in so far as he/she is *by or under the Constitution* required to exercise his/her functions in his/her discretion) must act only with the aid and advice of his/her Council of Ministers (Article 163[1]). This had been treated as settled law way back in 1974 in a bench decision of seven judges of the Supreme Court in *Shamsher Singh.*[18] But the apex court has often looked the other way on subsequent occasions! For instance, it has permitted the governor of a state to act unilaterally as the state's 'moral custodian' even against an elected chief minister of a state – who has indulged in corrupt practices as in the case of the Maharashtra Chief Minister A. R. Antulay in the early 1980s.[19]

In a later judgment of the Constitution Bench of the Supreme Court of India (in 2004[20]) – a case arising under the Prevention of Corruption Act 1988 (which repealed and re-enacted, with some changes, the Prevention of Corruption Act 1947) – Governor Bhai Mahavir's unilateral grant of sanction for prosecution (for corruption) of two ministers of the Government of Madhya Pradesh (B. R. Yadav and Rajendra Kumar Sindi) was upheld by India's Supreme Court although the then chief minister, Digvijay Singh, along with his Council of Ministers, had expressly refused to grant sanction for their prosecution under Section 19 of the 1988 Act.[21] The reason given by the five-judge bench for its conclusion (in the case of the *MP Special Police Establishment* vs *State of Madhya Pradesh* 2004) is diametrically opposed to the law laid down in the decision of the seven-judge bench in *Shamsher Singh* (1974). In *MP Special Police Establishment* (2004), the court said:

> There are two competing orders: one of the Council of Ministers, another by the Governor, one refusing to grant sanction, another granting the same. The Council of Ministers had refused to grant sanction on the premise that there existed no material to show that Respondent 4 in each [of the] appeals (i.e., the two concerned ministers) had committed an offence of conspiracy, whereas the

> Governor in his order dated 24-09-1998 was clearly of the view that the materials did disclose their complicity ...
>
> Certainly, the Council of Ministers has to first consider grant of sanction. We also presume that a high authority like the Council of Ministers will normally act in a bona fide manner, fairly, honestly and in accordance with law. *However, on those rare occasions where on facts the bias becomes apparent and/or the decision of the Council of Ministers is shown to be irrational and based on non-consideration of relevant factors, the Governor would be right, on the facts of that case, to act in his own discretion and grant sanction.*

As a result of this decision, the contours of (state) governors' powers have been enlarged – not by statute but by judicial fiat! All in the cause of effectively combating corruption. Such transgressions of constitutional powers by the governor of a state have been *advisedly* overlooked by the Supreme Court – when allegedly 'corrupt' ministers, shielded by a chief minister, are involved!

But Rashtrapati Bhavan has not countenanced such a flexible approach to constitutional imperatives. India's head of state has acted strictly as the Constitution has directed. One of the last orders passed by President R. Venkataraman, before he demitted office on 25 July 1992, was on a petition that prayed for sanction of India's president for prosecuting a senior member of the Council of Ministers (the Union minister for human resource development, Arjun Singh) under Section 19 of the Prevention of Corruption Act 1988. In a brief communiqué, the decision of the president rejecting the petition was communicated[22] to the applicant. This is how it read:

> To
>
> Mr Kailash Joshi,
>
> Sir,
>
> *Subject: Sanction under Section 19 of the Prevention of Corruption Act, 1988, to prosecute Shri Arjun Singh, Union Minister for Human Resource Development.*

The President is not the competent authority to remove a Minister of the Union Government (without the advice of the Prime Minister) for the purpose of Section 19 of the Prevention of Corruption Act, 1988.

Sd. R. Venkataraman
President of India

Yours faithfully,
(P. Murali)

If the president of India, in his/her discretion, is not empowered by the Constitution to sanction the prosecution of a Union cabinet minister, it is difficult to comprehend how the governor (of a state), acting on his/her own, can overrule the state's chief minister and lawfully sanction the prosecution of a state minister (even for the heinous offence of corruption) in the teeth of the provisions contained in Article 163(1), although, there are some judgments that suggest that he can.[23] But in my view, this remains a grey area in our constitutional law and must await a more definitive pronouncement by India's highest court.

* * *

If the role of our constitutional court was intended to be that of a policeman in federal conflicts, the high constable of India has been far too indulgent towards the Centre and not overzealous in checking transgressions of an overactive Central Government: there exists a law enacted by Parliament known as the Commission of Inquiry Act 1952, which empowers both the Central Government and the state governments to appoint commissions of inquiry into matters of 'public importance'. For nearly 30 years, matters of public importance pertaining to the states, and falling within the executive purview of states, were dealt with by commissions of inquiry appointed by state governments, and matters of public importance pertaining to the Centre were dealt with by commissions of inquiry set up by the Central Government. But, in 1977, the past practice was reversed. Although the chief minister of the state and his colleagues forming the (state's) Council of Ministers were answerable only to the State Legislature of Karnataka – and not to Parliament or to the government at the Centre – the Government of India took it upon itself to appoint (in May 1977) a Commission of Inquiry (under the 1952 Act) to inquire into charges of corruption, nepotism and favouritism levelled against Karnataka's chief minister, Devaraj Urs, and against members of his Council of Ministers. Such a power was not specifically conferred on the Union Government by the Constitution; but the width of any power is tested only by its exercise. When exercised, it was challenged by the state government of Karnataka in a suit filed in the Supreme Court of India under Article 131 of the Constitution. Surprisingly, the challenge was negatived by a seven-judge bench of the country's highest court (6:1). Justice P. S. Kailasam alone dissented. He held that the Centre had no right to appoint a commission of inquiry to enquire into charges against state ministers, including its chief minister, since this constituted 'a grave danger of interference with the functioning of state governments'. But the plea of Justice Kailasam (like that of Justice Subba Rao 14 years before)[24] was addressed (as with all dissenting opinions) only to 'the brooding spirit of the future'.

In the instances cited, the distinct centrist slant in our federal Union has been prompted not by the plain meaning of the constitutional provisions, but by the highest court's strained interpretation of them! Under our system (as in all federal systems of government) the supremacy of the Constitution is protected by an independent judicial body (the Supreme Court) that is empowered to act as the final arbiter in a scheme of distribution of powers between the Centre and the states. There is no remedy when the highest court acts with JUSTICE (stated upfront in the Preamble) on its side even though this be in apparent disregard of constitutional provisions! At this level the plaintive query in the Latin quote, *Quis custodiet ipsos custodes*? (who will guard the guardians?), gets answered as follows: by the wisdom and good sense of the guardians themselves!

***

In the State of the Nation, these have been the emerging trends – in our federalism – since 1950.

***

In the *S. R. Bommai* case (1994), a majority in a nine-judge bench of the Supreme Court held (I believe rightly so) that *secularism* was a basic feature of our Constitution – hence unamendable by reason of the court's judicial interpretation of the amendment clause in our Constitution (Article 368). But the majority then went on to say that *federalism* too was a basic feature of the Indian Constitution. In this expression of opinion, I believe, the court went too far. It meant that there could be no amendment in the existing articles of the Constitution to disturb the type of federalism originally envisaged in it, which takes us back to the now-discredited American constitutional doctrine of 'original intent'. 'Original intent' is a theory concerning constitutional interpretation, which means that a court should determine what the authors of the text were trying to achieve and to give effect to what they originally intended to accomplish, notwithstanding an evolving change of meaning in the language of the text in later years.

The members of the Constituent Assembly, whilst finalizing the draft of our Constitution, deliberately approved of a 'hybrid' type of federalism. Professor K. C. Wheare aptly described India's Constitution, when enacted, as 'a unitary, flexible Constitution with federal features'!

But with the apex court's decision in *S. R. Bommai* (1994), what had been left flexible has now been straitjacketed by judicial fiat – in my view, an unfortunate aberration. The play-in-the-joints, so useful in every written constitution, has been constricted. But the decision in *S. R. Bommai*'s case (holding that federalism is a basic feature of our Constitution) is erroneous for yet another reason as well: because judges (or a majority of them) did not pay heed to the then-recent constitutional history.

Article 2 of the Constitution provides that any state may be admitted into the Union on such terms and conditions as Parliament thinks fit. Sikkim was admitted into the Indian Union in May 1975 by the Constitution 36th Amendment Act, as India's twenty-second state. The terms and conditions according to which Sikkim was admitted were set out in Article 371-F (also introduced by the Constitution 36th Amendment Act), which provided that 'notwithstanding anything contained in the Constitution', Parliament may, for the purpose of protecting the rights and interests of different sections of the population of Sikkim, make provision for the number of seats in the Legislative Assembly of that state, which may be filled by candidates belonging to such sections of the population as may be prescribed [Clause (f) of Article 371-F]. In pursuance of this objective, the Representation of Peoples Act 1950 was amended to provide for reservation of seats in the Legislative Assembly of Sikkim on the basis of racial and ethnic origin. Out of 32 seats, 12 were reserved for Sikkimese of Bhutia-Lepcha origin, two for the Scheduled Castes of the state and one for the Sanghas (a religious denomination to be elected by an electoral college of the Lamaic monasteries).

In *R. C. Poudyal* vs *Union of India* (1993),[25] Article 371-F was challenged in India's Supreme Court as violating the 'basic structure of the Constitution'. The questions raised before the Constitution Bench were:

1. Could Parliament, by imposing terms and conditions in exercise of its power under Article 2 of the Constitution, stipulate aspects inconsistent with the basic features of democracy?
2. Could the Constitution adopt provisions for reservation of seats in a particular state Legislative Assembly in violation of the one-person-one-vote rule deliberately introduced after independence?

On 10 February 1993, the court held (by a majority of 4:1) that special electoral laws for the new state of Sikkim were essential to maintain the delicate balance between Bhutia-Lepchas on the one hand and Sikkimese of Nepalese origin on the other, so that the social stability of the mountain-state was not affected. On the question as to whether or not seats could be reserved on a *religious basis* for the Sangha constituency, the majority was narrower (3:2). Chief Justice L. M. Sharma – expressing the minority view – unreservedly said:[26]

> It has to be remembered that if the Constitution is so interpreted as to permit, by an amendment, a seat to be reserved in the legislature for a group of religious institutions like the Buddhist monasteries,

> it will follow that such a reservation would be permissible for institutions belonging to other religions also. There will not be any justifiable reason available against a similar provision for the Christian missionary institutions in the country on the ground of their services to the cause of upliftment of Adivasis, their contribution in the field of education and their efforts for medical assistance to the underprivileged; or, for the innumerable other religious institutions of Hindus, Muslims, Sikhs and other religions providing invaluable relief to the helpless. And all this may ultimately change the very complexion of the legislatures. The effect that only one seat has been reserved today for the monasteries in Sikkim is the thin end of the wedge which has the potentiality to tear apart, in the course of time, the very foundation, upon which the democratic republic is built. *In this background the question to ask is whether all this is prohibited as being abhorrent to the basic feature of the Constitution. I have no hesitation in answering the issue in the affirmative* [emphasis added].

Justice S. C. Agrawal joined the dissenting view expressed by Chief Justice Sharma. However, the majority verdict, handed down by Justice M. N. Venkatachaliah (speaking for himself, Justice J. S. Verma and Justice Jayachandra Reddy), simply said:

> It is true that the reservation of seats of the kind and the extent brought about by the impugned provisions *may not, if applied to the existing States or the Union, pass constitutional muster* [emphasis added].

But whilst sharing Chief Justice Sharma's apprehension, the majority (with somewhat questionable reasoning) then added:

> *But* in relation to a new territory admitted to the Union, the terms and conditions are not such as to fall outside the permissible constitutional limits! (Para 129.)

The introduction of Sikkim into the Indian Union on special terms and conditions is one glaring instance of what Dr B. R. Ambedkar (in the Constituent Assembly) had called 'the flexibility of Indian federalism'.

***

What of the future of federalism in India? As I see it, Article 3 of our Constitution (the provision enabling Parliament to virtually extinguish a state without its consent) will remain – but only in theory. In practice, no Parliament of the future could risk destroying the integrity of the Union by abolishing or destroying any of the existing states. Besides, financial dependency on the Centre has been so far one of the main disincentives to the working of true federalism in India. But the situation is fast changing. Growing investment opportunities from abroad and the tapping of global markets (as recent events have shown) are not to the advantage of the Centre alone. States find that they too can directly embark on joint ventures with multinational foreign corporations and find new and much-needed resources for raising funds on their own exclusively for themselves. Greater financial independence on the part of the states will necessarily herald less political dependence on the Centre. And such a change will, in turn, get slowly reflected in the views of state representatives in Parliament. This is because India (apart from union territories, which are few) is geographically only an agglomeration of the states within it. And so, Article 3 (formation of new states and alteration of areas, boundaries or names of existing states) will, in course of time, be only a reminder of theoretical possibilities.

In *W. H. Coyle* vs *Thomas Smith*, 1911 (the case that challenged the right of the US Congress to deny equality to the new state of Oklahoma joining the union), the US Supreme Court emphasized that the constitutional equality of the states was essential for the harmonious operation of the scheme on which the Republic was organized. 'When that equality disappears,' a majority of the judges said, 'we may remain a people, but the union will not be the union of the Constitution.' This realization had dawned on the independent judicial branch of the government in the USA 135 years after gaining independence from British rule! But it was just 16 years after independence that, in the Supreme Court of India, the erstwhile champion of state rights (Justice K. Subba Rao) had expressed sentiments somewhat similar. Subba Rao was a judge who functioned ahead of his time. The majority in *State of West Bengal* vs *Union of India* (1963) did not agree with him, perhaps because India had become one nation just a little more than a decade ago! Justice Subba Rao's dissenting opinion took the long-term view and is for this reason worth quoting:

> The future stability of our vast country with its unity in diversity depends upon direct adherence [to] the federal principle, which the fathers of our Constitution have so wisely and foresightedly incorporated therein. This Court has the constitutional power and the correlative duty – difficult and delicate one – to prevent encroachment, either overtly or covertly, by the Union on State field or vice versa, and thus maintain the *balance of the federation* [emphasis added].[27]

Maintaining the balance of the federation – of 'our federalism' – is a fine and noble sentiment not so far heeded in the politics of India.

* * *

The need of the hour is new judicial thinking on the subject of Indian federalism. The concept of a strong and a united India is praiseworthy, but the union of a strong Centre and weak states has not worked as effectively as it was expected to do 60 years ago. We must realize that, in the long run, it is only strong and self-reliant states that would go to make a powerful and united India. Justice Subba Rao's emotional appeal to the 'brooding spirit' of the law might still strike a responsive call in the intelligence of a future day: if not in our own lifetime, at least in the lifetime of our children.

INDIA – the India of our dreams – will definitely someday become (in the evocative words of Article 1 of the Constitution) a real 'Union of States', not (as it is today) a mere conglomeration of territories, euphemistically described as 'states'.

Notes and References

1. Quoted in Granville Austin: *The Indian Constitution: Cornerstone of a Nation*, Oxford University Press, Bombay, 1966, p.186.
2. See *W. H. Coyle* vs *Thomas Smith*, 221 US 559 (1911), p. 580, and also Kermit L. Hall (ed.): *Oxford Companion to the Supreme Court of the United States*, Oxford University Press, New York, 1992, p. 205.
3. Quoted from by Kermit L. Hall, op. cit., p. 278.
4. See Wikipedia.
5. *Babulal Parate* vs *State of Maharashtra*, AIR 1960, SC 51.
6. *State of West Bengal* vs *Union of India*, AIR 1963, SC 1241 (bench of six judges).
7. Eminent domain is authoritatively defined (in *Black's Law Dictionary*, 9th edition, Thomson West, 2009, Eagan, Minnesota, p. 601) as: '*The inherent power of a governmental entity to take privately owned property, esp. land, and convert it to public use, subject to reasonable compensation for the taking.*'
8. K. C. Wheare: *Federal Government*, Oxford University Press, London, 1967: cited in AIR 1994, SC 1918, at 1949 to 1950 (*S. R. Bommai* vs *Union of India*).
9. A retired judge of the Supreme Court of India had noted ruefully (in his Report on Centre–State Relations: 1988) that 'despite the hopes and expectations so emphatically expressed by the framers, in the last 37 years, Article 356 had been brought into action no less than 75 times'!
10. *Rameshwar Prasad* vs *Union of India*, AIR 2006, SC 980.
11. The (Second) Commission on Centre–State Relations (the Justice M. M. Punchhi Commission) (Vol. II) recommended in its report of March 2010:

    That the phrase 'during the pleasure of the President' in Article 156(i) should be substituted by an appropriate procedure under which a Governor who is to be removed for whatever reasons is given an opportunity to defend his position and the decision is taken in a fair and dignified manner befitting a Constitutional office.

    But this recommendation has not been so far acted upon by the Central Government.
12. During the Emergency (June 1975 to March 1977), the Constitution 38th Amendment Act 1975 had expressly stipulated that all proclamations issued under Article 356 were to be beyond the scope of judicial review 'in any Court on any ground', but, by the Constitution 44th Amendment Act 1978, this constitutional impediment was removed.
13. *Sunderlal Patwa* vs *Union of India*, 1993, *Jabalpur Law Journal*, 387 (full bench).
14. AIR 1994, SC 1918 (bench of nine judges).
15. Justice S. R. Pandian (para 2), Justices P. B. Sawant and Kuldip Singh (para 153) and Justices Jeevan Reddy and S. C. Agrawal (para 435).

16. In its report the Second Commission on Centre–State Relations (the M. M. Punchhi Commission) has recommended the following guidelines –

> 11.10: Conditions for exercise of power under Article 356:
> 11.10.01: On the question of invoking Article 356 in case of failure of Constitutional machinery in States, the Commission would recommend suitable amendments to incorporate the guidelines set forth in the landmark judgment of the Supreme Court in *S. R. Bommai* vs *Union of India*, AIR 1994, SC 1918. This would remove possible misgivings in this regard on the part of States and help smoothen Centre–State relations. Of course, the proper use of Article 356 can ultimately be governed by the inherent decency and honesty of the political process.

No action has as yet been taken on the above recommendations of the Punchhi Commission.

17. See para 2, p. 1942; para 90, p. 2003; para 91 (X), p. 2004; para 199, p. 2049; and para 365 (XII), p. 2113 of the judgment of the Supreme Court reported in AIR 1994, SC 1918.
18. *Shamsher Singh* vs *State of Punjab*, AIR 1974, SC 2192.
19. *State of Maharashtra* vs *R. S. Nayak*, 1982 (2), SCC 463: a case under Section 6 of Prevention of Corruption Act 1947 in which a bench of two judges observed:

> 10: ... in the facts and circumstances of the present case, we have no doubt in our mind that when there is to be a prosecution of the Chief Minister, the Governor would, while determining whether sanction for such prosecution should be granted or not under Section 6 of the Prevention of Corruption Act, as a matter of propriety, necessarily act in his own discretion and not on the advice of the Council of Ministers.
> 11: ... we are satisfied that in deciding to sanction or not to sanction the prosecution of a Chief Minister, the Governor would act in the exercise of his discretion and not with the aid and advice of the Council of Ministers.

20. *MP Special Police Establishment* vs *State of Madhya Pradesh*, 2004 (8), SCC 788 (bench of five judges). The Second Commission on Centre–State Relations (2010) has approved of this decision: para 11.7.05 of the report (Recommendations and Conclusions).
21. Section 19: Previous sanction necessary for prosecution:

> (1) No Court shall take cognizance of an offence punishable under Sections 7, 10, 11, 13 and 15 alleged to have been committed by a public servant, except with the previous sanction
> (a) in the case of a person who is employed in connection with the affairs of the Union and is not removable from his office save by or with the sanction of the Central Government, of that Government;
> (b) in the case of a person who is employed in connection with the

affairs of a State and is not removable from his office save by or with the sanction of the State Government, of that Government;

(c) in the case of any other person, of the authority competent to remove him from his office.

(2) Where for any reason whatsoever any doubt arises as to whether the previous sanction as required under Subsection (1) should be given by the Central Government or the State Government or any other authority, such sanction shall be given by that Government or authority which would have been competent to remove the public servant from his office at the time when the offence was alleged to have been committed.

22. Letter from the president's secretary to Kailash Joshi, who had sought sanction to prosecute Arjun Singh. Kailash Joshi of the Janata Party (a political rival of Arjun Singh, a Congressman) was the chief minister of Madhya Pradesh from June 1977 to January 1978.
23. For example: *State of Maharashtra* vs *R. S. Nayak*, 1982 (2), SCC 463 and *MP Special Police Establishment* vs *State of Madhya Pradesh*, 2004 (8), SCC 788. The report of the Punchhi Commission (Centre–State Relations: Conclusions and Recommendations), para 11.7.05, states:

> On the question of granting sanction for prosecution of a State Minister in situations where the Council of Ministers advised to the contrary, the Commission would endorse the interpretation given by the Supreme Court to the effect that 'if the Cabinet decision appears to the Governor to be motivated by bias in the face of overwhelming material, the Governor would be within his rights to disregard the advice and grant sanction for prosecution'. The Commission recommends that Section 197 Criminal Procedure Code may be suitably amended to reflect the position of law in this regard.

There has been no such amendment till date of Section 197 of the Code of Criminal Procedure 1973.

24. In *State of West Bengal* vs *Union of India*, AIR 1963, SC 1241.
25. AIR 1993, SC 1804.
26. AIR 1993, SC 1804, pp. 1822-23, para 27.
27. AIR 1963, SC 1241, para 99, p. 1278.

Chapter IV

Have We Forgotten the Common Man?

If we search for the main reason why we have floundered, over the past 60-plus years, and why we have not been able to successfully work the Constitution – despite the genuine efforts of politicians, lawyers and a string of commissions and committees – it is only because we have not had the will to implement the Directive Principles of State Policy, principles declared fundamental to the governance of the country ... making of laws is not enough. Applying and enforcing laws – which is also the primary duty of the state – require a certain idealism, a certain awareness of constitutional norms, which, alas, over the years, those in governance have totally ignored.

NEWS
FINE
GREAT
VERY GOOD
PLENTY
VERY HAPPY
VERY ROSY

The most eloquent words in our Constitution are the first three, WE THE PEOPLE, which are also the opening words of the world's oldest Constitution: that of the United States of America. But what about the overwhelming majority of India's one billion plus who were not born before 1950? They were not included in WE THE PEOPLE. How are they accommodated? A shrewd Congresswoman in the United States (Barbara Jordan) answered this conundrum some years ago. With reference to the opening words of the US Constitution, she said (on 25 July 1974):

> '*We the People.*' It's a very eloquent beginning. But, when that document was completed on 17 September 1787, I was not included in that '*We the People*'. I felt somehow for many years that George Washington [the first president of the USA] and Alexander Hamilton [the first US secretary of the treasury] just left me out by mistake. But it's through the process of amendment, interpretation and Court decision[s] that I have been finally included in '*We the People*'.[1]

Nicely put. In a nutshell, it describes the role of India's Supreme Court. By judicial interpretation, the court has broadened the reach of the Constitution's provisions. It has included within the range of its beneficent provisions the millions who were not born when India got independence on 15 August 1947!

That is how our judges, present and past, have interpreted and sustained this Constitution – a Constitution framed for only about 330 million people, most of whom are not alive today! This is one of the ways in which a written constitution is made to grow into a dynamic living document.[2]

The late Ronald Dworkin, academic jurist, had a theory about the legitimacy of *judicial governance*: Present-day judges (he said), who may have had nothing to do with the written Constitution when it was framed, by reason of their position as judges have become – and must act like – *partners* with the framers of the Constitution in an ongoing project (since it is, and always will be, an *ongoing project*) to interpret a historical document in the best possible light.[3] This shows the significance of a living Constitution being interpreted by members for the time being of the country's highest court. And so, an amendable Constitution like India's must keep evolving with the experience gathered in its working.

***

'We the People' tells us at the start who this Constitution is for. But in a pluralistic society like India's – in this land of a 'million mutinies' (as the Nobel Laureate Sir V. S. Naipaul described it[4]) – *WHO* really are the people? For me, they are typified by the renowned cartoonist R. K. Laxman's endearing representative of Indian humanity: '*the common man*'! During a successful tenure as president of India (from July 1997 to July 2002), K. R. Narayanan once made a special trip to Pune (in Maharashtra) in December 2001 to unveil an 8-foot-high bronze statue extolled as the '*world's tallest metal statue of a cartoon character*'. It typifies – as no other single manifestation does – the quizzical doubts of the 'common man' for whom (we must assume) this Constitution of ours was drafted. Every generation throws up its 'common man' – a 'generation' being defined as a whole body of individuals born about the same period and spanning a period of about 30 years.

By this computation, there have been two successive generations since 1950 and, if we are to present to members of the current generation (typified by the 'common man') our document of governance, he is bound to ask (on behalf of the people he represents): '*Tell me, what has it done for us? How are we better off?*' In answer, we can perhaps point to the chapter on Fundamental Rights (Part III), which owed much to the standard-setting Charter of the United Nations (1945) and the almost contemporaneous Universal Declaration of Human Rights (1948). But it is questionable whether the chapter on Fundamental Rights has worked as effectively as was expected to.

***

In his exhilarating (50th) Hamlyn Lecture, the Right Honourable Lord Justice Stephen Sedley[5] reminded his audience that the *rule of law*, of which we speak so glibly, is a necessary but not a sufficient condition for a decent society. The proposition that the rule of law is an unqualified good has to be examined in the light of modern experience of regimes that function strictly *according to law*, i.e., without arbitrariness, but whose very laws are discriminatory and oppressive! There is more to a decent society than the rule of law. Judicial enforcement of rights by courts of law does not necessarily guarantee public understanding and support for those rights. Such understanding or awareness needs to be inculcated, which can only be achieved through meaningful *education*.

* * *

We are living in an age marked by an all-pervading 'rights culture'. The experience of 60-plus years of working a written Constitution has shown that a rights culture generates greater dissatisfaction amongst persons propounding different sets of rights. For instance, how far does the right 'to profess, practise and propagate one's religion' (guaranteed by Article 25) extend?[6] Do Christians have a fundamental right to convert to Christianity persons professing another faith, or persons having no faith at all? And do Hindu religious bodies have a right to object? This controversy has caused much disquiet and soul-searching in recent times. Christian minorities feel threatened. Hindus, in turn, resent what they believe to be an assault on their age-old culture. Too much of an emphasis on *rights* serves only to divide and fragment society, apart from spreading discontent. We have somehow forgotten our heritage of accommodation and tolerance. We have completely overlooked the word FRATERNITY in the Constitution's Preamble. It is time we remembered.

A year after Jawaharlal Nehru wrote *Discovery of India* (1946), the first Human Rights Commission of the UN carried out an inquiry into the theoretical problems raised by a Universal Declaration of Human Rights. A questionnaire was circulated to various thinkers and writers of member-states of UNESCO (the United Nations Educational, Scientific and Cultural Organization) about ideas for a declaration of human rights.

They were asked, as individual experts, to give their views. One of the chosen experts was Mohandas Karamchand Gandhi, who responded in a letter, written in a moving train – those were troublesome times when the Mahatma was constantly on the move! The following is an excerpt from the letter:

> 25 May 1947
>
> Dear Dr Julian Huxley,
>
> ... I learnt from my illiterate but wise mother that all rights to be deserved and preserved came from duty well done. The very right to live accrues to us only when we do the duty of citizenship of the world. From this one fundamental statement, perhaps it is easy enough to define the duties of Men and Women and correlate every right to some corresponding duty to be *first* performed. Every other right can be shown to be a usurpation hardly worth fighting for.[7]
>
> Yours sincerely,
>
> M. K. Gandhi
>
> Dr Julian S. Huxley,
> Director-General, UNESCO,
> Paris

When we gave ourselves a Constitution, it was certainly good to provide for rights enforceable *against* the state and state agencies. But I believe that it would have made a difference to our attitudes and our national consciousness if we had also stressed the duties and responsibilities of one citizen towards another. The subsequent inclusion of Part IVA in the Constitution of (the chapter on fundamental duties)[8] has not inspired much enthusiasm amongst India's citizenry – simply because this part was added during the (unpopular) period of the internal Emergency (June 1975 to March 1977).

* * *

Every Constitution must have an ideal and a purpose, and the more I get acquainted with India's, the longest in the world, the more I believe that its heart is in Part IV (Directive Principles of State Policy).

If we search for the main reason why we have floundered, over the past 60-plus years, and why we have not been able to successfully work the Constitution – despite the genuine efforts of governments, politicians and a string of commissions and committees – it is only because we have not had the will to implement the Directive Principles of State Policy, principles declared fundamental to the governance of the country. The Constitution, having imposed a duty on the state to apply these principles in making laws, has also said that the provisions contained in Part IV 'shall not be enforceable by any court' (Article 37).[9]

In the course of the debates in the Constituent Assembly, Dr B. R. Ambedkar had explained the true purpose of the Directive Principles:

> The Directive Principles are like the Instruments of Instructions which were issued to the Governor-General and the Governors of Colonies by the British Government under the Government of India Act 1935. *What is called 'Directive Principles' is merely another name for the Instruments of Instructions.* The only difference is that they are instructions to the legislature and the executive. Whoever captures power will not be free to do what he likes with it. In the exercise of it he will have to respect these instruments of instructions which are called Directive Principles.[10]

The sanction behind these directives was political, not juridical:[11] 'If any Government ignores them' [Dr Ambedkar had said] 'they will certainly have to answer for them before the electorate at election time.'[12] But, alas, it has not worked out that way.

* * *

The framers of the Constitution had not foreseen the proactive or hyperactive judiciary that we have today: a judiciary that tells the government when and how to distribute excess food; what crops to grow and what not to grow; which economic projects are good for the country and which are not; what fuel should be used in the engines of our vehicles; and whether 2G/3G (second generation/third generation) spectrum licences should be allotted only through auctions! If the founding fathers had envisaged this state of affairs, I believe that they would have made the provisions of Part IV enforceable by courts! However, as the role of the judiciary was perceived in the late 1940s and 1950s, these Directive Principles were not conceived to be juridically enforceable. They were looked upon as homilies, and, consequently, ignored by successive governments both at the Centre and in the states! The legislative and executive wings of state – the elected representatives of the people – were exhorted to, and were therefore expected to, provide for the welfare of the people. They have failed miserably, not because our laws (both Central and state) do not take into account the provisions of Part IV of the Constitution, but simply because making of laws is not enough. Applying and enforcing laws – which is also the primary duty of the state – requires a certain idealism, a certain awareness of constitutional norms, which, alas, over the years, those in governance have totally ignored.

To me, it is a matter of regret that our Constitution, which borrowed from a host of written documents from around the world, did not choose to pick out the most evocative words in that democratic exemplar of modern times – the Declaration of Independence adopted by the American colonies in the year 1776. Its material part reads:

> We hold these truths to be self-evident, that all men are created equal, that they are endowed by their Creator with certain unalienable Rights, that among these are Life, Liberty *and the pursuit of Happiness* … [emphasis added].

* * *

The framers of our Constitution knew that giving freedom and rights to the people without the wherewithal for exercising them was meaningless. Hence, they made provision, for instance, in Article 45 that: 'The state shall endeavour to provide *within a period of 10 years from the commencement of this Constitution* [emphasis added] free and compulsory education for all children until they complete the age of 14 years.' But this Article now stands truncated. More than 50 years after the Constitution was enacted, Parliament passed, at the instance of the government in power, the Constitution 86th Amendment Act 2002 by which the original Article 45 was substituted. It now reads:

> Article 45: The State shall *endeavour* to provide early childhood care and education for all children until they complete the age of six years.

A new Article 21A was also inserted in the Fundamental Rights chapter, which read:

> The State shall provide free and compulsory education to all children of the age of six to fourteen years *in such manner as the State may, by law, determine* [emphasis added].[13]

With this new constitutional provision, the clock has been effectively put back in time. A Constitution Bench of the Supreme Court had already held as far back as 1993 (in *Unnikrishnan* vs *the State of Andhra Pradesh*[14]) that since the framers of the Constitution had mentioned a specific time limit in the original Article 45, which had long since expired, the aspiration mentioned in Article 45 had already matured into a Fundamental Right! This significant part of the decision was overlooked by the government when it introduced the Constitution 86th Amendment Bill, and also by the Parliament that passed it!

If several post-Second World War democracies have gone to seed – replaced either by dictatorships or anarchy – the reason has been that when giving themselves freedom, they neglected to educate themselves! The lack of education lies at the root of all problems – the problems of poverty, of overpopulation, and of the intolerance that is tearing apart the fabric of our society.

The particular Article in Part IV – fundamental to the governance of the country – which mentioned a time limit was (the original) Article 45. The Constitution contemplated a crash programme being undertaken by the states to achieve the goal set out in Article 45 within 10 years, and unlike matters of higher education mentioned in Article 41, it was not subject to the limits of the states' economic capacity and development.

In the USA, in his celebrated decision in *Brown* vs *the Board of Education* (1954),[15] Chief Justice Earl Warren emphasized the importance of education in society:

> Today, education is perhaps the most important function of state and local governments .... It is required in the performance of our most basic responsibilities, even service in the armed forces. It is the very foundation of good citizenship. Today, it is the principal instrument in awakening the child to cultural values, in preparing him for later professional training, and in helping him to adjust normally to his environment. In these days, it is doubtful if any child may reasonably be expected to succeed in life if he is denied the opportunity of an education.

Words of wisdom by one of the great chief justices of modern times, who (incidentally) also believed that important constitutional decisions must be 'unanimous, short, readable by the lay public, non-rhetorical, unemotional and above all non-accusatory ....' Useful advice to justices in India and around the world!

* * *

According to the UNDP (United Nations Development Programme) Human Development Report 2002, India has a very high 'polity score',[16] i.e., '*institutional factors necessary for democracy*' (one of the subjective indicators of governance) – a plus nine in the range of minus ten to plus ten! And yet, as revealed in the later UNDP Report of 2010,[17] expenditure in India on public education as a percentage of the GNP has remained abysmally low. During the entire period from 1985–87 to 1995–97, and again from 2000 to 2002, it was only 3.2 per cent! Underdeveloped countries, such as Swaziland and Botswana, have been spending between 7 and 8 per cent of their GNP on education! India's overall ranking in human development based on 'subjective indicators of governance' stood at 124.[18] In 2011,[19] it had plummeted to 134! India has not been ranked either 'high' or 'very high' in human development: just 'medium'.

Besides, as the Report of the Education Commission 1996 records, educational development in India 'has been benefiting the "haves" more than the "have-nots"', which is a negation of social justice; we are spending increasingly lesser amounts on primary education and increasingly larger amounts on secondary and tertiary education.

In 1992, the Supreme Court of India observed in *Mohini Jain* vs *State of Karnataka* (1992)[20] – reiterated later in *Unnikrishnan* vs *the State of Andhra Pradesh* (1993)[21] – that without primary education being provided to the citizens of this country the objectives set forth in the Preamble to the Constitution would not be achieved. 'The Constitution would fail', the court had warned. But the dire warning has fallen on deaf ears.

When a vast range of Christian and other missionary schools – private institutions set up in various parts of the country – have been striving to ensure good primary education, many states have adopted a policy of hounding out these missionaries without substituting anything worthwhile in their place. In fact, the Ramakrishna Mission has shown the way. It too has established many missionary schools in the hope that children who study in them would become good Hindus (and therefore good Indians) – which has stimulated to some extent the spread of primary education.

***

The reason for the emphasis on Directive Principles of State Policy is because international trends point in the same direction. Many of the provisions of the International Covenant on Economic, Social and Cultural Rights (ICESCR), 1966 (to which India is a party), are similar to the Directive Principles of State Policy in Part IV of the Constitution of India. In 2001, Mary Robinson, then UN high commissioner for human rights (who specially flew in to India to attend a one-day workshop for judges on the Justiciability of Economic, Social and Cultural Rights in South Asia), said:

> The topic of this workshop is well framed. It does not refer to '*whether*' economic, social and cultural rights are justiciable. Instead the focus is on how best to address them within the justice system.

> The practical perspective finally puts aside the jaded debate as to whether these rights can be considered as 'rights' at all. Similarly, it goes beyond the mistaken and anachronistic discussion as to whether economic, social and cultural rights are of equal standing with civil and political rights.
>
> That we can take this approach is, in no small measure, thanks to the pioneering work of the judiciary over a number of years. Today, I express deep appreciation of these judges and [of] advocates who have argued before them. I am particularly pleased to be able to do so here in South Asia. For there can be no doubt that, in the field of economic and social rights, it is here in this subregion that the most significant advances have been made and key precedents established. It is my hope that this workshop may harvest achievements, with a view to sharing the experience with the justice system of other Asia-Pacific subregions and indeed globally.[22]

If there is one single aspect in which governments can be more popular with the people – not populist, but popular – it is by speedily implementing programmes of primary education and by refraining from interfering with the work of missionary schools – whether Christian, Muslim, Buddhist, Hindu or any other institution – *that provide primary secular education.*

The international community has responded to the need and importance of the right to education, as emphasized in Article 13 of the ICESCR.[23] The general comments of the UN Committee on Economic, Social and Cultural Rights on this Article during its meeting in Geneva (November-December 1999) are now quoted:

> Education is both a human right in itself and an indispensable means of realizing other human rights. As an empowerment right, education is the primary vehicle by which economically and socially marginalized adults and children can lift themselves out of poverty and obtain the means to participate fully in their communities. Education has a vital role in empowering women, safeguarding children from exploitative and hazardous labour and sexual

> exploitation, promoting human rights and democracy, protecting the environment, and controlling population growth. Increasingly, education is recognized as one of the best financial investments [the] State can make. *But the importance of education is not just practical: a well-educated, enlightened and active mind, able to wander freely and widely, is one of the joys and rewards of human existence* [emphasis added].[24]

In other words, education contributes a great deal to the pursuit of happiness!

***

At defining moments of history – by events seared in human memory (e.g., '9/11' in the US, with its subsequent repercussions in the Indian subcontinent as well) – the role of economic, social and cultural rights becomes critical. Critical – as brought out in one of the masterpieces in the English language *A Christmas Carol* by Charles Dickens. In this story, the ghost of Christmas reveals the faces of two emaciated children and describes them as follows:

> This boy is ignorance, this girl is want: look upon them and beware of them both. Because on their brow is written: Doom – unless the writing is erased.

Ignorance and want spell doom. They are fertile breeding ground for terrorists, and we must strive, as Dickens said, to ensure that 'the writing is erased'. One of the ways to do this is for judges and lawyers around the world to comprehend the vital significance of economic, social and cultural rights as given in UN Instruments and in our own Constitution.

Remember there are vast areas of uncharted ignorance amongst judges and lawyers – even in the West. In her foreword to a book published by the Oxford University Press in 1995 (and titled *The International Covenant on Civil and Political Rights and United Kingdom Law*) Justice Rosalyn Higgins, the judge from the UK in the International Court of Justice (from 1995 to 2009), had this to say:

> Even those judges who are now publicly calling for the incorporation of the European Convention know virtually nothing of the Economic and Social Covenant. They are surprised when one tells them that there is another unincorporated human rights treaty that they might like to be thinking about at the same time. What is it, they say, and where do I find a copy?

The book then goes on to point out that in the teaching of human rights in England, students of law and even legal practitioners are blissfully unaware of international human rights instruments – illustrative of the humbling experience of Dr Samuel Johnson, the great lexicographer. When he was asked by an inquisitive lady why he defined the word 'pastern' in his dictionary as 'the knee of a horse', he confessed: 'Ignorance madam, pure ignorance!'

* * *

Ultimately, in a vast, motley nation like India, despite declaration of guarantees of Fundamental Rights, only such beliefs can be accommodated and protected in society that do not conflict with strong sentiments of the vast majority of people. An illustrative case in point is the frustration of a decree of the Supreme Court of India (upholding the Fundamental Right of freedom of conscience of a very small minority group) on account of its unpopularity with a large cross-section of general public opinion. The case (decided in 1987) concerned the adherents of a minuscule sect of Christians known as Jehovah's Witnesses.[25]

They number a few thousand and live mostly in Kerala. Their children used to attend public schools in the state. In one such school, India's national anthem ('*Jana Gana Mana …*') was regularly sung during the daily assembly. Children belonging to this particular Christian sect stood up respectfully but refused to sing, not because they were opposed to the words or thoughts expressed in the national anthem, but because of the tenets of their religious faith. No one considered this act disrespectful. There was no problem until July 1985, when a member of the Legislative Assembly of Kerala, on an inspection of the particular public school, noticed that three children (whose parents were Jehovah's Witnesses) did not sing the national anthem at the morning assembly. He felt that this act was unpatriotic. He raised a question in the Kerala Assembly. A commission of inquiry was appointed. It reported that the children were law abiding, showed no disrespect to the national anthem and stood in respectful silence when it was sung, *but they did not sing*. On the instructions of the inspector of schools, the three children were expelled.

A writ petition was filed in the High Court of Kerala seeking a prohibitory order against the authorities preventing the children from attending the school. The high court rejected the plea. I was consulted. We took an appeal to the Supreme Court of India, which reversed the verdict of the high court and held that the children did not join the singing of the national anthem in the morning assembly because of their conscientiously held religious faith, which did not permit them to join in any rituals, except prayers to Jehovah. The apex court noted: 'Jehovah's Witnesses, wherever they are, do hold religious beliefs which may appear strange, even bizarre to us, but the sincerity of their beliefs is beyond question.' The court held that the expulsion violated the Fundamental Right of freedom of conscience guaranteed in Article 25(1) of the Constitution of India. At the end of their judgment, the justices eloquently remarked:

> We only wish to add: our tradition teaches tolerance; our philosophy preaches tolerance; our Constitution practises tolerance; let us not dilute it.

The Supreme Court then directed the authorities to readmit the children to the school and permit them to pursue their studies without insisting on their singing in the morning assembly.

But the public ('We the People') would have none of it. Tolerance in the face of 'unpatriotic' behaviour? Never. The then prime minister (Rajiv Gandhi) expressed shock and amazement at the decision. The then speaker of the Lok Sabha (Balram Jakhar) said he could not understand how anyone who called himself an Indian could refuse to sing the national anthem. There were murmurs of 'treason'. The then attorney general of India (K. Parasaran) petitioned the Supreme Court of India to review the judgment. The review petition was (at first) admitted though, ultimately, the judgment was not reviewed or recalled.[26]

Justice O. Chinnappa Reddy, who spoke for the bench (that directed that the children of Jehovah's Witnesses be readmitted to the school from which they were expelled) was castigated by a high-ranking leader of the ruling Congress Party (Mohammed Yunus) as having forfeited his right to be called 'either an Indian or a judge'! A contempt petition filed by a spirited citizen against Mohammed Yunus was dismissed by a bench of three judges (companion justices of Justice O. Chinnappa Reddy) on the specious ground that the consent of the attorney general of India (required under Section 15 of the Contempt of Courts Act 1961) was not taken. This bench of three judges refused to take *suo motu* cognizance against the contemnor – which the law empowered them to do – *Conscientious Group* vs *Mohammed Yunus*, 1987 (3), SCC 89: a case (amongst many) illustrative of the tendency of (some) judges who profess too much, but do too little!

The judgment, in *Bijoe Emmanuel* (1987) though correct in law, was unacceptable to a large majority of so-called 'right-thinking' people. The result was that despite the verdict of the highest court, the children would not be admitted to any school in Kerala. Unpopular beliefs evoke a great deal of resentment. Jehovah's Witnesses had won their constitutional case in the Supreme Court, but lost their constitutional right, which the decision in the case had affirmed!

It is not a comforting thought, yet it is true that, in the end, in a pluralist society, no matter what the law or the Constitution says or how it is interpreted, it is only '*as good as it works*'.

***

Our Constitution did work and worked well for the first 20 years after independence. In Granville Austin's book *Working a Democratic Constitution – The Indian Experience* (Oxford University Press, New Delhi, 1999, p. 173), the opening paragraph reads:

> The early hours of 11 January 1966 brought India two ends and a beginning. The life of Jawaharlal Nehru's successor, Prime Minister Lal Bahadur Shastri, ended that morning in Tashkent [then in the Soviet Union], where he had gone to sign an agreement with Pakistan ending the previous year's war between the two countries.

Shastri's death also ended the Nehru years, for he had led the country in the Nehru tradition even while being his own man as Prime Minister. A new era, one that would be marked by confrontation over institutional and personal power, began with the arrival in the Prime Minister's office of Nehru's daughter, Mrs Indira Gandhi.

Thereafter, in 1969 the old Congress Party, which had led the country to independence, split down the middle between supporters of Indira Gandhi (Congress R)[27] and supporters of her opponents led by Morarji Desai (Congress O).[28] Post-1969 politics became immoral and unprincipled, and has so remained. We cannot make the parliamentary system work; we cannot make any system of government work, unless we reinject some degree of idealism and morality into politics!

* * *

Many years ago (19 November 1990) the prestigious British weekly, *The Economist*, expressed an opinion (which was both frank and brutal) and to which (I am convinced) we must all pay heed: 'India will continue to be misgoverned until politics becomes more of a vehicle for policies instead of the other way round' – that is, instead of policies being fashioned to suit the politics of the day!

To govern this country well, we must recognize (and then attempt to overcome) certain problems that hinder good government:

The *first* problem with governing India begins with numbers and the immense pressure they exert on national resources. We are just too many to be governed *with equality and justice to all*. Politicians have not dared to address themselves to this 'mother-of-all-problems(!)', particularly after the nightmare of forced sterilizations during the internal Emergency era (June 1975 to March 1977). It was one of the major factors that led to the resounding defeat of the single-party Congress Government (led by Indira Gandhi) in the general elections of March 1977.

And yet, even into the late 1980s, governments at the Centre kept urging citizens to embrace 'population control' as a panacea for economic hardships, though with somewhat diminishing fervour! And then in the 1990s, government policies changed. The new mantra now was that growth in population was a 'good thing'. That it meant a larger workforce, which, in turn, would drive economic growth to new heights. And (for once) the government appeared to be right – or so it seemed. The Indian economy grew from 6 per cent per annum in the early years of the first decade of the twenty-first century to 8 per cent in 2009. Members of Parliament, and public officials, returning from trips abroad (mostly sponsored!), spoke ecstatically about *the inevitable wonders of the demographic dividend*. 'See how China has prospered with its burgeoning population' was the refrain. But in the first half of 2012, we appear to have been halted and put back to where we started – to be content (at least in 2012 and in 2013) with a growth rate of no more than 6 per cent. In his most recent book, author Ruchir Sharma is more pessimistic. He predicts that India will, sooner rather than later, rediscover the menace of the 'population-bomb'.[29] I believe that his prediction is 'spot-on'!

The *second* problem stems from our failure to learn from the legacies of our political past. The British built for themselves a 'wall' that separated those who governed from those who were governed. After they left, we kept this 'wall' intact but discarded the idealism that had inspired generations of public officials in British India. Ministers and public servants in British India, as a class, were not dishonest. But more than 60 years after independence, we cannot say the same. There are two types of corruption. The first relates to secret isolated instances. They happen everywhere; they are endemic. They take place without infecting the body politic. The other type – known as tidal corruption – is what has now engulfed us. It floods the entire state apparatus including those at the centre of power. I cannot visualize an era of good government in India until we take emergent steps to exorcise graft and corruption from public life at all levels.

The *third* problem arises when it is widely believed that the leaders and officials (or a majority of them) are corrupt. Such a belief devalues and debases the people as well. In fact, actions of governments have an ever-widening ripple effect on the general social milieu of the time. In our country, those in positions of power are looked up to – indeed fawned upon – as 'great'. The Bhagvad Gita says that whatsoever a great man does that very thing other men also do; whatever standard he sets up, the majority of human beings follow the same. Our Constitution starts with the hallowed words: 'WE THE PEOPLE.' *We the People* learn by the actions of our leaders, not by the precepts they hypocritically profess and proclaim!

The *fourth* problem is that constitutional functionaries fail to function in the manner they are expected to, especially when times are bad. In India, politics begets power, but the men and women in power assume that they owe no responsibility to the people who elected them till election time comes around once again! The connivance in, and the acceptance of, the internal Emergency imposed on 25 June 1975 by constitutional functionaries in high places can only be explained on this basis. They may be forgiven, but the lesson they have taught us must never be forgotten.

The *fifth* problem is the crisis of competence. Those who propagate a presidential form of government for India – and I don't doubt their bona fides – sometimes speak glowingly of the American system and its form of government. They would be disillusioned when they read Irving Stone's *They Also Ran*,[30] the incisive story of the men who were defeated in their contest for the US presidency. In the nineteenth century, the United States was still a developing country – like India is today. In 1872, an outstanding journalist, Horace Greeley, stood against Ulysses Grant for president. He was defeated. Grant romped home to victory with a margin of one million votes. History records that President Grant's innocence of the nature of American government was as astounding as his ineptitude! On his induction to the highest office, he loaded government payrolls with so many relatives that a wag observed that he had never seen anyone getting in the family way so fast! But his relatives were his best appointments. His friends turned out to be 'the worst set of rascals the country had yet experienced'. Even in the 1920s, when America had matured and become a rich nation, presidential elections did not necessarily help to put the right man at the top. James Middleton Cox was a case in point – believed to be one of the clearest cases in all American history of the best man having been defeated. When Cox was asked what he thought to be the most important quality in a president, he replied: 'The power to take a situation by the nape of the neck and the seat of the trousers and shake a result out of it.' But Cox was soundly defeated by Warren Harding in the 1920 presidential election. Irving Stone says that if the United States had been on a treasure hunt to find the worst possible candidate for the presidency, it is hardly conceivable that they could have done better than the Republican Harding. Harding broke all laws that interfered with his pleasures, and made a mockery of government agencies by selling pardons and concessions. Even the Republicans held their noses at the stench of (what was called) 'the debris of decency of the Harding Administration'! At the half-way mark of American presidential history (ending with the First World War), Irving Stone says that the box score was astonishingly poor. Mediocre weaklings got elected as president whilst many brilliant men lost. Things improved after the 1920s – FDR (Franklin Delano Roosevelt) brought up the average, as no one else had. But despite the glorious years of the Roosevelt presidency (1933–45), students of American politics have come up with statistics that show that in the fifty-odd presidential elections since 1788, the American electorate has rejected good and superior men 50 per cent of the time! Not a very flattering score for the presidential system of government in the world's oldest democracy!

***

In India, every election after 1951 has thrown up increasingly less proficient (and less scrupulous) men and women. The downward trend is not only noticeable but it is also very significant. It points not to the inadequacy of the parliamentary system of government but to the crying need for reforms in the electoral process. Successive political parties have come to power with promises to reform the electoral system but they have just remained promises. So long as a politician is voted to power by employing corrupt means, he (or she) will remain in power with like methods. It should not be forgotten that citizens have a vital stake in the reformation of the electoral system. There is no dearth of solutions; only a lack of the will to adopt them.

The *sixth* problem is that in the euphoria created by India's economic progress and recognition as a world power, post-1991, those in governance have omitted to notice that, whereas current policies have certainly made the affluent richer and more prosperous, a very large majority of India's populace is still struggling to keep body and soul together, often without much success. The great divide is getting wider. In April 2011, a bench of the Supreme Court of India (Justices Dalveer

Bhandari and Deepak Verma), whilst hearing a case relating to acute malnutrition amongst the poor and needy, said in open court:

> We cannot have two Indias. You want the world to believe we are the strongest emerging economy but millions of poor and hungry people are a stark contrast.[31]

We face the problem of a 'Second Partition': partitioning one people into two almost warring camps – the very affluent and the very poor. In 2010, the 20th anniversary year of the United Nations Development Programme's flagship Human Development Report (UNDP HDR), the HDR introduced a new international measure of poverty – the Multidimensional Poverty Index or MPI – which directly measures the combination of deprivations experienced by each household. The new MPI supplants the Human Poverty Index or HPI used in previous Human Development Reports. Using the MPI, a UNDP/Oxford University study concluded (in 2010) that eight states in India have more poor than 26 of the poorest African nations put together! The eight states (Bihar, Chhattisgarh, Jharkhand, Madhya Pradesh, Odisha, Rajasthan, Uttar Pradesh and West Bengal) account for 421 million people, 11 million more 'MPI-poor' than in the 26 poorest countries in Africa.[32] All the financial wizardry with which this country is endowed has not been able to find acceptable and viable solutions to the problems of the poor and hungry masses, not to mention the poorly educated or illiterate sections of the population. Our Constitution cannot survive long if we only pay lip service to the Directive Principles of State Policy. We must implement them in earnest. The neglect of the poor and needy in our country poses the greatest single serious threat to our survival as a nation in more than 60 years of independence.

Notes and References

1. Barbara Charline Jordan: Statement on the Articles of Impeachment of Richard Nixon, dated 25 July 1974, House Judiciary Committee (USA), p. 1.
2. In his book *The Law of Peoples* (Harvard University Press, Cambridge, Massachusetts, 1999), John Rawls contends that population – 'peoples' – and not governments should be treated as fundamental entities. He believes that governments may be meaningfully categorized on the basis of how they ordinarily deal with people within their territories. Liberal states are those that treat resident populations as liberal peoples. Such states also regard the well-being of the population in general as the ultimate preoccupation of government.
3. Ronald Dworkin: *Law's Empire,* Harvard University Press, Cambridge, Massachusetts, 1986, pp. 61-63. Dworkin passed away on 1 February 2013.
4. V. S. Naipaul: *India: A Million Mutinies,* Vintage, London, 1998.
5. Justice Stephen Sedley: *Freedom, Law and Justice – The Hamlyn Lectures* (now published) Sweet & Maxwell, London, 1999. (He retired as Lord Justice of the Court of Appeal in April 2011.) He states in the Preface:

   > These, the 1998 Hamlyn Lectures, are the 50th in an unbroken series. The honour of being asked to deliver them was made more daunting by the fact that the author of the first Hamlyn Lectures, Lord [Alfred Thompson] Denning, was now in his hundredth year. Denning's 1949 lectures were an instant classic: so much so that the great line we have learned to attribute to Lord Mansfield [aka William Murray] in [James] Somersett's case [1772] – 'The air of England is too pure for any slave to breathe: let the black go free' – which appears in no contemporary report of the judgment, seems to have originated there.

6. Article 25(1) reads:

   > Subject to public order, morality and health and to the other provisions of this Part, all persons are equally entitled to freedom of conscience and the right freely to profess, practise and propagate religion.

7. The entire letter has been reproduced in Ruud Lubbers: *Inspiration for Global Governance,* Kluwer Publications, Deventer, The Netherlands, 2008, on the 60th anniversary of the Universal Declaration of Human Rights 1948.
8. Article 51A in Part IV as it stands today reads as follows:

   > Fundamental duties – it shall be the duty of every citizen of India – (a) to abide by the Constitution and respect its ideals and institutions, the National Flag and the National Anthem; (b) to cherish and follow the noble ideals which inspired our national struggle for freedom; (c) to uphold and protect the sovereignty, unity and integrity of India; (d) to defend the country and render national service when called upon to do so; (e) to promote harmony

and the spirit of common brotherhood amongst all the people of India transcending religious, linguistic and regional or sectional diversities; to renounce practices derogatory to the dignity of women; (f) to value and preserve the rich heritage of our composite culture; (g) to protect and improve the natural environment including forests, lakes, rivers and wild life, and to have compassion for living creatures; (h) to develop the scientific temper, humanism and the spirit of inquiry and reform; (i) to safeguard public property and to abjure violence; (j) to strive towards excellence in all spheres of individual and collective activity so that the nation constantly rises to higher levels of endeavour and achievement; (k) who is a parent or guardian to provide opportunities for education to his child or, as the case may be, ward between the age of six and fourteen years.

9. Article 37 reads:

   Application of the principles contained in this part: The provisions contained in this part shall not be enforceable by any court, but the principles therein laid down are nevertheless fundamental in the governance of the country and it shall be the duty of the State to apply these principles in making laws (official series, Lok Sabha Secretariat, New Delhi).

10. Constituent Assembly Debates, official series, Lok Sabha Secretariat, New Delhi, Vol. VII, p. 84.
11. D. D. Basu: *Commentary on the Constitution of India* (6th edition) Vol. E, S. C. Sarkar and Sons, Calcutta, 1981, p. 84.
12. Constituent Assembly Debates, official series, Lok Sabha Secretariat, New Delhi, Vol. VII, p. 41.
13. Inserted by the Constitution 86th Amendment Act 2002. The law enacted for that purpose (seven years later) was the Right of Children to Free and Compulsory Education Act 2009, which envisages that each child, especially a poor child, must have access to a neighbourhood school. As later stated in a bench decision of three justices reported in 2012 (6), SCC 1: the word *free* in the title to the RTE Act, 2009, stands for removal by the state of any financial barrier that prevents a child from completing eight years of schooling; the word *compulsory* in that title stands for compulsion on the state and parental duty to send children to school.
14. AIR 1993, SC 2178, p. 2232, para 145:

    It is noteworthy that among the several articles in Part IV, only Article 45 speaks of a time-limit; no other article does. Has it no significance? Is it a mere pious wish, even after 44 years of the Constitution? Can the State flout the said direction even after 44 years on the ground that the article merely calls upon it to 'endeavour to provide' the same and on the further ground that the said article is not enforceable by virtue of the declaration in Article 37. Does not the passage of 44 years – more than four times the period stipulated in Article 45 – convert the obligation created by the article into an enforceable right? In this context, we feel constrained to say that allocation of available funds to different sectors of education in India discloses an inversion of priorities indicated by the Constitution. The Constitution contemplated a crash programme being undertaken by the State to achieve the goal set out in Article 45. It is relevant to notice that Article 45 does not speak of the 'limits of its economic capacity and development' as does Article 41, which inter alia speaks of right to education. What has actually happened is more money is spent and more attention is directed to higher education than to – and at the cost of – primary education. (By primary education, we mean the education, which a normal child receives by the time he completes 14 years of age.) Neglected more so are the rural sectors and the weaker sections of the society referred to in Article 46.

15. 347 US, 483 (1954). A later case – *Cooper* vs *Aaron*, 358 US, 1 (1958), equally celebrated – arose out of a state governor's resistance to a judicial order to integrate the public schools, which the Supreme Court of the US went so far as to say that *Brown* vs *the Board of Education* (1954) was itself 'the Supreme Law of the Land', which meant that what the Union (USA) stood for could be saved only by regarding the court's earlier unanimous judgment in *Brown* as supreme law.
16. *UNDP Human Development Report*, Oxford University Press, New York, 2002, pp. 38- 40.
17. Ibid., 2010, p. 204.
18. Ibid., 2002, p. 38.
19. Ibid., 2011, p. 133.
20. AIR 1992, SC 1858.
21. AIR 1993, SC 2178.
22. Opening address of Mary Robinson, high commissioner for human rights, 17 November 2001, New Delhi, www.unhchr.ch/huricane (paras 3 and 4).
23. Article 13 of the ICESCR reads (in part):

    1. The States Parties to the present Covenant recognize the right of everyone to education. They agree that education shall be directed to the full development of the human personality and the sense of its dignity, and shall strengthen the respect for human rights and fundamental freedoms. They further agree that education shall enable all persons to participate effectively in a free society, promote understanding, tolerance and friendship among all nations and all racial, ethnic or religious groups, and further the activities of the United Nations for the maintenance of peace.
    2. The States Parties to the present Covenant recognize that, with a view to achieving the full realization of this right:

    (a) Primary education shall be compulsory and available free to all;
    (b) Secondary education in its different forms, including technical and vocational secondary education, shall be made generally available and accessible to all by every appropriate means, and in particular by the progressive introduction of free education;

(c) Higher education shall be made equally accessible to all, on the basis of capacity, by every appropriate means, and in particular by the progressive introduction of free education;
(d) Fundamental education shall be encouraged or intensified as far as possible for those persons who have not received or completed the whole period of their primary education;
(e) The development of a system of schools at all levels shall be actively pursued, an adequate fellowship system shall be established, and the material conditions of teaching staff shall be continuously improved.

24. United Nations Committee on Economic, Social and Cultural Rights, 21st session, Geneva, 15 November to 3 December 1999. The right to education (Article 13), pp. 1 and 2 (para 1).
25. *Bijoe Emmanuel* vs *the State of Kerala*, AIR 1987, SC 748.
26. See Order dated 22 November 2001, reported only in 2003 (7), SCC 137 (Constitution Bench).
27. In 1971, it was renamed Congress I, after Indira Gnadhi.
28. Congress Organization.
29. Ruchir Sharma: *Breakout Nations: In Pursuit of the Next Economic Miracle*, Penguin/Allen Lane, New Delhi, 2012.
30. Irving Stone: *They Also Ran: The Story of the Men Who Were Defeated for the Presidency*, Doubleday (revised edition), New York, 1966.
31. 'Indian High Court Takes Activist Role', *The Wall Street Journal*, 17 May 2011.
32. Source: *The Tribune*, 28 June 2011.

Chapter V

Corruption

Just as it is impossible not to taste honey or the poison that one may find at the tip of one's tongue, so it is impossible for one dealing with government funds not to taste a little bit of the king's revenue.

Just as it is impossible to know whether fish moving in water are drinking it, so it is impossible to find out when government servants employed in government work are taking money for themselves.

– Kautilya, *Arthashastra* (circa fourth-century BCE or before the Christian era)[1]

The new moral order is best appreciated in terms of our response to graft and corruption in public service. We cannot afford a government of thieves unless we can tolerate a nation of highwaymen.

– Joaquin 'Chino' Roces (veteran journalist from the Philippines)[2]

INCREASE PROSPERITY
COMMUNALISM MUST GO!
POVERTY MUST BE REMOVED!
CORRUPTION SHOULD BE ERADICATED--
SOCIAL JUSTICE
EMPLOYMENT--
DEMOCRATIC VALUES SHOULD BE RESTORED--
ILLITERACY MUST BE ABOLISHED
WAITING FOR THE SECOND FREEDOM STRUGGLE
POVERTY, CORRUPTIO
INJUSTICE, CRIME
50

The experience of former colonies that emerged as independent developing nations after the end of the Second World War was that *freedom brings in its wake corruption*: a theme to which the Polish Nobel Laureate, Czeslaw Milosz, gave eloquent expression:

Ill at ease in the tyranny
Ill at ease in the republic
In the one I longed for – freedom,
In the other – the end of corruption.[3]

But in our part of the world, people's expectations are that whatever be the form of government, corruption will ultimately corrode it!

In a weighty tome of 800 closely printed pages titled *Bribes*,[4] its author (John Noonan Jr) links prosecutions for bribery to society's search for purity. He says that just as sexual purity has decreased as a social objective, insistence on purity in government has gone up! After studying the problem over the ages, Noonan declares that the damage that bribe givers and bribe takers inflict is inestimable; their actions subvert the trust that accompanies public office and obliterate the distinction between office and power. He also cautions that our judgment about corruption in society should never rest on a statistical basis: the common mistake is to use the number of laws enacted or convictions obtained as an index of corruption; *the only real index is the visible degree of tolerance of corruption, amongst people who individually abhor it.*

* * *

I am convinced that we have to fight the menace of corruption with whatever weapons we can call in aid: with laws, with education, with persuasion, with instilling in the dishonest and fraudulent the fear of God – and the like. *But will the fight succeed*? Noonan believes it will, because (as he puts it) 'the nature of bribes is antithetical to the nature of human power in its full development'. At the end of the book, the author ventures a prediction:

> [Just] as slavery was once a way of life and now has become obsolete and incomprehensible, so the practice of bribery in the form of exchange of payment for official action will become obsolete.[5]

True – slavery did 'become obsolete' in the US by the passing of the 13th Amendment (to the US Constitution), but by means that were far from praiseworthy! Noonan gives us a blow-by-blow description as to how (in his words) 'the greatest measure of the nineteenth century (the 13th Amendment) was passed by corruption, aided and abetted by the purest man in American history (Abraham Lincoln)!'[6] Here is the story – but only 'in capsule form'.[7]

In the elections held in 1864 in the USA, the Democrats in Congress (the House of Representatives) were reduced in strength: from 64 to 35 members. The newly elected Republican members could not take office until March 1865, when the new Congress would first meet. Meanwhile, the old Congress, where the Democrats were still in a majority, assembled in a traditional lame-duck session – a session that ran from December 1864 to March 1865. In his presidential message to this session, Lincoln (a Republican) asked the members to pass the 13th Amendment. But under the US Constitution, the passage of a Constitutional Amendment required a two-thirds majority of members present and voting. And there were two votes lacking to make up the requisite majority. Lincoln said that '*these votes must be procured*'. Two 'trusted' members of the House were sent for and Lincoln again told them that those two votes *must* be procured. When asked how, all he (reportedly) said was:

> I am President of the United States, clothed with immense power. The abolition of slavery by constitutional provision settles the fate, for all coming time, not only of the millions now in bondage, but unborn millions to come – a measure of such importance that those two votes must be procured. I leave it to you to determine how it

> shall be done; but remember that I am President of the United States clothed with great power, and I expect you to procure those votes.[8]

According to the recollections, 28 years after the event, of one Albert Riddle,[9] a Republican Congressmen from Ohio, the task of procuring the needed two-thirds majority was entrusted to fellow Congressman James Ashley, also from Ohio. The Republicans were told in confidence that Ashley could report 'the acquisition' of the needed Democrats. One Democrat wanted 'a place' for his brother in New York; another was told that an election contest in the next Congress 'would depend entirely on his vote on the impending 13th Amendment'; the third was a lawyer representing a railroad in Pennsylvania, threatened by legislation, pending in the Senate: all three were 'satisfied'. Every hostile member who stayed away at voting time was helped: their absence reduced the number required to constitute two-thirds of those voting! Ultimately, on the day of voting (31 January 1865), the lawyer and seven other Democrats stayed away; 175 members voted and the Amendment was carried by a two-thirds majority 119–56: by a margin of just two votes!

If Lincoln had lived longer, and if the Democrats who controlled the House in 1874, had investigated the circumstances surrounding the passage of the 13th Amendment, it is possible that a price would have been exacted – in political terms and to the detriment of Lincoln's reputation. The investigation did not occur because Lincoln did not live that long. He was assassinated on Good Friday in 1865 (15 April) and his death overshadowed everything; it also sealed the emancipation of the slaves forever: An instance, rare in the history of politics, where a noble end was achieved by ignoble means!

***

In the nineteenth century, US politics had become so well oiled by 'corrupt practices', that in a work by an English observer – *The American Commonwealth* (1888) – it was recorded that one-quarter of the members of the US Congress took cash, stocks, land or other property for their votes(!), and that 'jobbery' – award of government business to political supporters – was common: so common that visitors returning to Britain from the US were being invariably asked the question: '*But isn't everybody corrupt over there?*'[10]

More than one hundred years later, in the 1990s, foreigners returning home from a visit to India would have been probably confronted with the same question! '*Isn't everybody corrupt over there?*'

* * *

It was in 1993 that *corruption got institutionalized in Indian politics*! That year, the Jharkhand Mukti Morcha (JMM) bribery scandal did not involve bureaucrats but sitting Members of Parliament! And this is how the scandal unfolded: After the general elections for the tenth Lok Sabha were held in May-June 1991, the Congress (I)* emerged as the single largest party and formed the government at the Centre, with P. V. Narasimha Rao as prime minister. In July 1993, during the monsoon session of the Lok Sabha a 'no-confidence motion' was moved against the Rao Government. At that time, the effective strength of the Lok Sabha was 528; the Congress (I) had only 251 members, 14 short of a simple majority. The issue was taken up for discussion on 26 July 1993 and the debate continued till 28 July when the no-confidence motion was put to vote. The result that was declared stunned all but those with inside knowledge! It so happened that 265 members voted against the motion – *the motion was defeated!* Something had gone wrong somewhere for the opposition parties!

After months of investigation, a criminal complaint was filed, alleging that there had been a criminal conspiracy to secure and prove a majority on the floor of the House on 28 July 1993 by offering large bribes (in cash) to named Members of Parliament belonging to different political parties to vote against the motion of no-confidence. On the basis of this complaint, the Central Bureau of Investigation (CBI) registered four cases under relevant sections of the Prevention of Corruption Act 1988.

It was the specific case of the CBI that three members of the Lok Sabha, owing allegiance to the the JMM, and six members of the Lok

*The 'I' stood for Indira Gandhi.

Sabha owing allegiance to the Janata Dal (AS)* – both recognized political parties – had voted against the no-confidence motion and that one member owing allegiance to the Janata Dal (AS) had abstained from voting. The CBI also stated that each of these 10 named members of the Lok Sabha had agreed to receive and did receive bribes, to the giving of which Prime Minister Narasimha Rao, along with three other MPs belonging to the Congress (I) and six Congress (I) Members of State Legislative Assemblies, were privy. A prosecution was launched against the bribe givers as well as the bribe takers, and cognizance of the offences was taken by the special judge, Delhi.

Writ petitions were filed by the accused in the Delhi High Court challenging the framing of charges against them – but the writ petitions were dismissed. In appeals filed in the Supreme Court of India, the provisions of Article 105(2) of the Constitution of India 1950[11] were invoked by the bribe takers: Article 105(2) provides that no Member of Parliament can be made liable to *any* proceedings in *any* court in respect of *any* vote given by him/her in Parliament.

A majority in a bench of five justices of India's Supreme Court upheld the challenge to the prosecution of the bribe takers (though not of the bribe givers), and the cases against the bribe takers were dismissed.[12] Many of us were disappointed at the verdict, reflecting that our founding fathers, honourable as they were, could never have anticipated that some 50 years down the road of parliamentary democracy, free India's 'shameless sons' would be selling their votes for monetary gain and doing so with impunity! Many years have gone by since the Supreme Court verdict in Narasimha Rao's case (1998) – better known as the JMM bribery scandal. In the interregnum, in India, no new law or Constitutional Amendment has been proposed or even suggested by any Member of Parliament. On the other hand, in the principal parliamentary democracies of the world – in Australia, in Canada and in the USA – courts had consistently held:

*'AS' stands for Ajit Singh, the son of Charan Singh, a former prime minister of India. Ajit Singh went on to become the Union food minister in the Narasimha Rao Government.

1. (in Australia) that a legislator who suffered his [or her] votes to be influenced by a bribe 'did that which was calculated to sap the utility of representative institutions at their foundations'; and that 'it would be a reproach to the common law if the offer to, or the acceptance of, a bribe by such a person were not an offence';[13]
2. (in Canada – in more flowery language) that a Member (of Parliament) being the watchdog of the public, 'Cerberus[14] must not be seduced from vigilance by a sop(!)'; and
3. (in the USA) that the Free-Speech-and-Debate Clause of the US Constitution (Article 1, Section 6)[15] would not exonerate a member of the US Congress or of the Senate who took a bribe: six judges (out of nine) said – in *US* vs *Daniel Brewster* (1972): 'The only reasonable reading of the clause consistent with its history and purpose is that it does not prohibit inquiry into activities that are casually or incidentally related to legislative affairs but not a part of the legislative process itself.'[16]

However, in Narasimha Rao's case, three of our justices (out of five) preferred to adopt the reasoning in the dissenting judgments of the US Supreme Court in *US* vs *Daniel Brewster* (1972), viz.: the judgments of Associate Justice William J. Brennan (along with Justice William O. Douglas) and of Associate Justice Byron R. White. In *Daniel Brewster* the dissenting judge/s had said:

> I would hold this prosecution (of Senator Daniel Brewster being an extra-congressional inquiry) into legislative acts and motives as barred by the [Free] Speech [and] Debate Clause … [However] I yield nothing to the Court in conviction that this reprehensible and outrageous conduct, if committed by the Senator, should not have gone unpunished. But whether a court or only the Senate might undertake the task is a constitutional issue of portentous significance, which must of course be resolved uninfluenced by the magnitude of the perfidy alleged. (Justice Brennan along with Justice Douglas.)
>
> Bribery is most often carried out by prearrangement; if that part of the transaction may be plucked from its context and made the basis

> of criminal charges, the [Free] Speech [and] Debate Clause loses its force. It would be small comfort for a Congressman to know that he cannot be prosecuted for his vote, whatever it might be, but he can be prosecuted for an alleged agreement even if he votes contrary to the asserted bargain .... The [Free] Speech [and] Debate Clause does not immunize corrupt Congressmen. It reserves the power to discipline in the House of Congress. I would insist that those Houses develop their own institutions and procedures for dealing with those in their midst who would prostitute the legislative process. (Justice White.)

In India, the majority decision of the Supreme Court in the JMM bribery case remains *good* law!

But there is a silver lining to every cloud! Cheered by the confidence placed by the country's highest court in India's highest legislative body, Parliament took it upon itself (a few years after the decision in Narasimha Rao's case) to discipline some of its own errant members who (after due inquiry by Parliament) had been found guilty of corruption. This was in the *cash-for-questions case* – a 'case' not in court but in Parliament.

It was in December 2005, when, thanks to the somewhat dubious advantages of modern technology, a private TV channel aired to viewers a 'sting operation', in which was offered both audio and visual evidence of some Members of Parliament accepting money for questions to be asked in the two Houses during Question Hour. The Lok Sabha constituted a committee to inquire into the truth of these allegations and, on being satisfied that a 'scandal' had been correctly exposed by the media, passed Resolutions expelling these members. The Rajya Sabha did likewise. The errant members then filed writ petitions in the Supreme Court challenging their expulsions. Fortunately for parliamentary democracy, the writ petitions were dismissed by a Constitution Bench of the court (4:1[17]) – the exercise of the power of parliamentary privilege in a worthy cause was upheld! Four judges in a bench of five held that though the power to expel a Member of Parliament was neither expressly envisaged nor expressly provided for in the Constitution, it was implicit in the 'powers, privileges and immunities' of Members of Parliament. But the cash-for-questions case (in Parliament) turned out to be only a 'flash in the pan'.[18]

The Prevention of Corruption Act 1988 – a law made by India's Parliament replacing a pre-independence statute of 1947 with the same title – had provided for prosecution of 'public servants' for corruption. Under Section 19 of the 1988 Act, prior sanction was necessary for the prosecution of public servants for certain offences set out in the Act.[19] Such previous sanction had to be given by the person or authority competent to remove the public servant from office. Members of Parliament and members of state legislatures had been held to be public servants.[20] However, according to two judges (Justices S. P. Bharucha and S. Rajendra Babu) in the bench of five justices in Narasimha Rao's case, the statutory condition of prior sanction being incapable of being satisfied, it was 'hoped' that Parliament would address itself to the task of 'removing this lacuna with due expedition' (a pious hope, so far unfulfilled); the other three justices (Justices S. C. Agrawal, A. S. Anand and G. N. Ray) opined that since there was no statutory authority competent to sanction the prosecution of a Member of Parliament or a Member of a State Legislative Assembly, 'the Court could (nonetheless) take cognizance of the offences mentioned in Section 19(1) even in the absence of sanction, provided that before filing of a charge sheet in respect of an offence punishable under the relevant sections requiring prior sanction the prosecuting agency had first obtained the permission of the Chairman of the Rajya Sabha for members of the Rajya Sabha, or of the presiding officer of the Lok Sabha/State Legislative Assembly for its members'.[21] This dictum was 'judicial legislation' at its worst!

* * *

In corruption cases, the want of previous/prior sanction is not a popular rationale with modern-day judges since it is believed (rightly so) that such defence only affords an extra layer of protection for the corrupt! It is in this background that the Supreme Court has held that sanction for prosecution is not at all necessary in the case of a public servant who is no longer holding the same post or office during the currency of which the alleged offence was committed; similarly where the person ceases to be a public servant (e.g., after an order of dismissal is passed), the possibility of a public servant 'being needlessly harassed would not arise at all' and his trial could not be held to be bad for lack of sanction.[22]

There is another lacuna: as yet, there is no general law providing for forfeiture of property acquired by corrupt means: such a law had been suggested by the Law Commission[23] (in February 1999) and it had actually framed a ready-to-enact draft Bill! But the Bill was never introduced in India's Parliament – neither by the National Democratic Alliance (NDA) Government during its last two years in office (2003 and 2004) nor by the United Progressive Alliance (UPA) Government either in its first five-year term (May 2004 to May 2009) or at any time during its current (second) term in office (May 2009 onwards)!

However, nearing the end of its first term in office, the UPA Government did introduce Bill No. 70 of 2008 – the Prevention of Corruption (Amendment) Bill 2008 – in the Lok Sabha, inter alia, 'keeping in view the recommendations of the Law Commission of India ....' But instead of a separate law providing for the forfeiture of property acquired by holders of public office through corrupt means, the Government proposed to insert a new Chapter IV-A in the Prevention of Corruption Act 1988, which empowered a special judge to exercise powers of attachment-before-judgment of the property/assets of the corrupt public servant: a procedure (according to the movers of the Bill) 'more effective than outright seizure'. The Bill had also proposed an amendment to Section 19 of the Prevention of Corruption Act 1988 'to provide a safeguard to a public servant from vexatious prosecution from any bona fide omission or commission in the discharge of his official duty because presently this protection is not available for a person who has ceased to be a public servant'. Section 19 was therefore amended to provide protection to persons who had ceased to be public servants. But the Prevention of Corruption (Amendment) Bill No. 70 of 2008 never became law – it lapsed upon the premature dissolution of the 14th Lok Sabha (which functioned from 2 June 2004 up to 18 May 2009)! With the lapsing of this Bill – considered important by the executive – the government of the day was certainly not helpless; it was constitutionally empowered to promulgate an Ordinance to convert the provisions of the lapsed Bill into law, but it chose not to adopt this course. Nor was a new Bill (to the same effect) introduced by the UPA Government during its second term in office (post-May 2009).

* * *

To the general public it does appear that there is simply no will either amongst Members of Parliament or those in government to take effective steps to deal with the canker of corruption, despite professed ministerial intentions to the contrary!

In a revealing article in a national newspaper, my lawyer friend K. N. Bhat had related a story about Thomas Edison.[24] Edison was a great inventor. He invented, amongst other things, a tamper-proof voting machine and he presented it to the US Senate, hoping that its members would appreciate and applaud his efforts. But they were silent. In exasperation, Edison then wrote to the Senate chairman: 'Sir, my machine is tamper-proof – do you have any doubt?' The chairman then invited Edison to his chamber and privately told him: 'Yes, we have no doubt – *the problem ... is that it is tamper-proof*!' The story is probably apocryphal but it represents a nearly accurate representation of the current realities in India!

But we must not lose heart. Lawgivers are never very popular with the public – either in this country or in the world's oldest democracy: the USA. In the final chapter of a book (recently published), an American author quotes from the results of recent opinion polls in the US according to which over 80 per cent of Americans 'disapprove' of the US Congress![25] In reviewing this book (in *The New York Review of Books*, 11 October 2012), retired Supreme Court Justice John Paul Stevens says that an even more disturbing feature than the result of the opinion poll is the widespread ignorance of the American public. It is 'quite appalling', observes the judge, 'that far more Americans can name the Three Stooges than any Member of the US Supreme Court'!

* * *

There is another difficulty – that of tardy implementation. The anti-corruption laws that have been brought on the statute book have so far exhibited a marked tendency to grind slowly: too slowly for the likes of that great one-time doer: viz., Chief Vigilance Commissioner N. Vittal (1998–2002). Which of us can forget him? When in office he had publicly 'named' 94 civil servants who were under investigation (accused of corruption on the basis of documentary evidence, but not yet charged in any court of law): on his instructions, their names were posted on the Internet! 'Sue me if you dare', Vittal appeared to say, but no one sued him. His bravado had struck a sympathetic chord amongst many people – myself included! Vittal retired from government service several years ago; only recently was he remembered by an otherwise forgetful government: In January 2012, he was awarded the Padma Bhushan for his more-than-significant role in public affairs![26]

The lack of seriousness with which governments of the day tend to approach the problem of corruption is also illustrated by an incident, to which I was privy. Before it was passed into law, the Central Vigilance Commission Bill 2003 had come up for consideration before the Rajya Sabha – it had been already passed by the Lok Sabha. The Bill was meant to stem the rot of corruption in public life indulged in by some high government officials. It proposed a three-member commission, each with guaranteed tenure, appointed on the recommendation of a high-level committee so that it functioned independently of the Central Government. But hidden in the verbiage of that Bill was a provision tucked away in a third subclause of the sixth section dealing with what has been commonly known as the 'single directive'.[27] Under its provisions any suspicion of corruption about employees of the Central Government at the level of *joint secretary and below* was to be inquired into and investigated by the CBI over which the statutorily appointed CVC (Central Vigilance Commission) was to exercise hawk-like superintendence! But all employees of the Central Government at the level of joint secretary *and above* were immune even from inquiry or investigation into an offence alleged to have been committed by these high officials – '*except with the previous approval of the Central Government*'! The only rationale offered by the government for this differentiation on the floor of the House was that it was essential to protect officers at 'decision-making levels' and to relieve them of the anxiety and likelihood of harassment for making honest decisions – which by itself may well have been an adequate reason. But when I suggested to the minister who moved the Bill to substitute the words 'except with the previous approval of the Central Government' with 'except with the previous approval of the Central Vigilance Commission', he declined! This was totally incomprehensible to me. If the government could trust the independently appointed Central Vigilance Commission not to needlessly harass a director of a department or an undersecretary with threats of prosecution under the Prevention of Corruption Act, why could it not trust the same commission in respect of the conduct of a secretary, additional secretary or joint secretary? In fact, why otherwise have a Central Vigilance Commission at all? Was it only for vigilance over 'small fish'? Sadly, so it appears. The NDA Government then in power had a comfortable majority in Parliament and refused to accept my suggestion even though it was in tune with the professed purpose of the Bill: viz., to root out corruption *at all levels*. The Bill, as introduced in the Rajya Sabha, was ultimately passed and became (with presidential assent) the Central Vigilance Commission Act 2003. The single directive, set aside by the Supreme Court in 1998 (in Vineet Narain's case; details given later in this chapter), was revived by legislation! It strikes me now that the refusal of the minister who introduced the Bill to accept any suggestion for its amendment could have been only for one of two reasons: *either* (1) because of the increasing influence of the higher echelons in our bureaucracy over their respective ministers (ministers being inclined to follow what their 'heads of department' suggest) *or* (2) the arrogant headiness of political power: power does not always corrupt; it also exhilarates! As the 'dragon lady' of Asian politics (Trần Lệ Xuân alias Madame Nhu) had once put it: 'All power is delightful and absolute power is absolutely delightful.'[28]

* * *

What makes corruption particularly significant and dangerous in the developing world is that corrupt money can 'fly'; it is smuggled abroad to safe havens and not ploughed back into the domestic economy. If faith in the administration of anti-corruption laws is to be restored, something drastic needs to be done. For instance, it is believed that there are billions (if not trillions) of dollars stacked away by India's citizens in bank accounts in Switzerland and other countries.[29] Why can we not try (just try!) to introduce and then pass a Bill in Parliament nationalizing all bank accounts held by Indian citizens abroad, leaving claims of genuine holders with lawfully remitted credits to be dealt with (sans harassment) by the same law? I have often suggested this to ministers of the Central Government. The suggestion has always been received with a polite, but ominous, silence!

***

At one time, it was believed to be 'not good form' ('not cricket' – as the saying goes) to 'trap' a person into accepting a bribe! Two judgments of the Supreme Court delivered in the 1950s had endorsed this view: the court drew a distinction between a person demanding a bribe and being deliberately tempted (and trapped) into accepting a bribe! In one of these cases the Supreme Court had said:

> Whatever the criminal tendencies of a man may be, he has a right to expect that he will not be deliberately tempted beyond the powers of his frail endurance and provoked into breaking the law; and the more particularly by those who are the guardians and keepers of the law. (Justice Vivian Bose.)[30]

In the other case, Senior Justice N. H. Bhagwati (father of Justice P. N. Bhagwati also a judge of the Supreme Court and later the chief justice of India from July 1985 to December 1986) had said (speaking for the court):

> It may be that the detection of corruption may sometimes call for the laying of traps, but there is no justification for the police authorities to bring about the taking of a bribe by supplying the bribe money to the giver where he has neither got it nor has the capacity to find it for himself. It is the duty of the police authorities to prevent crimes being committed. It is no part of their business to provide the instruments of the offence.
>
> We cannot too strongly disapprove of the step which the police authorities took in this case in the matter of providing the sum of Rs 25,000 to [one] Nagindas who but for the police authorities thus coming to his aid would never have been able to bring the whole affair to its culmination.[31]

But we have come a long way from the halcyon days of 'good form'. Not only in India but in England as well. Besides, moral standards in the UK have also plummeted to new lows. Long years ago, someone in a speech on the floor of the House of Commons had said that a minister was seen taking a 'bribe'. In those days they had no simultaneous recording equipment. And the reporter in Hansard (the official reports) thought he had misheard: it was inconceivable that a Minister would take a *bribe*. So, instead, the reporter wrote in the official version of Hansard that 'the Minister had taken a *bride*'. Such were the standards then as contrasted with standards now!

When Tarun Tejpal of *Tehelka* fame[32] was asked sometime ago whether it was not unseemly to engage in an unlawful act like bribery to 'trap' someone in a sting operation, his response was:

> I did not consult lawyers on the legalities, I was more bothered about the *monumental illegalities involved* [emphasis added].

The background to the disclosures (in 2001) in the 'Tehelka tapes' first showed the need for a credible institution like a *lokpal* (or ombudsman). In the absence of such an institution the disclosures had proved to be a *damp squib*[33] *in the end*.

In the second week of March 2001, tehelka.com released the videotapes named 'Operation West End' purporting to show and expose corrupt practices in defence deals.[34] They were the alleged record of a sting operation in which representatives of tehelka.com, posing as agents of a fictitious arms company, were shown allegedly offering a substantial bribe to the then Bharatiya Janata Party (BJP) president, Bangaru Laxman. In the wake of this 'scandal', in the last week of March 2001, a one-man commission was set up under the Commission of Inquiry Act 1952 (consisting of Justice K. Venkataswami, then a sitting judge of the Supreme Court). He was to inquire into the allegations made in the video tapes (Tehelka tapes) – of four-and-a-half hours' duration and edited from over 100 hours of filming – and give his findings. The judge (after his appointment as a Commission of Inquiry) had accepted another appointment from the Central Government: viz., that of the Advance Ruling Authority under tax laws. This acceptance was fastened on to by some disgruntled persons, and charges of 'conflict of interest' were levelled against Justice Venkataswami. To his credit, the judge promptly resigned from both offices. The editor-in-chief of tehelka.com complimented Justice Venkataswami for his step![35]

In January 2003, Justice S. N. Phukan (a retired Supreme Court judge) was appointed in place of Justice Venkataswami. The Tehelka tapes, whose authenticity was questioned, were sent to the UK for forensic examination. The report of such examination, though received in early April 2004, was made public only in June 2004 in view of the impending general elections of April-May 2004. (The forensic report had confirmed the tapes as genuine.) After the general elections, the Congress-led United Progressive Alliance (UPA) Government came into office. In October 2004 the Cabinet Committee on Political Affairs of the Government refused to extend the term of the Justice Phukan Commission and the (incomplete) Phukan Commission Report was tabled in Parliament in May 2005. (It found no illegality or irregularity in any of the past 15 transactions of defence deals that had been identified for investigation by the Venkataswami Commission). The investigation into the Tehelka tapes was then handed over to the CBI. In 2006, CBI registered a first information report (FIR) against Bangaru Laxman and others. After taking evidence, a Special CBI Court (in April 2012) found Bangaru Laxman guilty of taking a bribe in a fictitious defence deal and sentenced him to a four-year term of imprisonment. His appeal to the Delhi High Court was admitted and he has been enlarged on bail. Investigation into the cases of the other accused has not yet been completed.

* * *

In different capacities, many of us have commented (favourably and unfavourably) on the Tehelka tapes, but it is now time to tear off the mask of hypocrisy with which many public personalities have spoken about their surprise and dismay at the disclosures. Their attitude reminds me of one of R. K. Laxman's graphic cartoons, which is now reproduced.

(*Source*: *The Times of India*, 16 March 2001.

I suggest we cut out all the tut-tutting and get down to brass tacks. We all know, for instance, that it is unlawful for anyone to bribe an MP or any other public servant. But we also know that it is unlawful for a public servant to accept a bribe. And we know that the practice is not infrequent. Let's develop the will to do something concrete about it.

The answer as to what the Tarun Tejpals of this world[36] can do, in a tsunami-like situation in which we now find ourselves, was given many years ago by the editor of a left-bank literary journal in France (*Nouvelle Revue Française*). He was the editor until he was ousted by his own kinsmen who collaborated with the invading German army in 1942. He then joined the French Resistance, and when asked what one Frenchman could do against such heavy odds, his answer was:

> You can squeeze a bee in your hand until it suffocates – it would suffocate after stinging you – that's precious little, you will say, *but if it did not sting you, bees would have become extinct a long time ago*.

Personally, I am averse to sting operations: clandestine clips that intrude and take unsolicited 'peeks' into the lives of ordinary people and transgress on the *right* (of citizens) *to be let alone*: a most precious right. But then I am also averse to, and dislike, the spectacle of a minister, or a prominent public figure, accepting wads of currency notes (a feature that was central to the Tehelka tapes). We still do not know (in the year of grace 2013) whether we will ever have a *lokpal* or what form that institution will take. But when we do have one and it does function effectively (like a 'stinging bee') that will be the 'sting operation' that I will appreciate and applaud!

* * *

There is a move afoot to enlarge Fundamental Rights by introducing privacy laws (laws that ensure complete privacy to individual citizens) in the Fundamental Rights chapter. It would be fine if the proposal meant only no harassment of citizens by police or government officials and the like – 'the right to be let alone'.[37] This right is already there in Article 21 of the Indian Constitution, as broadly interpreted by the Supreme Court of India.[38] But if it means something more – i.e., protecting by new law the reputation of people – then I would worry. Such a provision would be out of place in this country at this time. The vast millions of this country have no need for it because they are not important enough to be noticed in the media (print or electronic). As for the few who are in positions of governance and/or who are in the public glare, it is best that their reputation be taken care of by the ordinary laws of defamation. The law of defamation, after all, is a recognized exception to the Fundamental Right to freedom of speech guaranteed by Article 19(1)(a) of our Constitution (under Article 19[2]). These are trying and difficult times not only for India but also all around the world and we must leave the precious reputation of public figures to 'market forces'. Those who like to see their names and faces in the print and electronic media cannot shout 'foul' when some non-proven allegation is made against them. They are, after all, under public scrutiny, and they must not be prematurely rescued from exposure in the vagaries of the 'market'.

The greatest deterrent against combating corruption in public life, in my opinion, would be to arm every 'citizen' with a specific individual and Fundamental Right to *privacy*. By so doing, the government would not protect the *ordinary* 'citizen'; it would only be providing a shield for those constantly in the public eye.

Let me remind you of a story related by Roger Chongwe (a brave lawyer from Zambia) at the Madrid Congress of the International Commission of Jurists in the 1980s. Under the penal code in Zambia, it was an offence to express opinions defamatory of the country's president. In the 1970s, three candidates stood for the office of president of Zambia. Sometime later, one of the unsuccessful ones, became bankrupt. When the official receiver of the bankrupt individual came to seize his assets, he wrote on the court summons:

> Kenneth Kaunda [the president] is a bastard and a son of a b****. He should be told that the government of this country does not belong to him alone.

He was prosecuted and tried for defaming the head of state. In the course of the trial, the official receiver was questioned by the prosecutor and asked if he held the president in high esteem after he read the scribble on the summons. The prosecutor expected the government official to answer: 'Not after I read the writing on the summons.' But the official receiver instead truthfully said: 'I never at any time held the President in high esteem.' The case for the prosecution collapsed! So much for 'reputation' of the high and mighty!

* * *

With the Right to Information Act 2005 in place, a separate law of privacy would trench upon the beneficent provisions of this Act. There is already in the 2005 Act an entire catena of exemptions from disclosure of information (Section 8), one of which expressly provides that 'there shall be no obligation to give any citizen [inter alia] information which relates to *personal information* [emphasis added] the disclosure of which has no relationship to any public activity or interest, or which would cause unwarranted invasion of the privacy of the individual unless [the authorities empowered under the Act] are satisfied that the larger public interest justifies the disclosure of such information.' Neatly put – any extended right to privacy beyond what is provided for in Section 8(1)(j)[39] would be inimical to, and in conflict with, the beneficent provisions of the 2005 Act.

***

They say that corruption in politics is as old as the hills! But never forget that in India it is older!

In a comprehensive treatise on public administration and statecraft in ancient India (*Arthashastra*), it is believed that Kautilya (also known as Chanakya) had perceptively written (circa fourth-century BCE):

> Just as it is impossible not to taste honey or the poison that one may find at the tip of one's tongue so it is impossible for one dealing with government funds not to taste a little bit of the king's revenue.
>
> Just as it is impossible to know whether a fish moving in the water is drinking it, so it is impossible to find out when government servants employed in government work are taking money for themselves![40]

Kautilya is also credited with having enumerated in detail 'forty different ways of embezzlement'! We have come a long way since those Machiavellian times (marked by cunning and duplicity). But judged by what we hear today, there are folks (whom I would not like to name) who could have taught a thing or two even to the crafty Kautilya!

While corruption in one form or another has always been with us, it has taken on variegated hues in different times and at different places, always with serious consequences. The tenacity with which it tends to persist in some cases leads to despair and resignation on the part of those who are concerned about it; but surprisingly, there have been its occasional protagonists as well! They have pointed out that corruption is the much-needed grease for the squeaking wheels of a rigid administration! Or to put it even more bluntly: 'In terms of economic growth, the only thing worse than a society with a rigid, overcentralized, *dishonest* bureaucracy is one with a rigid, overcentralized, *honest* bureaucracy!'[41]

In the context of pervasive and cumbersome regulations in developing countries, it has been suggested that corruption may actually improve efficiency and help growth! If, for instance, there is competitive bidding by private firms for a government contract, and the corrupt official awards it to the *highest bidder in bribes*, then allocation efficiency is maintained, *as only the lowest-cost firm can afford the largest bribe*![42] Such convoluted reasoning is dangerous – it is sometimes known as 'the self-fulfilling equilibrium of corruption'; like when the middleman who has a vested interest in spreading disinformation, keeps saying: 'Nothing gets done without bribing the officials.' And when everybody believes this, it has the effect of persuading the official (even if initially disinclined to himself indulge in corruption) to do so, since he is assumed to be corrupt anyway!! The middleman's role in corruption somewhat resembles that of the Italian Mafia, as observed in a 1993 study by Diego Gambetta (a professor of sociology): 'The Mafiosi himself has an interest in regulated injections of distrust into the market so as to increase the demand for the product he sells – which is protection!'[43]

Swedish economist Gunnar Myrdal – a favourite of the Jawaharlal Nehru era – liked to quote India's first prime minister:

> Merely shouting from the house tops that everybody is corrupt creates an atmosphere of corruption. People feel they live in a climate of corruption and they get corrupted themselves.[44]

Perhaps Nehru was right at the time he spoke. But we live in vastly different times, times intolerant of corruption, eloquently described (in more topical terms) by Jeremy Pope, the founder and the first managing director of Transparency International (a global civil society organization leading the fight against corruption):

> People everywhere are on the move: In Bangladesh they choked the streets of Dhaka to bring down a corrupt President [Hussain Muhammad] Ershad [in 1990]; in Latin America thousands of 'painted faces' took to the streets to depose President Collar [Fernando Affonso Collor de Mello] of Brazil [in 1992]; [and] Guatemala's President [Jorge Serrano] Elias fled the country [in

> 1993] after Nobel Peace Prize winner Rigoberta Menchu addressed thousands of citizens on the streets of Guatemala City. Earlier [in 1986], the people of the Philippines had defied the army to shoot as they marched through the streets of Manila to bring down the corrupt regime of President [Ferdinand] Marcos. *The list goes on.*[45]

Yes! The list goes on – a list that definitely has India in it!

* * *

The Nehru era had produced great bureaucrats, who believed in, and practised, honour, integrity and self-denial. Dharma Vira was one of them – his life spanned almost a century.[46] He rose from a humble recruit to the highest rank: that of cabinet secretary of the Government of India. After retirement,[47] he wrote *Memoirs of a Civil Servant* (Vikas, New Delhi, 1975), in which he spoke of Percy Marsh, district magistrate of Aligarh (now in Uttar Pradesh), who had taken a keen interest in Dharma Vira then as a young service officer. One day Marsh told Dharma Vira:

> Now listen carefully. Two things you must always do. One is to take a decision and take it quickly, right or wrong. Most often you are likely to be right in your decision. But even if you are wrong, less damage will be done than by not taking a decision. And the second thing is that you are an executive officer. You should keep your mouth shut as far as possible. The less you speak the less trouble you will get into .... Talking is the task of politicians. You will be judged by your actions and not by your talks. So you better speak less and act more.

Dharma Vira greatly valued this advice. He once told me a fascinating story: As cabinet secretary, he had headed a government delegation that went abroad to purchase some aircraft. After the agreement was signed, the sellers' representative asked Dharma Vira as to in whose name should the amount of the customary discount be credited. Dharma Vira's reply was: 'Excellency, make out the cheque in the name of the Government of India.' When he came back to India and handed over the cheque to his prime minister, Jawaharlal Nehru roared at him: 'What have you done?' he asked. 'You have accepted a bribe from the sellers? The reduction in price was a bribe for you to clinch the deal.' 'Yes Sir', responded Dharm Vira, 'but would you have preferred it if I asked the sellers to open an account in my name in Switzerland and deposited the money there?' Nehru, still smouldering with rage, did not reply. The moralist in Nehru was quietened by the realist in Dharma Vira. In his lifetime Dharma Vira was typical of many generations of noble, upright public servants. After his passing (and of the likes of him) there has been a steep decline of standards in public life.

And not in India alone. A Harvard professor, Lawrence Lessig, recounts the story of Senator John Stennis, from Mississippi. Like Dharma Vira, the senator was of the old school. When Stennis retired in 1989, after 41 years, he was the most senior member in the Senate's history. He thought and acted differently from other senators. Asked by a colleague to hold a fund-raiser with defence contractors, Stennis recoiled and remarked: 'Would that be proper? I hold life and death over those companies. I don't think it would be *proper* for me to take money from them.' It is a story (Lessig writes) about a *change of norms*. Stennis wasn't concerned that holding a fund-raiser with defence contractors would break the law. Probably it would not. He was worried that it 'wasn't proper'! He was worried about breaking prevailing *norms* on Capitol Hill. Lessig says that it is this that has changed over the years.[48]

* * *

'Corruption' is one of the most elastic of words in the English language. To every individual, it is something of which he or she disapproves. Some years ago, at a seminar of the International Bar Association held in Berlin, Jeremy Pope (of Transparency International) gave what then struck me as the most comprehensive, and yet the most concise, definition: '*Corruption is the misuse of public power for private profit.*' How right he was. Or so it seemed. But recent events have shown that his definition was not as all-embracing as I had once thought it was, because there are simply no limits to where, when or how corruption rears its ugly head. For example, with the revelations of the match-fixing and drug-related scandals in the world of sports (in cricket, cycling and the like), Pope's definition needs restructuring. For instance, there is no leverage of public power in cricket; cricketers do not hold any public office, and yet they exercise *moral* power – the power to instil idealism among millions of cricket-loving fans. Such fans feel cheated when a player, due to corrupt motives, plays badly or does not play well. The word 'corruption' now embraces the '*misuse of power of any kind for private gain*'.

* * *

A former procureur general of France (the equivalent of an attorney general in the common-law countries), Pierre Truche, placed the problem of corruption in ancient and modern times in proper perspective. In a proceeding before the Court of Cassation (the highest court in France), he said: 'Corruption is ancient in behaviour, illegal for a long time, but it was a practice tolerated in the higher echelons and by public opinion. We have currently entered a period in which this illegal behaviour which was previously tolerated is tolerated no longer.'[49] Simply and effectively put, it is the level of intolerance in society that is the ultimate combating force to tackle corruption.

* * *

The need to combat corruption was vividly brought out in a UN Report (the tenth) – on Human Development in South Asia published in November 1999 – which covered India, Pakistan, Bangladesh, Sri Lanka and Nepal. This report was prepared by Mahbub-ul Haq – a Pakistani economist and a well-known pioneer of the theory of human development; he was founder of the Human Development Report (HDR). He died in July 1998 before the report could be published. It was ultimately brought out – dedicated to his memory – with a foreword by Mark Malloch Brown, the newly appointed administrator of UNDP.[50] In his foreword Brown wrote:

> The Human Development Report is a crown jewel of the UNDP. Its robust editorial independence and its unapologetic scholarship have led its authors to say the unthinkable, and they then have the pleasure of watching conventional opinion catch up.

After the publication of the report,[51] Khadija Haq, widow of Mahbub-ul Haq, told a news conference that she believed that Pakistan's (then) new military leaders, who cited high-level corruption as a justification for the overthrow of the civilian government, would use the report's findings in their anti-corruption campaign! (Unfortunately, they did not!) The report called for 'a bold, concrete anti-corruption agenda, which must begin from the top if it is to be credible.' It noted: 'Combating corruption in the region is not just about punishing corrupt politicians and bureaucrats, but [also] about saving lives.' The report called for: (1) the creation of exclusive courts to deal with corruption; (2) the requirement that public officials declare their assets; and (3) transparent procurement laws. It also called for legislation giving the public a right to information about the government and the use of independent private-sector auditors. The 1999 report (a pioneer in the field) had mentioned that corruption in 'South Asia has four key characteristics that make it far more dangerous and damaging than corruption in other parts of the world':

- Corruption occurs at the top, not at the bottom, distorting decisions on development programmes and priorities.
- Corrupt money 'has wings, not wheels' and is smuggled abroad to safe havens, not ploughed back into the domestic economy.
- Corruption often leads to promotion, not prison, and 'the big fish' – unless they belong to the opposition – rarely 'fry'!
- Corruption has been occurring in a region with over 600 million people living in dire poverty.

***

As to where corruption is the most damaging depends on the observer's viewpoint. For us lawyers, there are special reasons to point to the judicial system itself and the failure of the rule of law to successfully combat this malaise. The lack of trust in the legal system to fight corruption is not confined to the developing world. I read some time ago that an opinion poll conducted in Belgium showed that 98 per cent of the population had no faith in the judiciary and 95 per cent of the population did not believe that investigators or the judiciary would push the then current scandals to their logical end! Opinion polls in some African countries – Tanzania, Uganda and Nigeria – have reportedly yielded similar depressing results!

Most of the discussion on topics connected with corruption is built on *perception*, which tends to greatly amplify the phenomenon by introducing the element of *scandal*. The spiral of scandals reflects the true extent of corruption. It also demonstrates how and where the limits vary between what is legal and what is illegal, what is legitimate and what is illegitimate, and between practices that are tolerated and those that are not. If there is the infrastructure of a controlling institution in place (whether judicial or extra-judicial, like an ombudsman), it defines the degree to which the political system is amenable to an investigation. The need for an ombudsman is imperative in our polity – but more of that later!

* * *

All scandals, particularly when exposed by the judiciary, create high expectations in the minds of the public, because our highest court is the most highly regarded as far as probity is concerned – rightly so. But when public expectations are aroused and then scotched or yield no results, there is dissatisfaction and disillusionment. In one of William Shakespeare's great tragedies, the lead character, Macbeth (who after murdering Duncan, a royal guest in his home, proclaims himself king of Scotland) indulges in a short soliloquy about life in which he says: '… it is a tale told by an idiot, full of sound and fury signifying nothing.'[52] This would be an apt description of the Jain '*hawala*' cases – a scandal of the 1990s, which followed the revelation of the 'Jain diaries' (maintained by one Surender Kumar, or S. K., Jain). This scandal (exposed by a crusading journalist Vineet Narain) too was once 'full of sound and fury', though ultimately 'signifying nothing'.

It all started on 25 March 1991, when one Ashfaq Hussain Lone, alleged to be an official of the terrorist organization Hizbul Mujahideen, was arrested in Delhi. Consequent upon his interrogation, raids were conducted by the CBI on the premises of S. K. Jain, his brothers, relatives and business offices. Along with Indian and foreign currency, the CBI seized two diaries and two notebooks. They contained detailed accounts of large payments made to persons who were identified (in the diaries) only by their initials. The sustained interest that these notations aroused was because the initials were linked to the names of various high-ranking politicians, in and out of power, and of highly placed bureaucrats as well! For reasons not far to seek, nothing had been done for a long period of time in the matter of investigating the contents of the Jain diaries. This had led to writ petitions being filed by Vineet Narain on 4 October 1993 (in the public interest – to push things along through the courts) that invoked the provisions of Article 32 of the Constitution of India.[53] The gist of the allegations in the writ petitions was as follows:

- Governmental agencies such as the CBI and the revenue authorities had failed to perform their duties inasmuch as they had neglected to investigate matters arising out of the seizure of the 'Jain diaries';
- the apprehension of terrorists had led to the discovery of financial support to them by clandestine and illegal means using tainted funds obtained through '*hawala*'[54] transactions, which had also disclosed a nexus among politicians, bureaucrats and criminals, who were recipients of money from unlawful sources, given for unlawful consideration;
- the CBI and other government agencies had failed to investigate the matter and take it to its logical conclusion and prosecute all persons who were found to have committed an offence; and
- this was presumably done with a view to protecting powerful and influential persons who were allegedly involved. The writ petitions therefore prayed for the following reliefs:

> (a) that the abovesaid offences disclosed by the facts mentioned in the petition be *directed to be investigated* [emphasis added] in accordance with law;
> (b) that this Hon'ble Court may be pleased to appoint officers of the police or others in whose integrity, independence and competence this Hon'ble Court has confidence for conducting and/or supervising the said investigation; and

> (c) that *suitable directions be given by this Hon'ble Court and orders issued to ensure that the culprits are dealt with according to law* [emphasis added].

When hearing this PIL (public interest litigation), a bench of three judges (Justices J. S. Verma, S. P. Bharucha and S. C. Sen) sat daily in court for several weeks, in close conclave and in camera, excluding the public, the media and even interested members of the Bar! The judges examined the pages of the Jain diaries, taken possession of by the CBI, and noted the cryptic initials and the figures mentioned against each initial (presumably lakhs, if not crores, of rupees!). They also noted (with concern) that the initials did appear to correspond to the names of some well-known politicians! In these special circumstances, it was thought proper by the Supreme Court bench not merely to issue a writ of mandamus to the authorities (i.e., to do their duty of investigating these matters as prescribed by law) but to keep the PILs pending under *constant monitoring* by the court of the investigations being conducted by the CBI. The court then monitored ongoing investigations, passing a series of orders on different dates in 1995, 1996 and 1997.[55] The bench made it clear that its task of monitoring the investigations would end the moment charge sheets were filed in competent courts for being dealt with thereafter in accordance with law. The exercise, which the court described as a '*continuing mandamus*', was well publicized, though the actual proceedings in court were not. This prompted a fantastic upsurge of expectation in the public mind: viz., that the 'big fish' were at last likely to be brought to book!

But did that happen? We have on record the pithy but truthful answer given by senior advocate Anil Divan who appeared and assisted the court in the case – as amicus curiae ('friend of the court'):

> Let me start by answering a few questions which are frequently put to me: Is the Jain *hawala* case over?
>
> Yes, final judgment was given on 18 December 1997.
>
> Was any politician convicted?
>
> No.[56]

No – because by March 1998 the principal accused who were charge-sheeted were finally acquitted by a judgment delivered by (another) bench of three justices of the Supreme Court (reported in *CBI* vs *V. C. Shukla*, AIR 1998, SC 1406). This bench of three justices (not the bench that monitored the investigation into the Jain diaries) held that, in law, entries in the diaries of a third party without corroboration by independent evidence was not sufficient to 'hang a dog' (as the saying goes) – in other words it was not 'evidence' (as defined in the Indian Evidence Act 1872) on which a court could convict any person and send him/her to jail.[57] The court held that on a conspectus of a large number of decisions (which were detailed in the judgment) – what the court described as 'the existing state of settled law' – even correct and authentic entries in books of account or diaries *without independent evidence of their trustworthiness* could not fix liability on any person.

But surely, all this was known, or at least apprehended, by the learned judges of the Supreme Court (all senior judges of high repute) who had sat with counsel for the CBI in camera for weeks in the Vineet Narain case! It is obvious that the senior judges had, at that time, consciously refrained from assuming the 'invasively investigative' role of 'magistrates'[58] functioning in civil-law countries.[59] They did not direct the manner and mode of investigation; they did not give directions as to the persons against whom investigations should be carried out; and they did not question the CBI as to the independent evidence (if any), which it had gathered, to establish reliable links with the initials noted in the diaries. In retrospect, I believe that this was a mistake: a grave mistake. A common-law court[60] (that is a court in a common-law country like India) has a choice: either

1. to follow hallowed judicial precedent established in bygone days, in England (the last court of appeal for civil and criminal cases in India) when the Privy Council had authoritatively stated in its opinion in Nazir Ahmed's case (1945) that the functions of the judiciary and the police are complementary and not overlapping, and each was to be left to exercise its own separate function *without* interference[61] or else,

2. to assume directly the role of an active full-fledged investigating agency especially if there was good reason to believe that those entrusted by the criminal law with the investigation of a case were 'dragging their feet' – either because of the influence (actual or presumed) of 'higher-ups' or for some other extraneous reason.

There is no half-way house. If and when a writ court in a common-law country such as India considers it absolutely necessary in the special circumstances of a given case (e.g., where the police, or the CBI, is not investigating a case effectively in order to serve the ends of justice), it would have the constitutional power (and therefore the duty) to 'go the *whole hog*' (as the saying goes[62]) and – disregarding the limitations imposed on ordinary courts under the Criminal Procedure Code – arrogate to itself the task of a full and complete investigation to be conducted as it (the court) directs.

The collapse of the Jain *hawala* group of cases had its own backlash on public perception about the criminal justice system. It confirmed the worst fears of the general public: an innominate class of persons not bothered too much about the niceties of legal procedure! Their perception was that the *big fish* never appeared to get their just desserts through the legal process, either because the law was defective or for some other reason too complicated for them to comprehend! It was only the *small fish* that invariably got caught, sentenced and incarcerated! We cannot honestly say that the general public was wrong in its perception of our laws and of our complex criminal justice system

* * *

It was the dismal failure of the 'Vineet Narain approach' that inspired, in more recent times, a bench of the Supreme Court of India armed with '*the flaming sword of its inspiration*'[63] to directly intervene in the process of investigation in the 2G (second generation) spectrum scam cases. At the direction of the Supreme Court itself, criminal cases had been directed to be filed against persons whom a bench of two judges[64] believed to be directly involved (on the judges calling for and a perusing the files of the investigating authorities). One need not follow an opinion of the Privy Council of the pre-Constitution days only because it is there. If the ends of justice so require, the high courts or the Supreme Court can (if circumstances so compel or warrant) descend into the arena of conflict and not just supervise from afar the investigation of a criminal case, but assume an active role in it. But a 'mid-way solution' as adopted in the case of the Jain diaries case is self-defeating, as it was later shown to be!

Earlier I have mentioned that scandals – particularly when exposed by the judiciary – create great expectations in the mind of the public. But one has to admit that occasionally, even the Supreme Court of India – like Homer – 'nods'.[65] Thus, for instance, on two different occasions when a bench of two justices of the Supreme Court of India (a bench of the Supreme Court of whatever strength speaks for the entire court) came down hard and heavy on the high, the mighty and the powerful, raising great public expectations, there was extreme disappointment when each of these judgments was overturned or modified upon a review by another (larger) bench of three judges of the same court (again speaking as all bench judgments do for the entire court!).

Each of these two cases (illustrative in nature) conveyed the not-very-salutary message to those whose expectations had been aroused by the initial decision given in each of them, viz., that perceived wrongdoings by the high and mighty – such as ministers in the government – did not (in the perception of the public) appear to receive the same treatment as wrongdoings of other mortals with less power and influence. The judgments are found in the law reports for all to read – and I take the liberty of commenting on them.

In the first such case (picked at random as illustrative though not, I hasten to say, as indicative of any trend),[66] this is what a bench of two judges of the Supreme Court had initially said:

> All the 15 allotments ... (of petrol pumps) have been made by the Minister in a stereotyped manner. The applications have not been officially received by the Petroleum Ministry. There is no receipt entry on any of the applications. The applicants seem to have approached the Minister directly. None of the applications have been dealt with in any of the branches of the Ministry. There is nothing on the record to indicate that the Minister kept any criteria in view while

making the allotments. How the applicants came to know about the availability of the petrol pumps is not known. No advertisement was made to invite the applications. There is nothing on the record to show that any other method of inviting applications was adopted. There is no indication in the allotment orders or anywhere in the record to show that the Minister kept any guidelines in view while making these allotments. The allotments have been made in a cloistered manner. The petrol pumps – public property – have been doled out in a wholly arbitrary manner.

All these allotments are wholly arbitrary, nepotistic and are motivated by extraneous considerations.

We have no hesitation in holding that the Minister for Petroleum and Natural Gas deliberately acted in a wholly arbitrary and unjust manner. We have no doubt in our mind that he knew that the allottees were relations of his personal staff, sons of Ministers, sons/relations of Chairmen and members of the Oil Selection Boards and the members of the Oil Selection Boards themselves. The allotments made by him were wholly mala fide and as such cannot be sustained. We are further of the view that the Minister acted in a wholly biased manner inasmuch as he unfairly regarded with favour the cases of 15 allottees before him. The relevant circumstances available from the record and discussed by us leave no manner of doubt in our mind that the Minister deliberately acted in a biased manner to favour these allottees and as such the allotment orders are wholly vitiated and are liable to be set aside.

The Minister has acted in utter violation of the law laid down by this Court and has also infracted Article 14 of the Constitution of India. As already stated a Minister in the Central Government is in a position of a trustee in respect of the public property under his charge and discretion. The petrol pumps/gas agencies are a kind of wealth which the Government must distribute in a bona fide manner and in conformity with law. The Minister has betrayed the trust reposed in him by the people under the Constitution.

Exemplary damages were awarded and the concerned minister was directed to pay Rs 50 lakh to the Government Exchequer, since the property with which he was dealing was public property and the Government 'which is by the people' had therefore to be compensated.

Strong words – but more importantly – followed by strong action. And high expectations raised!

But now the downside: On review petitions being filed by the minister, a differently constituted bench of three judges (two long years later)[67] allowed the review, recalled the earlier direction for payment of Rs 50 lakh as exemplary damages and also recalled the order previously made for the registration and investigation of a criminal case (by the CBI) against the minister. The bench of three judges held (and it so recorded) that though the conduct of the minister was 'wholly unjustified' (mark you, 'wholly unjustified'), it fell short of 'misfeasance in public office', which was a specific tort and that since the ingredients of that tort were not met, there was, therefore, no occasion for awarding exemplary damages. The bench of three judges then went on to say:

> Mere allotment of petrol outlets would not constitute 'misfeasance' unless other essential elements were present. These allotments have already been quashed as having been arbitrarily made and we appreciate the efforts of Common Cause for having caused this exposure. But the matter must end here.

With great respect, the paragraph quoted above and especially the sentence 'But the matter must end there' sound more like *special pleading*, which, in the law books, is defined as 'an argument that is unfairly slanted towards the speaker's viewpoint because it omits unfavourable facts or authorities and develops only favourable ones'.[68]

In another (illustrative) case,[69] a PIL had been filed against the allotments of 52 shops/stalls made by the then minister for housing and urban development, Government of India. After going into the facts, the Supreme Court directed the minister to pay a sum of Rs 60 lakh as exemplary damages to the Government Exchequer because 'she [the minister was a lady] was dealing with the public property of the Government', which is 'by the people and has to be compensated'.[70] The court further directed the CBI to investigate the case and launch prosecution against the minister. After this judgment was handed down in 1997 and widely reported and commended, a review petition that had been filed by the minister was 'disposed of' – only five years later (on 23 January 2002) – again by a bench differently constituted of three honourable judges.[71] (The two judges who delivered the initial judgment had long since retired.) The review petitioner had relied on the judgment of the three-judge bench in the case previously mentioned (*Common Cause* vs *Union of India and Others*, AIR 1999, SC 2979). The bench of three judges in the 2002 case said (rightly I submit) that it did not agree with this decision, but, since it had been rendered by a three-judge bench, it was directed that the matter before them should stand referred to a Constitution Bench of five judges! So far so good. But then, this bench of three judges (in 2002) also went on to quash and set aside the damages part of the judgment of the bench of two judges with the following observations:

> Having regard to the peculiar facts and circumstances of the Minister for Housing and Urban Development who is stated to be old and ailing and the gross hardship of the case we think it appropriate to quash the damages part of the impugned judgment, but we make it clear that the direction to launch criminal prosecution on the basis of investigation by CBI is not being altered in any matter and if any criminal proceeding has already been instituted, that must take its own course on the materials produced. This petition stands disposed of accordingly.

Age and illness of a party to a case is not reason sufficient enough to set aside a prior final decision (against that party) solemnly given by the highest court, although though it may well be a ground for a subsequent pardon – the power to pardon under our Constitution is lodged only with the highest executive.

* * *

These two cases may well be aberrations – but if so, they are significant aberrations. Whatever tends to give a great institution a bad name must be avoided in the highest, and certainly the most prestigious, court of the land.

I also regret to say that the majority of our judges are far too busy with their normal gruelling work schedule that they appear, at times, to be out of touch with the realities of public expectations. Take, for instance, the securities' scam on the Bombay Stock Exchange. It surfaced in 1992 in various types of transactions relating to government securities. The basic allegation was that these transactions were made in active connivance with officials of banks, financial institutions and shareholders and the amount involved was estimated to be over Rs 4000 crore. The matter was brought to the notice of both Houses of Parliament and a Joint Parliamentary Committee (JPC) was appointed to inquire into the incident. Thereafter, a special law was passed by Parliament known as 'the Special Courts (Trial of Offences Relating to Transactions in Securities) Act 1992' (in short, the Special Courts Act). Prosecutions were launched against one Harshad Mehta (a stock broker) and several others in 1994, and, after four long years, many of the accused were found guilty (and were convicted) by the special court set up to try the offences. It was the first conviction under a special new law, specially enacted in public interest. An appeal was provided for under the 1992 Securities Act directly to the Supreme Court of India; of course, the appeal being a first appeal it had to be admitted: a convicted person must have at least one appeal. But there was no effort on the part of the Supreme Court to say: 'Yes we will of course admit the appeal, but the case has far-reaching ramifications, viz., financial implications of wrong doing of over Rs 4000 crore, so we will fix it next month or the month thereafter and hear it finally.' The appeal was heard in the normal course. To me, it appeared to be a case of missed opportunities. It was a disappointment to see that the judges who admitted the appeal did not take a cue from pent-up public reaction to the securities scam. One could almost hear the plaintive prayer of the public left unanswered: 'Give us, O Lord, a final judgment in a first conviction in a securities scam case at least within a year.' It was not to be. The appeal was admitted and the sentence was stayed, and I make bold to (impertinently) suggest that it was only because of the 'chilling' effect of the laws of contempt (contempt for 'scandalizing the court') that inhibited biting comment by the media about the law's delays! Ultimately, of course, in January 2003,[72] judgment *was* handed down by the Supreme Court of India and the convictions by the special court of most of the persons accused were upheld, but the principal accused, Harshad Mehta, 'escaped'. He was not acquitted; nor could his conviction be upheld. He had died (on 31 December 2001) before the appeal could be finally heard!

* * *

In 1995, in a compendium of biographies of several prominent figures of the twentieth century, titled *Eminent Churchillians*,[73] the author, Andrew Roberts, coined a new word – *declinology* (the belief that *mores*[74] in society are in decline). Roberts had asserted that it was a major factor in 'today's Britain'. It is also a major factor in today's India. There is a galloping 'declinology' in all aspects of our public life, reflecting the existing state of the nation. Many years ago (i.e., in 1991), the *Asian Wall Street Journal*[75] had mentioned the significance of a large population (it was then around only 850 million!) and concluded that India need not make any special effort to carve out a role for itself in the world: 'If the 850 million people start living a normal life that itself will make the necessary impact!' The paradox is that our strength lies in our swelling population. But so does our weakness! To govern a country under these unimaginably difficult conditions, we must lighten our burden and get rid of the main problems that hinder good governance.

Next only to population, the major problem in our country is the enormous divide between the governed and those who govern. We have inherited this legacy from over 200 years of Mughal rule, followed by more than a century of British rule. But this is not an indigenous characteristic. It has been true of most bureaucracies around the world. Valéry Giscard d'Estaing, president of France (from 1974 to 1981), was once interviewed by a correspondent of the *New York Times* (James Markham) about his two-volume memoirs. This is what he said:

> I was struck that, in this century, which is a period of intense communication, there is so little mutual knowledge between those who govern and those who are governed. *At least in my country, there is the idea that those who govern belong to another race.*[76]

* * *

When I was in college (in British India) way back in the 1940s, it used to be jokingly suggested that the fall of the British Empire began with the building of country clubs, because once you build a country club what is the point of it unless you keep somebody out? And when the locals – or the '*natives*'[77] – are the 'somebody', there is justifiable resentment! The great divide – the wall of separation – started with the British country club! The British could afford to operate behind a wall of separation because they ruled (and made no pretence about it). They *ruled*, they did not govern; hence they faced few problems when it came to governance. But the rulers had one great quality – they instilled in their officials a high sense of idealism in government service. This went a long way. It was important that an official in government remained (first and last) a public servant in the service of the people. When the British left, we discarded the idealism, which had inspired generations of public officials in British India. Officialdom (in independent India) has become more insular and secretive since independence! The Official Secrets Act 1923 (which remains on the statute book) is a standing threat to open government. As some wit accurately remarked, it was enacted (and continues in force) not to protect secrets, *but to protect officials*! Of course, this was said before the enactment of the Right to Information Act 2005, which has done wonders for open government! The RTI Act has effected a redistribution of political power, ensuring, as much as a law can ensure, *good governance.* That statutes so dissimilar (viz., the Official Secrets Act 1923 and the Right to Information Act 2005) can co-exist in the same country is only possible in 'Incredible India'! (This is the epithet with which the Ministry of Tourism proudly advertises to foreign visitors the sights-and-sounds of our great country!)

There were other aspects of the British rule, which we jettisoned with the Raj. They were mentioned, somewhat pompously, by the British historian G. M. Trevelyan: 'The reason why the British ruled India for so long was that we were looked upon as a nation which kept our promises; and *as rulers we took no bribes*.'[78]

We too started, as a nation, by making promises but did not keep them. The Government of India promised to grant the rulers of the Princely States privileges and privy purses if they joined the Indian Union. They joined but the promise was not kept. As everyone now knows, the real reason for the government of the day reneging on its promise was because a few of the erstwhile rajas and maharajas had 'conspired ' to form, in the late 1950s, a new political party – the Swatantra Party – in opposition to the ruling Congress! These rajas and maharajas had to be taught a lesson – so off with their privileges and privy purses: lock, stock and barrel! Not only those of the maharajas of the larger Princely States but even those of the rulers and *thakurs* (lords or chieftains) of the much smaller states, many of whom were entirely dependent for their livelihood on their privy purses. Certain privileges as well as privy purses were guaranteed not only by solemn covenants of Government but also by express constitutional provisions deliberately enacted to assure the erstwhile rulers of the government's pledge (Articles 291 and 362[79]). These Articles were simply deleted by the Constitution 26th Amendment Act 1971. When the constitutional validity of the 26th Amendment was challenged, a bench of five judges[80] of the Supreme Court solemnly held that whilst the courts were not powerless to correct the government, which had reneged on its solemn pledge and guarantees, the 26th Amendment, by deleting Articles 291 and 362, did not alter 'the basic structure of the Constitution'. This was the verdict despite a binding prior decision of a bench of eleven judges in *Madhavrao Scindia* vs *Union of India* (AIR 1971, SC 530), in which ten of them had clearly stated as a matter of constitutional law that 'the privileges of Rulers and the institution of rulership had been made an integral part of the constitutional scheme'!

* * *

The second part of the Trevelyan quote ('... *and as rulers we took no bribes*') – more relevant in this chapter on corruption – was a bit of hyperbole![81] However, in the main, it was not untrue. Public servants in British India were not dishonest as a class. But more than 65 years after independence, we cannot truthfully say the same today about public servants *as a class*. Those in government are so absorbed in the politics of governance that they have forgotten the true art of governing, and, above all, its true purpose. In the first place, officials (at all levels) will not take decisions. The will and the capacity to take decisions is the true rationale of every bureaucrat functioning as an official of the government. He or she is trained and expected to take decisions fearlessly. But that seldom happens now – because he or she tends to toe the line of 'political masters': either to gain favours or (more often) for fear of being harassed with peremptory orders of 'transfer': a dreaded word amongst government officials in India. Even amongst honest officials, the prospect of being transferred is the single greatest disincentive to the free and frank expression of opinion (to be expressed on the files) and a deterrent to good governance.

* * *

The honest government officials of today, more often than not, would prefer to leave decision making to the courts, lest someone point a finger at them! The rights of citizens, though legitimate, are denied by government officials. For redress, citizens must approach the courts, which is a major contributing factor to the vast backlog of arrears. Governments (both Central and state) have the largest number of cases pending in the courts of this country, estimated roughly at 60 per cent of the total number of pending cases. These are estimated as being in the range of 43 lakh (4.3 million) cases pending in the 21 high courts and 275 lakh (27.5 million) cases[82] pending in the subordinate courts! This is the damaging fallout of the corruption syndrome that has infected all aspects of public life. Politics has become so debased that everyone, howsoever high, is suspect, as witnessed by the 2G scam cases currently with the courts, which has so transfixed the electronic media. Corruption has eaten into the vitals of the body politic and has become deeply entrenched in the psyche of the citizenry.

* * *

Every government in India (since the 1970s), on assuming office, has promised the people a clean administration. But with each successive election, administration and governance have become murkier and murkier. This is true not only of India but of other countries as well. In the Philippines, that doyen of journalists – the veteran editor Joaquin 'Chino' Roces – had led a petition drive in 1985 against the corrupt government of Ferdinand Marcos. In early 1986, President Marcos was overthrown and was succeeded by Mrs Cory Aquino. But corruption in high places still went unpunished. Roces made his protest at a public function when Mrs Aquino conferred on him the country's highest award – the Legion of Honour. In his acceptance speech, Roces lashed out at the administration honouring him: 'The new moral order is best appreciated in terms of our response to graft and corruption in public service. *We cannot afford a government of thieves unless we can tolerate a nation of highwaymen.*'[83]

In India, I cannot visualize an era of good government until we take bold and drastic steps to exorcise graft and corruption from public life. The question is: how drastic? Sting operations, media publicity, interventions by social activists and the like do have their own shortcomings because they depend on people – different people possibly with their own predilections and biases. But so far, the institution of an effective *lokpal* (ombudsman) performing its functions effectively is not in place (a phenomenon not yet visible on the political horizon in India). The armoury of ordinary citizens (against corruption and other evils) remains ill-equipped. The observance of the *due process of law* – by a citizen going to a police station and lodging a complaint – is not helpful: at least not in matters considered 'sensitive' by the authorities. FIRs[84] (first information reports) envisaged in the criminal law have first to be investigated by the police and then reported to the jurisdictional magistrate. But when persons with important connections are involved as the accused, there are pressures (direct and indirect) from higher-ups to see that fair and honest investigations are delayed, doctored or even scotched. The only recourse then is for individuals (usually the courageous ones) to approach established courts (the high courts) to seek their writ jurisdiction for obtaining redress. High courts do intervene (they are all *high courts of justice*) – and when they do so promptly, they are appreciated and applauded. But dockets in the high courts – in fact, in all courts – remain crowded. And even when justice through the courts does get ultimately administered, it is tardy – often unduly delayed under our three-tier system of justice administration. Nothing is final until the Supreme Court has a look (or refuses to have a look) on the ground that there is a case (or no case) under its extraordinary superintending jurisdiction over courts and tribunals under Article 136 of the Constitution. Believe me, expressions like 'government of thieves' and 'nation of highwaymen' – though often uttered in exasperation even in this country – are not always inapt or exaggerated!

* * *

There is another downside to the moral degradation in Indian politics. When promises are broken by sovereign nations, when it is believed that their leaders and officials (or a majority of them) are corrupt and take bribes, such a belief devalues and debases the people. Actions of governments have an ever-widening ripple effect on the general social milieu of the time. Moral leadership plays a vital role in every state. Aristotle had said that those in government exercise a teaching function. The people see what they do and do likewise. And when those in power do things that are underhand and dishonest, the people follow suit!

In our country those in positions of power are looked up to – fawned upon – as 'great men'. And (as already mentioned) our Constitution starts with the hallowed words: WE THE PEOPLE. *We the People* learn by the actions of our leaders, not by the precepts they hypocritically profess and proclaim. After the first generation of leaders who had fought for independence had passed on, instances of irregularities, in the bending of rules in high places, had rapidly increased. I believe that the death of Prime Minister Lal Bahadur Shastri in January 1966 marked the turning point in the deliberate and conscious bending of rules! In the post-Shastri era, public confidence in men and women at the top of the political ladder began waning; over the years it has steeply declined, if not vanished. All this has had a cascading effect on bureaucrats and businessmen, and its impact has not been lost upon the general populace.

In a judgment handed down at the threshold of the new millennium, i.e., in early 2000, the Supreme Court of India likened the present state of corruption to 'a dreaded communicable disease (like HIV)'. The judges said that the socio-political system exposed to such a disease 'is likely to crumble under its own weight':[85] words of dire warning: unfortunately not heeded

* * *

Some years ago, in a public interest litigation, a Division Bench of the High Court of Madras struck down an exemption order issued by a state minister in favour of an applicant for a building licence – an exemption order that was 'procured' – as an act of rank favouritism or corruption. At the end of his judgment, the erudite Justice M. Srinivasan (speaking for the bench) took leave to remind the government of the state (Tamil Nadu) of a verse attributed to that great saint of South India, Tiruvalluvar:

> Behold the king who doth not oversee his administration every day, and remove irregularities there; his sovereignty will wear away day by day.[86]

This is the great tragedy of our times. As we keep on making more and more laws and rules, those in charge of their implementation bend them to suit powerful (individual or business) interests! Consequently, integrity in public life keeps getting devalued and debased, even faster than the humble rupee! The casualty in the fine art of bending the rules is always the larger public interest, to protect which laws and rules are (in the first place) promulgated! All such sordid developments must surely put the country on the road to a sweeping anarchy. Nirad C. Chaudhari (1897–1999), when alive, kept reminding us, from abroad, that 'the most dangerous aspect of a sweeping anarchy is that those on whom it advances never perceive it'.[87] But no one paid any heed. We Indians only appreciate it if people abroad say nice things about us; if they criticize us, they are unpopular. Nirad Chaudhari, a resident in the UK, was realistic and forthright and was, for that reason, unpopular in India!

* * *

Transparency International's Corruption Perception Index[88] is a relatively recent innovation. It is a composite index of a number of surveys (17 surveys from 10 independent institutions) covering a large number of countries. Despite numerous criticisms, it provides fairly reliable information (thousands of an indicative nature) as to the levels of corruption from an international comparative perspective. Its main purpose is to provide a standard measure of *perceptions* of corruption and to stir public awareness. Although its intention is not to come up with precise league tables, it has a 'shaming' effect at an international level. However, it is neither a monitoring tool nor does it provide for information-related responses to corruption. In that sense, it shares the biases of many other national or local corruption-level measures. Nevertheless, it also serves a secondary purpose of stimulating debate around the globe about problems of corruption within each country for which Transparency International (TI) periodically presents the score!

So great has been the impact of bribery over the years, that, in the UNDP annual Human Development Report (2002), it was felt necessary to introduce for the first time a new slot: 'People victimized by crime' (it records the percentage of people residing in principal cities of the world who have been asked *to pay or have paid bribes to public officials*). Two of India's largest and most-populated cities – Mumbai and Delhi – had qualified (!) for inclusion in this report. The figures compiled showed that the 'victims of bribery' in these two cities were 22.9 per cent in Mumbai and 21 per cent in Delhi: i.e., 22.9 per cent and 21 per cent of the total population of each of these cities![89]

The Human Development Report 2011 grouped countries under four heads: (1) Very high human development; (2) high human development; (3) medium human development; and (4) low human development. The HDI ranking for India (in the latest Human Development Index 2011) was in the medium human development category, which includes 47 countries from index nos. 95 to 141 with India finding a place only at index no. 134!

In the 2010 Report (20th anniversary edition), in one of the tables (Table 6: Empowerment), there was a new subheading: 'Corruption – victims' (i.e., the 'percentage of people who faced a bribe situation in the last year'). An estimation was given (for the first time) for the entire country (not restricted to only two cities): it was 15 per cent of the total population of India!

After more than 65 years of independence, the *state of the nation* in terms of human development, as assessed by the UNDP, looks pretty grim.

* * *

Exasperated by decades of inaction, and maladministration, it was not surprising, that in early 2011, a growing number of very disappointed, but also public-spirited, persons gathered around social activist Anna Hazare when he raised his clarion call against corruption – in high places.

For decades, there had been a clamour for a *lokpal* (or an ombudsman) – an institution not foreshadowed in the 1950 Constitution of India. Its history has been long and tortuous. It was way back in 1966 that the Administrative Reforms Committee (ARC) – appointed by the Government of India – recommended, for the first time, the institution of a *lokpal*: this recommendation was made for better governance. But it has so far proved to be one of the most ill-fated of recommendations: It is still a dead-letter[90] as set out below:

(1) Pursuant to the ARC recommendation of 1966 the first Lokpal and Lokayuktas Bill No. 51 1968 was introduced in 4th Lok Sabha in 1968 amidst high expectations. This Bill[91] was considered by a Joint Committee of the two Houses of Parliament and the Bill (as reported by the Joint Committee) was passed by the Lok Sabha in 1969. But whilst the Bill was pending in the Rajya Sabha, the 4th Lok Sabha was dissolved in December 1970, and, as a consequence, the Bill lapsed – Clause (5) of Article 107 of the Constitution provides:

> A Bill which is pending in the House of the People, or which having been passed by the House of the People is pending in the Council of States, shall, subject to the provisions of Article 108, lapse on a dissolution of the House of the People.

(2) The Lokpal Bill passed by the previous Lok Sabha was reintroduced in the 5th Lok Sabha as the Lokpal and Lokayuktas Bill No. 111 of 1971 – but this Bill met the same fate as its forerunner. It lapsed on the dissolution of 5th Lok Sabha in January 1977!

(3) A fresh Bill (materially different from the one in 1971) was introduced in the 6th Lok Sabha. It was titled the Lokpal Bill of 1977[92] and was referred to a Joint Committee of both Houses, which submitted its report in July 1978. When the Bill (as reported by the Joint Committee) was under consideration, the 6th Lok Sabha was

prorogued and ultimately dissolved. Consequently, the Lokpal Bill No. 88 of 1977 lapsed.

(4) Lokpal Bill No. 166 of 1985 was introduced in the 8th Lok Sabha,[93] but was subsequently withdrawn – there is no record as to why it was withdrawn.

(5) In the 9th Lok Sabha, Lokpal Bill No. 98 of 1989 was introduced in December 1989.[94] This Bill sought to include the office of Prime Minister within the jurisdiction of the Lokpal (subject to certain safeguards); in this Bill it was also proposed that the Lokpal should be a body of three members. This Lokpal Bill of 1989 also lapsed, in March 1991 – with the dissolution of the 9th Lok Sabha.

(6) Lokpal Bill No. 101 of 1996 was introduced in September 1996 in the 11th Lok Sabha and referred to a Standing Committee, which presented its report to Parliament on 9 May 1997, but before the various recommendations of the committee could be discussed and debated, the 11th Lok Sabha was dissolved in December 1997; as a consequence, the Bill lapsed.

(7) Lokpal Bill No. 98 of 1998 was introduced on 3 August 1998 in the 12th Lok Sabha and referred to the Standing Committee on House Affairs which submitted its report on 25 February 1999, but before the recommendations of the Standing Committee could be discussed and debated, the 12th Lok Sabha was dissolved in April 1999. Bill 98 of 1998 lapsed!

(8) The Lokpal Bill No. 73 of 2001 was introduced in the 13th Lok Sabha. But this Bill also lapsed in February 2004 upon the dissolution of the Lok Sabha.

(9) With a string of Lokpal Bills having lapsed by the premature dissolution of a succession of Lok Sabhas, it remains a mystery to me as to why the government of the day did not resort to its constitutional power to legislate by Ordinance! (Article 123 confers specific powers on the executive to issue Ordinances during periods when Parliament is not in session.) The only reason I can think of is that all governments formed with different combinations of political parties – at different times – were (and are) extremely reluctant to have a monitoring authority set up over their executive decisions.

But no political party in India will ever admit that it has been responsible for the stalling of an effective Lokpal Bill!

(10) The subject of the Lokpal Bill of 2001, which lapsed with the dissolution of the 13th Lok Sabha, was then severely left alone by the (UPA) Government in the 14th Lok Sabha – i.e., for 5 long years from 2004 to 2009. It was also not even thought of in the first two years of the 15th Lok Sabha, until 2011, when the hydraulic pressure of public opinion, first exerted though the efforts of Anna Hazare, began to be felt – felt I am happy to say in responsible circles of government!

(11) It was in early April 2011, under pressure of a mass public movement inspired by social activist and crusader-against-corruption, Anna Hazare (he had gone on a fast-unto-death unless an *effective* Lokpal Bill was introduced in Parliament), that the government of the day (for the first time) agreed to the active participation by named representatives of 'civil society' in the drafting of a new Bill. It had never ever happened before! *The Gazette of India* Notification dated 8 April 2011 (Union Ministry of Law and Justice), Resolution No. 1 (42/2004), announced the setting up a 'Joint Drafting Committee to prepare a draft of the Lokpal Bill'. This committee consisted of representatives of 'Team Anna' and those of the government. But then there was disagreement between the two sets of representatives in the course of their deliberations in the Joint Drafting Committee. The government then announced that it had considered all the suggestions of 'civil society' and went ahead and introduced in the Lok Sabha a new Bill – Bill No. 39 of 2011.

(12) The statement of objects and reasons of the (Government) Lokpal Bill No. 39 of 2011 read as under:

> 1. The need to have a strong and effective institution of Lokpal has been felt for quite sometime. The Administrative Reforms Commission, in its interim report on the 'Problems of Redressal of Citizens' Grievances' submitted in 1966, inter alia, recommended the setting up of an institution of Lokpal at the Centre. In this Administrative Reforms Commission,

eight Bills on Lokpal were introduced in the Lok Sabha in the past, namely, in the years 1968, 1971, 1977, 1985, 1989, 1996, 1998 and 2001. However these Bills had lapsed consequent upon the dissolution of the respective Lok Sabha except in the case of 1985 Bill which was withdrawn after its introduction.

2. A need has been felt to constitute a mechanism for dealing with complaints on corruption against public functionaries in high places. In this regard, the Central Government constituted a Joint Drafting Committee (JDC) on 8 April 2011 to draft a Lokpal Bill.

3. Based on the deliberations and having regard to the need for establishing a strong and effective institution of Lokpal to inquire into allegations of corruption against certain public functionaries, it has been decided to enact a stand-alone legislation, inter alia, to provide for the following matters, namely:

- To establish an Institution of Lokpal with a Chairperson and eight Members of which 50 per cent shall be Judicial Members;
- To set up Lokpal's own Investigation Wing and Prosecution Wing with such officers and employees as felt by it to be necessary;
- The category of public functionaries against whom allegations of corruption are to be inquired into, namely:

  A Prime Minster, after he has demitted office;

  A Minister of the Union;

  A Member of Parliament;

  Any Group 'A' officer or equivalent;[95]

  A Chairperson or member or officer equivalent to Group 'A' in any body, board, corporation, authority, company, society, trust, autonomous body established by an Act of Parliament or wholly or partly financed or controlled by the Central Government;

Any director, manager, secretary or other officer of a society or association of persons or trust wholly or partly financed or aided by the Government or in receipt of any donation from the public and whose annual income exceeds such amount as the Central Government may by notification specify but the organizations created for religious purposes and receiving public donations would be outside the purview of the Lokpal.

- To provide for a mechanism to ensure that no sanction or approval under Section 197 of the Code of Criminal Procedure, 1973, or Section 19 of the Prevention of Corruption Act, 1988, will be required in cases where prosecution is proposed by the Lokpal;
- To confer on the Lokpal the power of search and seizure and certain powers of a Civil Court;
- To empower the Lokpal or any investigation officer authorized by it in this behalf to attach property which, prima facie, has been acquired by corrupt means;
- To lay down a period of limitation of seven years from the date of commission of alleged offence for filing the complaints before the Lokpal;
- To confer powers of police upon Lokpal which the police officers have in connection with investigation;
- To charge the expenses of Lokpal on [*sic*] the Consolidated Fund of India;
- To utilize services of officers of Central or State Government[s] with the consent of the State Government for the purpose of conducting inquiry;
- To recommend transfer or suspension of public servants connected with allegation of corruption;
- To constitute sufficient number of Special Courts as may be recommended by the Lokpal to hear and decide the cases arising out of the Prevention of Corruption Act, 1988, under the proposed enactment;

- To make every public servant to declare his assets and liabilities, and in case of default or furnishing misleading information, to presume that the public servant has acquired such assets by corrupt means;
- To provide for prosecution of persons who make false or frivolous or vexatious complaints.

I must frankly say that to me this Bill (with its perceived faults) was worthy of being enacted into law – at least, by passing it and giving it a try! But 'civil society' (so-called) reacted differently. It was up in arms.

(13) From 16 to 28 August 2011 there were demonstrations against Lokpal Bill No. 39 of 2011. Another fast-unto-death call was given by Anna Hazare! (Untimely and also counterproductive in my view.) Other NGOs had also criticized the contents of the (Government) Lokpal Bill No. 39 of 2011; it was even said (with wild exaggeration) that if passed the Bill would facilitate the corrupt to go free! In the turmoil, on 27 August 2011, a special session of both Houses of Parliament was convened – a rare event – and a resolution was unanimously passed: viz., that Bill No. 39 of 2011 be referred to a Department-related Parliamentary Standing Committee for structuring and finalizing a report on the following subjects:

1. Citizens charter;
2. Lower bureaucracy also to be under the Lokpal through an appropriate mechanism;
3. Establishment of Lokayukta in the States.

The term of the Standing Committee lapsed on 30 August 2011 but it was extended (and reconstituted) on 23 September 2011. It held 11 sittings till 24 November 2011, and finally the 48th Report of the Standing Committee on the Lokpal Bill 2011 (along with dissents) was laid before the Lok Sabha on 9 December 2011, on which date it was also presented to the Rajya Sabha.

(14) The Government's *new* Lokpal and Lokayukta Bill No. 134 of 2011 was introduced in the Lok Sabha on 22 December 2011. In a special extended session, the 15th Lok Sabha passed the Lokpal and Lokayukta Bill No. 134C 2011 by a majority[96] – but the Lok

Sabha refused to grant it constitutional status (as was desired by the Government). Some of the amendments discussed (and defeated) were (i) proposals to include corporate, media and NGOs receiving donations and (ii) bringing the CBI under the purview of Lokpal. 'Team Anna' – which failed to maintain its objectivity – again rejected this Bill No. 134C, as passed by the Lok Sabha, as 'anti-people'. It was said by the opponents of this Bill that:

1. Only 10 per cent [of the] political leaders were covered by it.
2. Only 5 per cent of employees were within its ambit – Class C and D officers were not included.
3. The Bill was silent about handling of corruption within the Lokpal office!
4. The Bill offered free lawyer service even to the corrupt accused!
5. The Bill covered temples, mosques and churches.
6. Above all, it was felt that Government would have overall control over the Lokpal as it would have power to appoint and remove its members at will.

(15) Having been passed by the Lok Sabha, a special extended session of the Rajya Sabha [was] convened for three days, viz., 27 December, 28 December and 29 December 2011 to consider and pass the Bill. The debate on Bill 134C of 2011 (that had been passed by a majority of members of the Lok Sabha) commenced on 29 December 2011. There were 187 amendments tabled in the Rajya Sabha. The discussion was acrimonious – how acrimonious [it was] can only be truly appreciated by perusing the entire record of the proceedings (pp. 10 to 509 of the Rajya Sabha Debates of 29 December 2011). Some extracts of these debates are reproduced later in this chapter (with the kind permission of the honourable chairman, Rajya Sabha). The debate was inconclusive because those in the opposition pleaded that the session should continue beyond the midnight hour so that the Bill with amendments could be put to vote! But the government of the day and its supporters dragged their feet. They refused an extension of time – even though this was

the prerogative of the entire House and not … of the Government alone. The chairman, however (not expressing any opinion either way), adjourned the Rajya Sabha sine die on 29 December 2011 (just after midnight) without the Bill being put to the vote, which greatly deflated high public expectations in the country that a Lokpal would be definitely installed, if not in 2011 at least possibly by January 2012.

Here are some extracts from the debates:*

> SHRI SITARAM YECHURY [Communist Party of India, Marxist]: Sir, we will respect your ruling. We will allow the Hon'ble Minister to complete, but you please tell this House what will happen at 12 o'clock. Do we continue or do we go to the next day? Is it a Session in continuity or will there be a break? That is what is agitating many Members.
>
> MR CHAIRMAN: Business of the day will go on ... (*interruption*). We are a long way from 12 o'clock.
>
> SHRI SITARAM YECHURY: Shri [V.] Narayanasamy (who as Minister of State for Parliamentary Affairs was then replying to the debates but had not concluded) has the capacity to go a long way ... (*interruption*).
>
> SHRI V. NARAYANASAMY: Sir, the proviso clause is very clear ... (*interruption*).
>
> SHRI N. K. SINGH [Janata Dal, United]: Sir, we want a ruling from you on that issue ... (*interruption*).
>
> SHRI SUKHENDU SEKHAR ROY [Trinamool Congress]: Sir, the Hon'ble Minister is misleading the House ... (*interruption*).
>
> SHRI V. NARAYANASAMY: You have every right to say that ... (*interruption*).
>
> MR CHAIRMAN: will you please continue with your speech, Mr Minister?
>
> SHRI MOINUL HASSAN [Communist Party of India, Marxist]: Sir, we want a ruling because the clock is now near …12 o'clock. Sir, we want a simple ruling.

*pp. 419 to 421 and pp. 483 to 509.

MR CHAIRMAN: Let us get to 12 o'clock.

SHRI MOINUL HASSAN: Perhaps, the Hon'ble Minister will continue up to 12 o'clock. Nobody wants to hear him but he is continuing ... (*interruption*).

MR CHAIRMAN: You don't have to worry on that count ... (*interruption*). You don't have to worry on that count ... (*interruption*).

SHRI SITARAM YECHURY: Sir, give a ruling ... (*interruption*).

SHRI MOINUL HASSAN: What is the need of the reply of the Minister? (*Interruption.*) Nobody wants to hear him ... (*interruption*).

SHRI V. NARAYANASAMY: Shri Sitaram Yechury, I am coming to you ... (*interruption*).

MR CHAIRMAN: Please continue ... (*interruption*).

Shri Narayanasamy continued, at which there were the following interrupters:

SHRI PRASANT CHATTERJEE [Communist Party of India, Marxist]: Sir, we want your ruling ... (*interruption*).

SHRI V. NARAYANASAMY: Sir, here, in this august House knows [*sic*], most of the Hon'ble Members know that CBI is an independent investigating agency ... (*interruption*).

DR V. MAITREYAN [All India Anna Dravida Munnetra Kazagham]: We want an assurance from you that this House ... (*interruption*).

MR CHAIRMAN: We have the listed business ... (*interruption*).

SHRI PYARIMOHAN MOHAPATRA [Biju Janata Dal]: Sir, give some ruling ... (*interruption*).

The proceedings indicate that, at 11.28 p.m., the House was adjourned for 15 minutes and after that it reassembled:

SHRI M. VENKAIAH NAIDU [Bharatiya Janata Party]: Sir, there was no reason to adjourn the House.

MR CHAIRMAN: Just one minute, please. I have received a request from the Minister for Parliamentary Affairs [Shri Pawan Kumar Bansal]. He wishes to say something ... (*interruption*). Please, sit down.

SHRI PAWAN KUMAR BANSAL: Sir, we all know that when the House had been summoned earlier, it was supposed to conclude on the 21st of this month [December]. That was extended by one day because we had a holiday in between. Since the work relating to the Lokpal Bill could not be taken up, and the Government was committed to bringing the Bill during the Winter Session, we had requested for three days' extension. The extension was granted and then, the BAC [Business Advisory Committee] allocated time for the Lokpal separately, as far as the Rajya Sabha is concerned, for eight hours …. We have been discussing it at length. The Bill was discussed in Lok Sabha the day before yesterday. Yesterday, the Bill could not be transmitted to this House by afternoon because of certain procedural requirements and the Bill was then circulated. We wanted the Bill to be taken up for discussion right from yesterday onwards. There was an objection when we met and then, of course ... (*interruption*).

MR CHAIRMAN: One minute, please ... (*interruption*).

DR V. MAITREYAN: They did not want to discuss the Lokpal ... (*interruption*).

MR CHAIRMAN: Dr Maitreyan, please ... (*interruption*).

SHRI PAWAN KUMAR BANSAL: After our discussion we said that time had been allocated separately both for the Whistle Blowers' Bill and the Lokpal Bill. The Whistle Blowers' Bill could be completed yesterday only but that was not permitted. Therefore, it was decided that both the Bills will be taken up today. The amendments given by different Members run to over 135, maybe there are some more after that ... (*interruption*).

SHRI ARUN JAITLEY [Bharatiya Janata Party]:[97] We are committed to fighting corruption. We will sit the whole night ... (*interruption*).

SHRI PAWAN KUMAR BANSAL: We are committed to fighting corruption ... (*interruption*) ... and that is precisely the reason we brought this Bill ... (*interruption*).

SHRI ARUN JAITLEY: You did not bring this Bill yesterday ... (*interruption*).

Shri Pawan Kumar Bansal: The Government is committed to fighting corruption ... (*interruption*).

Mr Chairman: One minute please ... (*interruption*).

Shri Pawan Kumar Bansal: The Government is committed to the cause ... (*interruption*). They are dilating the issue ... (*interruption*). The Government is committed to the cause and that is precisely ... (*interruption*).

Mr Chairman: Let him finish ... (*interruption*).

Shri Pawan Kumar Bansal: Sir, the Government is committed to fight corruption ... (*interruption*). The Government is committed to fighting corruption and that is why a number of Bills and plethora of laws this Government has brought. The Honourable Minister of Personnel referred to them. And if you are referring to that, there are good many Bills which you have stalled in this House relating to education which was also intended to fight corruption ... (*interruption*). But I am not coming to that point ... (*interruption*).

Mr Chairman: Please conclude ... (*interruption*).

Shri Pawan Kumar Bansal: Sir, what I am saying is that all those amendments require detailed discussion and study. The Government has to formulate its view. You want the Government to respond to those amendments. There are good many amendments. And I just want to point out that an amendment which should have been brought in Subclause (6) of a particular clause is being suggested for Subclause 5 ... (*interruption*). When we are referring to Section 173 of the CrPC [Criminal Procedure Code], something which should find mention in Subclause (6) is being suggested in Subclause (5). We are framing a law and if we incorporate all those things it will ultimately lead to hotchpotch of [*sic*] the Bill. We have to consider them ... (*interruption*). The amendments are running across each other. The discussion was going on. I don't know what prompted our honourable friends from the other side to immediately get agitated about it. We feel, and that is what you all wanted, that we have to have a Lokpal which is a well-considered one and based on right information on the matter. And what are we now doing? You want all those amendment notices for which have been given here to be taken up immediately ... (*interruption*).

SHRI BHUBANESWAR KALITA [Congress]: How can you ... (*interruption*).

MR CHAIRMAN: Mr Kalita please ... (*interruption*).

SHRI PAWAN KUMAR BANSAL: Sir, our honourable friends know this. Part of one amendment covers the part of another amendment. But its other part is not covered in that. How will the Secretariat decide which one becomes redundant and which one doesn't? Therefore, if we are committed to fighting corruption ... (*interruption*).

MR CHAIRMAN: What is the suggestion?

SHRI PAWAN KUMAR BANSAL: My suggestion is [that] the Government decides when the Parliament has to meet. That is the prerogative of the Government. The business is fixed by the Government. The time is allocated by the Business Advisory Committee. Sir, in all earnestness, I wish to say that we are really true to the cause and we want to bring about a Bill which does not have lacunae therein. Only one day's time was given. In Lok Sabha we discussed those amendments. The Government had the time; Government responded to some of the amendments which were moved by the Honourable Members from the opposition and the Government accepted a good many of those amendments. Here the case is like this. In the morning, when we came at 10.30, we saw the amendments here. Mr [S. S.] Ahluwalia's amendment came as late as 6 p.m. today ... (*interruption*).

SHRI S. S. AHLUWALIA [Bharatiya Janata Party]: No ... (*interruption*).

SHRI PAWAN KUMAR BANSAL: That amendment came as late as 6 p.m. ... (*interruption*).

MR CHAIRMAN: What is the suggestion? ... (*interruption*).

SHRI PAWAN KUMAR BANSAL: I am saying, Sir, in order to have a lacunae-free Bill ... (*interruption*). The Minister has to reply. The session is coming to an end at 12.00 [midnight] today, the 29th ... (*interruption*) .... That is the time up to which we have extended the session. That is what the Government had given. Sir, we can continue with this Bill and I wish to assure all the Honourable Members that we will consider all the amendments. If need be, we will talk to you. We will come up with whatever amendments the Government feels [are needed], whatever has to be the response of the Government, we will come with that to the House. But, there is some prerogative of the Government. The Government has to decide when the session meets. We wanted to complete it in three days. The Bill finally concluded in Lok Sabha at 12 o'clock like this, and, thereafter, Sir, there were lot many formalities, which had to be gone through. And, we could not have brought the Bill before 2 p.m. yesterday.

SHRI ARUN JAITLEY: Mr Chairman, Sir, it's ironical for democracy today that I am a Member of the Opposition and, curiously, I speak for majority of this House. The Government, today, is running away from this House because it is in a hopeless state of mind ... (*interruption*). Sir, after a day-long discussion ... (*interruption*).

SHRI PAWAN KUMAR BANSAL: You pass the Bill, as passed by Lok Sabha, we will pass it immediately ... (*interruption*). Pass it immediately ... (*interruption*). Lok Sabha is an elected House. Lok Sabha has passed the Bill. You pass it immediately ... (*interruption*). Pass it in two minutes ... (*interruption*). You have the Bill, as passed by Lok Sabha ... (*interruption*).

MR CHAIRMAN: Let him complete.

SHRI ARUN JAITLEY: Sir, I am not yielding.

MR CHAIRMAN: Please, go ahead.

SHRI ARUN JAITLEY: Sir, even after the sense of this House, every issue was clear and three principal amendments put up by the Opposition, in my respectful submission, are likely to succeed. Faced with such a situation, we have seen a situation where the Bill was ready, circulated yesterday, Mr Ahluwalia got up ...

SHRI V. NARAYANASAMY: Can you yield for a minute?... (*Interruption*).

MR CHAIRMAN: Please, don't do this ... (*interruption*).

SHRI V. NARAYANASAMY: Sir, if he yields for a minute, I will ... (*interruption*).

DR V. MAITREYAN: Sir, they want to postpone ... (*interruption*).

MR CHAIRMAN: Please, sit down. Yes, continue please.

SHRI PAWAN KUMAR BANSAL: Sir, the Honourable Leader of the Opposition was an author of the Resolution regarding the sense of the House that we wanted Lokayukta ... (*interruption*). Now, they want that to be deleted. Sir, we have to consider what do we do ... (*interruption*).

SHRI ARUN JAITLEY: A Government, which did not have the numbers in this House, consciously – and I say this 'consciously' – has choreographed this entire debate in such a manner that the debate can't be concluded today and the votes can't be taken today ... (*interruption*).

SHRI PAWAN KUMAR BANSAL: This is not the situation ... (*interruption*).

SHRI ARUN JAITLEY: It's a choreography of a minority Government ... (*interruption*). If the Government runs away from the Parliament ... (*interruption*). Sir, my last appeal to you is, and I beseech you, as the Chairman of this House, this House will decide how long to sit. The Government will not decide how long this House is to sit ... (*interruption*). And, as the custodian of this House, as the Chairman of this House, you must rule that the House will go on as long as the voting takes place ... (*interruption*).

MR CHAIRMAN: What is this going on? (*Interruption.*)

SHRI SITARAM YECHURY: Sir, there is a point on which I want your ruling.

MR CHAIRMAN: Yes, Mr Yechury ... (*interruption*).

SHRI SITARAM YECHURY: Sir, we are waiting for your ruling. That apart, the Minister has said, 'I want to respond in three bullet points'.

SHRI PAWAN KUMAR BANSAL: Let me respond to this ... (*interruption*).

MR CHAIRMAN: Okay. Let us hear the Minister's reply … (*interruption*).

SHRI PAWAN KUMAR BANSAL: Sir, while I reiterate the Government's commitment ... (*interruption*). Sir, while I reiterate the Government's commitment to pass a strong Lokpal Bill, I have to say only one thing with humility that there are certain Constitutional proprieties, which have to be respected ... (*interruption*). The year comes to an end on 31 December. The New Year begins with the President's Address. We can't really decide matters sitting here, Sir … (*interruption*). The New Year has to begin with the President's Address, and, then, the Motion of Thanks to the President's Address is important ... (*interruption*). Sir, what I said was ... (*interruption*). Sir, what I said was ... (*interruption*). Sir, there are Constitutional proprieties ... (*interruption*).

MR CHAIRMAN: I am sorry ... (*interruption*).

SHRI S. S. AHLUWALIA: Mr Chairman, Sir, today, we have ... (*interruption*).

SHRI RAM JETHMALANI [Bharatiya Janata Party]: Sir, we have already ... (*interruption*).

SHRI PAWAN KUMAR BANSAL: Sir, there are 187 amendments ... (*interruption*).

SHRIMATI MAYA SINGH [Bharatiya Janata Party]: Mr Chairman, Sir ... (*interruption*).

MR CHAIRMAN: Please ...

SHRI PAWAN KUMAR BANSAL: Sir, there are 187 amendments … (*interruption*). And some of them are contradictory. It is a web of confusion …. We have to consider these amendments ... (*interruption*). Sir, the Government ... (*interruption*). Sir, the Honourable Leader of the Opposition was one of the authors to that Resolution reflecting the sense of the House, and, now, when we have to decide, they are backing out, Sir … (*interruption*).

MR CHAIRMAN: Will you please resume your places?

Shri M. Venkaiah Naidu: Sir, let the voting start ... (*interruption*). Let the voting start, Sir … (*interruption*).

Mr Chairman: Please … (*interruption*). Please. This is not right ... (*interruption*). You can't do this. This is disgraceful ... (*interruption*). Honourable Members, an unprecedented situation has arisen. There appears to be a desire to outshout each other .... (*interruption*). Please … (*interruption*). Let me finish ... (*interruption*). Let me finish.

Shri Arun Jaitley: Sir, there is a desire to avoid the vote ... (*interruption*).

Mr Chairman: There is total impasse ... (*interruption*).

Shri S. S. Ahluwalia: They are not ... (*interruption*).

Mr Chairman: Just a minute … (*interruption*). The House cannot be conducted in this noise ... (*interruption*).

Dr V. Maitreyan: No, Sir … (*interruption*).

Shri Tapan Kumar Sen [Communist Party of India, Marxist]: Sir, let them … (*interruption*). Let the Bill be taken up for consideration ... (*interruption*).

Mr Chairman: I know, but that requires … (*interruption*) … that requires orderly proceedings ... (*interruption*) … I am afraid … (*interruption*) … I am afraid, the Chair has no option ... (*interruption*) … most reluctantly ... (*interruption*). Please ... (*interruption*). Just a minute ... (*interruption*).

Shri S. S. Ahluwalia: You can call for voting ... (*interruption*).

Mr Chairman: I am afraid ... (*interruption*) ... you can shout and nobody is heard ... (*interruption*).

Shri Sitaram Yechury: Sir, I asked for your ruling ... (*interruption*).

Mr Chairman: What ruling can I give in this noise? (*Interruption.*)

Shri Sitaram Yechury: Can we sit after 12 o'clock? (*Interruption.*)

Mr Chairman: I am afraid ... (*interruption*) … I am afraid I can't do anything. If this is how the Rajya Sabha is going to behave, then we all better go home ... (*interruption*).

(*The national song, 'Vande Mataram', was then played.*)

> MR CHAIRMAN [at 00.02 hours: Now, I adjourn the House sine die.

(16) In March 2012, the prime minister called a meeting of the floor leaders of the Rajya Sabha to 'narrow the differences'. The Rajya Sabha then referred the Lokpal and Lokayukta Bill 2011 as passed by the Lok Sabha to a Select Committee of the Rajya Sabha on 21 May 2012. The Select Committee was to submit its report within three months – it has not so far done so. Expectations were – but there was no assurance of this – that the Bill would be taken up for consideration by the Rajya Sabha (if at all) only in the 2012 winter session of Parliament. But it was not to be.

It would not be not be wrong to say that if the frustration of the majority of our people were to be expressed in drumbeats, the sound would have been simply deafening!

***

In this frustrating atmosphere, the only useful thing that can be said about combating corruption is to impress upon persons with a vision (judges, lawyers, editors, journalists and citizens – and there are still many of them in each category who have strong public consciences) to *keep up the pressure and never lose heart.* Remember what they said in the centuries gone by about slavery: that it could never be abolished and that human nature would never permit it. But, ultimately, slavery *was* abolished, human nature notwithstanding!

***

We must also never forget to applaud public officials when they do the right thing.

I offer an illustrative instance. In early 2000 there was a strong builders' lobby in Delhi – there still is! But at that time, there was an honest-to-God 'bulldozing' Union minister, Jagmohan, who stood firm against all the shenanigans of the builders. An editorial in the *Hindustan Times* (29 April 2000) set out why Delhi citizens owed a debt of gratitude to the minister:

A Measure of Gratitude

The Urban Development Minister has a reputation for being stubborn. When Mr Jagmohan was in charge of the Communications Ministry, many of his colleagues despaired of ever being able to persuade him to change his mind. Eventually they had to move Mr Jagmohan out before they could change the policy. Mr Jagmohan may or may not have been right in refusing to alter the telecom policy but few people will dispute that it is good to have an Urban Development Minister who is as stubborn as Mr Jagmohan. Ever since he announced a drive against unauthorized constructions, members of his own party have been using every trick in the book to get him to desist from following through with his crusade. A less stubborn man may have been amenable to some kind of compromise. But fortunately for the people of Delhi, Mr Jagmohan has lived up to his reputation for stubbornness.

Nobody who lives in Delhi can deny that a mafia of unscrupulous builders, corrupt municipal officials and venal politicians has conspired to destroy the character of this beautiful city. Some of the greatest architectural vandalism has occurred in south Delhi where quiet and pleasant colonies have been transformed by the illegal construction of ugly multistorey apartments and hideously repulsive shopping centres. The law states that residential premises must not be used for commercial enterprises. Yet, in such previously charming localities as Defence Colony, this law has been flouted with cheerful impunity. Greedy house owners have pulled down their bungalows to construct ugly four-storey complexes, where rooms are let out to offices, slimming clinics, restaurants, computer institutes, so-called 'health clubs' and grocery stores. Those who run these establishments have paid off the municipal authorities so they do not even bother to be discreet. Large neon signs, banners and hoardings litter the frontage of these houses, breaking the law with an arrogant indifference to its provisions. It is clear, by now, that municipal officials are on the take. It is as clear that politicians also get their cut of the bribes. So, who can the honest citizen turn to? The sad answer is that city's powers-that-be care more for their wallets than they care for Delhi. *That is why the citizens of the Capital owe Mr Jagmohan a measure of gratitude. He is the only man who has had the guts to launch this long-overdue drive. And only he has the stubbornness to see it through* [emphasis added].

I wrote a letter congratulating the editor of *HT*. It was published on 4 May 2000:

Doing the Right Thing

Sir,

I CONGRATULATE you on your leading editorial in the *Hindustan Times* (29 April) as to why citizens of Delhi owe Mr Jagmohan a measure of gratitude. It needed to be said. Corruption must not only be fought by laws and through courts, but must be combated through the hearts of men and women.

Jean Monnet, father of the European Union, used to say there are two types of people in this world – those who want to *be* somebody and those who want to *do* something. Being somebody, the Urban Development Minister has also done great things – notably the drive against unauthorized constructions. Doing the right thing has a trickle-down effect.

Fali S. Nariman, Delhi

* * *

There is an old school song made famous by Rudyard Kipling whose last stanza reads:

Bless and praise we famous men
Men of little showing!
For their work continueth
And their work continueth
Broad and deep, continueth
Great beyond their knowing.[98]

* * *

When good people, people in positions of power, sometimes do the right thing, it does have a trickle-down effect for the common man, the proverbial man-in-the-street. For as the great book says: 'Whatsoever a great man doeth, that other men also do; the standard he setteth up, by that the people go.'[99]

The need of the hour is *great men (and women)* And quite frankly they are in short supply.

Notes and References

1. Kautilya: *Arthashastra*, Penguin Classics Series, New Delhi 1992; first translated by R. P. Kangle (1972), now edited, rearranged and introduced by I. N. Rangarajan. The full text of the *Arthashastra* was not available until discovered (on palm leaf) in the first decade of the twentieth century by Dr R. Samasastry of Mysore (in Karnataka).
2. In an acceptance speech (1988) when he was conferred by the president of Philippines the country's highest award: the Legion of Honour.
3. Quoted in Nadine Gordimer: *Living in Hope and History*, Bloomsbury, London, 1999, p. 73. Milosz was awarded the Nobel Prize for literature in 1980.
4. John T. Noonan (Jr): *Bribes*, Macmillan, New York, 1984. The blurb commends it as 'a brilliant and provocative chronicle – from Biblical days to the present – of the men and women involved in one of the most pervasive and least understood crimes against society'.
5. Ibid., p. 706.
6. In the *Oxford Companion to the Supreme Court of the United States* (Oxford University Press, New York, 1992), the editors record the passage of the 13th Amendment as follows:

   > Although the amendment [was] passed easily in the Senate in 1864, during the Thirty-Eighth Congress, Republicans lacked the required two-thirds majority in the House of Representatives. When the House first considered the amendment in 1864, proponents were unable to attract the necessary Democratic votes. The Republican victory in the elections of 1864 changed the political dynamic, however. After that election, an *intensive lobbying effort* [emphasis added] by the White House changed enough Democratic votes to allow the amendment to pass the House on reconsideration in 1865.

7. A favourite expression of one of the brightest judges of his time in the Supreme Court of India (from 1964 to 1969). Justice R. S. Bachawat always told practising lawyers appearing before him (in clipped English) to address their oral arguments only 'in capsule form'!
8. Noonan: op. cit., pp. 453–56.

9. Albert Riddle: *Recollection of War Times*, G. P. Putnam' Sons, New York, 1892, pp. 324–25.
10. 'No impression regarding American politics is more generally diffused in Europe than that contained in the question which the traveller who has returned from the United States becomes so weary of being asked, "Isn't everybody corrupt there?" It is an impression for which the Americans themselves, with their airy way of talking about their own country, their fondness for broad effects, their enjoyment of a good story and humorous pleasure in exaggerations generally, are largely responsible'. Viscount James Bryce: *The American Commonwealth*, Vol. 2 (1888), Chapter 67, 'Corruption'; republished by the Liberty Fund Inc., Indianapolis, 1995.
11. Article 105 (Powers, Privileges and Immunities of Parliament and its Members):

    (1) ...
    (2) No Member of Parliament shall be liable to any proceedings in any court in respect of anything said or any vote given by him [or her] in Parliament or any committee thereof, and no person shall be so liable in respect of the publication by or under the authority of either House of Parliament of any report, paper, votes or proceedings.
12. *P. V. Narasimha Rao* vs *State*, AIR 1998, SC 2120 (3:2): where decisions of foreign courts are cited.
13. Ibid. Here the decisions of foreign courts are cited.
14. According Greek and Roman mythology, Cerberus is a multiheaded hound (usually three-headed) that guards the gates of the Underworld to prevent those who have crossed the river Styx from ever escaping!
15. Section 6, Clause 1: The Senators and Representatives ... shall in all cases ... be privileged from Arrest during their Attendance at the Session of their respective Houses, and in going to and returning from the same; and for any Speech or Debate in either House, they shall not be questioned in any other Place.
16. 408 US 501 (1972) (6:3 – Justices William J. Brennan, William O. Douglas and Byron R. White dissenting) followed in *United States* vs *Henry Helstoski* (1979), 442 US 447 (6:1): in the latter case, the only dissent was that of Justice Brennan.
17. *Raja Ram Pal* vs *Hon'ble Speaker, Lok Sabha*, 2007 (3), SCC 184 (not reported in the AIR series of law reports).
18. 'Something that disappoints despite a showy beginning': source http://www.phrases.org.uk/meanings.
19. Section 7 – public servant taking gratification other than legal remuneration in respect of an official act; Section 10 – punishment for abetment by public servant of offences defined in Section 8 (taking gratification in order, by corrupt or illegal means, to influence public servant) or Section 9 (taking gratification for exercise of personal influence with public servant); Section 11 – public servant obtaining valuable things, without consideration from person concerned in proceeding or business transacted by such public servant; Section 13 – criminal misconduct by public servant.

20. *P. V. Narasimha Rao* vs *State*, AIR 1998, SC 2120, para 180, p. 2202.
21. Justice G. N. Ray in his judgment (concurring in part and dissenting in part) held – agreeing with Justices Bharucha and Rajendra Babu – that a Member of Parliament enjoyed complete immunity under Article 105(2) from being prosecuted before a criminal court for an offence involving acceptance of a bribe for the purpose of speaking or giving his vote in Parliament.
22. The following cases have involved chief ministers of different states. *Prakash Singh Badal* vs *State of Punjab*, 2007(1), SCC 1; *Lalu Prasad* vs *State of Bihar*, 2007 (1) SCC 59; *K. Karunakaran* vs *State of Kerala*, 2007 (1), SCC 49; and *V. S. Achuthanandan* vs *State of Kerala & Anr.*, 2007 (1), SCC 61: these cases are not all reported in the AIR Series of law reports.
23. One hundred and sixty-sixth Report of the Law Commission of India (February 1999).
24. See *The Tribune*, 1 October 2004 (Chandigarh edition).
25. Sanford Levinson (professor of constitutional law, University of Texas): *Framed: America's Fifty-One Constitutions and the Crisis of Governance*, Oxford University Press, New York, 2012. His conclusion is that:

    > We need a new constitutional convention, one that could engage in a comprehensive overview of the US Constitution and the utility of many of its provisions to twenty-first-century Americans.

26. Vittal has recorded his experiences as chief vigilance commissioner in a book (*Ending Corruption? How to Clean Up India*, Penguin, New Delhi, 2012) that has been commended by N. R. Narayana Murthy (chairman emeritus of Infosys Ltd.) in glowing terms: 'Mr Vittal's informed insights and systematic assessment of the role that each of the stakeholders in society can play are a useful guide to eradicate the menace of corruption!'
27. The single directive was an order issued by the Government of India in 1969 (and thereafter frequently amended); it required prior sanction of the designated authority to initiate investigation against officers above a certain rank in the government, in public sector undertakings and in nationalized banks. The single directive was struck down in Vineet Narain's case (AIR 1998, SC 889) on the ground that it was not permissible under the Central Government's general power of superintendence under Section 4(1) of the Delhi Special Police Establishment Act 1946.
28. Madame Nhu, was the *de facto* first lady of South Vietnam from 1955 to 1963. She was the wife of Ngô Đình Nhu who was the brother and chief adviser to President Ngô Đình Diệm. As Diệm was a lifelong bachelor, and because she and her family lived in the president's palace, she was considered to be the first lady (*Source*: Wikipedia).
29. According to an article in the *Hindu Business Line* (13 August 2010), which created quite a stir, unofficial estimates indicated that Indians had over US $ 1456 billion (approximately 1.4 trillion US dollars) in black money stored in Swiss and other banks! But these statistics have been refuted by the Swiss Bankers' Association. According to a White Paper on Black

Money (*http://finmin.nic.in/reports/WhitePaper_BlackMoney2012.pdf*) issued by the Ministry of Finance, Government of India, May 2012, the Swiss National Bank estimates reveal that the total amount of deposits in all Swiss banks at the end of the year 2010 by Indian citizens were roughly US $ 2.1 billion. It has been stated that the Swiss Ministry of External Affairs has confirmed these figures upon request for information by the Ministry of External Affairs, Government of India (700fold less than the alleged figure of 1.4 trillion US dollars). It is further stated in the White Paper that the share of Indians of the total bank deposits of citizens of all countries in Swiss banks stood reduced from 0.29 per cent in 2006 to 0.13 per cent in 2010.

30. *Ramjanam Singh* vs *State of Bihar*, AIR 1956, SC 643, p. 651, para 37.
31. *Rao Shiv Bahadur Singh* vs *State of Vindhya Pradesh*, AIR 1954, SC 322, pp. 334-35.
32. In 2009, the magazine *Business Week* named Tarun Tejpal amongst 'India's 50 Most Powerful People'. In March 2000, he started tehelka.com, an online independent news and views magazine, which soon came to be known for its sting operations, such as the cricket and defence scams. The website was relaunched as a national weekly newspaper, *Tehelka*, in January 2004 and subsequently as a weekly magazine.
33. A squib is a type of firework (a small container filled with chemicals that explodes to produce bright light and loud noises) and if it becomes wet, it will not explode. The expression 'damp squib' is used to describe an event that people think will be exciting but which is disappointing when it occurs.
34. Tehelka's exposé has been documented by veteran Indian journalist, Madhu Trehan in her book titled *Tehelka as Metaphor* (Roli Books, New Delhi. 2009), a forensic study of the sting operation. For details go to 'Tehelka as Metaphor' on Wikipedia.
35. 'Venkataswami Resigns as Tehelka Commission Chairman'. See http://www.rediff.com/news/2002/nov/23teh.htm.
36. And many more public-spirited 'do-gooders': which include social activist Anna Hazare, Magsaysay Award winner Arvind Kejriwal and advocate Prashant Bhushan. The list is open-ended. Despite their alleged infirmities (and which of us are without blemish?), I am on the side of the 'do-gooders'. With Abou ben Adhem in the poem, I would say: 'May the tribe increase.' (The poem by Leigh Hunt is titled 'Abou ben Adhem'.)
37. A celebrated phrase first used by Justice Louis Brandeis (dissenting) in *Olmstead* vs *United States*, 277 US 438 (1928), p. 478:

> The makers of our Constitution undertook to secure conditions favorable to the pursuit of happiness. They recognized the significance of man's spiritual nature of his feelings and of his intellect. They knew that only a part of the pain, pleasure and satisfactions of life are to be found in material things. They sought to protect Americans in their beliefs, their thoughts, their emotions and their sensations. They conferred, as against the government,

the right to be let alone – the most comprehensive of rights and the right most valued by civilized men.

38. See, for instance, *Gobind* vs *State of Madhya Pradesh*, AIR 1975, SC 1378, para 20, quoting Justice Brandeis in *Olmstead*.
39. Section 8 (exemption from disclosure of information): (1) Notwithstanding anything contained in this Act, there shall be no obligation to give any citizen …(j) information which relates to personal information the disclosure of which has no relationship to any public activity or interest, or which would cause unwarranted invasion of the privacy of the individual unless the Central Public Information Officer or the State Public Information Officer or the appellate authority, as the case may be, is satisfied that the larger public interest justifies the disclosure of such information.
40. It was Kautilya who was responsible for Chandragupta Maurya being on the throne of Magadh. Kautilya being an Acharya (or teacher) of Chandragupta was directly involved in statecraft, with the king invariably seeking his advice. The *Arthashastra* contained 15 books covering several topics. The chance discovery in 1909 of an authentic text of the *Arthashastra* has emphasized the difficulty of stating anything with certainty about the distant past. It is believed that the *Arthashastra* predated the *Manusmriti*, being written sometime in, or prior to, the fourth-century BCE when powerful warrior emperors like Chandragupta reigned. The accession of Chandragupta (reckoned anywhere between 325 and 321 BCE) itself constitutes a significant landmark in Indian history because it inaugurated the first Indian empire! Kautilya was his chief minister. It was the Maurya dynasty (which included the Emperor Ashoka) that ruled virtually the entire subcontinent (except areas south of Mysore) under a centralized imperial system. After the death of Ashoka (circa 232 BCE), political decline set in and about half a century later the empire was reduced to only a part of the Ganges Valley! In 185 BCE, the last of the Mauryas was assassinated by his Brahmin commander-in-chief Pushyamitra. See this author's *India's Legal System: Can It Be Saved?* Penguin, New Delhi, 2006, p. 8.
41. Samuel Huntington: *Political Order in Changing Societies*, Yale University Press, New Haven, USA, 1968, p. 386.
42. See the interesting and well-researched article by Pranab Bardhan of the University of California, Berkeley: 'Corruption and Development: A Review of Issues', *Journal of Economic Literature*, Vol. 35, September 1997, pp. 1320-46, where the quote from Huntington (1968) is also mentioned. In the corruption/no-corruption scale of 0 to 10, Bardhan has placed India at 5.25. According to Transparency International (1996) India's perceived corruption ranking – in comparison with all other countries – has been put at No. 46 with a score of 2.6 (in the range of 0 to 10).
43. Diego Gambetta: *The Sicilian Mafia: The Business of Private Protection*, Harvard University Press, Cambridge, Massachusetts, 1993.
44. Gunnar Myrdal: *Asian Drama: An Inquiry into the Poverty of Nations*, Pantheon Books, New York, 1968, p. 941.

45. Jeremy Pope had also laid the foundation of the Commonwealth Lawyers' Association. In 2008, Pope was appointed for a five-year term as human rights commissioner on the New Zealand Human Rights Commission, which he served till his death in August 2012. The Indian Chapter of Transparency International was chaired for many years with great distinction by Admiral Ram Tahiliani: now mentor.
46. Dharma Vira lived from 20 January 1906 to 16 September 2000.
47. After retirement he was appointed governor of Punjab, then of West Bengal and then of Karnataka.
48. From an article by columnist Ezra Klein: 'Our Corrupt Politics: It's Not All about Money', *New York Review of Books*, 22 March 2012. The article reviews Lawrence Lessig's book: *Republic Lost: How Much Money Corrupts Congress – and a Plan to Stop It*, Grand Central Publishing, New York, 2011.
49. Pierre Truche was the procureur general of the Cour de Cassation (France's highest court) until 1996 before becoming its president, a post from which he retired in 1999. The quote is from a periodical, whose particulars I had then noted but which have been misplaced.
50. The Human Development Centre, Islamabad, was later renamed as the Mahbub-ul Haq Human Development Centre.
51. Human Development Report, Oxford University Press, New York, 1999.
52. William Shakespeare: *Macbeth*, Act V, Scene 5.
53. An article enabling a writ petition to be filed against the state (as broadly defined in Article 12) directly in the Supreme Court of India for the enforcement of one or another of the Fundamental Rights conferred in Part III.
54. A traditional system of transferring money in Arab countries and in South Asia, whereby the money is paid to an agent who then instructs an associate in the relevant country or area to pay the final recipient. It is basically a parallel remittance system that operates outside the traditional banking or financial channels: Oxford Online: http://oxforddictionary.com/hawala.
55. Almost all were decisions in the form of orders, which have been reported in that almost-instant law report *Scale*. The orders were dated as follows: 18 April 1995, 16 January 1996 (*Vineet Narain* vs *Union of India*), 30 January 1996 (*Vineet Narain* vs *Union of India*), 22 February 1996 [1996 (2), *Scale* 84], 1 March 1996 (*Vineet Narain* vs *Union of India*) [1996 (3), *Scale* (SP) 15], 13 March 1996 [1996 (4), *Scale* (SP) 3], 1 May 1996 [1996 (4), *Scale* (SP) 56], 26 July 1996 [1996 (6), *Scale* (SP) 24], 9 July 1997 (*Vineet Narain* vs *Union of India*). Orders passed in similar matters were dated 12 February 1996 [1996 (3), *Scale* (SP) 35], 2 April 1996, 26 April 1996 [1996 (4), *Scale* (SP) 71] and 26 July 1996 [1996 (6), *Scale* (SP) 23]. A series of directions were ultimately issued by the Supreme Court in December 1997 (by Chief Justice J. S. Verma, Justice S. P. Bharucha and Justice S. C. Sen), reported in AIR 1998, SC 889. The first paragraph of the judgment describes the innovative exercise undertaken by the judges, viz., activating by judicial fiat the investigative process in a criminal case. The paragraph reads as follows:

Chief Justice Verma: These writ petitions under Article 32 of the Constitution of India brought in public interest, to begin with, did not appear to have the potential of escalating to the dimensions they reached or to give rise to several issues of considerable significance to the implementation of rule of law, which they have, during their progress. They began as yet another complaint of inertia by the Central Bureau of Investigation (CBI) in matters where the accusation made was against high dignitaries. It was not the only matter of its kind during the recent past. The primary question was: Whether it is within the domain of judicial review and [whether] it could be an effective instrument for activating the investigative process which is under the control of the executive? The focus was on the question whether any judicial remedy is available in such a situation? However, as the case progressed, it required innovation of a procedure within the constitutional scheme of judicial review to permit intervention by the court to find a solution to the problem. This case has helped to develop a procedure within the discipline of law for the conduct of such a proceeding in similar situations. It has also generated awareness of the need of probity in public life and provided a mode of enforcement of accountability in public life. Even though the matter was brought to the court by certain individuals claiming to represent public interest, yet as the case progressed, in keeping with the requirement of public interest, the procedure devised was to appoint the petitioners' counsel as the amicus curiae and to make such orders from time to time as were consistent with public interest. Intervention in the proceedings by everyone else was shut out but permission was granted to all, who so desired, to render such assistance as they could, and to provide the relevant material available with them to the amicus curiae for being placed before the court for its consideration.

56. Paper by Anil Divan, senior advocate: 'Public Interest Litigation: The Jain Hawala Case' (unpublished), presented to the Rotary Club, Mumbai, 17 December 1998.

57. *CBI* vs *V. C. Shukla*, AIR 1998, SC 1406, decided on 2 March 1998 by a bench of three judges (Justices M. K. Mukherjee, S. P. Kurdukar and K. T. Thomas) affirming the decision of the Delhi High Court. Relying on the provisions of Section 34 of the Indian Evidence Act 1872, it was held that entries made in the Jain diaries, though admissible under Section 34, were not sufficient to fasten liability on persons whose initials corresponded with the initials in the diaries, *since the truthfulness of these entries had not been corroborated by any independent evidence*.

58. In common-law systems, a magistrate has limited law enforcement and administration authority. In civil-law systems, a 'magistrate' might be (and generally is) a judge in a superior court; the magistrate's court has jurisdiction over both civil and criminal cases. A related, but not always equivalent, term is chief magistrate, which historically denotes a political-cum-administrative officer.

59. Civil law (or civilian law) is a legal system inspired by Roman law and whose

primary feature is that laws are written into a collection, and codified, and not (as in the common law) created by judges.

60. Common law (also known as case law or precedent) is law developed by judges through decisions of courts and similar tribunals rather than through legislative statutes or executive branch action. A 'common-law system' is a legal system that gives great precedential weight to common law, on the principle that it is unfair to treat similar facts differently on different occasions.

61. In the celebrated case of *Emperor* vs *Nazir Ahmed*, AIR 1945, Privy Council 18, p. 22, it was stated:

> In India as has been shown there is a statutory right on the part of the police to investigate the circumstances of an alleged cognizable crime without requiring any authority from the judicial authorities, and it would, as their Lordships think, be an unfortunate result if it should be held possible to interfere with those statutory rights by an exercise of the inherent jurisdiction of the Court. The functions of the judiciary and the police are complementary not overlapping and the combination of individual liberty with a due observance of law and order is only to be obtained by leaving each to exercise its own function, always, of course, subject to the right of the Court to intervene in an appropriate case when moved under Section 491, Criminal Procedure Code, to give directions in the nature of habeas corpus. In such a case as the present, however, the Court's functions begin when a charge is preferred before it and not until then.

62. An idiom: to do something as entirely or completely as possible; to reserve or hold back nothing.

63. An evocative expression used by the eloquent Supreme Court Justice Vivian Bose way back in 1954:

> We have upon us the whole armour of the Constitution and walk henceforth in its enlightened ways, wearing the breast plate of its protecting provisions and *flashing the flaming sword of its inspiration* (*Virendra Singh* vs *State of UP*, AIR 1954, SC 447, p. 454).

64. A bench consisting of Justices G. S. Singhvi and A. K. Ganguly in *Dr Subramanian Swamy* vs *Dr Manmohan Singh*: judgment dated 31 January 2012, reported in 2012 (2), *Scale* 12.

65. Even a great person like Homer (an ancient Greek poet known for his epics the *Iliad* and the *Odyssey*) can make mistakes!

66. *Common Cause* vs *Union of India and others*, AIR 1997, SC 1886 (Justices Kuldip Singh and Faizan ud-din). This case, fought almost single-handedly by the great H. D. Shourie (founder of Common Cause, a public interest organization), gave PILs a new face and a good name. Common Cause has helped lakhs of people in getting justice. He was the recipient of the Padma Bhushan in 1999. His motto was: 'I believe in living for people.' And he did.

67. *Common Cause* vs *Union of India and others*, AIR 1999 SC 2979 (Justices Saghir Ahmed, K. Venkataswami and Rajendra Babu).

68. See *Black's Law Dictionary*, ninth edition, Thomas West, Eagan, Minnesota, 2009, p. 1526.
69. *Shiv Sagar Tiwari* vs *Union of India*, AIR 1997, SC 1483 (Justices Kuldip Singh and B. L. Hansaria).
70. Ibid.
71. *Shiela Kaul* vs *Shiv Sagar Tiwari*, AIR 2002, SC 2868 (Justices G. B. Pattnaik, R. P. Sethi and B. P. Singh).
72. See *Ram Narayan Popli* vs *CBI*, AIR 2003, SC 2748.
73. Andrew Roberts: *Eminent Churchillians*, Orion Books, London, 1995.
74. Origin in Latin: 'The (ethical) customs or conventions of the community.'
75. *The Asian Wall Street Journal*, September 1991.
76. Valéry Giscard d'Estaing: *Power and Life*, Sullivan, Paris, 1988, quoted in an article entitled 'Paris Journal: The Giscard Best Seller: Is It Run, Valéry Run?' *New York Times*, 6 January 2009.
77. Local inhabitants – but with derogatory implications.
78. David Cannadine: *G. M. Trevelyan: A Life in History*, Penguin, London, 1992.
79. Article 291 – privy purse sums of rulers:

    (1) Where under any covenant or agreement entered into by the Ruler of any Indian State before the commencement of this Constitution, the payment of any sums, free of tax, has been guaranteed or assured by the Government of India to any Ruler of such State as privy purse –

    (a) such sums shall be charged on, and paid out of, the consolidated Fund of India; and

    (b) the sums so paid to any Ruler shall be exempt from all taxes on income.

    (2) Where the territories of any such Indian State as aforesaid are comprised within a State specified in Part A or Part B of the First Schedule, there shall be charged on, and paid out of, the Consolidated Fund of that State such contribution, if any, in respect of the payments made by the Government of India under clause (1) and for such period as may be subject to any agreement entered into in that behalf under clause (1) of Article 278, be determined by order of the President.

    Article 362 – rights and privileges of rulers of Indian states:

    In the exercise of the power of Parliament or of the Legislature of a State to make laws or in the exercise of the executive power of the Union or of a State, due regard shall be had to the guarantee or assurance given under any such covenant or agreement as is referred to in clause (1) of Article 291 with respect to the personal rights, privileges and dignities of the Ruler of an Indian State.
80. In *Raghunath Ganpatrao* vs *Union of India*, AIR 1993, SC 1267. This decision of five judges was not a correct interpretation of constitutional law. Shedding of judicial tears for erstwhile princes was neither popular nor populist!
81. 'Exaggerated statements that are not meant to be taken in the strict sense of the words.'

82. From a report dated September 2011 prepared by a Planning Commission Panel on the Department of Justice for the 12th five-year plan (2012–2017).
83. Joaquin 'Chino' Roces: 'A Call for New Moral Order', *The Manila Chronicle*, 27 July 1988, p. 3. The article has been reproduced in Mina Roces: 'Kinship Politics in Post-War Philippines: The Lopez Family (1945–1989)', *Modern Asian Studies*, **34**, 2000, pp. 181-221, Cambridge University Press, London, 2000.
84. The number of FIRs filed in India has risen steeply – from approximately 6 lakh cases in 1953 to approximately 31 lakh cases in 2011 (from the Bureau of Criminal Statistics). Of these, only some are investigated and then either dropped or pursued further by filing of charge sheets.
85. *State of Madhya Pradesh* vs *Ram Singh*: the judgment of a bench consisting of Justice K. T. Thomas and Justice R. P. Sethi, 1 February 2000, AIR 2000, SC 870, p. 873 (para 7) reads as follows:

    Corruption in a civilised society is a disease like cancer, which if not detected in time is sure to malignise [*sic*] the polity of the country leading to disastrous consequences. It is termed as plague which is not only contagious but if not controlled spreads like a fire in a jungle. Its virus is compared with HIV leading to AIDS, being incurable. It has also been termed as Royal thievery. The socio-political system exposed to such a dreaded communicable disease is likely to crumble under its own weight. Corruption is opposed to democracy and social order, being not only anti-people, but aimed and targeted against them. It affects the economy and destroys the cultural heritage. Unless nipped in the bud at the earliest, it is likely to cause [turbulent] shaking of the socio-economic-political system in an otherwise healthy, wealthy, effective and vibrating society.

86. 1995, *Writ Law Reporter*, 737 at 769, *Palani Hill Conservation Council* vs *State of Tamil Nadu*, Justices M. Srinivasan and S. Jagadeesan (High Court of Madras). Justice Srinivasan was elevated to the Supreme Court on 25 September 1997. He died whilst in office (on 25 February 2000).
87. Nirad C. Chaudhari: *The Autobiography of an Unknown Indian*, Jaico, Bombay, 1951.
88. Since 1995, Transparency International (TI) publishes the Corruption Perceptions Index (CPI), annually ranking countries 'by their perceived levels of corruption, as determined by expert assessments and opinion surveys'. The CPI generally defines corruption as 'the misuse of public power for private benefit'. As of 2010, the CPI ranked 178 countries on a scale from 10 (very clean) to 0 (highly corrupt). Transparency International had commissioned Johann Graf Lambsdorff of the University of Passau (in Germany) to produce the CPI. The 2010 CPI draws on 13 different surveys and assessments from 10 independent institutions: The African Development Bank, the Asian Development Bank, the Bertelsmann Foundation, the Economist Intelligence Unit, Freedom House, Global Insight, International Institute for Management Development, Political and Economic Risk Consultancy, the World Economic

Forum and the World Bank. Countries have to be assessed by at least three independent institutions out of the ten sources to 'qualify' for being included in the CPI! (http://en.wilkipedia.org/wiki/Corruption_Perceptions_index). India's place is low: between 2 and 3 in the CPI scoreboard. However, in the CPI for 2010, from 2002 to 2010, India's ranking has ranged from 2.7 to 3.3 – an improvement (if you can call it that), but at the slowest possible pace!

89. Human Development Report 2002 (July 2002), p. 220 (the figures given are for the year 1995). India was ranked at No. 124 in the Human Development Index (in the Human Development Report 2002).
90. That is, it still does not have any legal force.
91. The Bill seeks to give effect to the recommendations of the Administrative Reforms Commission insofar as they relate to matters within the purview of the Union Government. In its scope, it differs from the draft bill proposed by the Administrative Reforms Commission in two major respects: First, it does not extend to public servants in the states. Secondly, it does not confine itself to ministers and secretaries alone. In other words, the Bill seeks to provide a statutory machinery to enquire into complaints based on actions of all Union public servants, including ministers (para 2 of the Statement of Objects and Reasons of Bill No. 51 of 1968).
92. The Statement of Objects and Reasons read as follows: The matter has been re-examined having regard to the recommendations of the ARC, the provisions of the 1971 Bill, other laws on the subject enacted in various States from time to time and the experience of the functioning of such institutions in the States where they have been set up. In the light of this re-examination, it is proposed to alter the scheme of the Lokpal as incorporated in the 1971 Bill in material respects for making the institution of Lokpal an effective instrument to combat the problem posed by corruption at higher political levels. Under the scheme now proposed, the jurisdiction of the Lokpal will cover any complaint of misconduct (pertaining to a period not exceeding five years prior to the date of the complaint) against a person who is or has been a public man as defined in Clause 2(g) of the Bill. The Prime Minister, Members of Parliament and Chief Ministers of States are being brought within the purview of the Lokpal. Allegations against civil servants will not come within the purview of the Lokpal; and grievances, as distinct from allegations of misconduct, will be excluded from his jurisdiction. The Lokpal will have under his direct administrative control an independent investigating machinery to assist him in the discharge of his functions.
93. The Bill sought to set up the office of Lokpal as a high office with a fixed tenure. With a view to ensuring that the Lokpal was able to act independently and discharge his functions without fear or favour, the Bill provided that the Lokpal shall not be removed from his office except by an order made by the President on the ground of proved misbehaviour or incapacity after an inquiry made by the Chief Justice of India or by any other Judge of the Supreme Court nominated by the Chief Justice of India for this purpose. Under the scheme

of the Bill, the Lokpal was to inquire into complaints alleging that a public functionary as defined in the Bill has committed an offence punishable under Chapter IX of the Indian Penal Code or under the Prevention of Corruption Act 1947 and the expression 'public functionary' covers Ministers, Ministers of State, Deputy Ministers and Parliamentary Secretaries of the Union. It sought to carry out in this respect the object and purpose of the recommendations of the Administrative Reforms Commission for enabling the citizen to have recourse to a convenient and effective forum for determination of complaints and thereby save him from pursuing his remedy through the process of courts, which may prove expensive or dilatory and may not facilitate in speedy determination. The Bill also sought to make special provisions for discouraging frivolous, vexatious and false complaints.

94. The Statement of Objects and Reasons for this Bill read as follows: The Lokpal Bill has had a chequered history going back to 1968. Having studied the interim report of the Administrative Reforms Commission submitted in 1966 on the subject and all the four Bills which were introduced in the Parliament earlier, the Government has come to the conclusion that such legislation for constituting the institution of Lokpal is imperative to combat the problem of corruption at higher political levels. In the interest of democracy, it should be the endeavour of every public functionary at top political levels to maintain high standards of public morality. Hence this Bill.

95. Group A officers are classified by the Department of Personnel and Training Notification No. 13012/2/87 Estt (D) dated 30 June 1987. The classification serves an important administrative purpose. Group A posts (officers) carry a pay or a scale of pay with a maximum of not less than Rs 39,100. Group A services and other groups are as follows:

    Indian P & T [Post and Telegraph] Accounts and Finance Service; Indian Audit and Accounts Service; Indian Revenue Service (Customs and Central Excise); Indian Defence Accounts Service; Indian Revenue Service (IT or Income Tax); Indian Ordnance Factories Service (Assistant Works Manager, Administration); Indian Postal Service; Indian Civil Accounts Service; Indian Railway Traffic Service; Indian Railway Accounts Service; Indian Railway Personnel Service; Post of Assistant Security Commissioner in Railway Protection Force; Indian Defence Estates Service; Indian Information Service (Junior Grade); Indian Trade Service, Group 'A' (Grade III); Indian Corporate Law Service.

96. Ayes 250, noes 180.
97. Leader of the opposition in the Rajya Sabha.
98. Rudyard Kipling: A school song of 13 verses.
99. Bhagavad Gita: text and translation by Annie Besant, Theosophical Publishing House, Chennai, 17th reprint, 1998, p. 53 (Chapter III, Verse 21).

Chapter VI

Combating Corruption in the Higher Judiciary

Corruption is another challenge we face both in the Government and the judiciary.

– Prime Minister Manmohan Singh in his address to a Conference of Chief Ministers and Chief Justices of High Courts (19 April 2008)

A court which is final and unreviewable needs more careful scrutiny than any other. Unreviewable power is the most likely to self-indulge itself and the least likely to engage in dispassionate self-analysis .... In a country like ours, no public institution, or the people who operate it, can be above public debate!

– Justice V. R. Krishna Iyer[1] (quoting Justice Warren E. Burger, chief justice of the US Supreme Court from 1969 to 1986)

For the judge there is one absolute standard, one implacable test – unswerving honesty. The few who have deviated, who have dishonoured themselves and the judicial process, comprise the main subject of this book ...

From the blurb of *The Corrupt Judge* by Joseph Borkin[2]

All persons possessing a portion of power ought to be strongly and awfully impressed with an idea that they act in trust and that they are to account for their conduct in that trust ...

– Edmund Burke:
Reflections on the Revolution in France *

* First published 1790; reprinted by Oxford University Press, New York, 1999, p. 77.

During his tenure in the Supreme Court of India from 1973 to 1980, Justice V. R. Krishna Iyer (born in 1915) gave equal space to *justice*, *compassion* and *the law*. In retirement he has been the voice of conscience of India's higher judiciary.

In an article ('Majesty of the Judiciary', *The Asian Age*, 17 February 2007), he expressed his sense of anguish at the

> … corruption and decline now creeping into the vitals of the Higher Courts and the urgent need to arrest this trend.

Since what he then wrote received scant attention from lawmakers, governments (at the Centre and the states) and courts, this outspoken judge wrote once more – nearly 30 years after he had retired – regretting that the number of delinquent judges was on the rise and calling for a commission to enquire into a candidate's fitness before appointment as a judge and also for a performance accountability commission to oversee the functioning of judges appointed in the high courts and in the Supreme Court of India.[3]

* * *

Delinquencies in the judicial branch of the state occur everywhere – but they have to be addressed and the injustices caused by such delinquencies have to be remedied.

Around 50 years ago, in the modern world's oldest democracy – the USA – there was enough judicial misbehaviour to justify the publication of a book titled *The Corrupt Judge – An Inquiry into Bribery and Other High Crimes and Misdemeanors in the Federal Courts*![4] It detailed allegations of bribery against individual American judges – state and federal – including an account of the proceedings for their impeachment. Since its publication (in 1962), there have been five more proceedings brought to light by the Judicial Council of the United States[5] about *errant* US federal judges:

1. Federal District Judge Harry Claiborne was removed from his post on 20 October 1986;
2. Federal District Judge Alcee Hastings was removed from his post on 20 October 1989;
3. Chief Judge Walter Nixon of the Southern District of Mississippi was removed from his post on 3 November 1989;
4. Federal District Judge Samuel Kent resigned on 30 June 2009 during proceedings for his impeachment; and
5. Federal District Judge Thomas Porteous was removed from his post on 8 December 2010.

As in India, the fight against judicial corruption in the USA is far from over.

In England, judicial corruption was rampant even before the Magna Carta (A.D. 1215). A fascinating book (*Tipping the Scales*) written by a county-court judge (under the pseudonym Henry Cecil[6]) records that for over six centuries the character of at least four of England's Lord Chancellors (the highest judicial office in the land) had been attacked to such an extent that each one of them had to stand trial in one or both the Houses of Parliament! They were:

1. Sir Michael de la Pole, who was impeached in 1386 before both the Houses on various charges of improper conduct;
2. Lord Chancellor Francis Bacon, who preached but failed to practise how a judge should behave: his lame excuse was that he was following the custom of the age! In 1620, however, his misdeeds caught up with him – he was charged with a slew of judicial misdemeanours, to which he later confessed; He was found guilty and fined £40,000 and imprisoned in the Tower of London: to remain there during the King's pleasure. He was also declared forever incapable of holding any office, or place in Parliament or in the state or Commonwealth;
3. Lord Chancellor Macclesfield (aka Thomas Parker) was impeached for corruption in 1720 before the House of Lords; he was found guilty, sentenced to undergo imprisonment in the Tower of London and ordered to pay a fine of £30,000;

4. In 1865, Lord Westbury (aka Richard Bethell) was compelled to resign his office of Lord Chancellor by a vote of censure passed on him by the House of Commons, although he was acquitted of the specific acts of corruption with which he had been charged.

Since 1865, the judiciary in England is reportedly free from corruption: a belief that has prompted Henry Cecil to moralize. 'Integrity', he has written, 'comes haltingly into public life and without watchfulness it could slip away.'

In the foreword to Henry Cecil's book (*Tipping the Scales*), the Right Honourable Lord Patrick Arthur Devlin ('Law Lord'[7] from 1961 to 1964) says that 'the integrity of British judges that we now take for granted is not a virtue that belongs exclusively to them; judges are not now, neither have they have been in the past, much better or worse than other public servants of their time'.

* * *

Corruption means dishonest or fraudulent conduct by those in power: whether it be political power or judicial power; it connotes a deviation from an ideal. The sin of corruption is not confined to politicians, ministers and bureaucrats. In India it has infiltrated into all organs of the state – with one difference: whereas the media, print and electronic, is not constrained when questioning or publicizing wrongdoing amongst public officials (except for the sanctions imposed by the general law of defamation), the same is not the case with regard to questioning alleged lapses of good conduct amongst judges in the higher judiciary. These judges enjoy almost complete protection under the laws of contempt: laws that are administered and interpreted solely and finally by the judges themselves.

In 2001, an article with the provocative title 'Judged Out!' was published in a fortnightly magazine circulating in New Delhi (*Wah India*). It described the result of what was characterized as a 'Delhi High Court judges' survey'. A form had been circulated by the editors of the magazine to '50 senior lawyers' (who were not named or identified). They were required to allocate marks to sitting judges of the Delhi High Court under each of the following heads: (i) manners in court;

(ii) general reputation for personal integrity; (iii) quality of judgments delivered; (iv) depth in basic law; (v) observance of punctuality in court; and (vi) receptiveness to arguments addressed. The maximum marks to be allotted under each head were 10. Based on the responses received from these unnamed 50 senior lawyers, an evaluation was presented for each of the sitting judges, along with their photographs published for instant identification! This article created a sensation.

On contempt proceedings being initiated by the Bar Council of Delhi, those responsible for the publication (the editor, the printer and the publisher) were called upon by the Delhi High Court to show cause why they should not be committed to prison (or fined) for contempt of court. A full bench of five judges of the Delhi High Court specially sat to hear the case, which was presided over by the then chief justice, Arijit Pasayat. In a unanimous decision, the bench held that the publication was based on conjectures and surmises and that this was one of 'the rarest of the rare cases' in which the court must intervene 'to protect the faith of the people who had an abiding interest in the administration of justice'. After administering a warning against such an exercise being undertaken in the future, a majority of the judges on the bench (viz., Chief Justice Arijit Pasayat, Justice D. P. Jain and Justice Arun Kumar) proceeded to accept the unqualified apology tendered on behalf of the magazine's editor, printer and publisher, saying that they would 'give a decent burial to the unwarranted controversy'! But two of the other judges on the bench – Justice Anil Dev Singh and Justice O. P. Dwivedi – dissented: whilst agreeing that gross contempt of court had been committed, they said that the apology offered was neither genuine nor made in good faith and should not be accepted. The view expressed by the majority prevailed and the case was closed! Chastened by the order passed by the Delhi High Court (which was widely publicized), no one has since attempted to 'rate' members of the higher judiciary (anywhere in India) on their overall performance as judges; nor has anyone undertaken an assessment of their 'reputation for personal integrity'. In the absence of the establishment of an institutionalized body like a judicial ombudsman (which I believe is imperative), assessments about judges' reputations (good or bad) are presently left to the tender mercies of hearsay and rumour.

***

The profession of law (that includes lawyers and judges) is one in which there is still very little transparency. When enacted laws are abstruse and unclear, we lawyers do little or nothing to educate the public about them. Our clients are, quite deliberately, left ignorant of the 'mumbo-jumbo'[8] that we utter in courts; the vast majority of people can neither understand the purpose or tenor of prolix legal proceedings nor can they comprehend the drift of judgments (often, of enormous length) handed down from the bench. Under our Constitution, the higher judiciary enjoys pride of place – well-deserved no doubt – but its inevitable consequence is to put justices of the high courts and of the Supreme Court on the highest pedestal: on cloud nine.[9]

How are judges appointed? How are they selected and recommended? What are their shortcomings and how are they remedied within the judicial fraternity? And why are judgments sometimes not delivered at all or (more often) interminably delayed? Before the advent of the RTI[10] (and even thereafter), such impertinent queries were met with responses such as: 'It is none of your business to ask us questions' and 'we (the judges) know what is best for the system.' Similar attitudes have been exhibited by the higher judiciary in other parts of the world.

* * *

At an international law conference that I had attended in the garden city of Bangalore many years ago, a prominent American journalist told me how he had been 'cited' by a US court for reporting a pending case in colours too fanciful for the presiding judge. The American journalist (backed by the proprietor of his newspaper) told the federal judge: 'We want no accommodation from you. The First Amendment[11] is on our side. We will fight it out.' The judge quietly responded: 'Have it your way. But don't forget, who the umpire is in this battleground!'

With a few exceptions, the 'umpire' in India continues to exhibit a dark and forbidding countenance. A case in point is that of author and activist Arundhati Roy. Some years ago, she had commented on a court order in language too brash for the then chief justice of India, Adarsh Sein Anand, and for Justice B. N. Kirpal. This occurred when the majority in a bench of three judges passed an order (2:1, with Justice S. P. Bharucha dissenting) permitting the raising of the height of the dam across the Narmada river in Gujarat, the necessary consequence of which was the flooding of the homes of tribals who had traditionally lived for centuries on its high banks. According to the dissenting judge, rehabilitation efforts had not kept pace with the height of the dam. Arundhati Roy (not a party to the proceedings in court) used some vituperative epithets about this order. Ultimately (and commendably) all three judges simply ignored Arundhati Roy's remarks,[12] saying 'the Court's shoulders are broad enough to shrug them off'.

But soon after, the same lady was involved in a dharna outside the Supreme Court, participating in the shouting of slogans and name-calling. It was felt that this simply could not be ignored! On a contempt notice being issued, she responded by filing what the court characterized as a 'contemptuous affidavit', for which she was asked to show cause why she should not be committed for contempt.[13] In her affidavit to show cause, she repeated what she had said earlier; on this occasion, the court (a bench of two justices) held that she was guilty of 'scandalizing the court' and sentenced her to simple imprisonment for one day and ordered her to pay a fine of Rs 2000.[14] Unchastened, the indefatigable Arundhati Roy stuck out her chin with an almost defiant: 'My head is bloody but unbowed!'[15] The sentence imposed on her was neither harsh nor improper (given the circumstances and the state of the law) but the very initiation of contempt proceedings against her had sent shivers down the spine of all and sundry (especially members of the media). The very initiation of proceedings for contempt of court was sufficient to convey the message: '*Don't trifle with us – you will never succeed*.'

'Scandalizing the court' is an aspect of 'criminal contempt' (where the accuser is also the judge); it has long since fallen into disuse in most of the civilized countries around the world, but not in India![16]

The origin of this branch of contempt law known as 'scandalizing the court' is shrouded in antiquity. In textbooks it has been described as 'both *dubious* and *controversial*':[17] dubious, since it originates from a dictum of one judge, Justice J. E. Wilmot, in the John Wilkes case[18] way back in 1765 and controversial since the dictum was recorded in a judgment that was never delivered. It was published by Justice Wilmot's son after his father died: the judgment had been reserved after argument, and when it was ready to be delivered, it was found that the writ (case) against Wilkes was incorrectly titled; since the procedural law of the time did not permit an amendment to the writ unless consented to by both parties, the entire case had to be abandoned! This then is the ancestry of that part of the law of contempt that goes by the name '*scandalizing the court*'; it is based on a judgment never delivered in court in a case that had already abated!

Strange are the ways of providence; sometimes, stranger are the ways of courts! There are no rules and no precise circumstances as to when it can be said that the administration of justice is brought into 'contempt'. Judgments of courts are strewn with pious platitudes that give little guidance to newsmen (and newswomen), editors or commentators. This part of the law of contempt – although necessary in extreme cases – constitutes a standing threat to a cherished Fundamental Right: the freedom of expression. It leaves too much to the predilections of the individual judge (or judges). Even the decisions rendered in contempt cases sometimes give the uncanny feeling that the status of the person who 'scandalizes' the court may well have influenced the ultimate result. In *P. N. Duda* vs *P. Shiv Shankar* (AIR 1988, SC 1208 at 1213), a cabinet minister of the Government of India was exonerated though he had compared the judges of the Supreme Court to 'anti-social elements, foreign exchange violators, bride burners and a whole horde of reactionaries who have found their haven in the Supreme Court'. The court said that the speech of the minister had to be read 'in its proper perspective' and, when so read, it did not bring the administration of justice into disrepute!! But in a later case (also reported) – *Mohd. Zahir Khan* vs *Vijai Singh and Others* (AIR 1992, SC 642) – an impetuous (but insignificant) litigant, merely said in a loud voice in court: 'Either I am anti-national or the judges are anti-national.' He was immediately cited for contempt, pronounced guilty and sentenced to undergo simple imprisonment for one month!

* * *

In India the higher judiciary has inherent (and almost unbridled) powers of contempt – even beyond laws enacted by Parliament.[19] And for that reason, the media and the whole lot of information-seeking agencies – not sure of how the contempt law will be interpreted – are tight-lipped. No one dares come out with what they believe to be the FACTS (in any matter pertaining to judges or the administration of justice) even though the law (amending the Contempt of Courts Act 1971) now permits 'justification by truth' as a valid defence.[20] But let a complaint be made even by a responsible individual against a reputedly corrupt judge in the higher judiciary, and no newspaper will publish it! Give the newspaper as much proof or evidence as you will – it will still not publish anything! Regrettably – with a few notable exceptions – the fraternity of justices in the higher judiciary in India tend to stick together when anyone speaks of any wrongdoing about one of them – alas, even when some of its members themselves entertain a shrewd suspicion of *some wrongdoing*! There pervades, in the higher echelons of the judiciary, what I would characterize as a *spirit of trade unionism.* Trade unionism amongst lawyers is different. It is also a closed shop but there are many leaks! One instance of wrongdoing about a colleague at the Bar and a dozen other 'lawyer-friends' will spread the word about more such wrongdoings! No, the trade unionism of lawyers is just no match to the trade unionism of judges. The latter close their ranks when one of their own is involved.

In 2003, there were unsubstantiated reports about three sitting judges in one of the high courts in South India being found in some shady joint outside Bangalore city. Their reported shenanigans (or 'secret activities') were publicized, but met with instant denials. An independent inquiry into the alleged incident was not *immediately* ordered by the then chief justice of Karnataka. Instead, contempt proceedings were promptly initiated by the high court against the concerned newspapers that had reported the alleged incident. It was only later – much later – that the chief justice of India set up a high-powered committee consisting of the chief justices of three high courts in the country (Bombay, Madhya Pradesh and Kerala) to look into the incident and report back to him. When this Inquiry Committee of Chief Justices took up its task, contempt notices had been already issued by the Karnataka High Court to representatives of the media (editors, printers and publishers), so that the latter were not quite sure whether, if they revealed to the committee, what they knew, or what they had heard, it may not be also used as evidence against them as contemnors. By that time the so-called 'scandal' had been blown out of all proportion – not by *fact*, but almost entirely by *rumour*. Everyone – almost everyone – seemed to know (or suspect) what had happened, but no one would tell! The leading national newspapers having been cited (by the High Court of Karnataka) in proceedings for contempt of court, they approached the Supreme Court of India for ultimate redress. I was appointed amicus by the court (to assist it to arrive at a decision), and a wise chief justice of India (V. N. Khare) – wise beyond his years – after hearing what I had to say passed an order staying all contempt proceedings initiated by the High Court of Karnataka. They remain stayed till this day! Meanwhile, the Inquiry Committee of Chief Justices proceeded with a very detailed investigation and its findings were reported to the chief justice of India. Unfortunately, these findings have never been published or publicized. In my view, this was a mistake, because *if* the finding of the committee was that there was no basis for any of the allegations initially made, the person/persons found responsible for making them should have been dealt with severely; this was the only way to clear the fair name of the higher judiciary in Karnataka.. 'Sunlight is the best disinfectant', as a former chief justice of India, Justice M. N. Venkatachaliah, always liked to say! But in the absence of a full public disclosure of the report, busybodies assumed the worst, on the facile (and often erroneous) assumption that 'there can be no smoke without fire'! It was definitely in the larger interests of propriety and justice that the report of the committee should have been promptly made public.

***

An aside about V. N. Khare would not be out of place here.

'Wise' is the encomium I give to him since he was the judge, who, as chief justice, came to the aid of upholding the supreme dignity of the apex court. Sometime in February 2004, I was sitting in Court Room No. 2 on a Miscellaneous Day (i.e., when matters other than final hearings are taken up for disposal). A party in person was arguing his own case and raised his voice a bit, in order to emphasize the point that he was making. Unfortunately for him, the judges asked him not to raise his voice, but he wouldn't listen, and kept on arguing in a loud tone, which prompted the judges to send for the court marshal to physically remove him. This was too much for me. I got up from my seat in the second or third row and shouted to the court marshal not to touch him since I felt that no litigant could be removed physically from court premises for arguing his case – howsoever unreasonably. But the marshal did as the judges in court had directed and removed the party in person under duress and the case was dismissed. I was so enraged that I stomped out of the room and finding that the chief justice of India had risen for the day, I phoned his secretary and asked him whether I could see Chief Justice Khare at his residence. On receiving a favourable reply, I then went directly to the residence of the chief justice and told him about the incident and said that in my (then) over 50 years at the bar I had never witnessed a litigant being thrown out of the court whilst arguing his own case. And the fact that this was done in the Supreme Court had set a most unhealthy precedent. Chief Justice Khare was visibly disturbed and thanked me for bringing this to his notice. He then sent for the litigant in person, personally apologized to him on behalf of the court and ordered that his dismissed case be restored and heard once again by the same bench! Here was a 'Daniel-come-to-judgment', I said to myself! When Chief Justice Khare retired at age 65 on 2 May 2004, we honoured him with a farewell dinner at the Hotel Imperial in New Delhi. Apart from Chief Justice M. N. Venkatachaliah, no other retired chief justice of India has been so honoured by the Bar Association of India. I believe that a judge must have *good* instincts and *good* responses – qualities that I greatly admire more than the writing of *good* judgments!

* * *

The role of the media in India in highlighting judicial corruption in the higher judiciary (or some other wrongdoing of one of its members) has drawn a blank. We have to try different measures to root out 'judicial corruption' (or rather, root out manifest perceptions of it); first of all we must try to *shame* the (few) wrongdoers.

How do we do this? It is the lawyers who have to do it, not with a view to exposing 'skeletons in the cupboard', but for the good of the institution (the judiciary) and for the cleansing effect that transparency always has. But then, this is, at least for now, foreclosed, because we have to live with that (regrettable) decision of our own apex court in *C. Ravichandran Iyer* vs *A. M. Bhattacharjee* (1995), popularly known as Bhattacharjee's case.[21] A. M. Bhattacharjee was chief justice of the Bombay High Court (from April 1994 to April 1995), and allegations about his 'wrongdoings' (along with those of one other high court judge in Bombay at the time) became (as the expression goes) 'the talk of the town'. The Bombay Bar Association (under its then president, senior advocate I. M. Chagla) took up the matter, and a resolution was passed by the association requesting Chief Justice Bhattacharjee to demit his office as a judge in the interest of the institution. Bhattacharjee resisted.[22] In court proceedings initiated thereafter, a bench of two judges of the Supreme Court (Justices K. Ramaswamy and B. L. Hansaria) said (in Bhattacharjee's case) that even associations of lawyers could not on their own take up matters and pass such resolutions with regard to allegations of corruption against sitting judges. The bench also said that the associations must first take up the matter with the chief justice of the high court and, if there is no redress, then with the chief justice of India and await a response for a 'reasonable period'. But what constitutes a 'reasonable period'? And what if the chief justice of India failed to respond? The bench of two judges gave no answer. In my view, the judgment in *Bhattacharjee* is a dampener to transparency in cases of 'perceived judicial corruption' but it remains declared law and operates – with 'chilling effect' (as the popular American expression goes).

In Bhattacharjee's case, the judgment of the Supreme Court noted (with approval) the opinion of Harry T. Edwards, chief judge of the US Court of Appeals of the District of Columbia. He was at one time chairman of what is known as the Judicial Council in the United States, a statutory body set up by the US Congress for disciplining federal judges (who are appointed for life). Many years ago, when a team of Indian judges and lawyers (under the aegis of the Indo–US Legal Forum) had been invited to Washington D.C., I had visited Harry Edwards in his court. It was he who told me how the Judicial Council in the USA (of which he was one of the twelve members) dealt with all manner of charges against all manner of judges (including his own colleagues, i.e., federal judges). When litigants or lawyers there made complaints against sitting judges, the complaints were investigated and the result of the investigation was pronounced upon in open court. He handed me a judgment of his own with respect to a colleague (whom I later saw sitting on the bench with him) where a litigant had made certain allegations against that judge about his conduct in a case that had been previously heard. The allegations were investigated and dealt with by a speaking order in a judgment that was printed and widely circulated. There were no hard feelings amongst the judges. The *in-house* procedure in the United States is both open and transparent.

It was in Bhattacharjee's case that the bench of two judges quoted from an article written by Chief Judge Harry T. Edwards:[23]

> Ideal of judicial independence is not compromised when judges are monitored and regulated by their own peers. This limited system of judicial self-regulation presents no constitutional dilemma as long as the removal power remains with Congress. I argue that the judiciary alone should monitor this bad behavior *through a system of self-regulation* [emphasis added].

True. But we in India have so far lacked a system of *transparent* 'judicial self-regulation'. The concluding paragraph in the judgment in Bhattacharjee's case has told us why:

> 42. It would thus be seen that [the] yawning gap between proved misbehaviour and bad conduct inconsistent with the high office on the part of a non-cooperating Judge/Chief Justice of a High Court could be disciplined by self-regulation through in-house procedure. This in-house procedure would fill in the constitutional gap and would yield salutary effect. *Unfortunately, recourse to this procedure was not taken in the case at hand, may be, because of absence of legal sanction to such a procedure* [emphasis added].

* * *

Regarding associations of lawyers being inhibited from taking action in respect of *errant* judges, the matter has necessarily to be left (under existing circumstances) to the justices themselves. How have they reacted?

Stopping of work is an ad hoc measure 'invented' by the judges of the higher judiciary – for errant colleagues. It has been judicially approved in India in J. P. Mitter's case[24] by a bench of five justices of the Supreme Court; that was a case arising out of a dispute about the age of a judge (J. P. Mitter) then sitting in the High Court of Calcutta. And the controversy was whether he had or had not crossed the mandatory retirement age of 62 years for a high court judge. Chief Justice P. B. Gajendragadkar speaking for the Supreme Court said (in his reported judgment) that 'any prudent and wise Chief Justice would naturally think of avoiding unnecessary complications by refusing to assign any work to the sitting judge if when the dispute about age had been raised it *appeared* that at the relevant time the Judge in question had already reached the age of superannuation'.[25] The test propounded by the Constitution Bench of five judges of the Supreme Court of India was one of *perception*, not of *proof or certainty* (viz., that the judge at the relevant time had – or had not – reached the age of superannuation).

Nearly 25 years later, not giving work to certain judges because of their perceived wrongdoings was resorted to by Bombay's chief justice, this time under different circumstances. And it proved effective: it worked in what I like to describe as the 'Bombay experiment'. In June

1990, two bar associations in the High Court of Bombay resolved (almost unanimously) that none of its members would appear before four named judges (of the high court) against whom there had been constant allegations of nepotism and corruption by responsible members of the Bar, allegations which had gone unheeded by the then chief justice of Bombay as also by the then chief justice of India. Resentment had been building up and was simmering among all sections of the Bar not just for a few months, but for nearly a year. When I was invited to speak (at Aurangabad, Maharashtra, in October 1987) at the 125th anniversary celebration of the Bombay High Court, I had mentioned in my address the problem of the two great C's – Corruption and Caste – creeping into the higher echelons of the judiciary in the state of Maharashtra. Chief Justice C. S. Dharmadhikari, who presided at the anniversary celebration, acknowledged that the high court was faced with problems of corruption and caste and said that he was glad I had openly raised it. But alas, this able judge could do nothing about it, as he was only the *acting* chief justice of the Bombay High Court. But his successor, Chief Justice Chittatosh Mookerjee, did do something.

Mookerjee was just finding his feet in the Bombay High Court when members of the two associations of the Bombay Bar, exasperated at the lack of response even from the then chief justice of India, took the unprecedented step of virtually declaring 'guilty' four sitting judges of the high court. Yes, without even hearing them, on the principle that the hand that holds the scales of justice must not be *seen* to be soiled; 200 members belonging to the two bar associations sent a signed petition and representation to Chief Justice Mookerjee.

On a later visit to Bombay (in late 1990), the Chief Justice of India Ranganath Mishra upbraided the office bearers of the bar associations (wrongly, in my view) for having taken this 'hasty step'. Some of the judges of the Supreme Court shared the CJI's views. My sympathies were, and remain, with the Bombay Bar, not because I believe in the 'boycott' of courts by lawyers (I have for long openly protested against lawyers' strikes[26]) but because I believe the Bar was left with no choice. The higher judiciary, repeatedly given the opportunity, could not – only because it would not – take care of its own domestic problem. If the Bombay Bar had not acted when it did, I believe that the entire high court would have soon been swamped with ill-founded rumours by disgruntled litigants.

To his abiding credit, Chief Justice Chittatosh Mookerjee (1987–1991) – long since retired[27] – after a cursory inquiry into the veracity of the complaints made in the representation (again, a matter of perception since the allegations were not yet proven) promptly took action. Since the chief justice of a high court sets the roster of work amongst judges, Mookerjee refused to assign any work to any of the three judges named in the resolution of the bar associations (the fourth judge having resigned earlier). The chief justice did this not in deference to the near-unanimous wishes of the practising members of the Bar, but because he had satisfied himself that the allegations made were not lacking in substance. The concerned judges protested. Chief Justice Mookerjee told them that they were at liberty to challenge his administrative order on the judicial side of the high court under the provisions of Article 226 of the Constitution: the writ jurisdiction of the high courts (a course of action well established in law). Not one of them did! One of the judges was transferred some months later to the High Court of Kerala and the other two continued drawing emoluments due to them as 'sitting judges' – sitting only in their chambers with no work assigned to them till they retired at the constitutionally prescribed retirement age (62 years)! Although not giving work to errant judges increased the backlog of cases, it also helped to put a stop to the spread of frequently irresponsible talk of judicial wrongdoing.

***

What happened in the Supreme Court of India – also in the year 1990 – was equally disquieting. But again, in the absence of the establishment of a judicial ombudsman, the manner in which the matter was handled by India's Chief Justice Sabyasachi Mukherjee (no relation of Justice Chittatosh Mookerjee) was as admirable as it was unique.

Charges of financial impropriety had been made by a state comptroller and auditor general against a sitting judge of the Supreme Court who (prior to his elevation to the apex court) had been functioning as chief justice of Punjab and Haryana. To maintain the unsullied image of the apex court, the then chief justice of India, Sabyasachi Mukherjee, took the unprecedented step of announcing in open court his resolve (the decision was his own as chief justice of India) that the judge – Justice V. Ramaswami[28] – should proceed on leave till he was cleared of the charges. By an unconventional, but neatly surgical method (not warranted by any provision of law but justified only by the superior wisdom of experience), Chief Justice Mukherjee successfully isolated the concerned judge from the rest of the members of his court. His 'order' of 20 July 1990 (headed 'Re: Ramaswami J.: CJI's Statement to the Bar') announced in open court was applauded by the legal fraternity – although some of the chief justice's own colleagues, at the time, had demurred! In my view it is a practice – a precedent[29] – of great significance in the weeding out of perceived wrongdoing of members in the higher judiciary by the head of the judiciary. But since it has not been used since, the 'order' needs to be more widely known. It is for that reason reproduced here in full (with important portions italicized for emphasis):

> Re: Ramaswami, J.
>
> CJI's Statement to the Bar (20 July 1990)
>
> In the beginning of May 1990, some learned advocates of this Court drew my attention to certain newspapers about the audit report investigating the expenses incurred in furnishing the residence of a former Chief Justice of the Punjab and Haryana High Court, namely, Shri V. Ramaswami, who is now a sitting Judge of this court. I was requested by the learned lawyers to take action suo motu. The matter was mentioned more than once. On 1 May 1990. I had received a communication from the editor of a magazine enclosing therewith a copy of April [19]90 issue of the magazine *The Lawyers*, stating that it contained the full text of the audit report of the Chandigarh Administration. Thereafter, the learned Attorney General, Sri Soli Sorabjee, the former Attorney General, Sri [K.] Parasaran, Mr [K. K.] Venugopal, the President of the Supreme Court Bar Association, and Dr Y. S. Chitale, former President of the Supreme Court Bar Association, also met me and drew my attention to these reports and expressed concern on the contents of the publications. The Union Minister of Law and Justice called on me and expressed the concern of the members of Parliament about the alleged extravagance by Justice Ramaswami and the contents of the report, while working as the Chief Justice of the Punjab and Haryana High

Court. Sharing their concern, I had told the Law Minister and have since assured the learned Attorney General and other members of the Bar that I would look into the matter.

Legally and constitutionally the Chief Justice of India, as such, has no right or authority to inquire into the conduct of a sitting Judge of the Supreme Court. However, the Chief Justice of India, as the head of Judicial Family has, I believe, the duty and the responsibility to maintain the judicial propriety and attempts to secure the confidence of the public in the working of the judicial process.

This was an unprecedented and an embarrassing situation. It called for caution and establishment of a salutary convention.

I have obtained from the Chief Justice of Punjab and Haryana High Court the necessary papers.

There are three kinds of reports:

(i) Reports submitted by the Internal Audit Cell of the High Court;

(ii) Fact-finding Reports submitted by District and Sessions Judges (Vigilance) both of Punjab and Haryana; and

(iii) Reports and audit paras submitted by the official of the Accountant General's Office to the High Court for reply. The reports and audit paras last mentioned seek clarifications and justifications in respect of the transactions which prime facie appeared to be irregular.

I have looked into [the reports] and then arrived at a certain tentative impression it is not necessary to recapitulate, in detail, the alleged irregularities. I understand from the authorities of the High Court that the officials involved in the alleged irregularities have been suspended and departmental inquiries have been instituted against them. The final result of these departmental inquiries is awaited. In the meantime, I took Brother Ramaswami into confidence and made known to him the contents of the audit reports with a view to ascertaining his position in relation to the disclosures made in the reports. He has given his version. I have also requested Brother Ramaswami to communicate his views to the Registrar, High Court of Punjab and Haryana so that the High Court may reply to the audit objections raised by the Government.

I understand that the High Court had directly sought Brother Ramaswami's clarifications with regard to certain audit objections and he has written to the officers of the High Court in this behalf. The proceedings, as mentioned before, against some of the officers of the High Court on alleged irregularities are still pending. In respect of some of the irregularities which I have considered and the tendency of the departmental inquiries against the suspended officers, I am of the opinion that it would be appropriate to wait for a closer examination of the replies to the audit objections and the various queries submitted by the High Court to Brother Ramaswami before one can come to a final conclusion.

The processes initiated for unearthing facts relating to the alleged irregularities should be completed to determine whether rules have been breached. I have asked the Registrar of the Supreme Court to write to the Registrar of the High Court to complete the departmental inquiries that are to be conducted in respect of the alleged irregularities committed by the officers and employees of the High Court, and a report of the same should be forwarded to me. I have also personally requested the Chief Justice of the Punjab and Haryana High Court in respect of the same. I have also directed the Registrar of the Supreme Court to write to the Accountant General (Audit), Haryana ... to come to a final opinion on the audit objections and determine whether any amount has been illegally or improperly withdrawn and whether the advance taken by Brother Ramaswami under the rules is justified or regularized. I have personally advised Brother Ramaswami to check if there had been any excessive drawings of account of salary, LTC [leave travel concession], etc., and if so, to voluntarily repay such drawings which are contrary to rules. It must be reiterated that the audit objections by the Government should also be expedited and disposed of. I have directed the Registrar of this Court to so write to the appropriate Government to expedite the inquiry. Maturity requires that we do not jump to conclusions unless the facts are ascertained and the questions involved are decided.

The Supreme Court must uphold the rule of law. It is, therefore, necessary that those who uphold the rule of law must live by law and judges must, therefore, be obliged to live according to law. The law, procedure and the norms applicable in this case enjoin that the expenses incurred by the Court for the Judges must be according to the rules, norms and the practice. No man is above law or the rules. The Judges either of the Supreme Court or of the High Courts and the Chief Justices are all subject to the rule of law and procedure like any other citizen of this country and must abide by the norms and regulation prescribed inasmuch as these and to the extent [sic] *are applicable to them I always thought this was clear and needed no reiteration.* We must, therefore, ensure that there is no conduct of the Judges, which affects the faith of the people that Judges do not live according to law. Judges cannot afford to be involved in disputes, which have to determine the question whether the Judges while functioning as Judges or Chief Justices have attempted to subvert the law either designedly or in utter negligence or recklessness.

In this matter, the questions involved are, namely:

(i) whether the Chief Justice was entitled to the expenses of his telephone at Madras because Chandigarh was declared a disturbed area;

(ii) Whether the Chief Justice was obliged to obtain leave to avail the facility of LTC;

(iii) Whether the Chief Justice was entitled to direct the cars to be taken to Madras when he was on vacation from Chandigarh for the reasons mentioned by him;

(iv) Whether the silver maces ordered by the High Court have been done at the rate similar to the rate applied in respect of those supplied to the Madras high Court; and

(v) Whether even though the Judges of the Punjab and Haryana High Court did not approve the idea of having maces for each individual Judge, the Chief Justice was entitled to direct the purchase of these maces. These are the matters on which interpretation of the rules or on the permission or relaxation of rules, certain consequences will follow, and if the Chief

Justice was not so entitled or these could not be sanctioned as has been done under the circumstances mentioned in the aforesaid objections and communications, reimbursement or recovery would be directed. These matters, therefore, will have to await adjudication by the appropriate authorities, namely, the Government and the sanctioning authorities dealing with audit objections, in respect of the permissions sought. Though one would like to think that there has been extravagance and ostentatiousness but these by themselves do not involve determining questions of moral or legal impropriety of a judge functioning as a Judge in the Court.

But there are some other aspects involved in this matter, namely, the questions of not accounting for all the furniture or items that were in the residence and office of the Chief Justice, the alleged replacement of superior quality items by inferior quality items, the missing items and the splitting up of the bills in order to have the sanction of the authorities or to conform to the rules, are matters which are also pending determination and adjudication.

Involvement in any investigation on the conduct of a sitting Supreme Court Judge on such matters as aforesaid is embarrassing, in the circumstances and the background in which these questions have arisen in the instant case. For one who should attempt to uphold the rule of law, it is embarrassing to be involved in such a dispute. But no final decision on this aspect can be arrived at until the investigations and inquiries are completed. I have, on these aspects after looking into the matter and the points involved, no doubt that those who aspire to uphold the rule of law must strive to live according to law and they necessarily expose themselves to the danger of perishing by law. I am aware and deeply conscious that in certain circumstances somebody may be a victim of a certain situation. I was constrained, in those circumstances, to advise Brother Ramaswami to desist from discharging judicial functions so long as the investigations continued and his name was cleared on this aspect.

I wrote to Brother Ramaswami on 18 July 1990 rendering my aforesaid advice. I have also conveyed to him my anguish in tendering

> *this advice and I have requested him to please be on leave until the investigations on the aforesaid conduct are completed.*
>
> On 18 July 1990 after receipt of my letter, Brother Ramaswami has applied for leave for six weeks in the first instance with effect from 23 July 1990. I have directed the office to process his application for leave.
>
> Since I had assured the learned Attorney General, the Law Minister, the President of the Bar Association and others that I will look into it [the Justice Ramaswami issue], I thought I must convey to you (members of the Bar) the result of my looking into it.

In my view, this statement of the chief justice of India constitutes a high watermark in the annals of India's Supreme Court. It shows that no man or woman, not even a judge of the Supreme Court of India, is above the law. It also shows what a chief justice of India can do, and should do, in the absence of enacted law in order to save the court and his own colleagues from ignominy and disgrace!

It was felt by the Bar that, at last, the highest court was *doing* something. Confidence in the Supreme Court of India – invariably high – was never higher. Great expectations were raised that the problems confronting some of the high courts (where immediate remedial measures had to be taken) would now soon be satisfactorily resolved. But it was not to be. Chief Justice Sabyasachi Mukherjee prematurely died in harness in September 1990. His decision about his own colleague was reversed (again, not finally but pro tem) a few months later by the entire court after perusing the prima facie views of a committee of three justices – a committee that had been constituted by Chief Justice Mukherjee himself during his tenure. V. Ramaswami J. then resumed sitting in court, suffering the indignity of some lawyers refusing to appear before a bench of which he was a member! (According to administrative orders of the chief justice, if any lawyer appearing in court objected to arguing before a bench that had Justice Ramaswami as member, the case was to go before another bench!) But all this embarrassment was short-lived.

A motion for the removal of Justice Ramaswami was moved in the Lok Sabha – under the Judges Inquiry Act 1968[30] – the only constitutional way in which a judge in the higher judiciary can be removed. The motion was admitted by the speaker of the Lok Sabha on 12 March 1991 – after which Justice Ramaswami did not sit in court. A three-member committee [as stipulated by Section 3(2) of the Judge's Inquiry Act 1968], was then set up with (i) a sitting judge of the Supreme Court: Justice P. B. Sawant as principal officer, (ii) a chief justice of a high court: P. D. Desai, chief justice of the Bombay High Court and (iii) O. Chinnappa Reddy (retired judge of the Supreme Court): who was appointed as 'eminent jurist'. Advocate Raju Ramachandran and myself were designated as counsel for the committee. Justice Ramaswami, though served with a notice to appear before the committee, refused to participate in the proceedings, which then went on ex parte – i.e., in his absence. Ultimately, after evidence was recorded, the committee found Justice Ramaswami guilty of 'proved misbehaviour' within the meaning of that expression in Article 124 (4)[31] of the Constitution and recommended that he be removed as a judge of the Supreme Court of India.

With this recommendation, the motion that had been initiated in the Lok Sabha (and was then pending) was taken up, and debated on 10 and 11 May 1993. Senior advocate, Kapil Sibal (who became a cabinet minister in the Manmohan Singh Government in 2004), appeared as counsel for Justice Ramaswami and was granted audience by the House. He argued his client's case with great acumen, but the outcome was not determined by arguments but by a decision already taken in unison by members of the Congress Party in Parliament to *abstain* from voting for or against the motion! The result was that 201 members of the Congress Party (then a large number) did not vote for or against the motion for the removal from office of Justice Ramaswami: the inevitable (but foreseeable and intended) consequence was that the requisite two-thirds majority required by Article 124(4) was not secured! The motion was defeated despite 196 votes being cast for removal of the judge and none against removal! The only satisfaction for the mover of the motion, Somnath Chatterjee of the Communist Party of India (Marxist), was that he had the last word in the debate! After the vote, he said (and this is recorded in the proceedings of the House): 'No Hon'ble Member of this House is against this motion. Therefore the Judge should understand that there is only one view!'[32] Justice V. Ramaswami then resumed sitting in the Supreme Court till he reached the constitutionally prescribed age of retirement for a judge of the Supreme Court of India: i.e., 65 years.

* * *

Since the Ramaswami incident, proceedings for the removal of judges of the higher judiciary for 'proved misbehaviour' have been initiated – on two subsequent occasions, both in 2009 – against two judges of different high courts.

First, in February 2009, 58 members of the Rajya Sabha gave Notice of Motion to its chairman (under the provisions of the Judges Inquiry Act 1968)[33] for the removal from office of Justice Soumitra Sen, a sitting judge of the High Court of Calcutta (under Article 217[1][c] read with Article 124[4] of the Constitution), on the ground of misappropriation of funds received by him as receiver appointed by the court when he was a practising advocate (he having continued as receiver till 2005 even after he was appointed as a judge in 2003). The ex-officio chairman of the Rajya Sabha (i.e., the elected vice-president of India) admitted the motion and constituted a three-member Committee of Inquiry in accordance with the provisions of the 1968 Act with Justice B. Sudershan Reddy of the Supreme Court of India as presiding officer and Chief Justice T. S. Thakur (of the High Court of Punjab and Haryana)[34] as member. I was appointed as the third member.

To enable Justice Soumitra Sen to object to the framing of 'definite charges', draft statements of grounds and charges were forwarded to him for his views, but he did not respond. Definite charges were then framed – in accordance with the rules – along with grounds (and documents in support), which were served on the judge on 4 March 2010, giving him an opportunity to appear before the committee. He did not personally appear, but, on 3 May 2010, he filed a 'reply to the charges', which was taken on record as his written statement of defence. Hearing of evidence took place from 24 to 26 June 2010, at which the concerned judge did not personally appear but was represented by advocates instructed by him. Finally, on 18 and 19 July 2010, arguments were heard from counsel for the committee (senior advocate Siddharth Luthra) and from senior advocate Shekhar Naphade, counsel for Justice Sen; after that, the hearing concluded.

The committee submitted its report on 10 September 2010 to the chairman of the Rajya Sabha with the finding that the charges framed were duly proved against the judge. The pending motion was then brought on in the Rajya Sabha. On 18 August 2011, Justice Soumitra Sen, who had neither participated personally in the proceedings before the committee nor given oral evidence before it, put up a spirited personal defence in a special session of the Rajya Sabha, which after hearing him, adopted the motion for his removal with 189 members voting in favour and 16 members against.

Under the Constitution, *each* of the two Houses of Parliament is required to pass the resolution for the removal of a judge with the requisite special majority. When the matter was to come up next before the Lok Sabha, Justice Sen sent an unconditional letter of resignation, which was accepted by the president of India. The proceedings against the judge then became infructuous and had to be 'dropped' (since a sitting judge who has already resigned cannot be removed). Justice Sen was, and is, to be regarded as a judge who had resigned from his office and not as a judge who was removed from his office.

* * *

The second proceeding for a judge's removal (in the same year, i.e., 2009) had an element of high drama. There were several complaints at the Bar of 'misbehaviour' against Justice P. D. Dinakaran who had been a judge of the High Court of Madras from December 1996 to August 2008 and was then transferred to the High Court of Karnataka where he was appointed chief justice (from 8 August 2008 onwards). There were reports in the *Hindu* (dated 28 August 2009) that Justice Dinakaran had been recommended by the 'collegium' of the Supreme Court of India to be elevated to the apex court.[35]

The practising lawyers, especially of the High Court of Madras, were greatly disturbed by the news and, in September 2009, they submitted representations to the chief justice of India, and to members of the collegium, containing allegations of a serious nature against Justice Dinakaran as also allegations about his having illegally amassed wealth/assets on a large scale. It appeared (from news reports) that the chief justice of India, K. G. Balakrishnan, had summoned Justice Dinakaran to Delhi and, at a meeting held on 11 September 2009, at the chief justice's residence, Justice Dinakaran was confronted with the allegations against him.

As president of the Bar Association of India, I was approached, more than once, by Ms R. Vaigai, a lawyer practising for many years in Chennai who (with her team of associates) had documented the judge's 'misdeeds' (whilst a judge in Chennai) and requested me to intercede. Along with senior advocate Shanti Bhushan, I called on Chief Justice Balakrishnan in his chambers in the Supreme Court and told him that although I had no personal knowledge about Justice Dinakaran, a large number of prominent lawyers both in Chennai (as well as Bangalore) were agitated and requested that he be removed as a judge in such circumstances, (I said) it was 'unthinkable that Justice Dinakaran should be at all considered for "elevation" to the Supreme Court of India, without first considering all these allegations'. The CJI said that he would see what could be done but I came away from my meeting with the CJI unconvinced and carrying the impression that the name of Justice Dinakaran had already been 'cleared' by the 'collegium' of justices (the five seniormost judges of the Supreme Court, including the chief justice)[36] for being appointed a judge of the highest court! When I told the contingent of lawyers from Chennai and Bangalore all this, and about my misgivings, they were very disturbed. As it is, they were already disheartened because their request that their representatives should meet Chief Justice K. G. Balakrishnan and members of the collegium had been turned down. Nor would the chief justice of India meet senior advocate K. K. Venugopal, who knew about Justice Dinakaran's functioning as a judge when the latter was sitting in the High Court of Madras.

In a special meeting of the Bar Association of India called for considering the emergent problems – held in New Delhi on 28 November 2009 and over which I presided – a number of advocates from Bangalore and Chennai recounted the 'misdeeds' of Justice Dinakaran. After listening to them all, I said that if Dinakaran was appointed judge of the Supreme Court of India – as then appeared to me likely – we in the Bar should resolve *not* only to refrain from appearing before him, but also to resolve not to appear before any member of the collegium who had recommended him for appointment. I said that most certainly I would not. (This was widely reported in the media the next day.)

I had been extremely disappointed that the collegium had refused to countenance the representations made by responsible advocates both from Bangalore as well as from Chennai and had refused to even grant them an audience, which had been requested. In my view, the judges in the collegium ought to have heard at first-hand the views of a vocal (and responsible) section of the Bar about Justice Dinakaran even though they may have already recommended him (as a collegium) for appointment as judge of the Supreme Court of India. These acts – of the collegium having first unanimously recommended the name of Justice Dinakaran without any detailed scrutiny or inquiry and then having refused to even listen to the views of responsible sections of the Bar – have not only destroyed the credibility of the collegium system but have also cast grave doubts about the entire method of recommendation laid down by a majority of justices in a bench decision of nine judges (in the case reported in AIR 1994, SC 268). This decision, which has since been admitted to a review and reconsideration, was summed up in the heading of a newspaper article published in the *Indian Express* on 10 November 2010 titled 'REVISITING COLLEGIUM SYSTEM: SUPREME COURT NOTICE TO CENTRE, AG [Attorney General]'.[37]

* * *

With the 'collegium system' as it now exists, it is not as if *good judges* are not appointed. But the possibility, and more often the probability, that better ones may have been appointed (sans the collegium) cannot always be ruled out. There is simply not enough 'homework' done in the matter of recommendation of judges to the highest court. If the collegium system is to remain, even temporarily, it must be strengthened at the roots to enable more meaningful inputs to go into the method of selection of judges to the highest court.

* * *

The next chapter in the Dinakaran saga, as it unfolded, was unedifying: it was also embarrassing to the members of the collegium who had recommended his name for appointment to the Supreme Court of India.

In December 2009, 75 opposition MPs in the Rajya Sabha moved a motion for the removal of Justice P. D. Dinakaran, former chief justice of the Karnataka High Court, under Article 217(1)(c) read with Article 124(4) of the Constitution, on various grounds: viz., possessing wealth disproportionate to known sources of income, land grabbing and abuse of judicial office. After admitting the motion, the ex-officio chairman of the Rajya Sabha (i.e., the elected vice-president of India) constituted (within the stipulated period of three months) a committee under the Judges Inquiry Act 1968: it consisted of a sitting justice of the Supreme Court Justice V. S. Sirpurkar (as presiding officer), Justice A. R. Dave (then chief justice of the High Court of Andhra Pradesh as member) and P. P. Rao, senior advocate, as eminent jurist. On his being elevated to the Supreme Court of India, Justice Dave resigned from the committee, and Justice J. S. Khehar (chief justice of the Karnataka High Court) was appointed in his place. Justice Sirpurkar later recused himself as presiding officer[38] and, in his place, Justice Aftab Alam, sitting judge of the Supreme Court, was appointed in September 2010.

On 16 March 2011, the Justice Alam Committee, after going through the relevant papers, issued notice to Justice Dinakaran (along with a statement of charges, supported by specific grounds with details and a list of documents as well as a list of witnesses) and required him to appear on 9 April 2011 to answer the charges. Justice Dinakaran did not respond, but, on 7 April 2011, filed two applications with the chairman of the Rajya Sabha praying that a direction may be issued for supply of documents specified therein and seeking an audience with the presiding officer of the inquiry committee. The next day (i.e., 8 April 2011), Justice Dinakaran also filed another representation, with the chairman of the Rajya Sabha praying that: (1) the order admitting the Notice of Motion be withdrawn; (2) the order constituting the inquiry committee be rescinded; and (3) the notice issued by the committee be annulled. Simultaneously, he also raised an objection of bias to the appointment of P. P. Rao as a member of the committee. On 9 April 2011, he sent a letter to the presiding officer of the committee, along with the copy of the representation (dated 8 April 2011) made to the Rajya Sabha chairman and requested that further proceedings be deferred till his objections were decided. His request for deferring proceedings was rejected by the committee on 9 April 2011 and Justice Dinakaran was asked to file his written statement of defence by 20 April 2011. But on 19 April 2011, Justice Dinakaran filed an application before the committee in which he made a request for supply of copies of several documents and, in another application, he raised several objections against the notice: viz., that the charges framed were beyond the scope of the notice presented before the Rajya Sabha and further that the charges had taken into consideration material that did not form part of the aforementioned notice in Parliament. He also objected (as stated earlier) to the continued participation of P. P. Rao in the proceedings of the committee on the ground of 'bias'. The application was disposed of by the committee on 24 April 2011, which rejected the request for the supply of documents and also rejected the preliminary objection as to the jurisdiction and procedure adopted by it (the committee) for framing of charges. The committee also held that the plea of bias against P. P. Rao was an afterthought and was untenable.

Justice Dinakaran then filed writ petitions in the Supreme Court of India: WP No. 217 of 2011 (challenging the appointment of P. P. Rao as member of the committee) and WP No. 218 of 2011 (against the order dated 24 April 2011 of the committee rejecting his prayer for supply of documents and details and rejecting his objection to the jurisdiction of the committee to frame certain charges). WP No. 217 was dismissed by a bench of two justices of the Supreme Court on 5 July 2011,[39] which concluded:

> We hold that belated raising of objection against inclusion of respondent No. 3 (P. P. Rao) in the Committee under Section 3(2) appears to be a calculated move on the petitioner's part.

The bench then added:

> 52: However, keeping in view our finding on the issue of bias, we would request the Chairman to nominate another distinguished jurist in place of respondent No. 3. The proceedings initiated against the petitioner have progressed only to the stage of framing of charges and the Committee is yet to record its findings on the charges and submit [its] report. Therefore, nomination of another jurist will not hamper the proceedings of the Committee and the reconstituted Committee shall be entitled to proceed on the charges already framed against the petitioner.
> 53: In the result, the writ petition is dismissed with the aforesaid observations.

WP 218 was also dismissed by the Supreme Court.[40]

Meanwhile, on 29 July 2011, Justice Dinakaran sent in a unconditional letter of resignation to the president of India, which was accepted, and further proceedings of the committee were thus brought to a premature end. Since Justice Dinakaran did not file a statement of defence before the Justice Alam Committee, we will never know what was his answer to the specific charges framed against him.

* * *

The common feature in the case of Justice Sen and in that of Justice Dinakaran was that each of them had avoided the possibility of a motion for their removal being proceeded with in Parliament by resigning their offices. It may appear – it so appeared to many – that this expedient had frustrated the entire procedure for removal. It has been said that the judge who resigns his office with immediate effect at any stage after the motion for his removal is moved and before the motion for his removal is passed 'conveniently extricates himself from the tentacles' of Article 124(4)! Such a step would enable errant judges to first test the waters, go through the tortuous process (under the rules) of evidence having to be led (and contradicting such evidence by crossexamining the witnesses called), submit arguments before the committee, and then, at any stage (even at the very last stage – as in the case of Justice Sen) to resign office. However, although there has been a clamour for an alternative method (and I myself at one time was in favour of it), on a mature consideration, I am now of the definite view that the option of resignation cannot and ought not to be taken away by law or by Constitutional Amendment and that the provisions contained in Article 124(4) in the case of a judge of the Supreme Court and in Article 124(4) read with Article 217 in the case of a judge of a high court – heavily loaded as they are in favour of the judge against whom charges are brought – should not be altered. Proceedings brought against an errant judge under the deliberately cumbersome procedure prescribed under the Judges Inquiry Act 1968 do serve a very useful purpose, viz., to emphasize the seriousness of the charges against a sitting judge and the almost Herculean efforts that are needed to be taken to pursue them. The prescribed procedure for removal under the Judges Inquiry Act 1968 (and the rules framed under that Act) are all for securing that the independence of the superior court judges is fiercely protected, because they *need* to be seen as truly independent judges dispensing justice without fear or favour. Besides, providing the judge – against whom charges are brought by a statutory committee (consisting of two judges and an eminent jurist) – a (last) opportunity to resign is a step in the right direction: good-riddance-without-stigma is always a better option than removal, not only for the errant judge but also (more importantly) for the system.

The Judicial Standards and Accountability Bill No. 136 of 2010, introduced by the law minister in Parliament in November 2010 (and still pending), offers an *additional alternative*: it is less tortuous (and likely to be preferred if and when passed) as the only method to be pursued for the 'removal' of a judge of a high court or of the Supreme Court. But

I do not favour it, because, under the Bill (as proposed), the procedure for the ultimate removal of a judge for 'proved misbehaviour' can now be initiated on the complaint of *'any person making an allegation'*, of course, with the safeguard that the complaint must first go to a Scrutiny Committee (of judges), which can dismiss it if it is 'frivolous or vexatious'. If not, it goes to a National (Judicial) Oversight Committee, which, after charges are framed against the judge, ultimately enables this committee to give a warning to the judge to behave better or to recommend his removal. The Bill is certainly well intentioned. But, in my view, in India at this time and in conditions as they are at present – of profound disbelief and suspicion about everyone, including judges of the higher judiciary – to permit complaints by all and sundry against judges of the superior courts is inadvisable and positively dangerous, simply because *so far good judges far outnumber the bad*. (Thank God – and I thank the *good* judges – for that!)

There is also another reason. 'Misbehaviour' is a word with many meanings. It encompasses gross and palpable acts of dishonesty, but it may even include persistent dereliction of duty. Much depends on the perception of those who sit in judgment. A former distinguished law minister (Shanti Bhushan) once told me that when he took a copy of the motion to remove V. Ramaswami (then a sitting judge of the Supreme Court) to his party leader Atal Bihari Vajpayee, the latter enquired what the judge's 'misbehaviour' was. When told that the principal charge was that, as chief justice of Punjab and Haryana, he had spent public moneys imprudently and excessively on decorating his house at Chandigarh and was also keeping for himself some pieces of furniture bought at the cost of the government, Vajpayee's response was: '*Yeh toh murgi chor ki baat hai*.' And yet on this *murgi chor ki baat* (in a matter thought to be allegedly as trivial as the theft of a chicken!), a committee of three eminent and fair-minded judges ultimately found V. Ramaswami guilty and recommended that he be removed from his office as judge of the Supreme Court! The recommendation was turned down only when it went through the political process – for want of a two-thirds majority in Parliament – a special majority being constitutionally required for the removal of a judge of the higher judiciary.

At one time, I was of the view that we should follow the American system of judicial councils, with judges (in the higher judiciary) sitting in judgment over the conduct of other judges (in the higher judiciary) on complaints made by anyone, including litigants. But not now.

Given the present-day media exposure (with over 270 licensed news channels in the electronic media), coupled with the burning desire of some unsuccessful and disgruntled litigants to seek 'revenge' (some governments and public corporations, which lose cases are often the most disgruntled of all litigants), it is always possible for a tutored private TV channel (no offence meant or intended to any one of them) to trump up a series of complaints of 'misbehaviour' against a sitting judge, howsoever fair and honest he (or she) may be, for ulterior motives. And, in any case, this Bill is unnecessary, because with the aid of PIL (public interest litigation), it has not been difficult for benches of judges of the superior judiciary to deal effectively with genuine complaints, under existing law and practice, against some errant members of their own fraternity (whether of the high courts or of the Supreme Court).

My own view NOW is that it is far better – and safer – to call to account the 'bad eggs' in the judicial basket when they retire (it must be admitted that there are a few). *What the law minister must do is to have the Judges (Protection) Act 1985 repealed.*[41] This, in my view, is essential and imperative. H. R. Bhardwaj, a former Union law minister (from May 2004 to May 2009) in an interview reported in the *Hindustan Times* of 25 September 2008, had said:

> There was a time when the judiciary was above suspicion and people had great respect for it. The same cannot be said today, serious allegations of corruption against judges are in the public domain. It needs to be corrected.

The 1985 Act has provided almost absolute immunity to sitting and retired judges of the higher judiciary. *Honourable* sitting judges in this country (and, believe me, most of them do deserve the prefix) do not need this additional protection. It is now used only as a shield for the few who belong to the class of erstwhile members of the higher judiciary whose integrity (according to common repute) is doubtful: And if a sitting judge does do something glaringly improper, then with prior permission of the chief justice of India, a criminal prosecution can be launched,[42] as was done (in 2011) in the case of a sitting judge of the High Court of Punjab and Haryana.

It may be true that *honest* judges have nothing to fear. But the harassment caused to such judges by the prospect of even frivolous or vexatious complaints is real. Judges of the higher judiciary take an oath when they enter upon their office to decide 'without fear or favour, affection or ill-will ....' Deciding without fear or favour, affection or ill-will is facilitated by the tortuous and cumbersome procedure prescribed under the Judges Inquiry Act 1968, an enactment that makes it extremely difficult to remove from office a judge in the higher judiciary. With the new Bill in Parliament, it would now be much easier to do so. But the Bill is premised on the assumption that more judges of the higher judiciary may become, in the foreseeable future, dishonourable or dishonest. Even if this assumption be correct, this is the wrong approach to lawmaking. Extreme care must be taken when appointing a person to the higher judiciary but, once appointed, its serving members must not be traumatized with the prospect of complaints by *anyone* and *everyone*, which will only make judges in the higher judiciary more populist and not necessarily less fearless. And in these fractious times, we need fearless judges.

However, the problem of what to do when 'sometimes something goes wrong' in the higher judiciary still remains unresolved. It lies in the lap of the judges; a serious judicial responsibility, not yet seriously attempted to be dealt with. It is time that a system of *transparent judicial self-regulation* is institutionalized and not left to be dealt with on a case-to-case basis by a group of judges in a high court or by a group of justices in the Supreme Court

* * *

At present, with that branch of the law of contempt known as 'scandalizing the court' firmly in place, it is next to impossible for anyone to attempt to assess – even for bona fide reasons – the true levels of corruption in India's higher judiciary.

In countries around the world, corruption rarely gets exposed by proof established in courts or before anti-corruption commissions. And it is more often than not well concealed. For instance, an otherwise reliable body – Transparency International – in its Bribe Payers Index for 2002 named Australia as the country where companies were the 'least likely to offer bribes to win business'. But at the time that Australia received this accolade, businessmen in the Australian Wheat Board were reportedly paying massive bribes to Saddam Hussein totalling US $225 million as part of the oil-for-food scandal! This fact was only revealed with the publication of the Volcker Report in October 2005 (written by a UN investigator Paul Volcker). In his report, Volcker made the finding that the Australian Wheat Board (later AWB Ltd.) was the biggest single source of kickbacks in exchange for trouble-free disembarkation of wheat purchased under the UN oil-for-food programme!

***

In my experience of over 60 years of practice at the Bar, there was one chief justice of India who showed how a perceived 'wrong' done by a judge could be remedied – without scandalizing either the judge or the court. It was deftly done. Years ago, a senior judge in the Supreme Court became (by convention) chief justice of India – he was to hold this post for only three weeks after which he would reach the age of superannuation. This CJI, a few days after his swearing-in, made a speech on the occasion of Law Day[43] stating that his priority would be to clear off arrears in criminal (and quasi-criminal) cases. The Supreme Court Registry was then directed to place on the board of the new chief justice's court a couple of cases filed against the Union of India – which were pending – known as the *Vanaspati group of cases* (which related to import of industrial coconut oil). The cases related to the illegal import of palm oil in containers of stainless steel – a prohibited item under the Import Tariff. The containers were allegedly painted over to give the impression that they were made of mild steel (a permitted item under the Import Tariff)! After a brief hearing, the chief justice, sitting with another judge, decided the cases against the Union of India and in favour of the importers.[44] By itself, nothing strange or wrong in that!

But the chief justice who took over after him was an inquiring sort (his uncle Sir Harilal Kania had been the first chief justice of India). The background in which this case had been decided left the new chief justice in some doubt, and the course he then pursued was noteworthy. Without reference at all to the manner in which the Vansaspati group of cases came to be listed and decided and without any finger pointing, Chief Justice M. H. Kania directed (administratively – as the CJI was empowered to do) that the Vansaspati group of cases in which judgment had been recently rendered (by the just-retired CJI) should be immediately placed for decision on review – a review that had been filed by the Union of India.[45] A special bench consisting of the three seniormost judges of the Supreme Court at the time (Justices M. N. Venkatchaliah, A. M. Ahmadi and J. S. Verma) was constituted. These three judges heard the review, reopened the cases already decided and arrived at a decision, which was contrary to the decision previously rendered: the cases filed by the importers against the Union of India were dismissed.

The Supreme Court did this all on its own, and in open court, and brought credibility to the functioning of the country's highest judiciary. No one even suspected that anything was amiss; after all, quite often, reviews are filed and are decided one way or another in respect of final judgments already delivered by the Supreme Court. But I feel proud that these judges, headed by Chief Justice Kania, lived up to the *motto* of the Government Law College in Bombay: my alma mater. The motto of this 150-year-old institution has been: '*Ne vile fano*' ('let nothing be done to defile the temple of justice'). Thanks to Chief Justice Kania and his three seniormost colleagues, the court ensured that nothing was said or done to 'defile' the temple of justice: a case was decided, a case was reviewed and the prior judgment was set aside, and it was made to appear as if it was all in a day's work!

***

My regret, however, is that more than 15 years later when a somewhat similar situation arose, the then chief justice of India and his senior colleagues omitted to follow the example set by their forebears (Chief Justice Kania and the three seniormost judges of the court at the time): perhaps because our highest court lacks 'institutional memory'! It was because of this omission to respond appropriately to yet another court decision by subjecting it to an internal review that proved to be a matter of considerable embarrassment to the higher judiciary.

I mention this with sadness but with a sense of responsibility. A former otherwise able and competent chief justice of India had, in a bench decision (and presiding over that bench whilst a sitting judge) strictly enforced the development control laws in Delhi: premises built or occupied contrary to law were ordered to be sealed and houses that were not in accordance with the building rules were directed to be pulled down. And all this had been widely reported in the media: it was generally felt that it was all for the good. But then, after a while, allegations were openly made in the media (with documentation) suggesting that there was more to it than met the eye. The allegations were that whilst stopping commercialization of residential areas, this particular now-retired chief justice had (whilst in office) fostered his sons owning and running three commercial companies from the official residence of the CJI in Delhi. The records of the Registrar of Companies bore witness to it. The sons' business included building of malls! Instead of subjecting the judgments of this judge to a fresh scrutiny – and suo motu review – and then dealing with the cases again strictly on merits (as was done during the time of Chief Justice Kania), contempt proceedings were initiated against the section of the media that had reported the allegations. This move set off a course of events that could well have been avoided.

Reports published in the *Mid Day* issues of 18 May 2007[46] and 19 May 2007[47] received prominence and notoriety by being brought to the notice of a bench of the Delhi High Court, which ordered the initiation of proceedings for contempt of court. A bench of two judges of the Delhi High Court promptly issued a notice, suo motu, to the editor the printer and the publisher of the newspaper (*Mid Day*) for scandalizing the court, even though it concerned a retired judge. 'Scandalous' stories about what a judge did whilst he was a sitting judge even after he had retired could be interpreted (it was said) as adversely affecting the image of the judiciary as a whole. The newspaper also carried a cartoon, which depicted the former chief justice of India in his robes holding a bag with currency notes flowing out, with a man sitting on the sidewalk saying: 'Help – the *mall* is in your court' (a pun on 'the ball is in your court')! The judges of the Delhi High Court were of the opinion that this was not just defamatory of the judge but was aimed at lowering the image of the judiciary.[48] The bench of two judges of the Delhi High Court then issued a notice to the editor, the printer, the publisher and the cartoonist (the whole lot of them) to show cause why action in contempt be not taken. The matter was argued for the newspaper by a senior lawyer, Shanti Bhushan. He said (in court) that the material brought on record (by his client) was ample proof of the fact that the sons of that particular retired chief justice were beneficiaries of sealing of the commercial premises (ordered by a bench, of which the chief justice of India in question was the presiding member) and the plea pointed to the impropriety of a chief justice sitting on cases and passing sealing orders of premises in which commercial activity was being conducted to promote (as counsel put it) 'his own sons' businesses'. But the bench of two judges of the high court said that 'all this tended to erode the confidence of the general public in the institution itself'. Besides, they said that 'it was a slur on the other judges of the Supreme Court who were parties to the order passed by the then Chief Justice of India.'

When news of this and of this case got around, the reaction of two distinguished former chief justices of India[49] (Justice J. S. Verma and Justice V. N. Khare) was that the facts as disclosed thus far did require investigation by an independent body and that the named former chief justice of India should submit himself to such an inquiry and clear his name. This was widely reported. Interviewed on television I said the same (also reported[50]). I later wrote an article to this effect.[51] Two retired judges of the Supreme Court of India (Justices V. R. Krishna Iyer and P. B. Sawant) also called for a probe 'so that the truth be brought out.'[52] But there was no probe and no submission to an inquiry – there were only impressions and comments. The judge did not 'clear his name' as recommended by his peers but contented himself with an article that was published in the *Times of India*.[53]

But how was this individual treated? How does one treat one's erstwhile colleague who has fallen from grace? Was he left severally alone by his peers? Regrettably he was not. On occasions when this person was invited to official parties, sitting judges of the court treated him as one of their old trusted senior colleagues and dealt with him as if no such allegation had ever been made! It is a common human failing amongst us that we treat all persons with civility – even those who may have indulged in some questionable conduct. Men and women who are otherwise upright in their own behaviour think it bad form to slight someone or ignore someone against whom even credible charges have been levelled.

All this shows that it will possibly take us as long to get rid of corruption in high judicial places as it took the Western world to get rid of slavery, which was – about 200 years! But to get rid of corruption in high judicial places, we just cannot afford to wait that long. We have to choose. Do you keep everything under the carpet until all that is under the carpet suddenly blows up in your face? Or do you dare to expose it on that healthy principle propounded by the great and beloved Chief Justice M. N. Venkatachaliah who always used to say that 'sunlight is the best disinfectant and electric light is the best policeman'?

To continue with the story: the judges of the Delhi High Court[54] held that clients of Shanti Bhushan – the editor, the printer, the publisher and the cartoonist – were all guilty of contempt of court and posted the matter for punishment after ten days. But thank God we have a Supreme Court. Before the contempt matter could be put up for sentencing in the High Court of Delhi, a bench of two judges of the Supreme Court (presided over by one of its senior judges[55]) admitted the statutory appeal and directed that the punishment imposed by the high court would not be executed without leave of the Supreme Court. There the matter rests – and there it will, in all probability (ultimately), get buried!

But grateful as I am to the Supreme Court, I must confess these are just sporadic fire-fighting measures. In my view this is not how judicial corruption in the highest places should be tackled. There is another way. Such measures have to be institutionalized. And they can be only institutionalized without damaging the general credibility of the judiciary as a body by putting in place (as soon as possible) the office of 'judicial ombudsman'. It can be filled by one, two or three persons. The holder/s of this office would be the recipient/s of all complaints, even taking up matters on his/her (or their) own. The judicial ombudsman would make a report, in writing, to the sitting chief justice of India with regard to the particular judge – either of the high court or the Supreme Court – against whom the complaint is made, after making due inquiries. Upon receipt of that report it would be incumbent on the chief justice of India to see that no work is assigned to that particular judge until the dilatory processes of the law (for removal of judges) are gone through.

I believe this is the only way in which we can accommodate the need for keeping *clean* and *bright* the image of our high (and our highest) judiciary.

* * *

Whilst I write this let me make one thing very clear. Just as two swallows don't make a summer, so a few reputedly corrupt judges amongst 555 in the higher judiciary do not make for a corrupt judiciary. We do have excellent, honest and upright judges in the high courts and in the Supreme Court of India. And I can confidently say that I am proud of them. But they too need to be protected – against themselves, against being branded as part of a group that is not honourable. We therefore need to weed out the bad ones. At present, only the collectivity of judges can do this. I am afraid that with the current state of the law, the media – and the lawyers – will continue to draw a blank.

Impressions are very important. Perceptions of the public – of right-thinking people – are important. The more one tries to bury the sporadic allegations, or hide them, the worse the situation becomes – it corrodes the entire judicial system. It is far better that the exposure be immediate and prompt and that powers be given to an institutional entity like a judicial ombudsman to act suo moto even on anonymous complaints. Like poverty, indiscipline and the rest, the law of contempt also will remain with us – it cannot be wished away. And where judicial corruption is concerned, to say that truth is a defence will never help to reveal the truth. It will not induce journalists to write what they hear or know (but often cannot prove as required in a court of law). So it is best to have an institutionalized system of surveillance, which is at once respectful to the judiciary as an institution and is respected by the judges themselves – it will then be believed in by the general public as well.

***

One aspect, indirectly linked to corruption, has prompted the need for greater humility as well as greater transparency in the higher judiciary. It concerned declaration of assets by judges of the Supreme Court. Many years ago, it had been resolved by all judges in the higher judiciary that a declaration of assets would be made by every judge – but only to his/her chief justice.[56] In 2009, an RTI activist (Subhash Chandra Agrawal) applied to the Central Information Commission (CIC) under the Right to Information Act 2005 to provide him with information as to whether or not any declaration of assets had been filed by the honourable judges of the Supreme Court of India (not their contents). A simple query, which was responded to by the CIC by directing the officer deputed by the Supreme Court under the RTI Act – the CPIO (central public information officer) of the apex court – to provide the necessary information within ten working days from the date of the receipt of the notice, viz., to disclose whether any declaration of assets had been filed by the honourable judges of the Supreme Court of India (not their contents).

Promptly, a writ petition (No. 288/2009) was filed in the Delhi High Court by the CPIO (later joined by the registrar of the Supreme Court) challenging the order of the CIC. At this extremely early stage, this very odd state of affairs – of the highest court seeking relief for its judges before a high court – was commented on in an editorial in a national newspaper:[57]

Supreme Folly

Transparency Strengthens Judiciary

The Supreme Court has not crowned itself with glory by challenging a Central Information Commission order in the Delhi High Court. It is, perhaps, the first time that the apex court has filed a case in a lower court. What provoked the Registrar to file it was an innocuous directive to the court's information officer seeking to know whether any declaration of assets had been filed by the Supreme Court judges or not. If the information was provided, it might have been asked to provide details of the assets. In order to rule out such a possibility, it decided to question the very basis on which the directive was issued. In doing so, the court has relied on legal quibbling.

The court says the Chief Justice of India is not a public authority, as defined under the Right to Information Act. Besides, the judges are not mandated to provide information about their assets to the Chief Justice. It claims that the practice in vogue whereby judges declare their assets to the Chief Justice was based on an informal resolution. In other words, the asset details are not to be revealed. The very purpose of declaring the assets is defeated if they have to remain a closely guarded secret. Whatever may be the soundness of the court's claim, it goes against the very grain of the RTI Act.

Declaration of assets has become mandatory for contesting elections and to hold high offices, including that of the President. Government officials have to periodically give details of the assets they have acquired while in office. There is, therefore, no logic for exempting judges from this provision. The RTI Act is considered one of the most enabling pieces of legislation for probity and transparency in public life. Unfortunately, it has run into a strong opponent in the judiciary. It is nobody's contention that the court should submit itself to questions on how judicial decisions are taken but it cannot use the same logic to deny the citizen's right to ask questions on the administrative decisions of the court. The heavens will not fall if judges have to declare their assets in public. It's a folly to claim that they are above the RTI Act.

In response to this editorial, I wrote a letter to the editor, which was published the next day (20 January 2009) to remind our judges and the public as to what happens in the world's oldest democracy: the United States of America:

Chuck It, My Lords

Congratulations on your centre-page (19 January) editorial, 'Supreme Folly'. This comment is about the editorial.

As to whether judges should or should not disclose their assets, I thought the chapter was closed after a group of our judges and lawyers, way back in 1995, went to the United States under the auspices of the Indo–US Legal Forum; I was a member of the team. It so happened that while we were there a short piece, headed: 'Clarence Thomas Discloses Box of 50 Cigars', appeared in *USA Today* [a daily newspaper]. (I had distributed copies to the four seniormost judges: Chief Justice [A. M.] Ahmadi and Justices Kuldip Singh, [J. S.] Verma and [M. M.] Punchhi who were part of our team of judges.)

In this article was given disclosures of assets of each and every judge of the US Supreme Court (Judge Ruth Ginsburg was the richest and then Chief Justice [William] Rehnquist the least wealthy!). This piece was to attract the attention of readers to a US law that all public officers, including Judges of the Supreme Court of the USA, were compelled to disclose not only their assets each year – publicly – but that any yearly gifts received by them in excess of 50 US dollars had also to be disclosed! On the occasion of the baptism of a godson of Justice Clarence Thomas, someone had given him a box of 50 cigars, which exceeded 50 dollars in value and he had disclosed it: which explained the catchy title!

Judges of the Highest Court who have powers of life and death over us citizens, judges who can (and do) send people to jail for contempt of its orders must – I repeat must – show that they too are amenable to *good practice*. That is how they earn the respect of us commoners. We in India learn by example – never by precept.

For judges of the highest court to litigate as to whether or not they should disclose their assets is as bad as judges going to court on whether it is lawful for income tax to be deducted from the salaries they get! We have good judges, but we need more judicial wisdom.

Fali S. Nariman, New Delhi

Their lordships did not accept the suggestion to 'chuck it'! The writ petition filed on behalf of the Supreme Court was pressed to a hearing before a single judge of the Delhi High Court (Justice Ravindra Bhat), who after hearing the arguments, reserved his judgment. Later, by his order dated 2 September 2009 the single judge directed the CPIO of the Supreme Court to release the information sought by the RTI activist (Subhash Chandra Agrawal) as to whether or not any declaration of assets had been filed by the honourable judges of the Supreme Court. But the matter did not rest there. Presumably, on instructions from above, an appeal was filed (on behalf of the Supreme Court) before a bench of two judges (called a division bench) in the Delhi High Court.

The division bench was informed that after the single judge had reserved his judgment in the case, the judges of the Supreme Court had themselves resolved to place the information about their assets on their website, but the appeal was, nevertheless, 'being pursued on the ground that fundamental questions of law with regard to the scope and applicability of the Act *with specific reference to declaration of assets by the Judges of the High Courts and the Supreme Court persist and need to be addressed*'.

The division bench then referred the appeal to a bench of three judges (known as a full bench) of the Delhi High Court. The full bench of the Delhi High Court by its judgment affirmed the decision of the single judge, upholding the dismissal of the writ petition of the registrar of the Supreme Court.[58] An appeal on behalf of the Supreme Court was thereafter carried to the Supreme Court itself.

How will their lordships now decide the case? Will they decide in favour of the view previously taken by the Supreme Court? No one can tell. My experience has been that innate prejudices or biases of individual judges are often overriden by a strict adherence to the discipline of the law. But howsoever the case gets decided, I believe it must reflect an attitude of mind expressed by the Lord Chief Justice of England and Wales (Lord Igor Judge). In a lecture on the Judiciary and the Media delivered in Jerusalem on 28 March 2011, he commended to all judges everywhere, the 'wise saying' of Michel de Montaigne:[59]

> No matter that we may mount on stilts, we must still walk on our own legs. And on the highest throne in the world, we still sit only on our own bottom!

Notes and References

1. V. R. Krishna Iyer, 'Of Justice, Justices and Justicing', *The Hindu*, 12 September 2008. See http://www.thehindu.com/2008/09/12/stories/2008091255791100.htm.
2. The long subtitle of this book is *An Inquiry into Bribery and Other High Crimes and Misdemeanors in the Federal Courts.* Clarkson N. Potter, New York, first and only edition published in 1962. (Library of Congress Catalog Card No. 62-19290.)
3. V. R. Krishna Iyer, op. cit. An extract from the article reads as follows:

   > Fortunately, judges generally maintain a high standard of behaviour on and off the Bench. Even so, the number of delinquents is on the rise. Bribery, sexism, communalism, corruption, vanity, arbitrariness and like vices are no longer uncommon. Also, colossal ignorance, indolence and utter indifference to writing judgments [are] sometimes evident. There is no commission of high status to enquire into a candidate's fitness before an appointment is made. Nor is there a Performance Accountability Commission; the basic obligation of a trustee of judicial power, it is a desideratum that cannot wait. Its absence weakens the people's faith in judicial justice which used to be held in high esteem.

4. See Note 2.

5. The Judicial Council of the USA consists of 12 seniormost federal judges of the land. In addition to normal judicial duties, these judges are required to oversee and adjudicate upon complaints against other federal judges.
6. Henry Cecil: *Tipping the Scales*, Hutchinson, London, 1964.
7. Lord of Appeal in Ordinary: one of the 12 Law Lords comprising the Judicial Committee of the House of Lords. In 2009 the Supreme Court of the United Kingdom took the place of the Law Lords as England's highest court.
8. Mumbo-jumbo is an English phrase or expression that denotes a confusing or meaningless subject. (*Source*: Wikipedia.)
9. The types of cloud are numbered according to the altitudes they attain, with nine being the highest. If someone is said to be on cloud nine, that person is floating high up, well above all others.
10. The Right to Information Act 2005: As recently stated in an editorial ('The RTI Power' in *The Hindu*, 5 November 2012): 'Of the slew of rights-based laws initiated by the first UPA government, only the RTI Act has met with an impressive degree of success. The law has been empowering for the common person. And it has played an invaluable role in uncovering scams and scandals that would have been shut out of sight in an earlier era.'
11. The First Amendment in the US Constitution is in absolute terms. It says:

    Congress shall make no law respecting an establishment of religion, or prohibiting the free exercise thereof; or abridging *the freedom of speech, or of the press*; or the right of the people peaceably to assemble, and to petition the government for a redress of grievances [emphasis added].
12. *Narmada Bachao Andolan* vs *Union of India*, order dated 15 October 1999, reported in AIR 1999, SC 33, p. 45.
13. AIR 2001, SC 3395, order dated 28 August 2001 of a bench of two justices: G. B. Pattnaik and Ruma Pal.
14. AIR 2002, SC 1375, order dated 6 March 2002 of a bench of two justices: G. B. Pattnaik and Ruma Pal.
15. From that moving poem 'Invictus' by the English poet William Henley: this is how the entire stanza reads:

    In the fell clutch of circumstance
    I have not winced nor cried aloud
    Under the bludgeoning of chance
    My head is bloody, but unbowed.
16. In the Contempt of Courts Act 1971, 'civil contempt' has been defined as:

    2 (b) 'Civil contempt' means wilful disobedience to any judgment, decree, direction, order, writ or other process of a court or wilful breach of an undertaking given to a court.

    It is a very important and indispensable part of the law of the land.

'Criminal contempt' (scandalizing the court, the judges and the administration of justice) is defined separately in the Contempt of Courts Act 1971. It reads:

2 (c) 'Criminal contempt' means the publication (whether by words, spoken or written, or by signs, or by visible representation, or otherwise) of any matter or the doing of any other act whatsoever which

(i) scandalises or tends to scandalise, or lowers or tends to lower the authority of, any court; or

(ii) prejudices, or interferes or tends to interfere with, the due course of any judicial proceedings; or

(iii) interferes or tends to interfere with, or obstructs or tends to obstruct, the administration of justice in any other manner.

17. Gordon Borrie and Nigel Lowe: *Law of Contempt*, third edition, Butterworths, Oxford (UK), 1996, p. 331.
18. *Rex* vs *Almon*, 1765, Wilmot 243.
19. So stated in RE: *V. C. Mishra*, AIR 1995, SC 2348. The enacted law is the Contempt of Courts Act 1971. But both the high courts and the Supreme Court have, in addition, undefined and, apparently unlimited, powers of contempt as recognized in the Constitution of India (Article 129 and Article 215): These articles read as follows:

Article 129: Supreme Court to be a court of record: The Supreme Court shall be a court of record and shall have all the powers of such a court including the power to punish for contempt of itself.

Article 215: High Courts to be courts of record: Every High Court shall be a court of record and shall have all the powers of such a court including the power to punish for contempt of itself.

20. Contempt of Court (Amendment) Act 2006, Section 13 (relevant part) reads as under:

S. 13: Contempts not punishable in certain cases: Notwithstanding anything contained in any law for the time being in force –

(a) ...

(b) the court may permit, in any proceedings for contempt of court, justification by truth as a valid defence if it is satisfied that it is in public interest and the request for invoking the said defence is bona fide.

21. 1995 (5), SCC 457 (no AIR citation).
22. Although much later at the personal insistence of the then chief justice of India – A. M. Ahmadi – Bhattacherjee handed in his resignation.
23. 'Regulating Judicial Misconduct and Divining Good Behavior for Federal Judges', *Michigan Law Review*, Vol. 87, February 1989, p. 765.
24. See AIR 1965, SC 961 (bench of five justices).

25. But stopping of work to a judge under administrative powers of the Supreme Court's chief justice has not been approved abroad. In *Rees and Others* vs *Crane*, 1994 (1), All England Law Reports (ALL ER) 883 (an opinion of the Privy Council) it was held that chief justice of Trinidad and Tobago had no power (as part of his administrative duties) to indefinitely suspend a judge of the high court by not allocating work to him. Stopping of work was regarded as a suspension of the judge: a punishment not permitted by the Constitution of Trinidad and Tobago.
26. See, for instance, my article published in *Indian Advocate* (a journal of the Bar Association of India), Vol. VIII, July–December 1978.
27. Chittatosh Mookerjee had judging in his veins. His father was Justice Rama Prasad Mookerjee who was a judge of the High Court of Calcutta from 1948 to 1956 and acting chief justice from August to November 1956. His illustrious grandfather, Ashutosh Mookerjee, was a judge of the Calcutta High Court from 1904 to 1924 and was acting chief justice of the same court from March 1920 to July 1920. He was the first Indian to be appointed acting chief justice of any high court in British India.
28. Not to be confused with Justice V. Ramaswami ICS, who sat with distinction in the Supreme Court of India from 4 January 1965 till he retired on 29 October 1969.
29. It is printed only in an unofficial law report, viz., 1990 (2), *Scale* (SP) 1.
30. The motion was supported by more than 100 sitting members of the Lok Sabha: the requirement of law (under the Judges Inquiry Act 1968) is that a motion for removal of a judge of a high court or the Supreme Court of India had to be supported by 50 members if moved in the Rajya Sabha and 100 members if moved in the Lok Sabha.
31. Article 124(4): Establishment and constitution of Supreme Court:

    (1) …
    (2) …
    (3) …
    (4) A Judge of the Supreme Court shall not be removed from his office except by an order of the President passed after an address by each House of Parliament supported by a majority of the total membership of that House and by a majority of not less than two-thirds of the members of that House present and voting has been presented to the President in the same session for such removal on the ground of proved misbehaviour or incapacity.
32. Lok Sabha Debates, 11 May 1993, sixth session, Vol. XXII, No. 41, p. 757.
33. Under the Judges Inquiry Act 1968, the process of removal starts with a notice of motion being admitted – in the Lok Sabha by the speaker and in the Rajya Sabha by the chairman – supported by signatures of 100 members of the Lok Sabha or 50 members of the Rajya Sabha.
34. With Chief Justice T. S. Thakur of the Punjab and Haryana High Court having been appointed, in November 2009, a judge of the Supreme Court of India,

Chief Justice Mukul Mudgal also of the High Court of Punjab and Haryana was appointed in his place.

35. The word 'collegium' was first used in the *First Judges* Case (*S. P. Gupta* vs *Union of India*, AIR 1982, SC 149, p. 204) in the judgment of Justice P. N. Bhagwati, in which he said that 'he would rather suggest that there must be a *collegium* (of justices) to make recommendations to the President in regard to appointment of a Judge of the Supreme Court or a Judge of the High Court'. This expression was adopted in the *Second Judges* Case, AIR 1994, SC 268, and also in the *Third Judges* Case, AIR 1999, SC 1. Prior to these decisions it was for the 'President of India with the aid and advice of his Council of Ministers' (a constitutional euphemism for 'the Government of India') to appoint judges of high courts in states and judges of the Supreme Court of India.
36. The names of the members of the collegium at the time were: Hon'ble Mr Justice K.G. Balakrishnan; Hon'ble Mr Justice S. H. Kapadia; Hon'ble Mr Justice Tarun Chatterjee; Hon'ble Mr Justice Altamas Kabir; and Hon'ble Mr Justice R. V. Raveendran.
37. By an order passed in writ petition *Suraz India Trust* vs *Union of India* by a bench of two hon'ble judges. Writ petition No. 204 of 2011 was placed before the chief justice of India for appropriate directions to be dealt with by a larger bench: the case involved the decision of a nine-judge bench (reported in AIR 1004, SC 268) and previous judgments on the same subject of appointments of judges under the collegium system. This order is reported only in the unofficial law reports 2011 (4), *Scale* 252. More recently, on 9 November 2012, a bench of three hon'ble judges presided over by the chief justice of India has adopted the contents of the previous order, and once again directed that the matter be placed before the CJI for appropriate orders for constituting a larger bench.
38. Ms R. Vaigai, a lawyer from Chennai, had earlier moved an application before the committee for his recusal.
39. *P. D. Dinakaran (I)* vs *Judges Inquiry Committee and Others*, AIR 2011, SC 3711, para 51 (Justices G. S. Singhvi and A. K. Ganguly: judgment dated 5 July 2011).
40. *P. D. Dinakaran (II)* vs *Judges Inquiry Committee and Others*, AIR 2011, SC 3777 (judgment dated 26 August 2011).
41. 3. Additional protection to Judges:

    (1) Notwithstanding anything contained in any other law for the time being in force and subject to the provisions of subsec. (2), no Court shall entertain or continue any civil or criminal proceedings against any person who is or was a Judge for any act, thing or word committed, done or spoken by him when, or in the course of, acting or purporting to act in the discharge of his official or judicial duty or function.

    (2) Nothing in subsec. (1) shall debar or affect in any manner the power of the Central Government or the State Government or the Supreme Court of India or any High Court or any other authority under any law for the time being in force to take such action (whether by way of civil, criminal or

departmental proceedings or otherwise) against any person who is or was a Judge.

42. As prescribed in *K. Veeraswami* vs *Union of India*, 1991 (3), SCC 655: Justice K. Veeraswami was elevated to the Madras High Court in 1960 and, in 1969, appointed chief justice. In February 1976, the CBI registered a case against him alleging that he had assets disproportionate to his income – beyond his known sources of income. The judge went on leave in March 1976 and retired the next month at the constitutional age prescribed for retirement of every high court judge (62 years). Investigation by the CBI continued and a final report [u/ section 173(2), Criminal Procedure Code or CrPC] was filed before a special judge, Madras. The special judge then summoned the appearance of the judge who then filed a petition (u/section 482, CrPC) before the Madras High Court for quashing the prosecution on the ground that it was wholly without jurisdiction, for want of sanction and was therefore unconstitutional, illegal and void. The high court (full bench) dismissed his case, but granted certificate of appeal to the Supreme Court. The Supreme Court held that the appellant, on retirement from his office, ceased to be a public servant. Therefore, at the time of filing the first information report (FIR), the appellant having ceased to be a public servant no sanction was necessary. The court therefore upheld the high court judgment dismissing the application u/section 482, CrPC, and ordered that the trial of the criminal case be proceeded with. However the prosecution was ultimately aborted by the death of Veeraswami on 29 April 2010. In Veeraswami's case a split verdict was recorded on the question whether the CJI was empowered to grant sanction for the prosecution of a sitting judge: three judges – Justices Jagannatha Shetty, M. N. Venkatachaliah and B. C. Ray – said he was so empowered as head of the judicial family of judges, but two justices (Justice L. M. Sharma and Justice J. S. Verma) held otherwise.
43. Every year, 26 November is celebrated by Supreme Court lawyers as Law Day because this was the day in 1949 on which the Constitution of India was framed and adopted by the Constituent Assembly of India.
44. Decision dated 29 November 1991 in *Jain Exports Ltd.* vs *Union of India* in 1993, Supp. 3, SCC 487.
45. See Review Petitions 75-76 and 635 of 1992, which were allowed on 21 October 1992. As a consequence the Supreme Court's earlier Order dated 29 November1991 ceased to be operative (so mentioned in 1993, 4, SCC 51, p. 57, para 5).
46. Front-page headline: 'Mall-aa-Mall', *Mid Day*, 18 May 2007. See also, in the same issue, Vitusha Oberoi and M. K. Tayal's news item 'Truth behind Sealing', p. 4.
47. Front-page headline: 'Gol Mall Hai', *Mid Day*, 19 May 2007. See also, in the same issue, news item: 'Shock, Anger at Mall-aa-Mall'.
48. The line between defamation of a judge and contempt by scandalizing the court is a thin one, but well drawn in a catena of cases: for instance, *Ambard* vs *Attorney General for Trinidad and Tobago*, 1936, AC (appeals case) 322–35

and *Perspective Publications* vs *State of Maharashtra*, AIR, 1971 SC, 221–30. In my view, if every allegation against a judge who had been a member of the higher judiciary is dealt with in the contempt jurisdiction of the court, past misdemeanours of justices would never be exposed.

49. *Hindustan Times*, 18 July 2007, pp. 5 and 12.
50. Ibid., 2 October 2007, p. 10.
51. *Sunday Tribune*, 4 May 2008, p. 13. This article was based on an earlier address delivered at a Transparency International Annual Function in New Delhi.
52. *Hindustan Times*, 18 September 2007.
53. *The Times of India*, 2 September 2007 (http://epaper.timesofindia.com/Repository/ml.asp?Ref=QOFQLzIwMDcvMDk).
54. *The Court on Its Own Motion* vs *M. K. Tayal and Others*, Contempt Case (Criminal) No. 7 of 2007. Orders dated 11 September 2007 and 21 September 2007 (Judges R. S. Sodhi and B. N. Chaturvedi).
55. *Vitusha Oberoi and Others* vs *Court on Its Own Motion*. Order dated 19 September 2007 (Justice Ashok Bhan and Justice V. S. Sirpurkar).
56. The Resolution adopted at the full court meeting of the Supreme Court of India on 7 May 1997.
57. *The Tribune*, 19 January 2009.
58. Full bench judgment dated 12 January 2010. *Secretary General Supreme Court of India* vs *Subhash Chandra Agrawal*, AIR 2010, Delhi 159 (decided by Chief Justice A. P. Shah along with Justices Vikramjit Sen and S. Muralidhar).
59. Michel de Montaigne (1533–92) was one of the most prolific writers of the French Renaissance (known for popularizing the essay in literature). His massive volume *Essais* (translated literally as 'Attempts') contains to this day some of the most widely influential essays ever written.

Appendix
Constitution Making (and Unmaking) in Pakistan and Bangladesh

Pakistan

Pakistan was brought into existence by Britain's Parliament (as a separate dominion) on 14 August 1947 and was to be governed by the provisions of the Government of India Act 1935 till a new constitution was framed. Pakistan's founder, Mohammad Ali Jinnah, became Pakistan's first governor-general and president of its first Constituent Assembly. The co-founder of Pakistan, Liaquat Ali Khan, was appointed the first prime minister. Jinnah died in September 1948 and Liaquat Ali Khan was assassinated in October 1951. Before Pakistan's first Constituent Assembly could produce a written constitution, it was summarily dissolved by Pakistan's third governor-general, Ghulam Mohammed. This was to pre-empt the Constituent Assembly from passing a law revoking the governor-general's power to dismiss the country's prime minister.[1] Pakistan's second Constituent Assembly was elected only in May 1955. From 14 August 1947 (Pakistan's Independence Day) till March 1956 (when the country's Constitution was promulgated), Pakistan continued to be governed by the provisions of the Government of India Act 1935 – an Act of the British Parliament adapted for Pakistan by the Provisional Constitution Order of 1947.

Thus, only nine long years after independence there was pieced together in the new state of Pakistan *the Constitution of the Islamic Republic of Pakistan 1956*: it was based on a parliamentary system of government and it represented the country's first experiment in constitution making. But the experiment was short-lived. The 1956

Constitution was abrogated in October 1958 by President Iskander Mirza (the first president of Pakistan under the 1956 Constitution) in exercise of *extra-constitutional powers*: he issued a Proclamation on 7 October 1958 appointing General Mohammad Ayub Khan (then chief of Army Staff) as chief martial law administrator. This Proclamation – known as the Laws Continuance in Force Act 1958 – was challenged in the Supreme Court of Pakistan, where its constitutional validity was upheld. In the majority judgment (3:1) in the *State* vs *Doso*,[2] Chief Justice Muhammad Munir had said:

> Victorious revolution or a successful *coup d'état* is an internationally recognized method of changing a constitution … and that after a change by way of revolution, the legal order must for its validity depend upon the new law-creating organ.

Fortified by the judgment of the Supreme Court in Doso's case, in October 1958, the chief martial law administrator (General Ayub Khan), acting in furtherance of the coup d'état initiated by President Iskander Mirza, forcibly removed the latter and had him exiled to London! General Ayub Khan then proclaimed himself president of Pakistan, and a year later, promoted himself to the rank of field marshal!

***

Martial law continued till the framing of the 'Constitution of the Republic of Pakistan 1962' by a Constitution Commission that had been set up by Field Marshal Ayub Khan. The 1962 Constitution provided for a presidential form of government.

In the January 1965 elections, President Ayub Khan was re-elected head of state (under the 1962 Constitution) and continued as civilian head of government till he voluntarily demitted office in March 1969, but he did so (contrary to the provisions of the 1962 Constitution) only after handing over the presidency to General Yahya Khan (then chief of Army Staff) – an extra-constitutional act. Yahya Khan then promptly abrogated the 1962 Constitution and imposed martial law!

After the December 1970 general elections and the secession of East Pakistan (that led to the creation of the new state of Bangladesh), General

Yahya Khan stepped down (in December 1971) and Zulfikar Ali Bhutto (who had emerged as the popular leader of the majority party in West Pakistan in the December 1970 general elections) took over control as president and martial law administrator.

In April 1972, Bhutto introduced an interim Constitution for (West) Pakistan, which contained provisions for the country's return to civilian rule and for revocation of martial law. The next year, a third Constitution – the Constitution of the Islamic Republic of Pakistan (1973) – was adopted by Pakistan's National Assembly and the country reverted once more to a parliamentary form of government.

Despite being re-elected in what was generally perceived to be a rigged election (held in March 1977), Zulfikar Ali Bhutto was deposed as prime minister (in July 1977) by the then chief of Army Staff, General Zia-ul Haq. The general next suspended the 1973 Constitution and reimposed martial law, proclaiming himself as the 'chief martial law administrator': this state of affairs continued until December 1985. General Zia-ul Haq had also assumed the office of president in August 1978, when the tenure of the then elected incumbent, Fazal Ilahi Chaudhry, came to an end.

General Zia-ul Haq continued as president (and chief executive head of Pakistan) till his death in August 1988. During his tenure as chief executive head of government, General Zia-ul Haq ordered the arrest and trial of Zulfikar Ali Bhutto for the murder (of a political rival) – a murder Bhutto swore (till his dying day) that he did not commit! Bhutto was tried, convicted and sentenced to death; his appeal to the High Court of Lahore was dismissed. The Supreme Court of Pakistan (in 1978) upheld the conviction and sentence of death: though in a split verdict.[3] Zulfikar Ali Bhutto was hanged in April 1979; General Zia-ul Haq ignored worldwide appeals to pardon Bhutto by exercising his presidential power of clemency.

* * *

In February 1985, general elections were held on an experimental, non-party basis. But before the elected National Assembly met, General Zia-ul Haq made sure that he would retain his hold on government in Pakistan. By a Presidential Order of 2 March 1985,[4] he made sweeping changes in the 1973 Constitution before reviving it: he granted himself the right to nominate and dismiss the prime minister at his discretion and to dissolve the National Assembly.

A civilian government was then formed during the period of martial law. Zia-ul Haq named Muhammad Khan Junejo (a veteran politician from Sindh) as prime minister. The National Assembly (with the blessings of General Zia-ul Haq) then passed the Constitution 8th Amendment Act 1985, which conferred *full powers* on the president (under the 1973 Constitution) to dismiss an elected government and its prime minister and to dissolve the National Assembly.

Martial law was lifted on 30 December 1985 and the Constitution of 1973 (as amended) revived. In exercise of powers conferred on him by the Constitution 8th Amendment Act 1985, General Zia-ul Haq dismissed the government of Prime Minister Muhammad Khan Junejo (in May 1988) on charges of corruption.

Elections were called in October 1988, but before they could be held the president (Zia-ul Haq) died in a plane crash (in August 1988). In the ensuring elections of October 1988, the Pakistan People's Party (PPP), then headed by Benazir Bhutto (daughter of Zulfikar Ali Bhutto), came to power. Benazir Bhutto became Pakistan's first woman prime minister. But not for long. She was dismissed by President Ghulam Ishaq Khan in August 1990, and, in the ensuing October 1990 elections, Nawaz Sharif – of the Pakistan Muslim League (N) Party (a part of the Islamic Jamhoori Ittehad or IJI alliance) – was voted into power. Nawaz Sharif was also dismissed by the (same) president in mid-1993.

However, in the general elections of October 1993, Benazir Bhutto's party (the PPP) was voted back to power and she became prime minister once again. She was again dismissed, this time by President Farooq Leghari in November 1996, on charges of corruption and, in February 1997, Nawaz Sharif was voted back to power.

In a spectacular military coup staged in October 1999, the then chief of Army Staff, General Pervez Musharraf, deposed Prime Minister Nawaz Sharif, and, for the first time (after 1985), imposed martial law, suspending the 1973 Constitution (which had worked – in a sort of way – for nearly 12 long years). The imposition of martial law by General Musharraf was challenged in court; the Supreme Court of Pakistan upheld its imposition, granting three more years to General Musharraf to achieve his professed objectives![5] In a referendum called and held in April 2002, General Musharraf consolidated his position as president for the next five years. Martial law was lifted soon after the general elections of November 2002.

***

On each of the occasions (from 1977 to 1985 and again from 1999 to 2002) when the imposition of martial law had been challenged, its constitutional validity was upheld by the Supreme Court of Pakistan. This was on the basis of a (questionable) political doctrine – 'the doctrine of necessity' – which was embodied in the Latin maxim '*sallus populi est supreme lex*' ('public welfare is the highest law'), with the court relying on its own precedents (of the years 1955[6] and 1978[7]) for invoking the same.

A significant feature of Constitution making (and unmaking) in Pakistan has been the too frequent invocation of the provisions of the Constitution 8th Amendment Act 1985: this amendment to the 1973 Constitution enabled successive presidents of Pakistan – under the (revised) 1973 Constitution – to unilaterally dissolve the elected National Assembly and provincial assemblies and to dismiss elected prime ministers virtually at the will of the head of state. As already mentioned, the 8th Constitutional Amendment was first invoked by President Zia-ul Haq in May 1988 to dismiss elected Prime Minister Muhammad Khan Junejo; it was later called in aid by President Ghulam Ishaq Khan to dismiss the civilian government of Benazir Bhutto in 1990, and, later, the successor government of Nawaz Sharif in 1993. The provisions of the 8th Amendment were also invoked by President Farooq Leghari to dismiss the government of Benazir Bhutto (in her second term of office as prime minister) in November 1996.

Upon being re-elected to power in the general elections of February 1997, Nawaz Sharif introduced and got passed in the National Assembly (with the support of the opposition parties) the Constitution 13th Amendment Act, 1997 – an enactment that repealed the provisions of the Constitution 8th Amendment Act 1985.

But what went out of the window came back in through the door! Because the 8th Amendment was restored by President Musharraf, when the Pakistan Muslim League (Q)* (with Musharaf's support and under his inspiration) got passed in the National Assembly the Constitution 17th Amendment Act 2003: this Act once again conferred the power on the president of Pakistan to dissolve the elected National Assembly and elected provincial assemblies and to dismiss elected prime ministers! However, in April 2010, by the Constitution 18th Amendment Act 2010, the coalition government headed by Prime Minister Yousuf Raza Gilani succeeded in getting the National Assembly to repeal the Constitution 17th Amendment Act 2003. Since then – so far (!) – the president of Pakistan has no power under the 1973 Constitution to dissolve the elected National Assembly and the elected provincial assemblies and to dismiss an elected prime minister! Gilani was disqualified by Pakistan's Supreme Court on 26 April 2012. He was succeeded by Raja Pervaiz Ashraf.

Bangladesh

The borders of East Pakistan (now Bangladesh) were established with the partition of Bengal in 1947: East Bengal became part of the newly formed *Dominion of Pakistan* – separated from its western wing by nearly 1000 miles of Indian territory! Since gaining independence as a separate state in 1971, Bangladesh and its people have witnessed military coups and two prolonged periods of martial law. Bangladesh is today a democratic nation governed by a parliamentary system of government and the rule of law.[8] But it was not always so.

In December 1971, when East Pakistan became a separate independent state known as Bangladesh, it had inherited an economy that had suffered more than two decades of exploitation and neglect. In January 1972, a Constituent Assembly for the state was set up and, before the year was out it, adopted a democratic Constitution (in December 1972). The Constitution of the People's Republic of Bangladesh 1972 was based on a parliamentary system of government. The 1972 Constitution declared the people to be the source of all power and pledged four

*'Q' stands for Quaid-e-Azam (great leader), the title given to Mohammad Ali Jinnah.

basic principles of governance: viz., nationalism, socialism, democracy and secularism. The Constitution envisaged a strong executive prime minister, a largely ceremonial presidency, an independent judiciary and a unicameral legislature on the Westminster model. It also provided for an independent Election Commission to ensure free and fair elections.

In March 1973, the first general elections were held, when Sheikh Mujibur Rehman's Awami League gained power with a popular mandate. But shortly thereafter, under the Constitution 2nd Amendment Act 1973, the democratic Constitution was amended in order to confer power on the executive to suspend fundamental rights during periods of emergency. This power was used (for the first time) in December 1974 by Sheikh Mujibur Rehman when emergency was proclaimed. He then used the parliamentary majority of his Awami League to pass the Constitution 4th Amendment Act 1975 (25 January 1975), which introduced a one-party political system: with this amendment in place Sheikh Mujibur Rehman became all-powerful, but not for long.

On 15 August 1975, the president (Sheikh Mujibur Rehman) and most of his family members were assassinated in Dhaka by a group of mid-level army officers. Sheikh Mujib's daughters, Sheikh Hasina (currently prime minister) and Sheikh Rehana, were then out of the country. A cabinet colleague of the Sheikh, Khondaker Mustaq Ahmed, by a Proclamation dated 20 August 1975, took over full power of the government and suspended the Constitution with effect from 15 August 1975.

On 3 November 1975, there was a coup by a group of military officers led by Brigadier General Khaled Mosharraf and Colonel Shaafat Jamil. Khaled Musharraf appointed himself the chief martial law administrator, but, within a few days (on 7 November), he himself was assassinated in a countercoup staged by one Colonel Abu Taher. The first chief justice of Bangladesh, A. S. Mohammed Sayem, then assumed office as president and chief martial law administrator. By a Proclamation of 8 November 1975, the provisions of the amended 1972 Constitution (which had provided for a one-party political system) were repealed, Parliament was dissolved and it was declared that elections would be held before February 1977.

Meanwhile, in November 1976, the president (Chief Justice Sayem) by a Proclamation appointed General Ziaur Rehman as the chief martial law administrator. Sayem relinquished office as president in April 1977 and General Ziaur Rehman took over that post and soon became all-powerful. By a Proclamation Order of 1977, General Rehman amended the 1972 Constitution to give the power to himself to dissolve Parliament at any time. He also deleted 'secularism' from the four basic principles of the Constitution.

In June 1978, in a referendum initiated by General Ziaur Rehman, he was re-elected as president. In February 1979, general elections were held (at a time when the country was still under martial law). The Bangladesh Nationalist Party (BNP) – initially formed by General Ziaur Rehman – won a majority of seats in Parliament. The new Parliament passed the Constitution 5th Amendment Act 1979, which ratified all the prior martial law proclamations and action taken under past regimes stood validated. Martial law was lifted a day after the passing of the Constitution 5th Amendment Act – on 7 April 1979.

Ziaur Rehman continued to face opposition both from army and civil organizations, having failed to curb corruption and lawlessness and, in May 1981, he was assassinated. Vice-President Abdus Sattar took over as acting president and declared a national emergency, which was approved by Parliament in July 1981. Abdus Sattar was elected as the new president and adopted the same policies as General Ziaur Rehman.

In March 1982, President Sattar was ousted by a bloodless military coup engineered by the army chief, General Hussain Mohammed Ershad. Martial law was declared and the 1972 Constitution was suspended. General Ershad became president in December 1983.

In the general elections of May 1986, the Jatiya Party (founded by President Ershad) was voted to power. Ershad was re-elected president. Martial law was withdrawn and the 1972 Constitution revived. General Ershad, like his predecessor General Ziaur Rehman, got Parliament to pass the Constitution (7th) Amendment Act 1986, which ratified and confirmed previous proclamations of martial law and orders given and actions taken thereunder.

President Ershad attempted to introduce military representation in local administrative councils in July 1987. In response, the opposition organized nationwide protests and strikes. Emergency was imposed, Parliament dissolved and general elections were announced for March 1988. The opposition boycotted the elections. Ershad's Jatiya Party emerged victorious. In June 1988, the Constitution (8th) Amendment Act was passed by Parliament, declaring Islam as the state religion; the judiciary was decentralized by setting up six permanent benches of the high court outside Dhaka. There was opposition to these moves. General strikes and protests intensified, and a three-party alliance (formed by opposition political parties) demanded elections under a caretaker government led by a neutral person. President Ershad finally yielded and handed over power to Chief Justice Shahabuddin Ahmed in December 1990, after appointing him as vice-president.

* * *

After the fifth general elections of 1991, two distinct political parties have emerged in Bangladesh enjoying political power almost alternately: viz., the Awami League led by Shiekh Hasina (daughter of Sheikh Mujibur Rehman) and the Bangladesh National Party (BNP) led by Begum Khaleda Zia (wife of late General Ziaur Rehman). Since then, politics in Bangladesh has been 'a tale of two ladies': a phrase used by Sir Mark Tully, commentator and political analyst.[9]

The winner in the 1991 general elections was Begum Khaleda Zia's BNP; she became Bangladesh's first woman prime minister.

The Constitution 13th Amendment Act 1996 (with the consent of all political parties) was passed in Parliament: it provided for a non-party caretaker government (interim government) prior to scheduled general elections to carry out routine functions of the government with no policy decisions being taken; the interim government was to hold general elections to Parliament 'peacefully, fairly and impartially'.

A caretaker (interim) government under Habibur Rehman as prime minister was appointed (in March 1996) prior to the general elections to be held in June 1996. In these elections, it was the Awami League that was voted to power, and, on this occasion, Sheikh Hasina became prime minister.

After five years, a caretaker (interim) government headed by Justice Latifur Rehman was appointed (in July 2001) to conduct the eighth parliamentary elections. In these elections, Begum Khaleda Zia's party (the BNP) secured a majority of seats, and she assumed the office of prime minister in October 2001.

Later, for the ninth parliamentary elections (due in 2006), a caretaker interim government headed first by Iajuddin Ahmed (23 October 2006 to 11 January 2007) and later by Fakhruddin Ahmed (12 January 2007 to 6 January 2009) was appointed. But general elections were not held till December 2008. In these elections, the Awami League and the Jatiya Party together won a majority of seats in Parliament. And, on 6 January 2009, Sheikh Hasina was once again appointed prime minister of Bangladesh. Having regard to the experience of the caretaker government appointed in 2006 – which had unduly prolonged its existence (with army support) till December 2008 – the provisions of the Constitution 13th Amendment Act were repealed by consent of all political parties in June 2011 (by the Constitution 15th Amendment Act 2011).

In a recent judgment of the Supreme Court of Bangladesh reported in 62 DLR (AD), 2010, pp. 298-406 – a decision of a Constitution Bench of five judges of the Supreme Court – it was held as a matter of constitutional law that although the Parliament of Bangladesh may amend the Constitution it cannot make the Constitution subservient to proclamations, nor can it legitimize 'illegitimate activities'. Chief Justice Mohammad Tafazzul Islam spoke for the court when he said:

> Let it be made clear that Military Rule was wrongly justified in the past and it ought not to be justified in future on any ground, principle, doctrine or theory whatsoever as the same is against the dignity, honour and glory of the nation that it achieved after great sacrifice; it is against the dignity and honour of the people of Bangladesh who are committed to uphold the sovereignty and integrity of the nation by all means; it is also against the honour of each and every soldier of the Armed Forces who [is] oath bound to bear true faith and allegiance to Bangladesh and uphold the Constitution which embodies the will of the people, honestly and faithfully to serve Bangladesh in their respective services and also see that the Constitution is upheld, it is not kept in suspension,

abrogated, it is not subverted, it is not mutilated, and to say the least it is not held in abeyance and it is not amended by any authority not competent to do so under the Constitution.

We express our total disapproval of Martial Law and suspension of the Constitution or any part thereof in any form. The perpetrators of such illegalities should also be suitably punished and condemned so that in future no adventurist, no usurper, would dare to defy the people, their Constitution, their Government, established by them with their consent. However, it is the Parliament, which can make law in this regard. Let us bid farewell to all kinds of extra-constitutional adventure forever.

Notes and References

1. The power had been previously exercised – when Governor-General Ghulam Mohammed had dismissed Pakistan's second prime minister (Khwaja Nazimuddin) in April 1953.
2. PLD (Pakistan legal decisions) 1958, SC (Pakistan) 533.
3. *The State* vs *Z. A. Bhutto*, PLD 1978. Lahore 523 (five judges) and *Z. A. Bhutto* vs *The State*, PLD 1979, SC 53 (4:3): Review dismissed (PLD 1979, SC 741).
4. No. 15 of the 1985 Revival of the Constitution of 1973 Order 1985 (dated 2 March 1985).
5. The Zafar Ali Shah case, PLD 2000, SC 69 at 1223 (16) (12 judges).
6. Reference of His Excellency the Governor-General, PLD 1955, FC (Federal Court) 435.
7. *Begum Nusrat Bhutto* vs *Chief of Army Staff*, PLD 1978, SC 657, followed in *Zafar Ali Shah* vs *Pervez Musharraf*, Chief Executive of Pakistan, PLD, 2000, SC 869 (full bench of 12 judges).
8. See the judgment dated 1 February 2010 of a Constitution Bench of the Supreme Court of Bangladesh reported in 62 DLR (Dhaka Law Reports), AD, 2010, pp. 298 to 406.
9. Reported in *Mail Today*, 3 May 2012.

Index